Abdullah samir Debbazi 9:1

EDEXCEL GCSE (9–1) RELIGIOUS STUDIES B

Beliefs in Action

Victor W. Watton
Robert M. Stone

Specification B

DYNAMIC LEARNING

HODDER EDUCATION
AN HACHETTE UK COMPANY

In order to ensure that this resource offers high-quality support for the associated Pearson qualification, it has been through a review process by the awarding body. This process confirms that this resource fully covers the teaching and learning content of the specification or part of a specification at which it is aimed. It also confirms that it demonstrates an appropriate balance between the development of subject skills, knowledge and understanding, in addition to preparation for assessment.

Endorsement does not cover any guidance on assessment activities or processes (e.g. practice questions or advice on how to answer assessment questions), included in the resource nor does it prescribe any particular approach to the teaching or delivery of a related course.

While the publishers have made every attempt to ensure that advice on the qualification and its assessment is accurate, the official specification and associated assessment guidance materials are the only authoritative source of information and should always be referred to for definitive guidance.

Pearson examiners have not contributed to any sections in this resource relevant to examination papers for which they have responsibility. Examiners will not use endorsed resources as a source of material for any assessment set by Pearson.

Endorsement of a resource does not mean that the resource is required to achieve this Pearson qualification, nor does it mean that it is the only suitable material available to support the qualification, and any resource lists produced by the awarding body shall include this and other appropriate resources.

In loving memory of
Abby Watton 1974–2015
A wonderful daughter, mummy, sister, friend and RS teacher

Photo credits: are listed on page 378.

Acknowledgements: Bible quotations are from The Holy Bible, New International Version®, NIV® Copyright © 1973, 1978, 1984, 2011 by Biblica, Inc.® Used by permission. All rights reserved worldwide. Qur'an quotations are from The Holy Qur'an translated by Abdullah Yusuf Ali.

An extract from the website of the Jewish Voice for Peace (https://jewishvoiceforpeace.org/mission/#peace) is used with kind permission. An extract from the website of the Muslim Peace Fellowship (https://mpf21.wordpress.com/about-2/) is used with kind permission. NHS Choices: Contains public sector information licensed under the Open Government Licence v3.0. ONS statistics: adapted from data from the Office for National Statistics licensed under the Open Government Licence v.1.0. 'Attack on Canada and the United States is Attack on Muslims Too' from the Islamic Supreme Council of Canada (www.islamicsupremecouncil.com/attack-on-canada-and-the-united-states-is-attack-on-muslims-too/).

Every effort has been made to trace all copyright holders, but if any have been inadvertently overlooked, the Publishers will be pleased to make the necessary arrangements at the first opportunity.

Although every effort has been made to ensure that website addresses are correct at time of going to press, Hodder Education cannot be held responsible for the content of any website mentioned in this book. It is sometimes possible to find a relocated web page by typing in the address of the home page for a website in the URL window of your browser.

Orders: please contact Bookpoint Ltd, 130 Milton Park, Abingdon, Oxon OX14 4SE. Telephone: +44 (0)1235 827720. Fax: +44 (0)1235 400454. Email education@bookpoint.co.uk Lines are open from 9 a.m. to 5 p.m., Monday to Saturday, with a 24-hour message answering service. You can also order through our website: www.hoddereducation.co.uk

ISBN: 978 1 4718 6659 3

First published in 2016 by
Hodder Education,
An Hachette UK Company
Carmelite House
50 Victoria Embankment
London EC4Y 0DZ
www.hoddereducation.co.uk

Impression number 10 9 8 7 6 5 4 3 2
Year 2020 2019 2018 2017

Cover photo: ShaunL/istockphoto.com and Getty Images/iStockphoto/Thinkstock
Produced and typeset in 10/12pt DIN by Gray Publishing, Tunbridge Wells, Kent
Printed in Italy

A catalogue record for this title is available from the British Library

Contents

Area of study 2: Based on a study of Islam or Judaism

Preface

This book covers all aspects of your Edexcel GCSE Religious Studies B Short and Full Courses:

- Area of study 1: Religion and Ethics (in Christianity)
- Area of study 2: Religion, Peace and Conflict (in Islam or Judaism).

For the Full Course, you will need to study all four sections in each area, each of which has eight topics. In each section of the book, all eight topics are covered separately. For the Full Course, you will have to take a separate exam for each area where you will have to answer one question on Section 1, one question on Section 2, one question on Section 3 and one question on Section 4.

For the Short Course, you will only need to study Sections 1 and 2 of Area 1 and Sections 1 and 2 of Area 2. For the Short Course, you will have to take a separate exam for each area where you will have to answer one question on Section 1 and one question on Section 2.

To help you understand how to relate the information in the book to the exam questions, a high mark answer to a specimen question is given at the end of each section.

How to use the book

This is our suggested way of using the book:

- Work through each topic. Words that you can use to show that you understand specialist vocabulary (6 marks are available for this in the exam) are in boldface type and defined in a useful words box in the margins of the pages.
- Pay special attention to quotations from the Bible, Creeds, Catechism, the Qur'an and hadith, the Tenakh, Talmud and Mishneh as these are sources of wisdom and authority which you may have to refer to in the examination.
- Answer the practice questions at the end of each topic. The appendix gives you hints as to the approach which will help you reach full marks.
- You should study all the topics in Area 1, but in Area 2 you have a choice of either Islam or Judaism. You only need to study one of these (your teacher will tell you which you are studying), and so wherever there is a choice, you should only work through the topic relevant to the religion you are studying.

We hope you enjoy your study of Religion and Life. Remember: Religious Studies is not about making you religious; it is about enabling you to think for yourself about religious and moral issues so that you become a responsible citizen of a multiethnic and multifaith society free from the ignorance which causes prejudice, hatred and violence.

We wish you the best of luck with your studies.

Victor Watton and Robert Stone

1 Christian beliefs

Area of study 1: Based on a study of Christianity

Area of study 1: Introduction

Before we look at the specific topics of the specification, it is important that you should understand some of the different groups within Christianity so that you can understand their beliefs and attitudes.

The history of Christianity

Christianity is the largest of the world religions, and began as a branch of Judaism. Jesus was a Jew and the first Christians were all Jews; indeed, the first split in Christianity was between those Christians who felt you had to be Jewish to be a Christian and those Christians who believed Christianity was a new religion which could be embraced away from Judaism.

Denominations of Christianity

A denomination is a sub-group within a religion and occurs as a result of a division in the Church. Different Christian Churches are often described as denominations of Christianity. As Christianity grew, more divisions appeared and by the time Christianity became the official religion of the Roman Empire in 356CE, there were several different Christian groups. In 1054CE Christianity divided into Orthodox and Catholic Christianity in the Great Schism. The Reformation in the sixteenth century divided the Western Church into Catholic and Protestant and the rise of Protestantism led to the development of many Protestant sub-groups.

Roman Catholic Christians (Western Europe)

Roman Catholic Christians are those who accept the authority of the Pope. They comprise the largest group of Christians (about 1.2 billion members) and believe that the Pope is the head of the Church since he is the successor of St Peter and so has the authority over the Church, which Jesus gave to St Peter. Catholic Christians believe it is the role of the Pope to rule and guide the Church and to pass on the true teachings of Christ. Catholics believe that the seven sacraments (events/rites of special significance) of the Church are essential for salvation. These sacraments are baptism, confirmation, Eucharist, reconciliation, anointing of the sick, marriage and holy orders.

Pope Francis on Palm Sunday in St Peter's Square at the Vatican.

Orthodox Christians (Eastern Europe and the Middle East)

Orthodox Christians believe that they follow the right beliefs and teachings of the Church (the meaning of Orthodox) because they can trace their origins back to the first Church founded by Jesus' disciples in Jerusalem. They also believe that the sacraments are essential for salvation, but reject the authority of the Pope and believe authority comes from councils of bishops or patriarchs acting together. They are organised on nationalistic principles (for example, the Russian Orthodox, the Serbian Orthodox and the Greek Orthodox), but accept leadership (not authority) from the Patriarch of Constantinople.

There are other Eastern Churches with slightly different beliefs such as the Coptic Churches, which believe Jesus was divine, not both human and divine. There are Egyptian, Ethiopian, Eritrean, Armenian, Syriac and Malankara (Indian) Coptic Churches, all with slight differences.

The Church of England (known as Anglican or Episcopalian Churches outside England)

At the time of the Reformation, Henry VIII declared the Church of England to be independent of the Pope and made himself the head of the Church. This Church became a mixture of Protestant and Catholic beliefs and practices – the Church has priests and bishops. The Church spread through English-speaking colonies and there are Anglican Churches throughout the world, but particularly in Commonwealth countries and the USA. Each separate country's Anglican Church is independent, but accepts the Archbishop of Canterbury as a spiritual leader – first among equals. The heads of the Anglican Churches meet at Lambeth Conferences to preserve and develop their unity. Some Anglican Churches are called High Church and their worship is quite similar to Catholic worship; some are called Low Church and their worship is similar to Protestant worship. The official head of the Church of England is the Queen and it is the established Church – the official Church in England whose bishops sit in the House of Lords and lead all official functions. There are about 80 million Anglicans worldwide.

Census facts on religion in England and Wales

Christians	33,243,175	59.3%
No religion	14,097,229	25.1%
No answer	4,038,032	7.2%
Muslim	2,706,066	4.8%
Hindu	816,633	1.5%
Sikh	423,158	0.8%
Jewish	263,346	0.5%
Buddhist	247,743	0.4%
Other religion	240,530	0.4%
(Source: Census 2011, Office for National Statistics.)		

You may be asked questions about this information.

Protestant Christians

Martin Luther's protest, in Germany, against the Pope's authority began the Reformation and led to the emergence of Protestant Churches in Western Europe whose main beliefs were:

- that the Pope has no authority to decide on beliefs
- that the Bible is the sole authority for Christians
- that salvation comes from faith rather than the sacraments
- that all Christians are equal and all are priests
- that Churches should be ruled democratically.

The Protestant Churches themselves split soon after they began into Lutheran Churches, Calvinist Churches and Baptist Churches. Other Protestant Churches (such as Methodists, Salvation Army and Quakers) broke off over the years. The Pentecostal Churches developed from the Methodist Church in America and are the most rapidly growing Christian Churches gaining many converts from the Catholic Church in South and Central America.

Full water immersion: Mount Zion Spiritual Baptist Church outing to Felixstowe for baptism in the sea.

Modern Christianity or traditional Christianity?

There is also a major division in Christianity today which goes across all the Churches: the division between liberals and conservatives. There are liberals in all Churches who want the Church to alter to fit in with the modern world and believe that the Bible is a book written by human beings inspired by God. There are conservatives who will not accept any changes to their traditional beliefs, and believe that the Bible is God's direct word.

Topic 1.1.1 The Trinity

Thinking points

In this topic you need to:

- think about the nature of the Trinity as expressed in the Nicene Creed
- think about the nature and significance of the oneness of God
- understand the nature and significance of each of the persons, including Matthew 3:13–17
- be able to evaluate how belief in the Trinity is shown in worship and belief.

The nature of the Trinity

Christians believe that there is only one God.

Christian beliefs about the Holy Trinity are clearly stated in the Nicene **Creed**:

> *We believe in one God, the Father, the Almighty ... We believe in one Lord Jesus Christ, the only Son of God, eternally begotten of the Father, God from God ... begotten not made, of one Being with the Father ... We believe in the Holy Spirit, the Lord and giver of life, who proceeds from the Father and the Son. With the Father and the Son he is worshipped and glorified.*

The Nicene Creed explains that there is one Being – God – experienced as three persons, Father, Son and Holy Spirit, who are all equal and all eternal.

Useful words

Creed – statement of Christian beliefs

Painting of the Trinity from the Holy Sepulchre Basilica in Jerusalem.

Activity

Look at the painting from the Holy Sepulchre Basilica and explain how it illustrates Christian beliefs about the Trinity.

The oneness of God

Believing in one God is called monotheism, and believing in the oneness of God is the basis of Christianity:

- The teachings of the Bible in both the Old and New Testaments show clearly that there is only one God.
- The belief in the oneness of God is the first of the Ten Commandments, which all Christians accept as God's rules about belief and behaviour.
- When asked what was the greatest commandment, Jesus replied,

  The most important one is this, 'Hear O Israel, the Lord our God, the Lord is one'. (Mark 12:29)

- The oneness of God is the teaching of the Church as seen in the Creeds, the decisions of Church Councils and the writings of Church leaders.
- Christians believe that the oneness of God is shown in the universe that God has created. They believe that the fact it is a universe working to one set of laws means it was created by one God.

The persons of the Trinity

Although Christians believe that God is one, he is experienced in the world as a Trinity: the Father, the Son (Jesus) and the Holy Spirit. When Christians speak of God at work in the world they refer to the three persons of God: Father, Son and Holy Spirit.

Christians feel that belief in the Trinity helps them to understand the different ways that God has shown his presence in the world:

- God the Father helps Christians to understand the power and creativity of God and his care for the world and its people. It also shows that God creates human life like a father does. God is not a creator who creates and then leaves his creation to get on with things, he has a relationship of love and care with his creation. In the **Lord's Prayer** or 'Our Father', Christians learn that God will provide their daily bread and protect them from evil precisely because he is 'our Father'. Because God is the Father, Christians can turn to God as they would to a human father when they are in need.
- God the Son helps Christians to understand the love of God. In his life and teachings, Jesus showed God's love by healing people and feeding people. In his death he showed how much God loves the world.
- The Holy Spirit helps Christians to understand the presence of God in the world. Christians believe that the Holy Spirit is the means by which God communicates with humans, revealing God's presence in the world. Christians believe that through the presence of the Holy Spirit in their lives, God can strengthen and empower Christians today.

It should never be forgotten that the Christian belief in God as the Holy Trinity is also belief in God's unity: Christians only believe in one God. As the Catechism of the Catholic Church says:

The Christian faith confesses that God is one in nature, substance and essence. (Catechism 200)

Then Jesus came from Galilee to the Jordan to be baptised by John. But John tried to deter him, saying, 'I need to be baptised by you, and do you come to me?' Jesus replied, 'Let it be so now; it is proper for us to do this to fulfil all righteousness.' Then John consented. As soon as Jesus was baptised, he went up out of the water. At that moment heaven was opened, and he saw the Spirit of God descending like a dove and alighting on him. And a voice from heaven said, 'This is my Son, whom I love; with him I am well pleased.' (Matthew 3:14)

Activity

Look at the quote from St Matthew's Gospel above. What does this tell us about the Trinity?

Useful words

Lord's Prayer – the prayer Jesus taught his disciples that begins 'Our Father'

The World Council of Churches

The non-Roman Catholic Christian Churches are members of the World Council of Churches, which states in its founding document:

> *The World Council of Churches is a fellowship of Churches which confess the Lord Jesus Christ as God and Saviour according to the Scriptures and therefore seek to fulfil together their common calling to the glory of the one God, Father, Son and Holy Spirit.*

Divergent Christian understandings of the Trinity

Many Christians find the Trinity a difficult concept, but believe it because of their experiences of God as the Father and as the Son and as the Holy Spirit. However, there are Christian groups that do not accept the belief in the Trinity expressed in the Nicene Creed, the main ones being:

- The Church of Jesus Christ Latter-day Saints (Mormons) believe that the Father, the Son and the Holy Ghost are not one in substance or essence; instead, they are three separate beings who are united in will and purpose, as one God.
- Jehovah's Witnesses believe that Jehovah is the only true God. Jesus was created by God and so is God's son; the Holy Spirit is God's power applied to the world and so is not a person.
- Unitarians believe that there is only one God and that Jesus was a man whose teachings and life give him moral authority, but not divinity. They believe that there is no difference between God and God the Holy Spirit.

There are other smaller non-Trinitarian Christians such as the Living Church of God, the Oneness Pentecostals, the Church of God International, Christian Scientists, the Christadelphians and the Unification Church.

None of these groups can be members of the World Council of Churches and they are often regarded as non-Christian by Christians.

Activity

Explain why there would be no Mormons or Jehovah's Witnesses at meetings of the World Council of Churches.

The logo of the World Council of Churches. All the main Protestant and Orthodox Churches that believe in the Trinity belong to the Council but the Churches that don't accept the belief in the Trinity do not.

Useful words

Holy Communion – the Christian service of thanksgiving using bread and wine (also called Eucharist)
Liturgy – a set form of public worship
Anglicans – members of the Church of England or a Church in communion with the Church of England

How the Trinity is shown in belief and worship

For all Churches that accept the Nicene Creed the belief in the Trinity is expressed in all forms of Christian worship:

- Participants repeat the Nicene Creed in every service of **Holy Communion** (also known as Mass, Eucharist, the **liturgy**, the Lord's Supper, breaking bread), which can be at least once a week for many Christians.
- Catholic and Orthodox Christians (and some **Anglicans**) express their belief in the Trinity by crossing themselves when they enter a church or when the name of the Trinity is invoked.

- Priests (known as ministers or pastors in Protestant Churches) begin their sermons with the words, 'In the name of the Father, and of the Son and of the Holy Spirit'.
- Priests bless a congregation at the end of services with the words, 'May the blessing of God Almighty, Father, Son and Holy Spirit be with you now and for evermore'.
- Baptisms and marriages are performed in the name of the Trinity.

All the mainstream Christian Churches have belief in the Trinity as the basis of their beliefs. The official teaching of the Catholic Church (the Magisterium) declares that,

> *The mystery of the Most Holy Trinity is the central mystery of the Christian faith and of Christian life. (Catechism of the Catholic Church: 262)*

The first principle of the United Methodist Church (the largest mainstream Protestant Church in the USA) is:

> *There is but one living and true God, everlasting, without body or parts, of infinite power, wisdom, and goodness; the maker and preserver of all things, both visible and invisible. And in unity of this Godhead there are three persons, of one substance, power, and eternity – the Father, the Son, and the Holy Ghost. (Articles of Religion of the United Methodist Church)*

The first Article of Faith of the Church of England also states:

> *There is but one living and true God, ever-lasting, without body, parts, or passions; of infinite power, wisdom, and goodness; the Maker, and Preserver of all things both visible and invisible. And in unity of this Godhead there be three Persons, of one substance, power, and eternity; the Father, the Son, and the Holy Ghost. (Church of England's Articles of Religion)*

Practice questions

c Explain two reasons why Christians believe in the Trinity. In your answer you must refer to a source of wisdom and authority.

d 'You can't be a Christian if you don't believe in the Trinity.' Evaluate this statement considering arguments for and against. In your answer you should:

- refer to Christian teachings
- reach a justified conclusion.

Activity

Explain how the Trinity is reflected in Christian worship today.

Summary

Christians believe there is only one God (God's oneness), who is experienced by humans as a Trinity. This is summarised in the Nicene Creed which is accepted by Protestants, Orthodox Christians and Catholics.

God's unity helps Christians to understand the power and importance of God because there is only one God who Christians should worship. God's Trinity helps them to understand God's activity in the world as Father, Son and Holy Spirit.

Groups such as Mormons and Jehovah's Witnesses do not believe in the Trinity as expressed in the Nicene Creed.

Topic 1.1.2 The creation of the universe and of humanity

Thinking points

In this topic you need to:

- think about the biblical account of creation and how it can be understood in different ways
- think about the role of the Word and Spirit in creation
- be able to evaluate the importance of creation for Christians today.

The biblical creation

All Christians believe that God was responsible for the creation of the earth and the whole universe. The Bible contains three accounts of how God created the universe. Two of these accounts are in the Old Testament book of Genesis.

The account of creation in Genesis 1

According to Genesis chapter 1, God created the whole universe in six days:

- He created heaven and earth, light and dark on day 1.
- He separated the earth from the sky on day 2.
- He created the dry land, plants and trees on day 3.
- He created the sun, moon and stars on day 4.
- He created fish and birds on day 5.
- He created animals and humans on day 6.

Each part of the creation came about because of God's words:

> *God said, 'Let there be light,' and there was light.* (Genesis 1:3)

Male and female were made at the same time and were made in the image of God. Humans were also made to have authority over the world:

> *Let us make man in our image, in our likeness, and let them rule over the fish of the sea and the birds of the air, over the livestock, over all the earth.* (Genesis 1:26)

When God had finished the creation, it was perfect:

> *God saw all that he had made and it was very good.* (Genesis 1:31)

The account of creation in Genesis 2–3

According to Genesis chapter 2, creation happened in the following way:

- God created the heavens and the earth.
- God formed man from the dust of the earth and breathed life into him.
- God made trees grow out of the ground and formed the Garden of Eden.
- God placed Adam in the Garden of Eden.
- God thought Adam would be lonely, so he created birds and animals which Adam named.
- The birds and animals were not suitable helpers for Adam, so God put Adam to sleep, removed one of his ribs, and from the rib he created woman, Eve.
- Adam and Eve lived in innocence in the Garden of Eden until the serpent tempted them to eat the fruit of the tree that God had forbidden them to eat, telling them that if they ate it they would

become like God and know good and evil. Eve ate the fruit and gave some to Adam. As a result of this first (original) sin, Adam and Eve were banished from the Garden of Eden. Eve was condemned to bearing children in pain and to be ruled over by her husband. Adam was condemned to working hard for his living.

Divergent Christian interpretations of Genesis creation

There are three Christian attitudes to the Bible which can also be seen in attitudes to the biblical accounts of creation:

- Some Christians are described as literalists. They believe that the Bible is the actual word of God. This means that they believe that every word in the Bible is the Word of God and so is true. As far as Genesis 1 and 2 are concerned, such Christians believe that both accounts are correct and do not contradict each other. Genesis 1 gives the overall broad picture of creation, whereas Genesis 2 zooms in on day 6 of creation and gives details of exactly how God created male and female and animals. Literalist Christians do not accept the scientific theories of the Big Bang and evolution.
- Some Christians are described as conservatives. They believe that the Bible is the Word of God, but not his actual words. This means that they think the writers of the Bible were inspired by God, and guided by God in what they wrote, but they used their own ideas. Conservatives see the Bible as a book about faith rather than a book about science, and so they do not regard Genesis 1 and 2 as absolute scientific fact. Most of them would see Genesis 2 as a commentary on chapter 1 rather than a different story. Conservative Christians tend to regard Genesis 1 as fairly factual (although they would see the days as eras lasting millions, or billions, of years rather than 24 hours) whereas Genesis 2 and 3 are poetic explanations of such things as how suffering and evil came into the world. Conservative Christians accept the Big Bang and evolution.
- Some Christians are described as liberals. They believe that the Bible is a book of words about God rather than the words of God. They feel that the Bible writers were people who had special insights or experiences of God which they wrote in their own way. This means that there may well be mistakes and contradictions in the Bible, but what matters are the great truths about God that the Bible contains. Such Christians regard Genesis 1–3 as a metaphor about creation where what is important is the truth that the universe was created by God, and that that creation was good. They see Genesis 2–3 as written by a different person, and so it is a different story of creation expressing some other truths, such as that evil in the world comes from human misuse of **free will**. Liberal Christians accept the theories of the Big Bang and evolution (see Topic 1.4.1, page 110).

Sources of wisdom and authority

Some questions will say that you must refer to 'sources of wisdom and authority in your answer'. Sources of wisdom and authority for Christianity are:

- the Bible
- the Creeds
- the Catechism of the Church
- decisions of Church Councils
- statements by Church leaders
- anything that is used by the faith to inform or express belief, such as the words of the Dalai Lama or Martin Luther King Jr.

Useful words

Free will – the idea that human beings are free to make their own choices

Activities

1. What are the main differences and similarities between the two biblical accounts of creation?
2. How do Christians interpret the two different biblical accounts of creation? How would you interpret them?
3. Do you think it is possible for us to know that God created the universe?

He (the Word) was with God in the beginning. Through him all things were made; without him nothing was made that has been made. (John 1:2–3)

Useful words

Ex nihilo – from nothing

So God created man in his own image, in the image of God he created him; male and female he created them. (Genesis 1:27)

Activity

Look at the quotation above from Genesis 1:27. What do you think it means?

The role of the Word and Spirit in creation

The Bible begins with the words:

> *In the beginning God created the heaven and the earth. (Genesis 1:1)*

Genesis 1 records that at the beginning of creation, 'The Spirit of God was hovering over the waters'. It was the Spirit of God that created the universe out of nothing (***ex nihilo***), showing that God is all-powerful and is the cause of all life (which is why the Christian Creeds teach that God is the Father Almighty).

John's Gospel records creation in the New Testament, claiming that:

> *In the beginning was the Word, and the Word was with God, and the Word was God. (John 1:1)*

John goes on to claim that everything was made through the Word and that without the Word 'nothing was made that has been made' (John 1:3). As John identifies the Word with Jesus, the Son, the biblical creation shows that the God who created is the God Christians believe to be a Trinity.

Christians believe that God's work did not stop with the creation of humans; he continues to care for the world and show his love for the world.

The importance of creation for Christians today

The major significance of Christian beliefs about creation is that they show God's goodness. The key teaching of the Bible is that God's creation is good. Genesis 1 states after each day of creation, 'and God saw that it was good' and at the completion of creation, 'God saw all he had made and indeed it was very good' (Genesis 1:31).

God created human beings in his image, meaning that humans occupy a unique place in creation. They are the only creatures who are able to know and to love their creator. The Catechism of the Catholic Church states that being in the image of God means that humans have dignity. They are capable of **self-knowledge** – knowing who they are, why they are here – and have free will, meaning that God has given them the freedom to choose between good and evil.

It is this freedom that reflects how humans have been made in the image of God but it also reflects the huge responsibility they have been given. Part of **human dignity** is to have responsibility for God's creation: to care for the planet God has made.

This is the basic Christian belief that God gave humans the **stewardship** of the earth and its resources. Stewardship means looking after something so that it can be passed on to the next generation. In the Parable of the Talents or Minas (Luke 19:11–26), Jesus taught that God expects humans to pass on to the next generation more than they have been given. Christians believe that stewardship not only means looking after the earth's resources, it also means making sure that the earth's resources are shared out fairly.

The responsibility, however, is great. How well Christians perform the task of being God's stewards of the earth will determine how they are judged by God after death.

Useful words

Self-knowledge – knowing who you are and why you are here

Human dignity – the belief that humans are persons, not things, and that they have self-knowledge and free will

Stewardship – looking after something so it can be passed on to the next generation

Activities

1. What does the Bible say is the role of the Word and the Spirit in creation?
2. Why do you think creation is important for Christians today?

Practice questions

c Explain three ways in which Christians interpret the biblical accounts of creation. In your answer you must refer to a source of wisdom and authority.

d 'It's hard to believe the biblical accounts of creation.' Evaluate this statement considering arguments for and against. In your answer you should:

- refer to Christian teachings
- refer to different Christian points of view
- reach a justified conclusion.

Summary

There are two accounts of creation in the Old Testament. Genesis 1 says that God created everything in six days beginning with light and ending with creating humans. Genesis 2 says that God created the heavens and earth, then created man (Adam), then vegetation, then animals and finally woman.

Christians who believe the Bible is the literal word of God interpret Genesis 2 as being just about Day 6 of creation. Conservative Christians believe that Genesis 2 is a commentary on Genesis 1. Liberal Christians think that the two accounts have different human authors and that they are stories giving the important truth that everything was created by God.

John's Gospel claims that everything was created by the word which was God and which became flesh in Jesus.

Topic 1.1.3 The incarnation

Thinking points

In this topic you need to:
- think about the nature and importance of the person of Jesus Christ as the incarnate Son of God
- know the biblical basis of this teaching
- be able to evaluate the importance of the incarnation for Christians today.

Useful words

Incarnation – the belief that God took human form in Jesus
Virgin birth – the belief that Jesus was not conceived through sex
Gospels – the books of the Bible (Matthew, Mark, Luke and John), which are the only record of Jesus' life

Jesus, the incarnate Son of God

The **incarnation** is the Christian belief that God became a human being in Jesus. Christians believe that when Adam and Eve disobeyed God in the Garden of Eden, they broke the previously perfect relationship between God and humankind. This meant that before the incarnation, it was only possible to have a partial relationship with God. However, through the incarnation (which led to the life, death and resurrection of Jesus) the power of sin was cancelled so that it became possible for humans to have a full relationship with God and go to heaven after death.

As the only Son of God, most Christians believe that Jesus did not have a normal conception but that he did have a normal birth. Because Jesus' father was God, his mother, Mary, was a virgin when Jesus was born.

Christians believe that all human beings are children of God but by giving Jesus the title the only Son of God, they express their belief that Jesus was God in human form. Christians believe that this means that Jesus had two natures. In his human nature he was a human being, but in his divine nature he was God. So Christians believe that Jesus, the only Son of God, was both fully human and fully divine.

The **virgin birth** is important to most Christians because it shows that Jesus was the Son of God. It shows that Jesus was conceived by the Holy Spirit and not by Joseph, so God was Jesus' Father. This is important for Christians to believe because if Jesus was not conceived of the Holy Spirit but was brought into the world by sex he would not be God incarnate, but just a man.

The biblical basis for the incarnation

Our knowledge of Jesus and his incarnation comes from the **Gospels** of Matthew, Luke and John.

Mark's Gospel says nothing about the incarnation and begins with John the Baptist baptising Jesus.

Matthew's Gospel

Matthew's Gospel tells how Mary became pregnant and how Joseph was told by an angel that the baby was conceived by the Holy Spirit and that the child was to be called Jesus because he would save the people from their sins. Matthew records that the birth took place in Bethlehem in the time of King Herod and that wise men came from the East to worship him. When Herod heard of Jesus' birth he planned to kill the baby, so that he wouldn't eventually challenge him for the throne. But when his plan to kill Jesus didn't work he organised the slaughter of all babies under the age of two in Bethlehem. Being warned by an angel, Joseph escaped with his family to Egypt and did not return until Herod was dead.

Jesus Christ, God incarnate, shown in a mosaic from Daphni, Greece, *c.*1080–1100. 'The Word became flesh' (John 1:14).

At Christmas, the Almighty becomes a child and asks for our help and protection. His way of showing that he is God challenges our way of being human. By knocking at our door, he challenges us and our freedom; he calls us to examine how we understand and live our lives. (Urbi et Orbi, *Pope Benedict XVI, Christmas 2005)*

Beyond all question, the mystery from which true godliness springs is great: He (Jesus) appeared in the flesh, was vindicated by the Spirit, was seen by angels, was preached among the nations, was believed on in the world, was taken up in glory. (1 Timothy 3:16)

Luke's Gospel

Luke's Gospel begins with the miraculous birth of John the Baptist (his mother Elizabeth was old and infertile), a relative of Mary. The Angel Gabriel then appears to Mary and tells her she will be made pregnant by the Holy Spirit and give birth to a child who will be called 'the Son of the Most High'. Mary and Joseph travel from Nazareth, where they live, to Bethlehem because of a Roman census and Jesus is born in Bethlehem. Shepherds are told of Jesus' birth by angels and they come to worship Jesus. Later, the family go to the temple in Jerusalem for the after-birth purification ceremony and then return to live in Nazareth.

John's Gospel

John's Gospel records the incarnation in a **theological** way rather than in story form. He identifies Jesus as the Word of God and begins his Gospel at the beginning of the universe:

> *In the beginning was the Word, and the Word was with God, and the Word was God. (John 1:1)*

John then goes on to say that the Word made everything that is and is the light and life of the world. After this clear description of the second person of the Trinity, John continues,

> *The Word became flesh and made his dwelling among us. We have seen his glory, the glory of the One and Only (or Only Begotten) who came from the Father full of grace and truth. (John 1:14)*

This is the basis of the incarnation: it means that Jesus was God in human form.

Useful words

Theological – academic study of God and religious ideas

Activities

1. Look at Pope Benedict's *Urbi et Orbi* message from 2005. What do you think it means?
2. What are the similarities and differences between the accounts of the incarnation in Matthew, Luke and John?
3. What do you think 'the Word became flesh' means?

The importance and significance of the incarnation

The incarnation is both important and significant for Christians because:

- It shows Christians that God cared so much about the world that he sent his Son to show humans what God is like and to teach them how to live.
- It is the basis of the Christian faith; without the incarnation of Jesus Christ, the Son of God, there would be no Christianity.
- In Jesus, the incarnate Son of God, humans can see what God is like. It is hard for humans to understand an infinite, non-material, omnipotent being, but an incarnate God brings God closer to human understanding.
- Through the incarnation, God began the process of salvation from sin, so making it possible for humans to have a full relationship with him and go to heaven after death.

Activities

1. Read the quotation from 1 Timothy on page 13. What does it say about the nature of Jesus?
2. Do you think the baby Jesus was God incarnate?

Practice questions

c Explain two reasons why Christians believe Jesus was God incarnate. In your answer you must refer to a source of wisdom and authority.

d 'Jesus was God incarnate.' Evaluate this statement considering arguments for and against. In your answer you should:

- refer to Christian teachings
- reach a justified conclusion.

Summary

Christians believe in the incarnation, which means that God became man in Jesus. They believe that this happened through the virgin birth and that Jesus, therefore, was both man and God. Jesus was conceived by the Holy Spirit and was God on earth. The evidence for this comes from the Gospels of Matthew and Luke, which tell the stories of Jesus' birth, and the Gospel of John, which explains how Jesus was God in human form.

Topic 1.1.4 The last days of Jesus' life

The events leading to the death of Jesus form the basis of the Christian faith. You need to know these events as they are recorded in Luke's Gospel chapters 22–24.

The Last Supper

The night before his crucifixion (**Maundy Thursday**), Jesus shared a final meal with his disciples, which is known as the Last Supper.

According to the Luke, the meal took place in the Upper Room in Jerusalem and Jesus **prophesied** that one of the disciples would betray him. Then at the end of the meal, Jesus 'took bread, gave thanks and broke it, and gave it to them, saying, "This is my body given for you, do this in remembrance of me" ' (Luke 22:19).

> *Then he took the cup, gave thanks and offered it to them, saying, 'Drink from it, all of you. This is the new covenant in my blood which is poured out for you.'* (Luke 22:20)

After this, Jesus and his disciples had a discussion about greatness in which Jesus taught that in his kingdom the greatest would be the one who served. Jesus then prophesied that Peter would deny him three times before the cock crowed.

Jesus and his disciples then went to the Mount of Olives and Jesus moved away from the disciples to pray. He prayed for God to 'take this cup from me, yet not my will but yours be done' (the cup being his crucifixion). Then Jesus returned to the disciples and found them asleep.

Thinking points

In this topic you need to:

- think about the Bible accounts of the Last Supper, the betrayal, arrest, trial, crucifixion, resurrection and ascension of Jesus
- be able to evaluate the importance of these events for understanding the purpose of the life of Jesus Christ.

Useful words

Maundy – refers to the washing of the disciples' feet
Maundy Thursday – the day before Jesus was crucified (Good Friday)
Prophesied – predicted events in the future

A painting of the Last Supper in St Nicholas Church, Brussels, Belgium.

Father, if you are willing, take this cup from me; yet not my will, but yours be done. (Luke 22:42)

Useful words

Sanhedrin – the supreme religious authority in Israel at the time of Jesus
Blasphemy – speaking disrespectfully about God or sacred things
Treason – attempting to overthrow a government or state
Tomb – a burial place

The betrayal and arrest

As Jesus talked to the disciples, Judas arrived with the chief priests and the temple guard. Jesus' followers wanted to fight, but Jesus told them to put their swords away. However, one of his followers struck a servant of the High Priest and cut off his ear, but Jesus healed it and ordered there to be no violence. Jesus was led away to the house of the High Priest. Peter followed, but when he was asked, three times, if he was a follower of Jesus, he denied it, then wept bitterly when the cock crowed.

The trial

Jesus was then taken for trial by the Jewish Council known as the **Sanhedrin**, who condemned him for claiming to be 'the Christ, the Son of God', which they regarded as **blasphemy**. Early the next morning, Jesus was taken before the Roman governor, Pontius Pilate, and accused by the Sanhedrin leaders of claiming to be the King of the Jews. Pilate then tried him for **treason** but could not find him guilty of the charges and so Pilate offered to release either Jesus or a Jewish freedom fighter, Barabbas. The crowd chose Barabbas and Jesus was condemned to crucifixion. The soldiers guarding Jesus put a crown of thorns on his head and mocked him as a pretend king, although in Luke's Gospel it is the soldiers of the Sanhedrin who mock Jesus before he is taken to Pilate.

All four Gospels agree that the disciples ran away; only Jesus' women followers stayed with him and stood by while he was crucified.

The crucifixion

The four Gospels all agree that Jesus was crucified on a Friday (Good Friday) and that Simon of Cyrene carried the cross for Jesus. The Gospels agree that a robber was crucified on either side of Jesus, that a sign above him said he was the King of the Jews and that the bystanders mocked Jesus and challenged him to come down from the cross.

As he was being crucified, Jesus said,

> *Father forgive them, for they do not know what they are doing. (Luke 23:34)*

One of the criminals asked Jesus to save himself and also the two criminals if he was the Christ. The other criminal said they deserved to die for what they had done, but Jesus had done nothing wrong. Jesus said to this criminal, 'today you will be with me in paradise'. The crucifixion lasted just over three hours before Jesus cried out, 'Father into your hands I commit my spirit', then Jesus died in agony. The centurion of the guard said, 'Surely this was a righteous man'.

The resurrection

A member of the Sanhedrin, Joseph of Arimathea, asked Pilate for permission to bury Jesus' body in his **tomb**. Early on the Sunday morning Jesus' women followers went to anoint the body with spices. However, when the women entered the tomb, they found it empty. Two men then appeared in gleaming clothes and told the women that Jesus had risen. The women then told the disciples, who came and saw the empty tomb.

Luke says Jesus then appeared to two disciples (not from the Twelve) travelling to a village near Jerusalem called Emmaus. They did not realise it was Jesus until he broke bread with them and then disappeared. They

Activities

1. What happened at the Last Supper?
2. Why do you think Judas Iscariot betrayed Jesus?
3. Why would Pilate have thought claiming to be the King of the Jews was worse than claiming to be the Son of God?
4. Why do you think the disciples ran away and the women went to the cross with Jesus?

returned to Jerusalem and told the eleven disciples what had happened and as they were talking, Jesus appeared to them and showed them his hands and feet and let them touch him.

The ascension

St Luke records that 40 days after his resurrection, Jesus told his remaining disciples to stay in Jerusalem where they would receive the power of the Holy Spirit. Then he was taken up from them into a cloud and two men in white appeared and told them that Jesus had been taken into heaven (Acts 1:4–11). This is known as the **ascension**. Christians believe that the ascension removed Jesus from the limitations of human flesh and allowed him to be present with his followers wherever they were.

Useful words

Ascension – the return of Christ to heaven

Differences in the records of the other Gospels

The other three Gospels have many differences in their descriptions of Jesus' last days, but perhaps the main ones are:

- In John's Gospel, there is no mention of the Upper Room and no mention of the bread and wine or Jesus' words. Instead, John records Jesus washing his disciples' feet and some long theological discussions.
- Matthew and Mark say that the betrayal and arrest took place in the Garden of Gethsemane.
- John's Gospel says that Joseph of Arimathea and another disciple, Nicodemus, anointed the body with spices before placing it in the tomb, whereas the other three Gospels say that women brought spices to the tomb on Sunday morning to anoint it.
- Matthew says that there was a violent earthquake on the Sunday morning, an angel came and rolled the stone away from the tomb entrance and the guards ran away, but this is not mentioned in the other Gospels and Matthew is the only Gospel to mention Pilate putting a guard on the tomb.
- Matthew alone states that the guards were paid to say that the disciples had stolen the body.
- According to Matthew, the angel told the women and disciples that Jesus would meet them in Galilee. He then reports that the eleven remaining disciples went to Galilee and met Jesus on a mountain where he commissioned them to convert the whole world.
- According to Mark, a young man told the women who came to anoint the body that they should tell the disciples that Jesus would meet them in Galilee.
- According to John's Gospel, Mary Magdalene found the empty tomb and told Peter and John, who came to see. She then met Jesus and mistook him for a gardener before he revealed his true identity. John says that Jesus would not allow Mary to touch him because he has not yet ascended, but John records that a week later Thomas was allowed to touch him when Jesus appeared to the disciples in Jerusalem. John then records some appearances in Galilee including one where Jesus helped the disciples to catch a large number of fish while they were out fishing on the Sea of Galilee, which Jesus then shared with them as a breakfast meal before he gave Peter a special commission to care for his sheep (usually taken to mean the Church).

Activities

1. Make a list of the differences in the Gospel accounts of the resurrection.
2. Do you think it matters that there are differences in the Gospel accounts of the resurrection?

Jesus' ascension as pictured in the Coptic Church of El Adra, Aswan, Egypt.

The importance of these events in understanding the purpose of the life of Jesus Christ

- The Last Supper is the basis of the Eucharist, the most important form of Christian worship, as the priest or minister blesses bread and wine using Jesus' words and the congregation shares the bread and wine just as the disciples did (see Topic 1.3.2, page 75).
- Christians believe that Jesus' death on the cross brought about salvation from sin (see Topic 1.1.5, page 19).
- The resurrection is the basis of Christian belief as St Paul said, 'If Christ has not been raised, our preaching is useless and so is your faith' (1 Corinthians 15:17), and is remembered and celebrated by Christians in most of their services today, especially those at which the Nicene or **Apostles' Creed** is recited by the congregation.
- The resurrection of Jesus is also the basis of the Christian belief in life after death and the promise that death is not the end (see Topic 1.1.6, page 23).
- The ascension reminds Christians that Jesus has gone to heaven to prepare a place for them so that they don't need to fear death. They also believe that through the ascension, Christ is no longer restricted by time and space and so can be with them on earth wherever they are.

Useful words

Apostles' Creed – a short statement of belief attributed to the disciples of Jesus

Summary

The Last Supper was when Jesus began the Eucharist by sharing bread and wine with his disciples on Maundy Thursday. They then went to the Mount of Olives, where Jesus prayed to be spared death, Judas betrayed Jesus, and Jesus was arrested. Jesus was tried by the Sanhedrin and then by Pontius Pilate and Herod. He was crucified on Good Friday and buried by Joseph of Arimathea. Jesus rose from the dead on Easter Sunday and appeared to the disciples before ascending to heaven.

The evidence for this is only found in the Gospels, which do not always agree with each other on precisely what happened.

Activities

1. Look at the painting of the Ascension. Does this painting make sense in the age of space exploration?
2. Why do you think the only accounts of Jesus' last days were written by Christians?
3. Do you think the events of Jesus' last days are important for people today?

Practice questions

c. Explain two reasons why the events of his last days show the importance of Jesus. In your answer you must refer to a source of wisdom and authority.

d. 'The resurrection was the most important event in the life of Jesus.' Evaluate this statement considering arguments for and against. In your response you should:
- refer to Christian teachings
- reach a justified conclusion.

Topic 1.1.5 The nature of salvation

The nature of salvation

Sin is an action that breaks God's law. Sin makes it difficult to have a relationship with God because sin separates a person from God. Sin can be:

- Original sin, which is inherited from the actions of Adam and Eve. Most Christians believe that when Adam and Eve disobeyed God in the Garden of Eden, they broke the perfect relationship between humans and God and as a result everyone is born with original sin.
- Personal sin, which is the consequence of a person's own actions.

Many Christians believe that those who die with unforgiven sins will not be able to get to heaven.

Salvation means being saved from sin, and Christians believe that salvation is essential to have a relationship with God while on earth, and to have eternal life with God in heaven after death.

The role of Jesus in salvation

At the time of Jesus, the Jewish people believed that salvation came from obeying the 613 laws given to Moses in the **Torah**. However, Christians believe that Jesus came to earth in order for Christians to receive salvation in a more permanent way.

They believe that when Jesus died on the cross, his death paid for human sins and gave people the chance of salvation. When people believe in Jesus they believe that they receive God's **grace**, which helps them lead a good Christian life.

> *For God did not send his Son into the world to condemn the world, but to save the world through him.* (John 3:17)

> *Salvation is found in no one else, for there is no other name under heaven given to men by which we must be saved.* (Acts 4:12)

Christians sometimes use the word atonement to describe the role of Jesus' salvation. **Atonement** means **reconciliation**, and the healing of the broken relationship between God and humans.

Roman Catholic, Orthodox and some Anglican Christians believe that they can receive the salvation offered by Jesus' death by:

- receiving the **sacraments** of baptism and confirmation
- receiving the sacrament of reconciliation/confession
- receiving the sacrament of the Eucharist (Holy Communion)
- leading a Christian life.

Many Protestants, especially Evangelicals, believe that salvation comes through a personal acceptance of Jesus as Lord and Saviour.

Thinking points

In this topic you need to:

- think about the nature of salvation (law, sin, grace and spirit)
- understand the role of Christ within salvation including reference to John 3:10–21 and Acts 4:8–12
- think about different attitudes to atonement within Christianity
- evaluate different understandings of the importance of atonement and salvation.

Useful words

Sin – an act that is against God's will
Salvation – the act of delivering from sin or saving from evil
Torah – the books of Moses (Genesis, Exodus, Leviticus, Numbers, Deuteronomy), the most holy book of Judaism
Grace – God's gift which gives the strength to be good and holy
Atonement – reconciliation between God and humans
Reconciliation – bringing together people who were opposed to each other
Sacrament – an outward ceremony through which God's grace is given

Activity

Look at the passages from John 3:10–21 and Acts 4:8–12. What do they tell us about the role of Jesus in salvation?

Catholics participating in the Mass, as the service including the Eucharist is known in the Catholic Church.

Why is salvation from sin important to Christians?

Salvation from sin is important because:

- Without salvation, a person's sins will prevent them from having a relationship with God in this life and send them to hell or **purgatory** after death.
- Salvation is the only way that Christians can have eternal life with God. This eternal life will be perfect and is beyond description.
- Salvation from sin was the purpose of the life, death and resurrection of Jesus. Jesus is the saviour of the world whose death on the cross brought forgiveness of sins and the assurance of eternal life.

Useful words

Purgatory – a place where Catholics believe souls go after death to be purified

Activities

1. Why do Christians think people need salvation from sin?
2. Look at the photo of the Mass. How do Roman Catholics believe Jesus brings salvation to people today?

Divergent Christian understandings of atonement

Atonement, as the word suggests, comes from 'at-one-ment': being in harmony with someone. Christians use it to describe how by paying the price for human sin, Jesus' death repaired the broken relationship between humans and God. It refers to the forgiving or pardoning of sin, especially original sin, through the death and resurrection of Jesus, allowing God to be reconciled with his creation. However, there are three different understandings of how exactly Jesus' death brought about atonement and salvation in Christianity:

1 The Roman Catholic understanding

The Catholic Church teaches that Christ offered himself as a sacrifice for human sin in an act of love. So Jesus' death on the cross made 'satisfaction' for our sins. In his act of self-sacrifice (**Christ's Passion**), Christ demonstrated his Father's love for humanity.

In this view, salvation comes through taking the sacraments of the Church.

Useful words

Christ's Passion – the betrayal, arrest, trials and crucifixion of Jesus
Faith – firm belief without logical proof

2 Evangelical Protestant understanding

Evangelical Protestants' understanding of how Jesus' death led to atonement is often known as the Protestant 'penal substitution theory'. They believe that God's justice meant that he needed to punish human sin. However, rather than punish humans he took the punishment on himself, through Jesus' death on the cross. So Jesus acted as a substitute and took the punishment of all humans.

In this view, salvation comes through **faith** in the atoning death of Christ by taking Jesus as one's Lord and Saviour.

3 Liberal Protestant understanding

Most liberal Protestants believe that the way Jesus brought about atonement was by acting as a moral example to humanity. They believe that through his teachings, the example he set in his life and most of all through his death on the cross Jesus showed God's love for humankind.

In response to the love Jesus showed, humans are inspired to follow his example and live a good life and to repent their sins. By doing these things humans can be reunited with God.

On this view, salvation comes from living the Christian life and following the teachings and example of Jesus.

Activity

Look at the placard in the photo below. Do you think this would make non-religious people look for salvation?

An Evangelical placard in Belfast.

The importance of atonement and salvation for Christians today

For conservative and fundamentalist Christians, salvation is important because they believe that without salvation from sin, they will never be able to have a proper relationship with God, their sins will not be forgiven and so they will not be able to enter heaven. Atonement is important because the atoning death of God's Son was the only way to bring salvation to humanity.

For liberal Christians, their understanding of the atonement makes it important because it inspires them to live a good Christian life, and living the Christian life will bring them salvation.

Activity

Which Christian understanding of atonement do you agree with the most?

Practice questions

c Explain two reasons why Christians believe salvation is important. In your answer you must refer to a source of wisdom and authority.

d 'Only those who have been saved from sin will get to heaven.' Evaluate this statement considering arguments for and against. In your response you should:

- refer to Christian teachings
- reach a justified conclusion.

Summary

Christians believe that they need salvation from sin because sin stops people from having a proper relationship with God. All Christians believe that Jesus saved people from sin (atonement) by his death on the cross. Catholics and Orthodox Christians believe that Jesus brings salvation through the sacraments of the Church. Some Protestants believe that salvation comes through believing in Jesus' saving work. Many Protestants believe that salvation comes through following the teachings and example of Jesus.

Christians believe that salvation is important, because without it many believe they will go to hell.

Topic 1.1.6 Christian eschatology

Eschatology refers to religious beliefs about death, judgement and life after death. All Christians believe that this life is not all there is. They believe that God will reward the good and punish the bad in some form of life after death. However, there are different attitudes in Christianity about the nature of life after death.

Resurrection of the body

Some Protestants believe that when people die, their soul remains in the grave until the time when God will end the world. This is known as the Last Day, which will follow the Second Coming of Jesus. This is the belief that Jesus will return to earth to declare the end of the world. At that time, the dead will be raised and both the living and the dead will be given **resurrection** bodies.

Everyone will then appear before God for the final judgement. This judgement will be based on both what people believe and how they have lived their lives on earth. Some Christians believe that those Christians who have been born again, and have repented of their sins, will go to **heaven** for eternity. Everyone else will go to **hell** for eternity because they have rejected God's love.

Some Christians believe in the resurrection of the body because it was Jesus' body which physically rose from the dead, and his resurrection body was different from his earthly body, so Christians' bodies will rise and become resurrection bodies. This is what is taught by St Paul in 1 Corinthians 15 and by John the Divine in Revelation.

Immortality of the soul

Many Christians believe that people are made up of a body and a soul. They believe that the soul is non-material and immortal (it will never die). They believe that when the body dies, the soul leaves the body to live with God.

These Christians believe that there is a spirit world where God can be experienced in a much more immediate way than on earth. Some of these Christians believe that the nature of the afterlife in the spirit world is determined by what people believe and how they have lived their lives on earth. Therefore, they believe that good Christians will go to heaven, but everyone else will go to a spiritual form of hell.

Others do not believe in any form of hell. They believe that all souls will have opportunities to learn from their mistakes on earth, and so move up in a variety of types of heaven until they reach the presence of God.

Belief in the **immortality of the soul** is based on the belief that after his ascension, Jesus became a spirit and went to the spirit world. Also, Jesus told the robber crucified with him that he would go straight to paradise, and there are references in the Gospels to Abraham, Moses and Elijah being able to be communicated with in heaven, therefore they must be living on in a spiritual world. Furthermore, the evidence of the paranormal (see Topic 1.4.5, page 128) seems to indicate the immortality of the soul rather than the resurrection of the body.

Thinking points

In this topic you need to:

- think about divergent Christian teachings about life after death
- think about the nature of resurrection, judgement, heaven and hell and purgatory
- know how these teachings are shown in the Bible, especially 2 Corinthians 5:1–10
- be able to evaluate the importance of the teachings about life after death for Christians today.

Useful words

Resurrection – the belief that, after death, the body stays in the grave until the end of the world, when it is raised

Heaven – a place of paradise in the presence of God

Hell – a place of horrors where Satan rules

Immortality of the soul – the idea that the soul lives on after the death of the body

Activity

What are the differences between resurrection and believing in the immortality of the soul?

Many Christians believe in a mixture of resurrection and immortality. They think their souls will live on after death and have a final judgement.

> *Christ has indeed been raised from the dead, the first fruits of those who have fallen asleep ... God gives it a body as he has determined ... The body that is sown perishable, it is raised imperishable ... it is sown a natural body, it is raised a spiritual body.* (1 Corinthians 15)

Useful words

Purgatory – a place where Catholics believe souls go after death to be purified

Catholic teachings about life after death

Catholics believe in a mixture of resurrection and immortality. The Roman Catholic Church teaches in the Catechism that when people die, Christians who are perfectly purified will go to heaven, Christians who have died with unforgiven sins (and possibly good members of other religions and good non-believers) will go to **purgatory** to be purified of their sins and evil people will go to hell. At the end of the world, God will judge everyone and make a new heaven and a new earth where the resurrected souls from heaven and purgatory will live, but the souls from hell will return to hell.

Heaven and hell

All Christians believe in heaven as a perfect place in the company of God, although they may describe it in different ways. All Christians believe that heaven is a place of everlasting life where Christians go after their death. Many Christians believe that hell is the opposite of heaven; it is a place of suffering away from the presence of God.

However, there are different attitudes about heaven and hell among Christians:

- Most Catholics believe that all Christians will eventually go to heaven and that good followers of any religion may go to heaven, but everyone else will go to hell.
- Some Christians believe that only good Christians will go to heaven, but bad Christians and all members of other religions will go to hell.
- Some believe that all good people will go to heaven whatever they believe, but bad people will go to hell.
- Other Christians believe that there is no hell, only levels of heaven, so everyone will eventually go to heaven.

Purgatory

Catholic Christians believe that purgatory is the place where those Christians who have died with unforgiven sins go to be purified of their sins so that they can go to heaven.

However, Protestant Christians believe that there is no such place as purgatory since it has no biblical foundation. As Article 22 of the 39 Articles of the Church of England (the statement of the beliefs of the Church of England) states:

> *The Romish Doctrine concerning Purgatory, Pardons, Worshipping and Adoration, as well of Images as of Relics, and also Invocation of Saints, is a fond thing, vainly invented, and grounded upon no warranty of Scripture, but rather repugnant to the Word of God.*

The final judgement

As we have seen, Christians believe that after death each person will be judged and the nature of their afterlife will depend on the outcome of this judgement.

Catholics and Protestants who believe in resurrection believe that this will be a final judgement at the end of the world when the living and the raised dead will be gathered before God. They will be judged on how they have lived and on what they have believed.

Christians who believe in immortality of the soul believe that each soul will be judged when they die and the basis of the judgement will be focused on how they have lived.

Christian beliefs about judgement are based on Bible teachings such as the Parable of the Sheep and the Goats. This parable says that the final judgement will be based on whether people have fed the hungry, clothed the naked, welcomed strangers, and visited the sick and those in prison: those who have done this will go to heaven, those who have not will go to eternal punishment (Matthew 25:31–46).

An angel leading a soul into hell. Oil painting by a follower of Hieronymus Bosch, *c.*1540.

How beliefs about life after death are shown in the Bible

As we have seen, Christian teachings about life after death come from the Bible. The belief in resurrection is based on St Paul's teaching in 1 Corinthians 15. Belief in the immortality of the soul comes from such verses as Jesus' promise to the robber crucified with him. Heaven is referred to as a place of paradise where God dwells and hell is referred to as a place of fire and punishment in many places in the Bible, especially in the parables of Jesus such as the Sheep and Goats. The final judgement is also taught in many biblical passages, perhaps most clearly in the Parable of the Sheep and Goats. The reason Protestants do not believe in purgatory is that it is not taught in the Bible.

Activities

1. Why do you think Christians have different opinions about heaven and hell?
2. If you were God what would you base the final judgement on?
3. How does St Paul's teaching in 2 Corinthians show the importance of belief in life after death for Christians?

Useful words

Atheist – someone who does not believe that God exists
Agnostic – someone unsure as to whether or not God exists

Summary

Some Evangelical Protestants believe in the resurrection of the body, the idea that everyone will be raised on the Last Day to be judged by God and sent to heaven or hell depending on whether they've been a good Christian or not.

Liberal Christians believe that the soul lives on after death in a spirit world and that their after-lives will depend on how they have lived this life.

Catholic Christians believe that those who die with all their sins forgiven go straight to heaven; those who die with unforgiven sins will go to purgatory to be purified. At the end of the world they will be judged and the good will go to heaven and the evil to hell.

These beliefs about life after death affect Christians' lives as they try to live a good Christian life so that they go to heaven and not hell.

A major Bible teaching on life after death comes from St Paul in 2 Corinthians 5:1–10, where he says:

- Christians know that if their body is destroyed they will have a non-physical home in heaven.
- Christians long to be in heaven, which is their goal.
- Because they are aiming for heaven, Christians do all they can to please God while living on earth.
- Christians do this because they know that everyone will appear before God to be judged on the good and/or bad deeds they have done on earth.

Why teachings about life after death are important to Christians today

- Christians believe that what happens to them after they die will be determined by how they have lived in this life. Many Christians believe that they will be judged by God and that only if they have lived a good Christian life will they be allowed into heaven. So Christians will try to live a good Christian life following the teachings of the Bible and the Church so that they go to heaven and not hell when they die.
- Christians believe that sin can prevent people from going to heaven. Some Christians believe that those who die with unforgiven sins will go to hell. The Catholic Church teaches that those who die with unforgiven sins will go to purgatory to be purified before they can reach heaven. Clearly, these teachings mean that Christians will try to avoid committing sins in their lives so that they will go to heaven.
- Beliefs about life after death give Christians' lives meaning and purpose. They feel that for life to end at death does not make sense. A life after death, in which people will be judged on how they live this life, with the good rewarded and the evil punished, makes sense of this life. If the purpose of life is for people to live their lives in such a way that they spend eternity in heaven, then that gives life a meaning. This may be why in surveys it is found that Christians suffer less from depression and are less likely to kill themselves than **atheists** and **agnostics**.

Practice questions

c Explain two reasons why beliefs about life after death are important for Christians. In your answer you must refer to a source of wisdom and authority.

d 'Only those who believe in Jesus will go to heaven.' Evaluate this statement considering arguments for and against. In your response you should:

- refer to Christian teachings
- refer to different Christian points of view
- reach a justified conclusion.

Topic 1.1.7 The problem of evil and suffering

Evil and suffering can take two forms: **moral suffering** and **natural suffering**.

Moral suffering

Moral suffering is suffering that is caused by humans misusing their free will (the human ability to make choices). It is always possible to choose to do something good or something evil. Humans choosing to do evil usually cause moral suffering.

War is a good example of moral suffering. Wars cause large amounts of suffering. Not only are military personnel on both sides made to suffer, but modern warfare also uses weapons that kill and injure large numbers of innocent civilians. All wars are caused by the actions of humans who could have chosen to act differently. Suicide bombers actively choose to cause suffering to innocent people, who are likely to include babies and children, in order to draw attention to their cause.

Rape, murder and burglary are clear examples of moral suffering. Less clear would be suffering such as famines, where humans making wrong choices may have caused the suffering, for example, landowners growing cash crops like cotton instead of food in order to make more money. However, the famine could have been caused by something out of human control, such as a drought.

Christians often call acts of moral evil sins because they are against what God wants humans to do (as revealed to them, for example, in the Ten Commandments):

> *You shall not murder.*
> *You shall not commit adultery.*
> *You shall not steal.*
> *You shall not give false testimony ...*
> *You shall not covet ... (The last five of the Ten Commandments, Exodus 20:13–17)*

Natural suffering

Natural suffering is suffering that has not been caused by humans. Earthquakes, floods, volcanoes, droughts, tsunamis, hurricanes, tornadoes, cancers and so on are not actually caused by humans but they result in massive amounts of human suffering. However, some suffering which appears to be caused by nature may actually be the result of human evil choices. For example, climate change is caused by humans polluting the atmosphere and results in more extreme weather and natural disasters.

Activities

1. Look at the last five of the Ten Commandments above. Would breaking these lead to moral suffering?
2. Look at the photo of a burglary. What reasons might the burglar have had for his action?

Thinking points

In this topic you need to:

- think about the problems that evil and suffering raise for Christians about the nature of God
- understand why these problems may lead some believers to reject belief or question their faith
- think about the differences between natural and moral suffering
- be able to evaluate the problems that evil and suffering cause for Christian belief.

What sort of suffering do criminals cause?

Useful words

Moral suffering – suffering caused by actions done by humans

Natural suffering – suffering which is caused by nature and has nothing to do with humans

Rescue workers in Japan two days after a powerful tsunami triggered by an earthquake hit the country's east coast in March 2011.

Activity

Look at the photo above. Who could be blamed for the massive suffering caused by the Japanese tsunami?

Useful words

Holocaust – the mass murder of the Jews by the Nazis in the Second World War
Omnipotent – the belief that God is all-powerful
Omnibenevolent – the belief that God is all-good

How evil and suffering may cause people to question or reject belief in God

Some people cannot believe that a good God would have designed a world that contained natural evils. They find it easier to believe that natural disasters are a result of the earth being formed by accident from the Big Bang and so they question or reject God's existence.

People find it hard to believe in a God who allows humans to cause so much evil and suffering when he could stop it if he wanted to. If God exists, he must have known what Adolf Hitler was going to do, so why not intervene before so many people suffered throughout the Second World War and the **Holocaust**? The existence of this suffering may mean that God does not exist.

Why this raises problems for Christian beliefs about the nature of God

- If God is **omnipotent** (all-powerful), he must be able to remove evil and suffering from the world.
- If God is **omnibenevolent** (all-good), he must want to remove evil and suffering from the world because they cause so much unhappiness.

The Lord is compassionate and gracious, slow to anger, abounding in love. He will not always accuse, nor will he harbour his anger forever. (Psalm 103:8–9)

- If God is **omniscient** (knows everything that is going to happen), he must have known all the evil and suffering that would come from creating the universe in the way he did. Therefore, he should have created the universe in a different way to avoid evil and suffering.
- It follows that, if God exists, there should be no evil or suffering in the world.
- As there is evil and suffering in the world, either God is not omnipotent, or God is not omnibenevolent, or God is not omniscient, or God does not exist.

A British soldier (left) guards Fritz Klein, the doctor of the Bergen-Belsen Nazi concentration camp, standing in front of a mass burial site for dead prisoners.

Christians believe that God is omnipotent, benevolent and omniscient. So, the existence of evil and suffering challenges their beliefs about God, and as these beliefs come from their holy book and creeds, it challenges the whole of their religion.

For many religious believers, evil and suffering only become a problem when they come into contact with them. So, if they experience the suffering caused by a natural disaster like an earthquake, or if their child dies from a disease, the problem can sometimes lead believers into rejecting religion and becoming atheist or agnostic.

Useful words

Omniscient – the belief that God knows everything that has happened and everything that is going to happen

Activity

Find out about the Holocaust, then look at the photo above and explain why some of the soldiers might have lost their faith in God.

Practice questions

c Explain two reasons why evil and suffering in the world cause problems for Christian beliefs about the nature of God.

d 'Evil and suffering are the fault of humans.' Evaluate this statement considering arguments for and against. In your response you should:

- refer to Christian teachings
- reach a justified conclusion.

Summary

Evil and suffering in the world stop some people from believing in God. They think that there should be no evil and suffering in a world created by a good and powerful God. A good God should not want bad things to happen, and a powerful God ought to be able to stop such things, yet they still exist and this leads people to doubt that there is a God.

Topic 1.1.8 Solutions to the problem of evil and suffering

Thinking points

In this topic you need to:

- think about how Christians respond to the problem of suffering biblically (Psalm 119, Job), theoretically and practically
- be able to evaluate the success of these solutions.

Useful words

Holiness – the state of being very moral and spiritual

Psalms – a book of the Old Testament containing 150 sacred songs

Biblical responses to the problem

Many Christians believe that there is no point in worrying about the problem of evil because humans cannot understand God's reasons for doing things. This view is based on the Book of Job in the Old Testament. Job was a sinless man who worshipped God faithfully. However, Satan argued with God that Job only worshipped him because God had given him a good life and that if his good life disappeared he would then stop worshipping God. God did not believe this and so allowed Satan to remove Job's good life and afflict him with terrible diseases. Job asked God why this was happening to him and demanded that God should speak to him directly. However, when Job came face to face with God and was presented with his greatness and **holiness**, he realised that God is so great, humans have no right to question him. God must have a reason for allowing evil and suffering, but people cannot understand the reason.

Christians often combine this response with the one shown in the Book of **Psalms** in the Old Testament. The Psalms show that suffering is intended to be a part of life and many of the Psalms tell of good, religious people suffering, but the Psalms show that life is more than suffering. The other side of suffering is joy and in the Psalms suffering and joy go side by side.

The Psalms also show that suffering can bring believers to a deeper knowledge of God, as shown in Psalm 119:

> *Teach me knowledge and good judgement, for I trust your commands. Before I was afflicted I went astray, but now I obey your word. You are good, and what you do is good; teach me your decrees. Though the arrogant have smeared me with lies, I keep your precepts with all my heart. Their hearts are callous and unfeeling, but I delight in your law. It was good for me to be afflicted so that I might learn your decrees.* (Psalm 119:66–71)

Having God's help and strength when suffering helps Christians to cope with the problem.

Activities

1. Make a list of the weak and strong points of the biblical responses.
2. Do you think Psalm 119 answers the problem of evil and suffering?

Theoretical responses

The free will response is how many Christians claim that evil and suffering are not God's fault. According to Genesis 1, God created humans in his image, which means he created them with free will. Christians believe that God wanted people to be free to decide whether to believe in him or not; he did not want to force them to worship him. However, to be free means to be free to do either good or evil. So when God created free people, he could not create people who always did good because such people would not be free. Creating free people has brought evil and suffering into the world, but the evil and suffering are problems caused by humans misusing their free will, and so are not God's fault.

Often connected with the free will response is the Christian belief that the evil and suffering in this life are not problems because they are part of a plan in which those who suffer will be rewarded by eternal paradise after they die. Most Christians claim that this life is a preparation for paradise. If people are to improve their souls, they need to face evil and suffering in order to become good, kind and loving. They claim that the evil and suffering of this life are things God cannot remove if he is going to give people the chance to become good people. But, in the end, he will show his omnibenevolence and omnipotence by rewarding them in heaven. This is often known as the '**vale of soul making** response'. God created this world as a place for people to develop their souls.

Christians often connect this to the belief that good can come out of evil. For example, in the evil of the Holocaust, Maximilian Kolbe, a **Franciscan friar**, was arrested and sent to **Auschwitz**. Here he continued his priestly ministry discreetly, hearing many confessions and smuggling in bread and wine for Mass. When a married man with children was to be executed, Maximilian offered to take his place. He was **canonised** in 1982, when the man whose life he saved was still living and able to attend the ceremony in Rome.

Maximilian Kolbe (1894–1941) celebrated in a stained-glass window of the Basilica of the Assumption of the Virgin Mary in Marija Bistrica, Croatia.

Practical responses

Many Christians believe that they should respond to evil and suffering in practical ways. The life of Jesus in the Gospels shows that even God's own son had to suffer, and that Jesus commanded his followers to respond to suffering by helping those who suffer. All Christians believe that they should respond to the problem by helping those who suffer and trusting in God for the answer to the problem. The New Testament teaches Christians that Jesus regarded evil and suffering as something to be fought. Jesus healed the sick, fed the hungry, challenged those who were evil, and even raised the dead. Christians feel that they should follow the example of Jesus and fight against evil and suffering by:

- *Praying for those who suffer*. Christians believe that prayer is a very powerful way of responding to the problem. They believe that by praying for those who suffer, God will ensure that the right type of relief for their suffering is provided. Such prayers are called **intercessionary prayers** and all Christian services include prayers of intercession asking God to help those who suffer from poverty,

Useful words

Vale of soul making – the idea that God gave people this life to make their souls good enough for heaven
Franciscan – a member of a religious order which follows the teachings and spiritual disciplines of St Francis of Assisi
Friar – a member of a religious order which does not own property and who has to either work or beg to earn a living
Auschwitz – a Second World War Nazi concentration camp in Poland where at least 1.1 million prisoners died
Canonise – make someone a saint
Intercessionary prayers – prayers asking God's help for other people

Activities

1. Make a list of the weak and strong points of the theoretical responses.
2. Look at the photo of Maximilian Kolbe above. Do you think he deserves to be a saint?

Activities

1. Make a list of the weak and strong points of the practical responses.
2. Look at the photo of a food bank opposite. Why do you think many food banks are run by churches?

Much Wenlock Methodist Church helping in collecting donated food for distribution by the Bridgnorth food bank.

sickness, famine, war and so on. Christians believe that the power of prayer can be seen in its results. Catholic Christians would see this especially in the prayers offered during pilgrimage to Lourdes and Protestant Christians in the healing services held in many churches.

- *Offering practical help to those who suffer.* Jesus did not just pray and preach, he healed the sick, brought sight to the blind and fed the hungry. Christians believe that they should follow Jesus' example and respond to evil in a practical way. As a result, many Christians try to overcome evil and suffering by becoming doctors, nurses, social workers and so on, so that they can help to reduce the amount of suffering in the world. Christians have also founded charities to help to eliminate suffering, such as Christian Aid and CAFOD to ease the suffering of those in less economically developed countries. In the UK, Christian churches organise food banks, campaigns to remove child poverty, charities to help refugees, groups promoting racial harmony and so on.

Summary

Christians respond to the problem of evil and suffering by:

- accepting the teaching of the Bible in Job that God has a reason for suffering but that humans cannot understand it
- accepting the Bible teaching in Psalms that suffering and joy are an essential part of life
- claiming that evil and suffering are the fault of humans misusing their free will
- claiming that evil and suffering are part of a test to prepare people for heaven
- praying for those who suffer
- helping those who suffer.

Practice questions

c. Explain two ways in which Christians respond to the problem of evil and suffering.

d. 'Evil is not a problem for religious believers.' Evaluate this statement considering arguments for and against. In your response you should:
   - refer to Christian teachings
   - refer to different Christian points of view
   - reach a justified conclusion.

How to answer questions

a) State three religious other than Christianity in Britain. [3]

Islam, Hinduism and Judaism are three non-Christian religious traditions in Britain.

A high mark answer because three non-Christian religions in Britain are clearly stated.

b) Explain two reasons why the Trinity is important to Christians. [4]

Christians feel that the Trinity helps them to understand how God works in the world: the Father who creates, the Son who saves from sin and the Spirit who empowers.

They also believe that the Trinity helps them to understand God's unity. There might be three persons but there is only one substance: God.

A high mark answer because two correct reasons are given and each reason is developed

c) Explain two ways Christians respond to evil and suffering. In your answer, you should refer to a source of wisdom and authority. [5]

Christians respond to evil and suffering by helping those who suffer as they were told to by Jesus in the Parable of the Sheep and Goats. They also respond to the problem by seeking an answer in the Bible such as in the Book of Job where they learn that God has a reason for evil and suffering, but humans cannot understand it.

A high mark answer because two ways are explained and each is developed by explicit reference to a Bible teaching.

d) 'Jesus had to die.' Evaluate this statement considering arguments for and against. In your response you should:

- **refer to Christian points of view**
- **refer to different Christian points of view**
- **reach a justified conclusion. [12 marks + 3 spelling, punctuation and grammar (SPaG) marks]**

Many Christians believe that Jesus had to die because otherwise there would be no salvation from sin or eternal life in heaven. Catholics believe that the Father had to hand his Son to sinners in order to reconcile sinners to himself. Evangelical Protestants believe that everyone has sinned and so deserves death ('the wages of sin is death', Romans 6:23) and only by his death could Jesus bear the curse of sin in the place of the whole of humanity and bring salvation.

However, most liberal Protestants do not think Jesus had to die. They believe that salvation comes through following the teachings and example of Jesus, which enables humans to behave like the children of God, and so reconciles them to God. They do not believe a loving, omnipotent God would require his son to die.

It seems to me that, although the idea that Jesus had to die is based on the Bible and Church teachings, the liberal view makes more sense because if God wants us to be saved from our sins, we must be able to do this by changing our behaviour rather than someone having to die.

[Continued]

A high mark answer because it gives two clear developed Christian reasons for thinking that Jesus had to die. It then gives three reasons for liberal Christians disagreeing and then reaches a fully justified conclusion.

SPaG

A high mark answer because the answer spells, punctuates and uses the rules of grammar with consistent accuracy and effective control of meaning. A wide range of specialist terms is used adeptly and with precision.

2 Marriage and the family

Topic 1.2.1 Marriage

Thinking points

In this topic you need to:

- think about Christian teachings on the importance and purpose of marriage, including Mark 10:6–9
- think about the importance of marriage in society; different Christian, non-religious (including Humanist and atheist) attitudes to marriage, including cohabitation, and the Christian responses to them
- be able to explain and evaluate different Christian and non-religious attitudes to marriage.

Useful words

Sacred bond – a joining together sanctified by God which cannot be broken by humans

Adultery – a sexual act between a married person and someone other than their marriage partner

Christian teachings about the importance and purpose of marriage

Jesus taught that:

Marriage was established by God when he created humans: 'But at the beginning of creation God made them male and female. For this reason a man will leave his father and mother and be united to his wife, and the two will become one flesh'. (Mark 10:6–8)

In marriage, God joins the couple together in a ***sacred bond*** *that humans have no right to break: 'So they are no longer two, but one flesh. Therefore what God has joined together, let no one separate'. (Mark 10:9–10)*

Consequently, marriage is for life because God's bonds cannot be broken: 'Anyone who divorces his wife and marries another commits ***adultery****'. (Mark 10:11)*

Two different Christian wedding ceremonies.

The implication of these verses is that Jesus believed in **monogamy** and that marriage should be between one man and one woman.

The Christian Churches follow Jesus in teaching that God created man and woman for each other and that marriage should be a **lifelong relationship** between them.

The Christian Churches teach that God created marriage:

- so that a couple can have a lifelong relationship of love, companionship and faithfulness
- so that a couple can have the support and comfort of each other and enjoy sex with each other in the way God intended for the **procreation** of children
- so that children can be brought up in a Christian family and become members of Christ's Church
- as a way for the couple to show their love for each other and to gain God's grace to help them in their married life.

Marriage is one of the seven **sacraments** of the Catholic and Orthodox Churches and as such it is a sign of **grace**, instituted by Christ himself and, through the Church, imparting God's grace and strength. As a sacrament, Catholic marriage involves not only the bride and groom, but also God himself.

Even though Catholic priests and all monks and nuns are forbidden to marry, marriage is very important in Christianity because:

- Christians believe that marriage was created by God as the way of establishing and preserving society.
- Christians believe that marriage is the only acceptable way for Christians to have a sexual relationship.
- Christian families are brought about through marriage and are the way new life is brought into the Church as the children of Christian parents are baptised and confirmed or dedicated and baptised as adults.

Humanist and atheist attitudes to marriage

Humanists believe that sex and marriage are matters for individual decisions. It is up to individuals whether they live together without marrying (**cohabitation**) or get married in a civil ceremony. However, Humanists expect sexual relations to be based on respect and trust. They believe that relationships should be exclusive (one partnership at a time) and many believe that marriage is a good thing when raising a family because it provides:

- a stable legal and financial backing for a relationship (there can be major problems for a cohabiting spouse if their partner dies)
- more social acceptance of the relationship
- a more stable home for a family
- a public ritual to declare and celebrate the couple's love.

Most atheists have a similar view to Humanists, although some would accept people having multiple sexual partners.

Useful words

Monogamy – marriage to only one person at a time
Lifelong relationship – the idea that marriage can only be ended by the death of a partner
Procreation – making a new life
Sacraments – an outward ceremony through which God's grace is given
Grace – God's gift which gives the strength to be good and holy
Cohabitation – living together in a sexual relationship without being married

Now for the matters you wrote about: It is good for a man not to marry. But since there is so much immorality, each man should have his own wife, and each woman her own husband ... I say this as a concession, not as a command ... Now as to the unmarried and the widows, I say: It is good for them to stay unmarried, as I am. (St Paul in 1 Corinthians 7:1–8)

Activities

1. What are the similarities and differences between the teaching of Jesus on marriage on page 36 and the teaching of St Paul in 1 Corinthians on this page? What are your views about marriage?
2. Why do Christians believe marriage is important?
3. Look at the two wedding photos on page 36. Which do you think is a more accurate reflection of British society today?

A civil wedding of a couple on a tropical beach.

Activity

Look at the photo of a civil wedding. Why do you think so many couples now have a civil rather than a religious wedding?

Humanists and atheists are often classed as non-religious and the number of non-religious people in the UK is increasing. The Census of 2011 and more recent surveys indicate that less than half of the British public believe in God.

Useful words

Spouse – marriage/cohabitation partner

It is now socially quite acceptable for couples to live together rather than marry and a greater percentage are doing so: 5.9 million people were cohabiting in 2012, which has doubled since 1996, and 80 per cent of 30-year-olds say they have cohabited at some point in their lives. In 2012, 70 per cent of weddings were between people who had been living together.

Marriage is still important for the non-religious

In 2012, the number of marriages in England and Wales actually increased by 5.3 per cent to 262,240, from 249,133 in 2011. Although the Civil Partnerships Act 2004 provided same-sex couples with the same rights and treatment as opposite-sex couples who enter into a civil marriage, there was great pressure for this to become a proper marriage. Eventually, this led to the Marriage (Same Sex Couples) Act 2013 that allowed for same-sex couples to marry in just the same way as heterosexual couples. However, the Act did not require religions to provide same-sex marriage ceremonies.

Research shows that most cohabiting couples would like to get married at some point because marriage provides:

- a stable legal and financial backing for a relationship (there can be major problems for a cohabiting **spouse** if their partner dies)
- more social acceptance of the relationship
- a more stable home for a family (many cohabiting couples decide to marry when they start a family)
- a public ritual to declare and celebrate the couple's love.

How Christians have responded to non-religious attitudes to marriage and cohabitation

There have been three very different responses from the Churches:

- The official response of the Roman Catholic Church and the conservative Protestant Churches has been to condemn the non-religious attitude and to insist that Christians should refrain from having sex until they have had a Christian marriage.
- The official response of the more liberal Protestant Churches has been to accept that couples may live together before marriage, but to expect couples to marry when starting a family. The Churches would only accept a sexual relationship between two people committed to a long-term relationship: 'recognising that for many [cohabiting couples] this is a step along the way to the fuller commitment of marriage' (*Something to Celebrate*, a report published by the Church of England's Board of Responsibility, 1997).
- The response of most under-40 churchgoers has been to ignore the Church's teaching. For example, research published in 2014 showed that in the USA (which might be considered a very Christian country), 61 per cent of Christians would have sex before marriage and 56 per cent thought it appropriate to move in with someone after dating for six months. A survey by Professor Linda Woodhead into British Catholic attitudes found 80 per cent of Catholics in favour of premarital sex and 90 per cent accepting of cohabitation.

Activities

1. Why do you think many young people cohabit before they marry?
2. Do you find anything surprising about the Christian responses to non-religious attitudes? Explain your answer.

Practice questions

c. Explain two reasons why Christians get married. In your answer you must refer to a source of wisdom and authority.

d. 'Marriage is more important for Christians than for non-religious people.' Evaluate this statement considering arguments for and against. In your response you should:
- refer to Christian teachings
- refer to different Christian or non-religious points of view
- reach a justified conclusion.

Summary

Christians believe that marriage was established by God for a lifelong relationship of love and faithfulness and bringing up a Christian family as taught by Jesus in Mark's Gospel. Marriage is important for Christians because it was created by God and taught by Jesus, and is the only way for Christians to have sex and raise a family.

Sex before marriage and cohabitation (living together) are much more common as society has become less religious, but many atheists and Humanists regard marriage as good when bringing up a family.

The Catholic and conservative Protestant Churches still condemn sex before marriage and cohabitation but most young Christians ignore this teaching.

Topic 1.2.2 Sexual relationships

Thinking points

In this topic you need to:

- think about Christian teachings about the nature and importance of sexual relationships
- think about different Christian teachings and attitudes towards sexual relationships outside marriage and homosexuality
- be able to explain and evaluate different Christian and non-religious attitudes to sexual relationships and explain Christian responses to them.

Useful words

Premarital sex – sexual activity before marriage
Homosexuality – sexual attraction to someone of the same sex
Extramarital sex – sex acts outside marriage, usually referred to as adultery
Promiscuity – having sex with a number of partners without commitment
Faithful – staying with your marriage partner and having sex only with them

Flee from sexual immorality. All other sins a person commits are outside the body, but whoever sins sexually, sins against their own body. Do you not know that your bodies are temples of the Holy Spirit, who is in you, whom you have received from God? You are not your own; you were bought at a price. Therefore honour God with your bodies.
(1 Corinthians 6:18–20)

Different types of sexual relationship

- **Premarital sex** is sex before marriage. Any sexual relationship between two people who are not married is classed as premarital sex.
- Cohabitation is used to refer to two people who are living together in a sexual relationship without being married.
- Same-sex sexual relationships are classed as **homosexuality**, although they are usually known colloquially as gay relationships. Females in same-sex relationships are known as lesbians.
- **Extramarital sex** is either when a married person has a sexual relationship with someone other than their marriage partner or when an unmarried person has a sexual relationship with a married person.

Christian teachings about the nature and importance of sexual relationships

Christianity teaches that sex is a gift from God to be enjoyed between one man and one woman who are married to each other. Christianity teaches that sex was given to humans by God for the joy, pleasure and bonding of a married couple and for the procreation of children.

Christian teachings about and attitudes towards sexual relationships outside marriage

Most Christians are opposed to any form of sexual relationship outside marriage because:

- The Bible says that fornication (a word used in religion for both premarital sex and **promiscuity**) is sinful and Christians should follow the teachings of the Bible.
- The Catechism of the Catholic Church teaches that premarital sex is wrong and Catholics are encouraged to follow the teachings of the Church.
- All Christians are against adultery because it breaks the wedding vows to be **faithful** to each other.
- Christians are also against adultery because it is condemned in the Ten Commandments, which all Christians should follow.
- Adultery is condemned by Jesus in the Gospels, and all Christians should follow the teachings of Jesus.

Some Christians accept that before marriage couples may have sex and live together. Liberal Protestants in particular do not regard sex before marriage as sinful, although they would expect couples to marry when starting a family and would only accept a sexual relationship between two people committed to a long-term relationship. The latest surveys indicate that at least 80 per cent of young Christians ignore the teachings of the Church and are having premarital sex.

Hollywood film actors Angelina Jolie and Brad Pitt cohabited for nine years before marrying in 2014.

Humanist and atheist attitudes to sexual relationships

Although Humanists and atheists do not disagree with sex before marriage, premarital sex is acceptable only within certain limits:

- Sex must be **consensual sex** – rape in any form is seen as totally unacceptable.
- Sex must be between people 'of age'. Paedophilia is regarded as wrong regardless of religious teachings.
- A sexual partner ought ideally to be single or separated from their partner. Non-religious people find cheating on a partner offensive.
- No payment should be involved in sex – there is still a stigma attached to prostitution.
- Sex should involve a degree of stability. High levels of promiscuity are frowned upon.
- Sex ought to be safe; given the risk of disease and pregnancy, barrier methods of contraception should be used.

Most atheists would have a similar view to Humanists, although some might not object to multiple sexual partners or payment for sex.

Homosexuality

- The various changes in the laws on homosexuality have made it easier to be openly homosexual and have made society more aware and accepting of homosexuality.
- Medical research has shown that homosexuality is most likely to be caused by genetic and hormonal factors when a baby develops.
- As society began to recognise homosexuality as an acceptable orientation, more institutions began to grant equal status and rights for homosexual couples.
- The increased openness of gay celebrities has led to a greater acceptance of all gay people.
- The work of such organisations as **Stonewall** changed many people's attitudes and led to a greater acceptance of equal rights for homosexuals.

Useful words

Consensual sex – when both parties freely agree to sexual activity
Stonewall – a group which campaigns for the equality of lesbian, gay, bisexual and trans people across Britain

[redacted]

Activities

1. Look at the photo of Angelina Jolie and Brad Pitt. Why might a cohabiting couple decide to marry?
2. Do you think Christians would regard adultery as worse than premarital sex?
3. Look at the quotation from 1 Corinthians 6 on page 40:
   - How would you define sexual immorality?
   - How would the Church define sexual immorality?
   - Do you think your body is a temple of the Holy Spirit?

Christian attitudes to same-sex relationships

There are several attitudes to same sex-relationships in Christianity. The main ones are outlined below.

1 The Catholic attitude

Catholics believe that being a homosexual is not a sin but that homosexual sexual relationships are sinful. The Catholic Church asks homosexuals to live without any sexual activity. The Church does not accept same-sex marriage, but is less opposed to **civil partnerships**. However, the Church also teaches that it is sinful to harass homosexuals or attack their behaviour. Catholics have this attitude because:

- The Bible condemns homosexual sexual activity.
- It is the tradition of the Church that sexual activity should be creative and it is not possible for homosexual couples to have sex with a creative purpose.
- The Catechism of the Catholic Church, which all Catholics should follow, teaches that marriage is for a man and a woman to join as one and to raise a family.
- The Church teaches that people cannot help their sexual orientation but they can control their sexual activity. Therefore, discriminating against people because of their sexual orientation is wrong.
- The Bible teaches that everyone has human dignity because they are made in the image of God.

Useful words

Civil partnerships – legal ceremonies giving homosexual partners the same legal rights as husband and wife

Homophobia – hatred or fear of homosexuals

With this new legislation, marriage has now become an institution in which openness to children, and with it the responsibility on fathers and mothers to remain together to care for children born into their family unit, are no longer central. That is why we were opposed to this legislation on principle. (Statement by the president and vice-president of the Catholic Bishops Conference of England and Wales, 17 July 2013, commenting on the passing of the Marriage (Same Sex Couples) Act 2013)

2 The Evangelical Protestant attitude

Many Evangelical Protestants believe that homosexuality is a sin. They believe that there should be no homosexual Christians and some hold special prayer meetings to give homosexuals the power of the Spirit to change their sexual preference (orientation). The reasons for this attitude are:

- They believe that the Bible is the direct Word of God, and the Bible condemns homosexuality in some passages of both the Old and New Testaments.
- They believe that the salvation of Christ can remove all sins, including homosexuality.
- They believe that homosexuality is sinful because all the Churches have taught it in the past, even though some now say homosexuality is acceptable.

However, the Evangelical Alliance has recently made this statement: 'At the same time we utterly repudiate **homophobia** and call upon Churches to welcome those of a homosexual orientation as they would welcome any other person.'

Activity

Look at the statement above by the Catholic bishops. Do you think this is a valid reason for banning same-sex marriage?

3 The liberal Protestant attitude

Many liberal Protestants have the attitude that lifelong homosexual relationships are acceptable and homosexuals are welcomed into the Church. They are happy to provide blessings for civil partnerships but not same-sex marriages, which they believe cannot be equated to Christian marriage. The reasons for this attitude are:

- They believe that the teachings of the Bible need reinterpreting in the light of modern knowledge and that the anti-homosexual texts in the Bible are a reflection of Jewish culture at the time rather than the Word of God.
- They feel that the major Christian belief in love and acceptance means that homosexuals must be accepted.
- Recent scientific research shows that homosexuality may be caused by biological factors and so is part of a person's nature.
- They believe that Christians should be open and honest, and refusing rights to gay Christians encourages them to be dishonest and hypocritical about their nature and life.

However, some Protestants, such as Quakers, are happy to celebrate same-sex weddings in their churches. They are happy for homosexuals to be ministers and priests.

Humanist and atheist attitudes to same-sex relationships

Humanists, and the vast majority of atheists and non-religious people, see no problems with same-sex sexual relationships. They regard people's sexuality as their own concern unless it interferes with other people's human rights. This could be because all the Christian arguments against same-sex relationships are based on religious reasons, so if people have no religion then the reasons for disapproving of homosexuality disappear.

Activities

1. Do you think churches should provide church weddings for gay Christians?
2. Look at the photo of the Bishop of Los Angeles on this page. Do you think gay people should have equal rights in the Church?

Mary Glasspool, Bishop of Los Angeles, was the first open lesbian to be elected an Anglican bishop.

Christian responses to the non-religious attitudes

Christian responses to the non-religious attitudes to sexual relationships have been dealt with on page 39.

Just as with sexual relationships, there have been three very different responses to same-sex relationships:

- The official response of the Roman Catholic Church and the conservative Protestant Churches has been to condemn the non-religious attitude and to insist that Christian homosexuals should refrain from having sex and that same-sex marriages should not be legal. The issue of homosexuality has caused major divisions in the Anglican Church (Churches in communion with the Church of England) since the USA's Episcopal Church appointed an openly gay priest, Gene Robinson, as Bishop of New Hampshire. A conference of worldwide Anglican bishops held in Canterbury in January 2016 agreed to impose sanctions against the liberal US church and issued a statement in support of the traditional doctrine that marriage should be between a man and a woman: 'The traditional doctrine of the church in view of the teaching of scripture, upholds marriage as between a man and a woman in faithful, lifelong union.'
- The official response of the more liberal Protestant Churches has been to welcome homosexuals into the Church and to allow gay clergy to become bishops. Quakers in Britain give homosexuals completely equal rights and celebrate same-sex marriages with a religious service. Some liberal Churches still insist that gay clergy should refrain from sexual activities.
- Most Christians no longer agree with the official teachings. In May 2015, Ireland, perhaps one of the most Catholic countries in Europe, held a referendum on whether to allow same-sex marriage and it was approved by 62 per cent of the voters. All research seems to show that most Christians are more in line with the non-religious than with the Churches in their attitudes to homosexual relationships.

Summary

The Catholic and Conservative Protestant Churches teach that sex before marriage is wrong. Many liberal Protestants accept premarital sex. All Christians believe that adultery is wrong because it breaks the marriage vows.

Humanists and most atheists believe that sex is up to the people involved as long as they are of age and agree to it.

As far as homosexuality is concerned:

- Catholics believe that there is nothing wrong with homosexual feelings or relationships as long as there is no sexual activity because this is the teaching of the Church.
- Evangelical Protestants believe that homosexuality is sinful because it is condemned in the Bible.
- Liberal Protestants believe that homosexuality is acceptable because it is natural and Christians should love and accept everyone.

Humanists and atheists believe in equal rights for homosexuals and approve of same-sex marriages, as do the vast majority of non-religious people.

The Catholic and conservative Protestant Churches are opposed to same-sex marriages.

Practice questions

c Explain two reasons why many Christians are against people having sex before they are married. In your answer you must refer to a source of wisdom and authority.

d 'Non-religious people have the most sensible attitude to homosexuality.' Evaluate this statement considering arguments for and against. In your response you should:

- refer to Christian teachings
- refer to different Christian or non-religious points of view
- reach a justified conclusion.

Topic 1.2.3 Families

The nature of families

Throughout history there have been many different types of family, from small clans (a large extended family) to families with **polygamous** parents (several spouses) to families with **monogamous** parents (husband and wife). Families have developed as children cannot survive on their own until adulthood. The main family types in the UK in the twenty-first century are considered below.

Nuclear families

Although technically a nuclear family is one where mother, father and children are living together as a unit, most people, especially religious people, think of it as a married couple of opposite sexes living together with their children. Fifty years ago, such a nuclear family was regarded as the normal family, and this is still the type of family often portrayed in television adverts. However, of the 7.9 million families with dependent children in the UK in 2014, only 4.75 million were married-couple families. This means that only 60 per cent of families are now nuclear families. Two million families consist of a single parent and dependent children and 1.17 million families are headed by cohabiting couples. (Source: **ONS**.)

The cast of *Outnumbered*, an award-winning television comedy programme aired from 2007 to 2014.

Thinking points

In this topic you need to:

- think about Christian teachings on the purpose and importance of the family, including procreation, and security and education of children with reference to Ephesians 6:1–14
- consider the different Christian and non-religious responses to the purpose of the family
- think about different types of family within modern-day society such as nuclear, single-parent, same-sex parents, extended and blended families
- be able to explain different Christian and non-religious attitudes to families.

Useful words

Polygamous – having more than one spouse at a time
Monogamous – having only one spouse at a time
ONS – Office for National Statistics

Activity

Look at the photo of a nuclear family. Do you think this family would be any different if the parents were cohabiting rather than married?

Activity

Why are there so many single-parent families?

Single-parent families

In the UK in 2013 there were 1.9 million families consisting of a single parent and dependent children, which meant that more than 3 million children were living in families headed by a lone parent. In fact, 25 per cent of all families with dependent children are now single-parent families. (Source: ONS.)

The main cause of the large number of single-parent families has been the significant number of divorces and the increasing number of family breakdowns where couples are cohabiting. However, the divorce rate has reduced over the past few years (see Figure 1). Overall, 42 per cent of marriages will end in divorce, inevitably producing many single-parent families.

As far as cohabiting couples are concerned, on average, cohabitations last for less than two years before breaking up or converting to marriage, indeed less than four per cent of cohabitations last for ten years or more. Over 120,000 families with dependent children separated in 2013. About half were married-couple families (1.3 per cent of 4.7 million married families) and half were from cohabiting couples (5.3 per cent of 1.2 million cohabiting families). See Figures 2 and 3.

All statistics on this page come from the ONS.

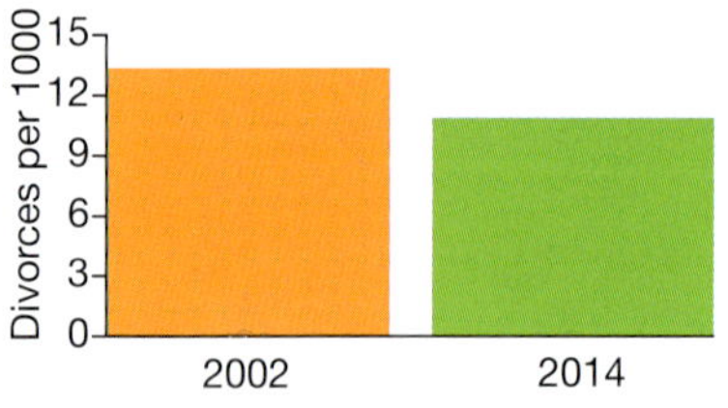

Figure 1 Divorces for every 1000 married couples for 2002 and 2014 in the UK. (Source: ONS.)

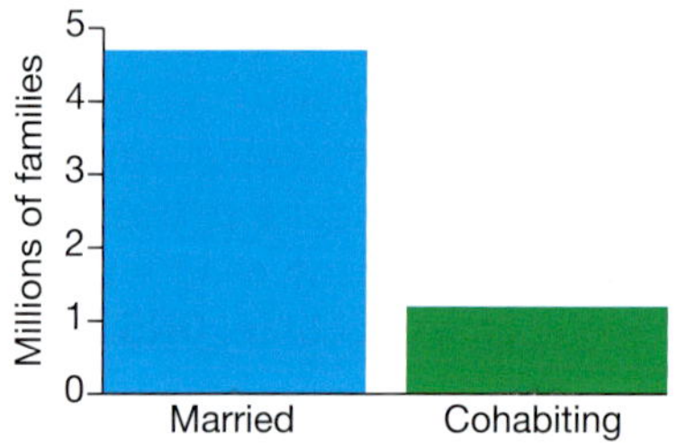

Figure 2 Families with married or cohabiting parents in the UK. (Source: ONS.)

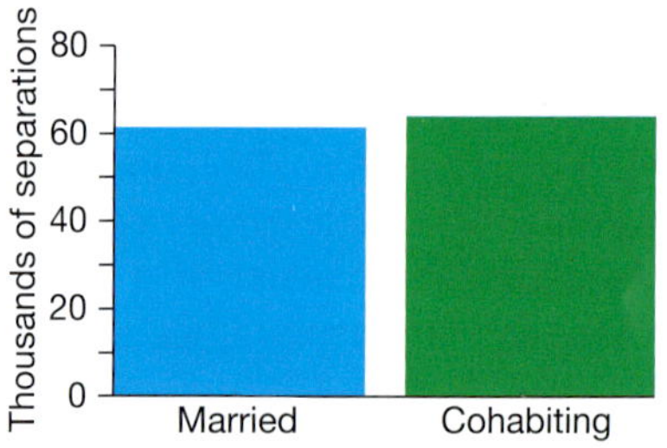

Figure 3 Separated families with married or cohabiting parents in the UK. (Source: ONS.)

Single-parent families allow children to escape from the emotional stress that can be caused when parents are quarrelling all the time. However, single parents can often have financial problems: 41 per cent of children living in one-parent families are living in poverty compared to only 23 per cent of children from two-parent households. Most (91 per cent) lone parents are women, so many children in single-parent families lack a **paternal** role model.

Useful words

Paternal – to do with the father
Heterosexual – attraction to the opposite sex

Same-sex parent families

The Civil Partnerships Act 2004 provided same-sex couples with the same rights and treatment as opposite-sex couples who enter into a civil marriage. The Marriage (Same Sex Couples) Act 2013 allowed same-sex couples to marry in just the same way as **heterosexual** couples, but did not require religions to provide same-sex marriage ceremonies. The Equality Act 2010 made discriminating against same-sex couples illegal, so giving them equal adoption and fostering rights.

In 2014, there were 21,000 families headed by a same-sex couple. Of these, 12,000 were in civil partnerships and 9000 were cohabiting. Many male same-sex partners have adopted hard-to-place children.

Singer–songwriter Sir Elton John (left) with husband David Furnish and their two children.

Activities

1. Look at the photo of Sir Elton John's family. Do you think it was a good idea to allow same-sex families?
2. Why do you think so many of the single parents in single-parent families are women?
3. Look at the quotation from Susan Golombok below. Why do you think many people were surprised at her conclusions?

Extended families

An extended family is one where three generations (parents, children and grandparents) are living in the same house or one where parents, children, grandparents, aunts and uncles live in close proximity and have frequent contact with and reliance on each other. The families are usually called multigenerational families.

According to the 2011 Census, only one per cent of families with dependent children were multigenerational, but research indicates that many more families live in close proximity and rely on grandparents and other family members for childcare. Indeed, more recent research indicates that there has been a big increase in multigenerational households since the 2011 Census because of the squeeze on incomes and jobs, and the increased cost of housing and both childcare and elderly care.

Blended families

A blended family is when two separate families are joined together when parents decide to marry or cohabit. The increase in divorce since 1969 has led to an increase in **remarriage** (most people who divorce before the age of 50 remarry), resulting in many more blended families (sometimes called step-families or reconstituted families). However, the number of blended families with dependent children actually fell by fourteen per cent between the 2001 Census (631,000 blended families) and the 2011 Census (544,000 blended families). Estimates from the General Lifestyle Survey in 2011 for Great Britain show that 85 per cent of blended families with dependent children include children from the woman's previous relationship, but only eleven per cent include children from the man's previous relationship, with even fewer, four per cent, coming from both partners' previous relationships.

Useful words

Remarriage – marrying again after a divorce

Whether children have one parent or two, whether their parents are male or female, whether their parents are of the same sex or the opposite sex, whether they have a genetic or gestational link to their parents and whether they have been conceived naturally or through assisted reproduction seems to matter less for children than does the quality of family relationships, the support of their community and the prevailing attitudes of the society in which they live.
*(*Modern Families: Parents and Children in New Family Forms *by Susan Golombok, Cambridge University Press, 2015)*

A multigenerational family.

The purpose and importance of the family in Christianity

All Christians believe that the family was created by God as the basic unit of society and as the only place in which children should be brought up. One of the main purposes of Christian marriage is to have children and bring them up in a secure and loving Christian environment so that they will come to love God and follow Jesus. Family is of particular importance in Christianity because:

- The family is the place where children are introduced to the faith through baptism/dedication and then through being taken to church for worship, Sunday school, festivals and so on.
- The family has the basic task of bringing up children safely and securely until they are mature enough to look after themselves. This means the parents have a duty to ensure that the **physical** and **material needs** of the children are met.
- The family has a duty of instilling **moral values** into the children so that they become good responsible citizens.
- Children have a duty to look after their parents when their parents are too old or infirm to care for themselves. The Commandments tell Christians to honour their mother and father.
- Christian teaching on divorce makes it clear that Christian parents should stay together and bring up their children together because the family is so important.

For many Christians, family is considered to be the most important part of society and without the family society would collapse.

However, there is a tradition dating back to Jesus, which says that there are more important things than the family for Christians. Marriage is not compulsory for Christians and many Christians feel they can serve God best by remaining single, for example Roman Catholic priests, nuns and monks leave their families to serve God.

Useful words

Physical needs – such things as housing and shelter from the elements
Material needs – such things as food, drink and clothing
Moral values – the standards of good and evil, which influence people's behaviour and choices.

Children, obey your parents in the Lord, for this is right. 'Honour your father and mother' – which is the first commandment with a promise – 'so that it may go well with you and that you may enjoy long life on the earth.' Fathers, do not exasperate your children; instead, bring them up in the training and instruction of the Lord. (Ephesians 6:1–4)

First Communion is a family occasion for Catholics.

Activities

1. Look at the photo of a First Communion. Do you think sharing in Christian events such as this will help a family?
2. Read the quotation from Ephesians. Do you think it is good advice for a twenty-first century family?

Different Christian attitudes to the family

The traditional Christian view of the family is that outlined above, but other Christians have different views:

- Some Christians believe that the purpose of the family is to provide love and security and to make sure that children are educated to think for themselves so that they can make up their own minds about religion when they are old enough. These Christians believe that it is not the role of the family to make Christians.
- Other Christians believe that while it is the duty of parents to provide love, security, education and a Christian upbringing, it is not the duty of children to obey their parents. A Christian family should encourage children to develop their own ideas, which may lead to different ideas from their parents.

Activities

1. What do you think would be the main differences between living in a Christian family and living in a non-religious family?
2. Do you think it is possible to honour your parents without always obeying them?

Non-religious ideas about the family

Most families in the UK are now non-religious. All recent surveys show that at least 60 per cent of people have little or no contact with religion. However, the family is very important to people regardless of religion. Falling in love and having a family is a goal in life for most people, no doubt because raising a family is part of what is known as the 'selfish gene': we want our genes to continue into future generations. Non-religious people see that the purpose of family life is as follows:

- To bring up children safely and securely until they are mature enough to look after themselves by making sure that the physical and material needs of the children are met.
- To pass on moral values to the children so that they become good responsible citizens.
- To provide emotional and financial support throughout life.

The importance of family life to non-religious people can be seen in the way that family members will come to the rescue in times of need regardless of religious commitment (for example, 80 per cent of parents expect to help their adult children with housing costs – General Lifestyle Survey 2011). Non-religious families also come together at times like Christmas just as much as religious families.

Practice questions

c Explain two reasons why there are more single-parent and blended families than there used to be.

d 'The family is more important for Christians than for non-religious people.' Evaluate this statement considering arguments for and against. In your response you should:

- refer to Christian teachings
- refer to different Christian points of view
- reach a justified conclusion.

Summary

There are lots of different types of families:

- Nuclear families where a married mother and father live with their children.
- Single-parent families where children are being brought up by either a mother or a father.
- Same-sex parent families where children are being brought up by two men or two women.
- Extended families where three generations of a family live together.
- Blended families where two sets of children from different families are being brought up together because their parents have remarried.

Christians believe that the family was created by God as the basis of society. It is where children are safe and nurtured, learn moral values and are brought up as Christians.

Non-religious people think the family is important for safety, nurture and moral values.

Topic 1.2.4 Support for the family in the local parish

Thinking points

In this topic you need to:

- think about how and why the local church community tries to support families through family worship, rites of passage, groups for children and counselling; and understand the importance of this support for Christians today
- be able to explain and evaluate Christian support for the family.

What is the parish?

The parish is an area round a local church. The Roman Catholic and Anglican Churches have an organisation based on parishes and **dioceses**. A diocese is a collection of parishes under the jurisdiction of a bishop (for example, the Bishop of London is head of the London diocese and its 413 parishes). There are 41 dioceses in the Church of England. Until recently, people wanting to get married in the Church of England had to marry in the parish where they lived. In some areas a parish council is part of local government.

Each parish has a **parish priest** (usually known as a **vicar** in the Church of England) and centres around a parish church (the church for the local area).

Other Churches in England and Wales are not based on the parish system, but any Baptist, Methodist or Pentecostal church, for example, will be doing similar things (although only the Church of England and the Roman Catholic Church have a large number of Church schools).

Useful words

Diocese – a Church area under the direction of a bishop
Parish priest – the clergy person responsible for a local church
Vicar – another name for a parish priest
Clergy – those ordained by the Church
First Communion – the first time a person receives the sacrament of the Eucharist; children receive special lessons before this important occasion

How the parish tries to help families

Parishes try to help families because they have a duty to help children baptised or dedicated in the Church. Indeed, in some Churches the **clergy** and the congregation make promises to God that they will help the parents with the Christian upbringing of the children. There are a number of ways in which parishes help and support families:

- Most parishes have a local Church primary and secondary school connected to them. These provide Christian education and worship alongside the standard education. The school buildings are provided and maintained by the Church. The teachers and equipment are paid for by the state.
- Many Churches are exploring new ways to be more family friendly including new forms of family worship. Churches believe that family life can be strengthened by families worshipping together. Family worship helps to unite the family and gives families an opportunity to discover religion together.
- Many churches run Sunday Schools where children can learn about the Christian faith in a child-centred environment while their parents attend the church.
- Parishes also help families through rites of passage. When a child is brought for baptism, the priest or minister meets the family before the sacrament and gives advice to the parents. The clergy also give advice to the Church members about their duty to help the child to come to the adult Christian life.
- Confirmation classes are run for children before they are confirmed (Catholic parishes also run classes to prepare children for First Confession and **First Communion**). These classes help parents with the Christian upbringing of their children as they bring children into full membership of the Church.

Activities

1. Why do you think the parish is important for Catholics and Anglicans?
2. Read the section on how the parish helps families. Can you think of anything churches near you do to help families which is not on this list?

- Most parish clergy spend some time reminding parents of the importance of the family and of the importance of keeping their marriage vows. Clergy in the local church are available for help with counselling families on family or marital problems.
- There are also counselling services run by the Church such as 'Good News Family Care', Catholic Marriage Care, the National Catholic Child Welfare Council and the Children's Society (Church of England). Dioceses in the Church of England have a special children and family officer to provide help for families in the diocese.
- Most Church services include prayers for families and for spiritual strength for parents to fulfil their responsibilities.
- Many Churches run toddler groups and Messy Church to help parents with young children to socialise and learn from each other.
- Many parishes run groups such as cubs, brownies, guides, scouts and the Boys' & Girls' Brigade which encourage children to become good citizens. Some parishes also run youth clubs and youth activities so that children are kept off the streets and away from bad influences. All these help parents to bring up their children as good Christians.
- The Churches are trying to ensure that the needs of young people are attended to by establishing such groups as the Methodist Youth Conference, Church of England Youth Council and International Anglican Youth Network.

Activity

Look at the photo of a Church school below. Make a list of arguments for and against having Church schools.

Then people brought little children to Jesus for him to place his hands on them and pray for them. But the disciples rebuked them. Jesus said, 'Let the little children come to me, and do not hinder them, for the kingdom of heaven belongs to such as these.' (Matthew 19:13–14)

A Church of England primary school.

Activity

Do you think it is important for Christian families to be given help by their local church?

Why parishes try to help families

Parishes try to help families because:

- They have a duty to help children baptised or dedicated in the church.
- The Church teaches that one of the main purposes of Christian marriage is to have children and bring them up in a secure and loving Christian environment, and it must be the responsibility of the parish to assist in that task.
- The Church teaches that the family is the only place in which children should be brought up, so the parish has a social as well as sacred duty to help parents with their family life.
- The family is the place where children are introduced to the faith. If the parish does not help the family in this, then Christianity will not grow and the Church will have failed.

Why support from the Church is important for Christian families

Support from the Church is important for Christians who are trying to raise a Christian family because:

- Raising children as Christians means taking them to church regularly and that requires the Church to be helpful to children.
- Teaching children about Christianity requires knowledge and expertise in the faith that parents are not likely to have, so Church schools, Sunday Schools and so on are vital.
- For Catholic, Anglican and Orthodox families, taking part in the sacraments is important and that requires the help of the Church.
- Being part of the larger family of the Church, which will give help if needed, is a great source of comfort and strength for a family.
- Christians believe in the power of prayer, and knowing that the local parish is praying for families brings them God's strength.

Summary

Local Christian churches (parishes) provide support for families by:

- supporting the local Church schools
- providing family worship and rites of passage
- providing advice and counselling for families
- running groups for young families
- running youth clubs and youth activities.

They do this because marriage and baptism teach the importance of bringing up children as Christians.

Practice questions

c Explain two ways in which local parishes provide support for families.

d 'Parents don't need help from the local parish church to raise their family.' Evaluate this statement considering arguments for and against. In your response you should:

- refer to Christian teachings
- reach a justified conclusion.

Topic 1.2.5 Family planning

The purpose of contraception

Contraception is something that allows a couple to have sex without conception occurring, so allowing a couple to control the number of children they have (sometimes known as regulation of births). The use of contraception in the West has become very popular (it is now estimated that 90 per cent of the sexually active population of **childbearing age** in the UK use some form of contraception). Throughout history, people have tried to control the number of children they have, for a number of reasons:

- for the health of the mother
- to avoid the risk of not having enough food for the existing family members
- to maintain a good standard of living for the family unit.

There are two fundamentally different types of contraception: artificial methods and natural methods.

Artificial methods of contraception

These are the most popular and effective methods of contraception. There are several types of artificial contraception:

Method of contraception	Effectiveness (%)	Number of pregnancies likely to occur (in 100)
Male **condoms**	98	2
Female condoms	95	5
Diaphragms	92–96	Between 4 and 8
Caps	92–96	Between 4 and 8
Combined contraceptive pill	>99	<1
Progestogen-only pill	99	1
Contraceptive injections	>99	<1
Contraceptive implants	>99	<1
Intrauterine system (IUS)	>99	<1
Intrauterine device (**IUD**)	>99	<1
Contraceptive patch	>99	<1
Vaginal ring	>99	<1

(Source: NHS Choices.)

Thinking points

In this topic you need to:

- think about different Christian teachings and attitudes about contraception and family planning, including reference to *Humanae Vitae*
- consider different Humanist and atheist attitudes to family planning and Christian responses to them
- consider the application of ethical theories such as Situation Ethics
- be able to explain and evaluate different Christian and non-religious attitudes to contraception.

Useful words

Childbearing age – the age when a woman is capable of having children

Condoms – thin rubber sheaths protecting against conception and STDs

IUD – intrauterine device (the coil); a type of contraceptive

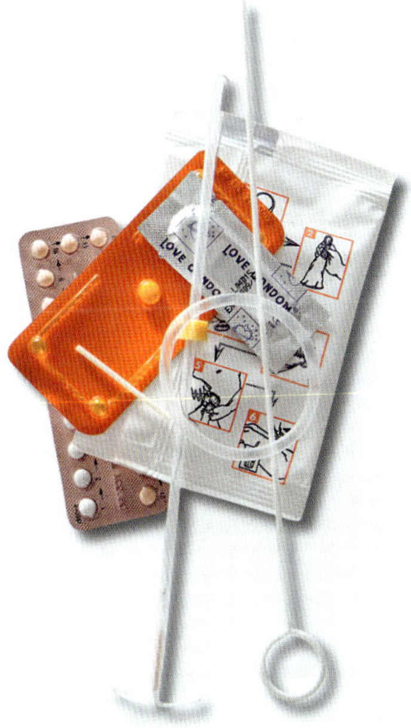

Some artificial contraceptives.

Useful words

STI – sexually transmitted infection
STD – sexually transmitted disease
Abortifacients – substances that bring about a very early abortion
NFP – natural family planning
Unitive purpose – sexual activity as a source of joy and pleasure to unite a married couple

For women who have had unprotected sex, there are two kinds of emergency ('morning-after') contraceptive pill: Levonelle has to be taken within three days of sex and ellaOne has to be taken within five days of sex (both pills work by preventing or delaying ovulation). It is also possible to have an IUD inserted into the uterus up to five days after unprotected sex. Emergency contraception does not protect against sexually transmitted infections (**STIs**).

Condoms, as well as being effective contraceptives, prevent the transmission of sexually transmitted diseases (**STDs**) such as HIV/AIDS.

Artificial methods can be used without much planning, and in any form of sexual relationship, however casual. However, they do involve either changes to a woman's body or interfering with the normal sexual process, and methods such as the IUD, IUS and the morning-after pill, which prevent a fertilised egg from attaching itself to the womb wall, are often called **abortifacients** because they bring about a very early abortion.

Natural methods of contraception

The most common form of natural contraception is known as natural family planning (**NFP**) or fertility awareness. It involves reducing the chance of becoming pregnant by planning sex around the most infertile times during the woman's monthly cycle. To be as effective as possible, it should be taught by an experienced NFP teacher.

Another method of natural contraception uses a device to measure hormone levels in the woman's urine. If used according to the instructions, these methods can be 94 per cent effective.

Natural methods require a couple to be in a loving, stable relationship as they require planning and sufficient love and concern for the partner to give up sex at certain times of the month. As they are natural methods they do not involve any drugs or any risk of promoting an early abortion. Natural methods do not prevent STDs.

A fertility chart combining several indicators or signs of fertility.

Christian attitudes to contraception

There are two main attitudes to contraception among Christians.

1 The Catholic attitude

The Catholic Church teaches that sexual intercourse is a gift from God as a source of joy and pleasure to married couples (the **unitive purpose**) as

The methods of birth regulation based on self-observation and the use of infertile periods … respect the bodies of the spouses, encourage tenderness between them … In contrast, 'every action which, whether in anticipation of the conjugal act, or in its accomplishment, or in the development of its natural consequences, proposes, whether as an end or as a means, to render procreation impossible' is intrinsically evil. (Catechism of the Catholic Church 2370)

well as a means of creating a family (the **creative purpose**). The Church also teaches that Christians should practise responsible parenthood by deciding on the number of children to have and when to have them. However, the Catholic way to achieve this is through using natural methods of family planning. The Church teaches that using artificial methods of contraception is going against God's intentions. Catholics believe this because:

- In 1968, Pope Paul VI's encyclical *Humanae Vitae* affirmed the teaching of Pope Pius XI which condemned all forms of artificial contraception, and the teaching of Pope Pius XII who declared that Catholics could use natural methods of contraception as these are natural and so part of God's creation. *Humanae Vitae* declared that the only allowable forms of contraception for Catholics are natural methods. This teaching has been confirmed in the Catechism of the Catholic Church.
- Artificial methods of birth control separate the unitive and creative aspects of sex, which is not what God intended.
- Some contraceptives have abortifacient effects (they bring about a very early abortion) and so are against the teaching of the Church.
- The Catholic Church regards contraception as a major cause of sexual promiscuity, broken families and the rise in the divorce rate and STDs.

2 The attitude of non-Catholic Christians

Almost all non-Catholic Christians believe that all forms of contraception are permissible as long as they are used to restrict the size of the family and not simply to stop having children altogether. They have this attitude because.

- Christianity is about love and justice, and contraception improves **maternal** health and raises the standard of living of children as families are smaller.
- God created sex for enjoyment and to cement the bonds of marriage. Within marriage, contraception allows the role of sex to be separated from making children and this is not against God's will.
- There is nothing in the Bible that forbids the use of contraception.
- In 1930, the Lambeth Conference of the worldwide Anglican Communion (Church of England) declared that it was legitimate for Christians to use contraception to limit family size. This has been followed by the major Protestant Churches and the Orthodox Churches.
- Non-Catholic Christians believe that it is better to combat HIV/AIDS by using condoms rather than by expecting everyone to follow Christian rules about sex and marriage.

Humanist and atheist attitudes to contraception

Humanist and atheist people are in favour of contraception because they assess the rights and wrongs of birth control by looking at its consequences. They argue that as contraception prevents unwanted children from being born, improves the material and emotional standard of living in families and prevents the spread of STDs, it must be morally right to use it. Humanists argue that if contraception 'results in every child being a wanted child, and in better, healthier lives for women, it must be a good thing' (British Humanist Association).

Useful words

Creative purpose – sex as a means of creating a family

Maternal – to do with the mother

Activities

1. Make a list of the similarities and differences between the Catholic and non-Catholic attitudes to contraception.
2. Explain why there are different attitudes to contraception in Christianity.

Most non-religious people think that contraception should be used by people having casual sex because it is important to avoid unwanted pregnancies and STDs.

Humanists played a major part in promoting contraception in modern times. Charles Bradlaugh, leader of the National Secular Society, and his partner Annie Besant were given prison sentences in 1877 for publishing a book that advocated birth control because it was thought that contraception would lead to sexual immorality. However, their advocacy of contraception gradually led to its acceptance in society: in the UK in 2010, 72 per cent of women of childbearing age were using contraception.

Ethical theories are philosophical theories to apply to moral issues. One such theory is Situation Ethics which believes that Christians should make moral decisions based on looking at the moral situation and deciding which choice would give the most loving outcome. This is based on Jesus' teaching that the greatest commandment is to love God and love your neighbour. Christians who believe in Situation Ethics would say that people should use contraceptives because contraception:

- improves women's health and well-being
- prevents many children suffering, because every child will be a wanted child
- by reducing rates of unintended pregnancies, it reduces the need for unsafe abortion
- reduces the risk of unintended pregnancies among women living with HIV, resulting in fewer infected babies and orphans
- provides dual protection against unintended pregnancies and against STIs including HIV if using male or female condoms.

Activity

Read the results of the Univision survey below. Do you find them surprising?

Christian responses to non-religious attitudes to contraception

As Protestant and Orthodox Christians agree with the non-religious attitudes to contraception, it is only the Roman Catholic Church which has responded to them. The Church continues to issue statements to Catholic couples that they must only use natural methods of contraception. It also opposes issuing free condoms to prevent the spread of HIV/AIDS and STDs.

However, Catholics seem to have responded by accepting the non-religious attitude. A survey by the US Spanish-language television network Univision of more than 12,000 Catholics in twelve countries discovered that 78 per cent of respondents worldwide supported the use of artificial birth control, and in some European and most Latin American countries, more than 90 per cent supported its use.

Summary

Contraception allows couples to control the number of children by allowing sex without pregnancy. About 90 per cent of couples in the UK use contraception.

Natural methods of contraception require planning to avoid having sex in a woman's fertile period. Artificial methods of contraception either prevent the sperm from meeting the egg, or stop a woman producing eggs or stop the fertilised egg from staying in the womb.

The Catholic Church teaches that using artificial methods of contraception to stop a baby being conceived is wrong. God gave sex in order to create children. However, natural methods of contraception are acceptable. Other Christians allow the use of contraception because they believe that God gave sex to strengthen a married relationship.

Humanists and atheists think contraception is a good thing as they believe that every child should be a wanted child.

Practice questions

c Explain two reasons why non-Catholic Christians support the use of contraceptives. In your answer you must refer to a source of wisdom and authority.

d 'The world would be a better place if everyone followed Catholic teachings on contraception.' Evaluate this statement considering arguments for and against. In your response you should:

- refer to Christian teachings
- refer to different Christian or non-religious points of view
- reach a justified conclusion.

Topic 1.2.6 Divorce and remarriage

In 1950 there were 30,870 divorces in the UK and in 2012 there were 118,140 divorces. Clearly, attitudes to divorce changed greatly between 1950 and 1975. This is probably because:

- New laws made divorce much cheaper and easier to obtain for ordinary people.
- Increased equality meant that women were no longer prepared to accept unequal treatment from men.
- Equal rights legislation meant that many women were financially independent and could afford to live well after a divorce.

Although 42 per cent of marriages are likely to end in divorce, 58 per cent of marriages today are unlikely to end in divorce, and around ten per cent of married couples should reach their diamond wedding anniversary (60 years of marriage).

Until about 2000, most people who divorced remarried within ten years of their divorce, but the remarriage rate is declining as more divorced people decide to cohabit if they meet a new partner. However, religious people who divorce are far more likely to remarry.

Thinking points

In this topic, you need to:

- think about Christian teachings about divorce and remarriage
- think about different Christian, atheist and Humanist attitudes to divorce and remarriage, including the application of Situation Ethics and Christian responses to them
- be able to explain and evaluate different Christian and non-religious attitudes to divorce and remarriage.

Christian teachings on divorce

In some places in the Gospels, Jesus seems to ban divorce and remarriage (see the passage from Matthew 19), but in others he seems to allow divorce on the grounds of adultery.

> *Some Pharisees came to him to test him. They asked, 'Is it lawful for a man to divorce his wife for any and every reason?' 'Haven't you read,' he replied, 'that at the beginning the Creator "made them male and female," and said, "For this reason a man will leave his father and mother and be united to his wife, and the two will become one flesh"? So they are no longer two, but one flesh. Therefore what God has joined together, let no one separate.' 'Why then,' they asked, 'did Moses command that a man give his wife a certificate of divorce and send her away?' Jesus replied, 'Moses permitted you to divorce your wives because your hearts were hard. But it was not this way from the beginning.*
>
> *I tell you that anyone who divorces his wife, except for sexual immorality, and marries another woman commits adultery.'*
> *(Matthew 19:3–9)*

> *Before the coming of this faith, we were held in custody under the law, locked up until the faith that was to come would be revealed. So the law was our guardian until Christ came that we might be justified by faith. Now that this faith has come, we are no longer under a guardian.*
>
> *So in Christ Jesus you are all children of God through faith, for all of you who were baptised into Christ have clothed yourselves with Christ. There is neither Jew nor Gentile, neither slave nor free, nor is there male and female, for you are all one in Christ Jesus.*
> *(Galatians 3:23–28)*

St Paul says Christians should not divorce, but if they do they must not remarry.

> *To the married I give this command (not I, but the Lord): A wife must not separate from her husband. But if she does, she must remain unmarried or else be reconciled to her husband. And a husband must not divorce his wife.* (1 Corinthians 7:10)

Useful words

Sacrament – an outward ceremony through which God's grace is given
Civil divorce – a divorce according to the law of the country but not the Church
Annulment – a declaration by the Church that a marriage was never a true marriage and so the partners are free to marry
Consummate – complete a marriage through sexual intercourse
Covenant – a religious agreement made between God and a religious group

1 The Catholic attitude

The Catholic Church does not allow religious divorce or remarriage. Catholic marriage is a **sacrament** and the exchange of vows means that the only way a marriage between baptised Catholics can be dissolved (religiously) is by the death of one of the partners or if the marriage is annulled.

However, the Catholic Church does allow for the legal separation of spouses if they find it impossible to live together, and even **civil divorce** (an ending of the marriage according to the laws of the country, but not the Church) if that will ensure the proper care of the children and the safety and security of the married partner. Neither of these routes, however, has ended the marriage: the couple are still married in the eyes of God and the Church and so cannot remarry.

As there can be no religious divorce, there can be no remarriage because that would be the same as bigamy and adultery, both of which are considered to be very serious sins. Catholics who remarry may be refused communion. However, the Catholic Church does allow **annulment** if it can be proved that the marriage was never **consummated** or that it was not a true Christian marriage.

Catholics have this attitude because:

- In Mark's Gospel Jesus taught that divorce is wrong and Christians should follow the teachings of Jesus.
- The couple have made a **covenant** with God in the sacrament of marriage and that covenant cannot be broken by any earthly power.
- The Church teaches very clearly in the Catechism that a marriage cannot be dissolved and so religious divorce is impossible. Catholics should follow the teachings of the Church and so should not divorce.

2 The attitude of non-Catholic Christians

Most non-Catholic Churches think that divorce is wrong, but allow it if the marriage has broken down. Most of these Churches allow divorced people to remarry, but the divorced people are sometimes asked to show repentance for the failure and required to promise that this time their marriage will be for life.

- Jesus allowed divorce in Matthew 19:9 for a partner's adultery.
- They believe that there are certain situations where Christians must choose 'the lesser of two evils'. If a marriage has really broken down then the effects of the couple not divorcing would be a greater evil than the 'evil' of divorce itself.
- Christians are allowed forgiveness and a new chance if they confess their sins and are truly repentant. This belief in forgiveness should apply to divorce and remarriage as much as anything else. So a couple should have another chance at marriage as long as they are determined to make it work the second time.

Activities

1. Read the passage from St Matthew chapter 19 on page 57. Make a list of the main points. What do you think of Jesus' advice?
2. Which Christian attitude to divorce do you think is most suited to life in the modern world?

A couple arguing in front of their children. Is it better to divorce than live in hatred and quarrel all the time?

Atheist and Humanist attitudes to divorce and remarriage

Atheists do not believe in God and so they regard marriage as a purely human and legal institution. Some atheists do not believe in marriage and would cohabit and so would have no need to divorce. Many atheists would have the same attitude to divorce and remarriage as Humanists (many of whom are atheists). The Humanist attitude is that:

- All married couples should have the right to divorce if they feel the marriage has failed.
- Divorce should make sure that the spouses are treated equally in the financial arrangements.
- Divorce should make sure that any children are well provided for.
- Any divorced person should be treated as a single person and so have the right to remarry if they so wish.

Christians, Humanists and atheists often apply an ethical theory to deal with the issue of divorce and remarriage. One such theory is Situation Ethics. This is a theory which began with an American Christian thinker, Joseph Fletcher. Fletcher taught that although the rules of the Bible or the Church are important, they can be altered by a situation. For example, the Bible and the Church say that stealing is wrong, but if we found a madman who had gained possession of a nuclear weapon, it would surely be right to steal the weapon from him.

Activities

1. Look at the photo above. Why do you think divorce is sometimes regarded as the lesser of two evils?
2. Do you think Catholic Christians would agree with the Humanist attitude to divorce?

Activity

Do you think Situation Ethics is a good way of deciding about an issue like divorce?

People who apply Situation Ethics look at the situation, decide on the pros and cons of the possible choices and then determine what would be the best thing to do. So they would look at the advantages of divorce:

- it brings domestic peace and emotional security as it removes the conflict between the spouses
- it gives opportunities for the spouses to gain personal fulfilment as they are not being forced to stay in a relationship they hate
- it ends children's exposure to damaging parental conflict since research shows it is unhealthy for children to be around parents who fight and criticise each other
- it gives a chance for fresh starts for the spouses and opportunities for new, better relationships.

And then they would look at the disadvantages of divorce:

- it is expensive – apart from the legal costs, divorce usually means selling the family home as it is costlier for two people to live separately than live together and so a family's standard of living is often lowered
- it can hurt children as they are forced to choose between parents and may have to select which one to live with
- it hurts family relatives as they can often lose contact with the children if their relation is not awarded **custody**
- it causes stress as it forces new relationships and new living situations.

After weighing this up, the next step is to look at the people involved and try to work out the best and most loving choice. The most likely decision would be, that if a marriage has broken down and there are no children involved, divorce has more advantages than disadvantages. However, if children are involved, the decision would be more difficult. Some research suggests that children suffer from a divorce, but other research suggests they don't, and that they might even benefit from their parents divorcing.

Useful words

Custody – one parent being made responsible for the care of the children

Summary

There has been a steep increase in divorce in the UK in the past 50 years as it has become easier and more socially acceptable.

Catholic Christians do not allow religious divorce and remarriage because they believe that marriage vows cannot be broken.

Other Christians disapprove of divorce, but allow religious divorce and remarriage if the marriage has broken down, because Christianity teaches forgiveness.

Humanists and atheists believe that everyone should have the right to divorce and remarriage if a marriage has failed and any children will not suffer as a result of the divorce.

Practice questions

c Explain two reasons why remarriage is a problem for Catholic Christians. In your answer you must refer to a source of wisdom and authority.

d 'Christians should never divorce.' Evaluate this statement considering arguments for and against. In your response you should:

- refer to Christian teachings
- refer to different Christian points of view
- reach a justified conclusion.

Topic 1.2.7 Equality of men and women in the family

Christians have different attitudes to the roles of men and women in the family, perhaps because the Bible has three different teachings:

- Genesis chapter 1 teaches the equality of men and women as they were created at the same time and were both created in the image of God:

  So God created man in his own image, in the image of God he created him; male and female he created them. (Genesis 1:27)

- However, Genesis chapters 2 and 3 say that woman was created after man and out of man's rib, therefore, woman is **subordinate** to man. These chapters also explain that evil came into the world because woman persuaded man to give in to the temptation of the Devil and eat the fruit of the tree which God had forbidden. As a result of this action, God says to the woman,

  I will make your pains in childbearing very severe; with painful labour you will give birth to children. Your desire will be for your husband, and he will rule over you.' Whereas he tells the man, 'Cursed is the ground because of you; through painful toil you will eat of it ... by the sweat of your brow you will eat your food.

- St Paul says in Ephesians chapter 5:21–30 that wives should submit to their husband because the husband is the head of the wife in the same way that Christ is the head of the Church. This implies that the wife should do as she is told by the husband, but St Paul also says that husbands should love their wives in the same way they love their own bodies. However, his words that a husband feeds and cares for his body imply that men should feed and care for women, reinforcing the subservience of women.

So the biblical teaching of Genesis 1 says that men and women should have equal roles in life because they were created equal. However, Genesis 2–3 and Ephesians say that men have the **dominant role** and could be used to justify the belief that the role of women is to care for the home and children and the role of men is to work and provide the material needs of the family.

Wives, submit yourselves to your own husbands as you do to the Lord. For the husband is the head of the wife as Christ is the head of the church, his body, of which he is the Saviour. Now as the church submits to Christ, so also wives should submit to their husbands in everything. Husbands, love your wives, just as Christ loved the church and gave himself up for her to make her holy, cleansing her by the washing with water through the word, and to present her to himself as a radiant church, without stain or wrinkle or any other blemish, but holy and blameless. In this same way, husbands ought to love their wives as their own bodies. He who loves his wife loves himself. After all, no one ever hated their own body, but they feed and care for their body, just as Christ does the church – for we are members of his body. (Ephesians 5:22–30)

Thinking points

In this topic you need to:

- think about different Christian teachings and attitudes towards the role of men and women in the family, including reference to Genesis 1–3 and Ephesians 5:21–30
- consider different atheist and Humanist attitudes about the equality of men and women in the family and Christian responses to them
- be able to explain different Christian and non-religious attitudes to the equality of men and women in the family.

Useful words

Subordinate – of inferior importance or rank

Dominant role – the major, most influential part

Activity

Why may biblical teaching on the equality of men and women cause problems for Christians?

Activities

1. Look at the photo of women worshipping with their heads covered, then read 1 Corinthians 11:1–10. What do you think of this passage?
2. Read the statement from the Southern Baptist Convention below. Do you consider this an acceptable viewpoint in the twenty-first century?

A wife is to submit graciously to the servant leadership of her husband even as the Church willingly submits to the leadership of Christ ... she, being in the image of God, as is her husband and thus equal to him, has the God-given responsibility to respect her husband and to serve as his helper. (Statement by the Southern Baptist Convention of the USA, June 1998)

Christian attitudes to equal roles of men and women in the family

1 Evangelical Protestants

Many Evangelical Protestants teach that men and women have separate and different roles. It is the role of women to bring up children and run a Christian home. It is the role of men to provide for the family and lead the family in religion. Many such Protestant Christians believe women should dress simply and keep their heads covered in church. Men must love their wives as themselves, but only men can be church leaders and teachers.

This attitude is based on:

- the teaching of Genesis 2 about Adam being created first
- the disciples of Jesus being men
- the teaching of St Paul in Ephesians about the husband being the head of the wife
- the teachings of St Paul in Corinthians 11:3–10 about women's appearance.

2 Liberal Protestants

Many Protestant Churches now accept that men and women are equal, and should have equal roles in life and the family. This attitude is based on:

- the teachings of Genesis 1 that male and female were created at the same time and equally
- the teaching of St Paul in Galatians that in Christ there is neither male nor female
- the evidence from the Gospels that Jesus treated women as his equals. He preached in the court of women in the Jerusalem Temple (Matthew 21:23–22:14). He treated a Samaritan woman as his equal (John 4). He had female disciples who stayed with him at the cross (Matthew 27:55, Mark 15:40–41, Luke 23:27, John 19:25–27), unlike the male disciples who ran away. It was to women that Jesus appeared first after the resurrection.

Women covering their heads with lace mantillas (veil or shawl) at an Evangelical service in Panajachel, Guatemala.

3 Catholics

The Catholic Church teaches that men and women should have equal roles in life and the family.

On the basis of Genesis 1:27, the Church teaches that men and women have equal status in the sight of God. In the new Roman Catholic marriage service, the priest says: 'May her husband put his trust in her and recognise that she is his equal and the heir with him to the life of grace.' In most Catholic families the husband and wife have equal roles.

Atheist and Humanist attitudes to equal roles of men and women in the family

Atheist attitudes

Atheists would tend to have the same attitudes to equal roles as the general, non-religious population. Their attitudes to equal roles of women have changed considerably: in 1965, 85 per cent of men agreed that, 'a man's job is to earn money, a woman's job is to look after the home and family', but in 1989, only 32 per cent of men agreed, and by 2008 only seventeen per cent of men agreed with the statement. The effect of these changed attitudes can be seen in this table based on research from British Social Attitudes.

Activity	Parent	Hours per week in 1965	Hours per week in 2011
Childcare	Mother	10	14
	Father	3	7
Housework	Mother	32	18
	Father	4	10
Paid employment	Mother	8	21
	Father	42	37

As can be seen from these changes, the most common non-religious attitude is that men and women are equal and should have equal roles in the family. The main reasons for this attitude are:

- The development of equal rights for women began in New Zealand and was followed in the UK by the Labour governments of 1964–79 making **sex discrimination** illegal in the Equal Pay Act and the Sex Discrimination Act.
- Social and industrial developments in the 1950s and 1960s led to the need for more women workers and for married women to provide a second income.
- The United Nations' Universal Declaration of Human Rights and the development of the feminist movement put forward a case for equal rights that could not be contradicted.
- The important contribution of women to politics and developments in health and social care demonstrated that women were the equals of men.
- The work of the **suffragette** and feminist movements to gain equal voting and political rights for women showed the men in authority that women were no longer prepared to be treated as second-class citizens.

Activities

1. Explain why Christians have different attitudes to equal roles of men and women in the family.
2. Look at the table of parental activities (1965 and 2011). What conclusions can be drawn from this about differences in family attitudes between 1965 and 2011?

Useful words

Sex discrimination – treating people differently on the ground of their gender

Suffragette – a woman seeking the right to vote through protest

Humanist attitudes

Humanists base their beliefs on science and reason and so most would say they are equalists: they believe that men and women are equal and should have equal rights and therefore have totally equal roles in the family. Many of the suffragettes and early feminists were Humanists and modern Humanism teaches that men and women should have equal roles in the family.

Activities

1. Select some people from different age groups and ask their reactions to the following statement: 'a man's job is to earn money, a woman's job is to look after the home and family'. Discuss your findings.
2. How do you think Evangelical Protestants would respond to Humanist attitudes to the roles of men and women in the family?

Practice questions

c. Explain two reasons why Christians have different attitudes to the roles of men and women. In your answer you must refer to a source of wisdom and authority.

d. 'Men and women are totally equal and so should have completely equal roles in the family.' Evaluate this statement considering arguments for and against. In your response you should:
   - refer to Christian teachings
   - refer to different Christian points of view
   - reach a justified conclusion.

Summary

Genesis 1 teaches that men and women are equal. Genesis 2 and 3 teach that women are subordinate to men. St Paul teaches that women should submit to their husbands but that men should love their wives.

Evangelical Protestants believe that men should provide for the family and be leaders in religion, whereas women should bring up the children and run a Christian home. Liberal Protestants believe that men and women should be completely equal. Catholic Christians believe that men and women should have equal roles in life and the family.

Atheists and Humanists believe in the complete equality of men and women.

Topic 1.2.8 Gender prejudice and discrimination

You will need to understand the following terms when reading this topic:

- *Gender prejudice* is believing that one sex is superior to another based on feelings rather than an assessment of evidence.
- *Gender discrimination* is putting the prejudice into practice and treating people differently because of their sex.
- *Sexism* is discrimination, prejudice or stereotyping on the basis of gender. Sexism is most often expressed towards girls and women.

Christian teachings about gender prejudice and discrimination

It is sometimes said that Christianity is full of gender prejudice because God is described as a man, all the great heroes of the Bible were men, Jesus chose only men as his disciples and all the writers of the books of the Bible were men.

There are three different Christian attitudes to gender prejudice and discrimination and these are considered below.

1 Evangelical Protestants

Evangelical Protestants (as we saw in the last topic) teach that men and women have separate and different roles and so cannot have equal rights in religion. They also believe that women should not speak in church, should not teach and must submit to their husbands. It is the role of men to provide for the family and to lead the family in religion. Men must love their wives as themselves, but only men can be Church leaders and teachers. They do not see this as discrimination because it is what God **ordained** in the New Testament, which they believe is the final Word of God.

St Paul teaches that women should not teach or speak in church. He also uses the story of Adam and Eve in Genesis to show that men have been given more rights by God because Adam was created first and it was the woman who was led astray by Satan and then led man astray.

2 The Catholic Church

The Catholic Church is against gender prejudice and discrimination because it teaches that men and women should have equal roles in life and equal rights in society, since Genesis 1:27 teaches that God created men and women at the same time and both in the image of God. Furthermore, it is the teaching of the **Catholic Catechism** that men and women are equal, and should have equal rights in life and society, and Catholics should follow the teachings of the Catechism.

As far as ministry is concerned, women are able to study and teach in theological colleges, be **extraordinary ministers** of Holy Communion (people who give out the bread and wine which has been consecrated by a priest), visit the sick and take funerals in certain circumstances (over half

Thinking points

In this topic you need to:

- think about the meaning of gender prejudice and discrimination
- consider different Christian teachings about gender prejudice and discrimination, with examples of Christian opposition to gender prejudice and discrimination, including Galatians 3:23–29
- understand divergent Humanist and atheist attitudes to gender prejudice and discrimination and Christian responses to them
- be able to explain and evaluate different Christian and non-religious attitudes to gender prejudice and discrimination.

Useful words

Ordained – either set down by God or to be made a priest

Catholic Catechism – the official teaching of the Roman Catholic Church

Extraordinary minister – a non-ordained man or woman who assists the work of priests

Activities

1. What is the difference between gender prejudice and gender discrimination?
2. Outline the similarities and differences between the Evangelical and Roman Catholic attitudes to gender prejudice and discrimination.

of the lectors and extraordinary ministers in the British Catholic Church are women).

However, the Catholic Church also teaches that only men can be ordained priests, although it claims this does not affect the equal status of women because it is the special function of the priest to represent Jesus at the Mass which prevents women from becoming priests. The Catholic Catechism also teaches that only men can be priests because the **apostles** were all men, and priests and bishops are successors of the apostles.

3 Liberal Protestant Churches

Liberal Protestant Churches believe not only that men and women should have equal roles in the family (as we saw in Topic 1.2.7, page 61) but also that they should have totally equal rights in life and in the Church. Consequently, they have women ministers, priests and bishops (for example, Church of England, Methodist, United Reformed Church and Baptist) because:

- the creation story in Genesis 1 says that God created male and female at the same time and of equal status
- the letters of Paul teach that in Christ there is neither male nor female and therefore men and women should have equal rights
- the evidence from the Gospels shows that Jesus treated women as his equals
- there is some evidence that there were women priests in the early Church.

Christian opposition to gender prejudice and discrimination

The Movement for the Ordination of Women (MOW) is an organisation of Christians who believe that the Church's refusal to have women priests is gender discrimination. The group campaigned for the **ordination** of women as deacons and priests in the Church of England by persuading Church members to get their representatives on the General Synod to allow women priests. They achieved their first aim in 1975 when the General Synod agreed that 'there are no fundamental objections to the ordination of women to the priesthood'. But there was too much opposition to take it any further. By 1978, the movement had persuaded the lay members and the bishops to vote for women's ordination, but the clergy refused. The movement did not give up, and by 1987 the first women were ordained. The movement did not give up, and in 1993 the first women priests in the Church of England were ordained in Bristol Cathedral.

Another group of Christian men and women, Women and the Church, was established in 1996 to campaign for **gender equality** (and especially for the ordination of women as bishops) in the Church of England, but it was not until 2013 that the first woman bishop in the Church of England was ordained (there had been women priests and bishops much earlier in the American and Canadian Anglican Churches).

Catholic Women's Ordination began in 1993 as a British group of women and men who want the Catholic Church to accept that believing that women are equal with men (as the Catholic Church does) means not only that women have the opportunity to fulfil their own vocation, but also that women can become priests. Several such national groups formed Women's Ordination Worldwide (WOW) in 1996 as a network of national and international groups

Useful words

Apostle – one chosen by Jesus to preach his Gospel (often used for the twelve disciples)
Ordination – the act of conferring holy orders (making a priest)
Gender equality – the sexes being treated equally

Before the coming of this faith, we were held in custody under the law, locked up until the faith that was to come would be revealed. So the law was our guardian until Christ came that we might be justified by faith. Now that this faith has come, we are no longer under a guardian.

So in Christ Jesus you are all children of God through faith, for all of you who were baptised into Christ have clothed yourselves with Christ. There is neither Jew nor Gentile, neither slave nor free, nor is there male and female, for you are all one in Christ Jesus. (Galatians 3:23–28)

Activities

1. Read the quotation from Galatians. What do you think it means?
2. Outline two examples of Christian opposition to gender discrimination.

Pat Storey (left) became Britain and Ireland's first female bishop when she was consecrated by the Anglican Church in a ceremony in Dublin in November 2013.

whose mission is to end gender discrimination and persuade the Vatican to allow Roman Catholic women to join the ordained ministries. They hold conferences and protests, and had hoped that Pope Francis would listen to them, but in September 2015 he said that 'women priests, that cannot be done. Pope St John Paul II after long, long intense discussions, long reflection said so clearly'.

Activity

Look at the photo above. Why do you think so many Christians were against having women bishops?

Atheist and Humanist attitudes to gender prejudice and discrimination

Most atheists and all Humanists believe that men and women are equal and should have equal rights. The pressure for equal pay for women and to end sex discrimination came from non-religious politicians.

Humanists are against sexism and have been keen supporters of legislation to promote women's rights. Humanists believe that it is wrong for religion to be able to discriminate against women and that refusing to ordain women or have women leaders should be made illegal.

However, most surveys show that there is still a good deal of gender prejudice and discrimination in the UK, perhaps showing that many non-religious people are still prejudiced:

- Two-thirds (65 per cent) of adults agreed that sexism is still a problem in many workplaces (YouGov survey 2014).
- On average, two women a week are killed by a violent partner or ex-partner in the UK (Department of Health 2005).

Activities

1. Look at the photo opposite. Why do you think this group has little chance of success?
2. Did you find the evidence of gender discrimination on pages 67–8 surprising?
3. Would your responses to the MTV survey have been the same?
4. How do you think the Roman Catholic Church would respond to the Humanist view on page 67?

Summary

Evangelical Protestants believe that men and women should have different roles in life and that women cannot have equal rights in religion. They believe that only men should be church leaders and ministers.

The Catholic Church is against gender prejudice and discrimination and believes that women should have equal rights, but teaches that only men can be priests because Jesus and the Apostles were men.

Liberal Protestants believe in complete equality, are against gender prejudice and discrimination, and have women priests or ministers.

Many Christians have opposed gender discrimination, especially the Movement for the Ordination of Women, which persuaded the Church of England to ordain women, and the Catholic Women's Ordination, which is trying to persuade the Catholic Church to allow women priests.

Atheists and Humanists are totally against gender prejudice and discrimination.

Activists of the Women's Ordination Advocates organisation hold a banner during their vigil in St Peter's Square at the Vatican in 2010, calling on Pope Benedict XVI to ordain women.

- Up to 3 million women and girls across the UK experience rape, domestic violence, stalking or other violence each year (academic research 2009).
- Almost one in three girls have experienced unwanted sexual touching at school (YouGov survey 2010).

In 2014, an MTV survey of young people's opinions found that:

- Ninety-two per cent of males and 94 per cent of females believe that nobody should be treated differently due to their gender.
- More than 76 per cent of males and 80 per cent of females say that favouring one gender is unfair.
- Eighty-five per cent of males and 90 per cent of females believe that gender inequality can lead to big problems for society.
- Only two per cent of young people say that men and women are totally equal today and only 23 per cent say that men and women are at least mostly equal.

Practice questions

c. Explain two reasons why Christians have different attitudes to gender prejudice and discrimination. In your answer you must refer to a source of wisdom and authority.

d. 'Christians should never treat women differently from men.' Evaluate this statement considering arguments for and against. In your response you should:
   - refer to Christian teachings
   - refer to different Christian points of view
   - reach a justified conclusion.

How to answer questions

a) Outline three Christian beliefs about marriage. [3]

Christians believe that God created marriage when he created humans. They believe that marriage is for life and that marriage should be between one man and one woman.

A high mark answer because three correct Christian beliefs are clearly outlined.

b) Explain two reasons why there are different Christian attitudes to contraception. [4]

Catholic Christians oppose artificial methods of contraception because they are condemned in *Humanae Vitae* published by Pope Paul VI. Protestant and Orthodox Christians allow artificial contraception because it is not condemned in the Bible.

A high mark answer because two correct reasons are given and each reason is developed.

c) Explain two reasons why Christian teachings about sexual relationships may be important today. In your answer you must refer to a source of wisdom and authority. [5]

Christian teachings may be important because they conflict with the generally accepted attitudes. Most people think cohabitation is all right, but the Catholic Church says it is wrong because it is condemned in the Catechism and the Bible. Most people think homosexuality is acceptable, but both Catholics and Evangelical Protestants think it is wrong because it is condemned by Paul in his letter to the Romans.

A high mark answer because two correct reasons are given and each reason is developed with a reference to the Catechism and Romans, which are both sources of authority for Christians.

d) 'Christians should work against gender discrimination.' Evaluate this statement considering arguments for and against. In your response you should:

- **refer to Christian points of view**
- **refer to different Christian points of view**
- **reach a justified conclusion. [12]**

Some Christians would disagree with this view. Evangelical Protestants believe that women should not speak in church, should not teach and must submit to their husbands because it is what God ordained in the New Testament letters of St Paul. Catholic Christians believe that they can discriminate against women in the priesthood because the Magisterium teaches in the Catechism that only men can be priests. This is because the apostles were all men, and priests and bishops are the successors of the apostles.

However, liberal Protestants believe that they should fight against gender discrimination because in the creation story in Genesis 1, God created male and female of equal status. Also, St Paul taught that in Christ there is neither male nor female, and there is evidence from the Gospels that Jesus treated women as his equals.

Looking at the evidence I am not sure what to conclude. The excellent women priests and bishops in the liberal Churches who came to be through a fight against discrimination make me want to agree with the statement, but the sources of authority seem to justify Christians not working to end all discrimination.

[Continued]

A high mark answer because it gives two clear developed Christian reasons for thinking that Christians should not work against gender discrimination. It then gives three reasons for liberal Christians disagreeing and then reaches a fully justified conclusion that the evidence is too finely balanced to come down on one side.

3 Living the Christian life

Topic 1.3.1 Worship

Thinking points

In this topic you need to:

- think about the nature of liturgical and non-liturgical worship, including examples of the different types and when each type might be used and why
- be able to explain the importance of having different types of worship.

Useful words

Homage – acknowledgement of superiority
Reverence – an act showing religious respect
Host – unleavened bread used in the Eucharist
Clergy – people ordained for religious duties in Christian Churches
Vestments – official robes for those leading Christian worship
Lectionary – a list of Bible readings to be read at certain times of the year
Liturgical year – the year in the Church's calendar based on the special festivals from Advent to Pentecost
Congregation – the people assembled for worship
Liturgy – a set form of public worship
Holy Communion – the Christian service of thanksgiving using bread and wine (also called Eucharist or Mass)

What is worship?

The dictionary says worship is '**homage** or **reverence** paid to a deity (God)'.

Just as there are many different Churches (denominations) in Christianity, there are also many different forms of worship.

Liturgical worship

This is public worship in a church that uses a service book with set prayers and rituals so that everything follows the same format. The worshippers can follow the service and join in certain parts as they read the prayers and responses. The words have been in use for many years, which allows worshippers to think about them and continually develop greater understanding. The set form also means that rituals have developed to help the worshippers feel closer to God (for example, the elevation of the **host** in a Catholic Mass (see photo) helps the worshippers to feel the presence of Christ coming into the unleavened bread). The **clergy** usually wear **vestments**.

The Bible readings for a year are set out in a **lectionary** that follows the **liturgical year**. This begins at Advent, and follows through Christmas, Epiphany, Lent, Easter and Pentecost. The readings follow a three-year cycle (there are different readings for each day every year for three years). In this way, **congregations** hear most of the Bible read and also follow the main events of the Church's year.

Liturgical worship is the main form of worship in Roman Catholic (using the Missal as the service book), Orthodox (the Divine **Liturgy** of St John Chrysostom) and many Anglican Churches (Common Worship), but is only used for **Holy Communion**, baptism, marriage and funerals in most Protestant Churches. It takes place at set times, especially on a Sunday.

Elevating the host during a Mass in a church in Germany.

Non-liturgical worship

This is public worship in a church without set prayers or rituals. The leader of the worship is free to choose the hymns, prayers and Bible readings and the main focus of the service is the sermon, which can be on a theme of the leader's choice.

Music is often a major part of non-liturgical worship, with hymns (accompanied by an organ in more traditional churches) or Gospel songs/choruses (accompanied by guitars, keyboard or bands in more Pentecostal-type churches). Prayers are **extempore prayers** rather than following a set form, although, like all liturgical services, they usually include thanksgiving, confession and intercession.

In Pentecostal-type churches, there will often be more congregational participation, with members of the congregation offering prayers or expressing their approval of what the leader says by saying such things as 'Amen', 'Hallelujah' and 'Praise the Lord'.

Non-liturgical worship takes place at set times, especially on a Sunday.

Useful words

Extempore prayers – prayers said without preparation

Informal worship

Many Christian families worship God at home by saying grace before meals, having family prayers, reading the Bible together and celebrating the festivals of the Christian year.

Many churches also have worship in much more informal ways, especially for families and young people. 'Messy Church' provides worship for families, which is based on fun, creativity (lots of craft activities), hospitality and celebration. Many organisations based in churches (for example, uniformed organisations, Mothers' Union) include an element of informal worship in their activities.

Private worship

Most Christians will worship God at certain times on their own as they pray to God in private, or read the Bible alone. Private worship is when Christians have the opportunity to talk to God and think about their faith.

Many Anglicans use the Book of Common Prayer in their daily devotions because it uses the language of Shakespeare, and the Authorised Version of the Bible which makes it feel special and very religious. The Book of Common Prayer also provides a structure, which includes all elements of prayer: adoration, thanksgiving, confession and supplication (intercession and petition).

Activities

1. Look at the picture on page 72. How do you know this is liturgical worship?
2. Look at the picture on this page. How do you know this is non-liturgical worship?
3. What are the differences and similarities between liturgical and non-liturgical worship?

Worship in a Nigerian Pentecostal church in London.

Activities

1. Do you think that Christians need to go to church every Sunday? Give reasons for your answer.
2. Which types of worship might you use?

Why different types of worship are used

- *Worship in the home*: people need to be able to worship in the home because this is the heart of people's lives and worshipping as a family brings the family together.
- *Private worship*: people need to be able to worship God in private so they can communicate with God one to one and express emotions they cannot express in front of others.
- *Informal worship*: this helps people to see God in the ordinary and to realise that worship can happen anywhere in any way.
- *Public worship*: worshipping with others in church gives a sense of belonging to a whole community of believers and gives an opportunity to feel the strength of the faith and make friends with others in the faith.

Different Christian attitudes to liturgical and non-liturgical worship

Those Christians who believe in the seven sacraments (Catholic, Orthodox, and some Anglicans) and those whose forms of worship were based on Catholic worship (Lutherans and most Anglicans) feel that the best form of worship is liturgical worship because:

- worshipping with set prayers and in set forms helps them to worship God in a familiar way so that worship becomes a part of their lives
- using ancient prayers and forms of worship makes them aware of their Christian heritage
- using the same prayers and forms of worship as the rest of the Church gives them a sense of solidarity and belonging
- following the liturgical year helps them to understand their faith and learn more about God
- liturgical forms of worship make the worship important rather than the person leading the worship.

Those Christians for whom the sacraments are less important (most Protestants but especially Nonconformists and Pentecostals) prefer non-liturgical worship because:

- a more free form of worship helps people to participate in worship
- it helps to reflect people's moods from joy to sadness so that the worship comes from people's own feelings
- it allows worship to include forms people identify with such as rock and Gospel music
- it helps to connect worship to the world of today.

Summary

Christians have two types of worship:

- liturgical worship, which is worship using a set form, with set prayers and Bible readings (the main worship in Catholic, Orthodox and most Anglican churches)
- non-liturgical worship, which has no set form and tends to focus on music and the sermon (the main form of worship in Protestant and Pentecostal churches).

All Churches have informal worship at gatherings such as Mums and Tots, and Christians also worship in private. It is important to have different types of worship because people have different feelings and interests.

Practice questions

c. Explain two reasons why some Christians prefer to use liturgical worship to worship God.

d. 'God doesn't need people to worship him.' Evaluate this statement considering arguments for and against. In your response you should:
   - refer to Christian teachings
   - refer to different Christian points of view
   - reach a justified conclusion.

Topic 1.3.2 The role of the sacraments in Christian life

The role of the sacraments as a whole

There are seven **sacraments** in the Catholic and Orthodox Churches. The sacraments are baptism, reconciliation (**penance**), Holy Communion (**Eucharist**), confirmation, the anointing of the sick, holy orders and marriage.

The sacraments of baptism and confirmation take place only once in a Christian's life but are essential to being a member of the Church (the importance of baptism is dealt with below). The sacrament of anointing of the sick is essential for Catholics and the Orthodox when they are very ill, as it ensures that their sins are forgiven so that if they die, they will not be sent to purgatory (this sacrament used to be known as the last rites).

Holy orders is the sacrament that ordains a man as a priest (or a man or a woman in the Anglican Church). It is important because only priests can administer the sacraments and so without men taking holy orders, there will be no sacraments. Marriage is not an essential sacrament but it is important because the sacrament of marriage makes God a part of the marriage and gives a couple **grace** and strength.

The sacraments are essential in the life of Catholic and Orthodox Christians because:

- through sacraments they receive grace and blessings from God
- sacraments mark the journey of faith that Christians go through in life
- sacraments make Christians stronger in their faith
- sacraments bring Christians closer to God
- a sacrament is an outward and visible sign of an inward, spiritual grace.

Most Protestant Christians have only two sacraments – baptism and Holy Communion.

As far as the Church of England is concerned, the 39 Articles say that only the sacraments of baptism and Holy Communion are authorised by God. However, some Anglicans believe in and practise all seven sacraments.

Some Protestant Christians, such as the Quakers and the Salvation Army, do not have any sacraments at all. They are not baptised and their non-liturgical worship (for Quakers, very informal worship) never includes the Eucharist.

> *There are two Sacraments ordained of Christ our Lord in the Gospel, that is to say, Baptism, and the Supper of the Lord.*
>
> *Those five commonly called Sacraments, that is to say, Confirmation, Penance, Orders, Matrimony, and Extreme Unction, are not to be counted for Sacraments of the Gospel, being such as have grown partly of the corrupt following of the Apostles, partly are states of life allowed in the Scriptures; but yet have not like nature of Sacraments with Baptism, and the Lord's Supper, for that they have not any visible sign or ceremony ordained of God. (Article 24 of the 39 Articles from the Book of Common Prayer)*

Thinking points

In this topic you need to:

- think about the role of the sacraments as a whole in two denominations
- understand baptism and the Eucharist and their importance in two denominations
- be able to explain the differing importance of the sacraments comparing Roman Catholics to Baptists and Methodists.

Useful words

Sacrament – an outward sign of an inward blessing
Penance – an action showing sorrow for a sin
Eucharist – a Christian rite considered by most to be a sacrament
Grace – God's gift which gives strength to be good and holy

The 39 Articles set out the basic beliefs of the Church of England as Church in between Catholic and extreme Protestant. They are not essential doctrines, but the Apostles' and Nicene Creeds are.

Activity

Why are sacraments important in the life of a Catholic?

The sacrament of baptism

The word baptism comes from the Greek *baptizein*, which means to dip, bathe or wash. It refers to the washing away of the old life and entering a new one, free of sin.

A denomination is a sub-group within a religion and is sometimes used to describe the different Christian Churches. In this section of the specification we will look at baptism in the Catholic and Baptist Churches.

Useful words

Infant baptism – baptising babies, with their parents and godparents making vows on their behalf
Paschal candle – the large candle kept in the church throughout Easter and first lit on Easter Day

Activity

Make a list of the similarities and differences between infant baptism and believers' baptism.

Catholics and baptism

Catholics are usually baptised as babies (**infant baptism**) and their parents make promises on their behalf during the ceremony, in which:

- There are readings from the Bible about baptism or new life in Jesus.
- The priest talks to the family about the meaning of the sacrament and the responsibilities of raising a child as a Catholic.
- Prayers are said for the needs of the family, the parish and the world.
- The parents and godparents mark the child with the sign of the cross on its forehead.
- The priest says a prayer which removes all evil and sin and then anoints the baby with the oil.
- The parents and godparents say vows that show that they believe in the Catholic faith and are willing to bring the child up according to Church teachings.
- Water is poured over the child's head as the priest recites the words, 'I baptise you in the name of the Father and of the Son and of the Holy Spirit. Amen'.
- The child is dressed in a white garment.
- The child is anointed with the oil of chrism.
- A candle is lit from the **Paschal candle** (Easter candle) and given to the godparents to hold.
- The sacrament ends with prayers and a blessing, but occasionally with Mass.

A baby being baptised by a priest.

Why baptism is important for Catholics

- Baptism is seen as necessary for the person to receive salvation.
- Through this sacrament the person becomes a member of the Church.
- Baptism shows publicly that the child is now a Christian and intends to live as one.
- Baptism washes away original sin and makes the person pure.
- The Catechism teaches that it is the basis of Christian life and without it, a person cannot receive the other sacraments.
- The sacrament gives the parents strength and help in bringing up their child as a Christian.
- It copies the example of Jesus being baptised.

Baptists and baptism

Baptist Christians practise '**believers' baptism**'. They usually have a **dedication** for their babies, but believe that people need to be old enough to make baptismal vows for themselves when they have made their own decision to become a member of Christ's Church.

Baptist churches have a baptismal pool which is half-filled with water for a baptismal service, although some Christians (especially Pentecostals who also practise believers' baptism) hire a swimming bath or baptise in the sea or rivers. The person to be baptised usually has a sponsor who stands next to them in the water. The main features of a service of believers' baptism are:

- The person to be baptised is asked if they believe that Jesus is Lord and that he died for their sins.
- They say a few words about how they came to believe in Christ as their Lord and Saviour.
- The minister lowers them completely under the water, saying, 'I baptise you in the name of the Father, and of the Son, and of the Holy Spirit'.
- The sponsor hands them a towel and helps them to dry themselves.
- They are congratulated by the congregation and welcomed into the Church.

Why baptism is important for Baptists

- It signifies the end of their old life outside the Church and of being born again to new life in Christ.
- Baptists believe that in baptism, God's presence and blessing come upon them.
- It is a moment when they make a personal commitment of faith in Jesus as Lord.
- It is a moment when they receive God's Spirit for service in the Church and in the world.

An adult's baptism at Kensington Temple Church, London.

Useful words

Believers' baptism – restricting baptism to those old enough to understand the meaning of the ritual

Dedication – a ceremony involving a child being presented to the congregation and vows being made to encourage the child to follow the Christian life

Activity

Do you think Christians should baptise believers or infants?

Activity

What are the main differences between Catholics and Methodists in their beliefs about the Eucharist?

The Eucharist

The word Eucharist comes from the Greek word *eucharistia*, meaning thanksgiving. The Eucharist began with the Last Supper that Jesus had with his disciples, when he gave them bread and wine and said it was his body and blood and told them to have it in remembrance of him. It was used by the early Christians; St Paul describes early eucharists in his letter to the Corinthians. The Eucharist is the earliest recorded act of Christian worship.

For this part of the specification, we will look at how the Eucharist is celebrated in Catholic and Methodist Churches.

The Eucharist in the Catholic Church

The Eucharist in the Roman Catholic Church is part of the service known as the Mass (meaning dismissal, but used to mean that the sacrament gives one strength to go out into the world and fulfil one's Christian mission). Catholics are expected to attend Mass every Sunday and on holy days of obligation (non-Sunday feast days such as Christmas Day). In the Catholic Church the wine is alcoholic and is drunk from a chalice; the bread is a thin wafer of unleavened bread known as the host. The main features of the sacrament are:

- The Penitential Rite, where the congregation members confess their sins and receive **absolution**.
- The Liturgy of the Word, with readings from the Bible and a sermon to learn more about the faith, and prayers of intercession to help others.
- The Liturgy of the Eucharist, where the Last Supper is re-enacted and the bread and wine are changed by a process called **transubstantiation** into the body and blood of Christ.
- The Rite of Communion, where the people exchange the peace and share the **Holy Communion** by receiving the consecrated hosts and (in most, but not all churches) the wine. Any remaining consecrated hosts are placed in the tabernacle to be used for the sacrament of the sick or, if no priest is available, for Mass.
- The Concluding Rite, where the priest blesses the people and sends them out into the world.

Useful words

Absolution – through the actions and words of a priest or minister pardon of sins is assured
Transubstantiation – the belief that during the service of Mass (also called Eucharist or Holy Communion) the bread and wine transform into the body and blood of Jesus
Holy Communion – a Christian rite

Why the Mass is important in the lives of Catholics

- Catholics believe that during the Mass, bread and wine are turned into the body and blood of Christ through the words and actions of the priest and the grace of God. Through transubstantiation Catholics believe that Jesus is really present with them during Mass.
- The Eucharist is a sacrament: it is a weekly gift of grace that Catholics wish to receive to give them God's strength for the coming week.
- The Mass is a celebration of the resurrection of Jesus. Attending Mass reminds Catholics that there is eternal life and assures them that they will inherit eternal life.
- Through attending Mass, Catholics come into the real presence of Christ and receive the body and blood of Christ. So the sacrament joins them with Jesus.
- Mass was instituted by Jesus, who commanded his disciples to 'Do this in memory of me'. By attending Mass, Catholics are obeying the command of Jesus.

The Eucharist in the Methodist Church

The Eucharist is known as Holy Communion in the Methodist Church and is usually celebrated once a month. Although members are recommended to attend Holy Communion, it is not compulsory. The wine used in the Methodist sacrament is non-alcoholic and is drunk from individual glasses; the bread is normal bread, often in the form of a small loaf that is broken by the minister. The main features of the sacrament are:

- general confession of sins
- sharing of the peace and recitation of the Nicene Creed
- thanksgiving including a remembrance of the Last Supper
- sharing of the bread and wine
- the minister blessing the people and sending them out into the world.

The meaning and importance of the sacrament for Methodists

- Holy Communion is a remembrance of the Last Supper, and of God's mercy. The bread and wine do not change, they are symbols of the presence of Christ.
- Holy Communion gives spiritual nourishment, filling Methodists with God's grace.
- Holy Communion brings unity to Methodists as they share the one body of Christ and share the peace.
- Holy Communion is a reminder of the Last Supper and the crucifixion and resurrection of Christ.

Practice questions

c Explain two reasons why baptism is important for most Christians. In your answer you must refer to a source of wisdom and authority.

d 'You don't need to take the sacraments to be a good Christian.' Evaluate this statement considering arguments for and against. In your response you should:

- refer to Christian teachings
- refer to different Christian points of view
- reach a justified conclusion.

Activity

What are the similarities and differences in the way Catholics and Methodists celebrate the sacrament of the Eucharist?

Summary

Sacraments are celebrations. They mark stages in life and are outward signs and symbols which show that an inward gift from God has been given. Catholics, Orthodox Christians and some Anglicans have seven sacraments, while most Protestants just have baptism and Eucharist.

Christians are baptised to become members of the Church and to remove their sins. Most Christians are baptised as babies, but some Christians such as Baptists and Pentecostals are baptised as adults. Some Christians (Catholic and Orthodox) believe that the bread and wine in the Eucharist change to the body and blood of Jesus, others (Protestants) call it Holy Communion and think it is just remembering the Last Supper, but all Christians believe that it unites them with Jesus and each other.

Topic 1.3.3 The nature and purpose of prayer

Thinking points

In this topic you need to:

- think about the nature and purpose of different types of prayer, including set prayers, informal prayer and the Lord's Prayer (Matthew 6:9–13)
- be able to explain why each type might be used and evaluate the value of prayer.

Useful words

Vocal prayer – prayer using words
Meditation – thinking about religious matters
Contemplation – communion with God
Adoration – praising or adoring God for what he is
Thanksgiving – prayers thanking God
Confession – prayers saying sorry for sins and asking God's forgiveness
Supplication – prayers asking for God's help

A boy praying.

The nature and purpose of prayer

Prayer can be defined as 'an attempt to contact God, usually through words'. So the main purpose of prayer is to contact God.

Most prayer is **vocal prayer**, when words are used, either out loud or mentally, to express the prayer. However, prayer can also include **meditation** and **contemplation**.

Prayer can have several subsidiary purposes:

- **Adoration**: praising or adoring God for what he is. For example, by praying 'O God, how great and marvellous you are'.
- **Thanksgiving**: thanking God either for his general goodness or for some specific thing such as getting better from an illness.
- **Confession**: confessing sins to God, asking his forgiveness and determining to do better.
- **Supplication**: asking for God's help either for oneself or for others (praying for God's help for others is known as intercession).

Different types of prayer

Set prayers

Liturgical worship is full of prayers expressing all the four types of prayer above. Many Christians come to know these prayers off by heart and use them as their own prayers, especially as their own private prayers.

They might use this prayer to confess their sins to God:

> *Almighty and most merciful Father, We have erred, and strayed from thy ways like lost sheep, We have followed too much the devices and desires of our own hearts, We have offended against thy holy laws, We have left undone those things which we ought to have done, And we have done those things which we ought not to have done, And there is no health in us. (General Confession from the Church of England Book of Common Prayer)*

Or they might use this prayer to help them to say thank you to God:

> *It is right to give thanks and praise. It is indeed right, it is our duty and joy at all times and in all places to give you thanks and praise, holy Father, heavenly King, almighty and eternal God. (Thanksgiving from the Church of England Common Worship)*

Activity

Why do you think people pray?

Christians tend to use the Lord's Prayer (known as 'Our Father' by some Christians) many times in their personal contacts with God as this is what Jesus asked them to do:

> *And when you pray, do not keep on babbling like pagans, for they think they will be heard because of their many words. Do not be like them, for your Father knows what you need before you ask him. This, then, is how you should pray: 'Our Father in heaven, hallowed be your name, your kingdom come, your will be done on earth as it is in heaven. Give us today our daily bread. Forgive us our debts, as we also have forgiven our debtors. And lead us not into temptation, but deliver us from the evil one.' For if you forgive men when they sin against you, your heavenly Father will also forgive you. But if you do not forgive men their sins, your Father will not forgive your sins.* (Matthew 6:7–15)

This prayer expresses:

- *Adoration*: '... hallowed be your name, your kingdom come, your will be done on earth as it is in heaven'.
- *Confession*: 'Forgive us our debts, as we also have forgiven our debtors'.
- *Supplication*: 'Give us today our daily bread ... And lead us not into temptation, but deliver us from the evil one'.

Informal prayers

Most Christians also use informal prayers as part of their devotions. They will express their innermost thoughts to God as a prayer, using their own words and their own language. In this way, they feel that they are in a personal relationship with God.

Those Christians used to liturgical worship tend to use other set prayers as a part of the informal prayers, for example the 'Hail Mary'.

When Christians use set prayers

Obviously, Christians use set prayers during liturgical worship, but many Christians who are only familiar with liturgical worship (Catholic and Orthodox Christians) also use set prayers as their personal prayers, which they pray at set times. For example, when they wake up or before they go to bed, or at any moment when the thought of God enters their mind, or if they become aware of someone's suffering when they may offer a prayer of intercession.

When Christians use informal prayers

Christians who are used to non-liturgical worship are familiar with extempore prayer and so they use informal prayers as their personal prayer – although all Christians use the set form of the Lord's Prayer on all sorts of occasions. Such Christians also tend to pray at set times, or when the thought of God enters their mind, or when they become aware of someone's suffering.

Why Christians pray

- Prayer (especially adoration prayers) can help a person to get things into perspective; by stepping aside from the pressures of daily life and focusing on God, they can be brought to realise the reality of life.

Activities

1. Read the set prayers on page 80. Why do you think set prayers use such respectful language?
2. Try to put one of the prayers into language you would be more comfortable with.
3. Why do you think some Christians have a set time for devotions?
4. What do you think about the Lord's Prayer?

Activities

1. Why might some Christians think set prayers are the most important type of prayers and some not?
2. Why might some Christians think informal prayers are the most important type of prayers and some not?
3. Why might some Christians think the Lord's Prayer is the most important type of prayer and some not?

- Prayers of thanksgiving help a person not to be selfish, to realise that they depend on others, and not to take things for granted.
- Prayers of confession stop a person from bottling up feelings of guilt, help them to come to terms with what they have done and help them to learn from their mistakes so that their life improves.
- Prayers of supplication can help a person to feel they are doing something for those who suffer, but these prayers can also inspire them to do something practical to help the less fortunate.
- Contemplative and meditative prayers can bring inner peace so that they feel refreshed from within.

Practice questions

c Explain two reasons why the Lord's Prayer is important for Christians. In your answer you must refer to a source of wisdom and authority.

d 'Everyone needs to pray.' Evaluate this statement considering arguments for and against. In your response you should:

- refer to Christian teachings
- refer to different Christian points of view
- reach a justified conclusion.

Summary

Prayer is an attempt to contact God. Christians use prayers to adore God, to thank him, to confess their sins to him and to ask his help either for others or for themselves. They can be set prayers said at set times, or informal prayers said whenever a Christian feels the need to communicate with God. Prayer is important for Christians because it helps them to get things in perspective and can bring inner peace.

Topic 1.3.4 Pilgrimage

The nature, history and purpose of pilgrimage

Pilgrimage is a journey to a location of importance to a religion.

People have gone on pilgrimages for many years. Many archaeologists think that the prehistoric relic of Stonehenge was once a place of pilgrimage. The ancient Greeks went on pilgrimage to Mount Olympus. Hindus have been going to Benares for thousands of years. The Muslim annual pilgrimage to Makkah (Mecca) has been happening since the time of Muhammad. Jesus went on pilgrimage to Jerusalem every year when he was a child and Christians have been going on pilgrimage to the Holy Land since Emperor Constantine's mother went there after she had converted to Christianity.

In the Middle Ages European pilgrims continued to make the difficult journey to the Holy Land, taking years as they travelled on foot. Rich people often paid professional pilgrims to go on pilgrimage for them so that they gained the spiritual benefits without having to interrupt their lives. Pilgrims wore special badges to show which sacred places they had visited. There were many centres of pilgrimage, usually connected with the **relics** of a saint preserved and displayed in a **reliquary** in a **shrine** at the pilgrimage site.

The medieval world was full of relics. The bones and skin, fingernails and even heads of saints were preserved; three European churches even claimed to have the foreskin of Jesus preserved after his circumcision.

Pilgrims undertook these journeys to holy places because it was important for their faith. If they had committed sins, they believed that going on a pilgrimage would show God how sorry they were. Sometimes priests sent people on such journeys as penance for a particularly bad sin. Sometimes they went to be healed of an illness.

The popularity of these pilgrimages can be seen in Geoffrey Chaucer's *The Canterbury Tales* (c.1400), which tells the stories of a group of pilgrims journeying from London to the shrine of St Thomas Becket at Canterbury Cathedral.

Opposition to pilgrimage

The Protestant Reformers were very much opposed to these pilgrimages as they thought that they broke the commandment not to worship idols (the relics at the shrines were worshipped) and that the relics were false and there to deceive the pilgrims. John Calvin (1509–64), the great Reformer, claimed the following about relics of the cross on which Jesus was crucified (known as the **True Cross**):

> *There is no abbey so poor as not to have a specimen. In some places there are large fragments, as at the Holy Chapel in Paris, at Poitiers, and at Rome, where a good-sized crucifix is said to have been made of it. In brief, if all the pieces that could be found were collected together, they would make a big shipload. Yet the Gospel testifies that a single man was able to carry it. (John Calvin,* Traité Des Reliques*)*

Thinking points

In this topic you need to:

- think about the nature, history and purpose of pilgrimage, including Luke 2:41–43
- think about the significance of the places people go to on pilgrimage, including Jerusalem, Iona, Taizé and Walsingham
- think about the differences between Protestant and Catholic beliefs about pilgrimage
- be able to explain why pilgrimage is important for Christians today.

Useful words

Relics – the physical remains of a saint or the personal effects of the saint or holy person

Reliquary – a container for holy relics

Shrine – a place of worship that holds the tomb or relic of a saint

True Cross – the actual cross on which Jesus was crucified

Every year Jesus' parents went to Jerusalem for the Festival of the Passover. When he was twelve years old, they went up to the festival, according to the custom. After the festival was over, while his parents were returning home, the boy Jesus stayed behind in Jerusalem, but they were unaware of it. (Luke 2:41–43)

Activities

1. Look at the photo. Do you think relics like this should be on public display?
2. Read the quotation from Luke chapter 2 on page 83. Why might this make Christians want to go on pilgrimage to Jerusalem?
3. Do you think the Protestant reformers had good reasons for opposing pilgrimages?

You shall have no other gods before me. You shall not make for yourself an idol in the form of anything in heaven above or on the earth beneath or in the waters below. You shall not bow down to them or worship them. (Exodus 20:3–5)

The head of St Catherine of Siena displayed in the Church of San Domenico in Siena. Other parts of her can be found in Venice and England.

Why Christians go on pilgrimage

- Some Christians feel that life is a search for God and that going on a pilgrimage helps them in their search for God.
- Many pilgrims feel that they become closer to God on a pilgrimage.
- Making a pilgrimage takes planning, time and effort, and this process can help in determining what your priorities in life are.
- Pilgrimage adds discipline to a Christian's spiritual life – they have to get up and do something.
- Jesus himself went on pilgrimage to Jerusalem every year, according to Luke chapter 2.
- Pilgrims go to places like Lourdes in the hope of being cured from an illness, and although few are cured, many claim that the pilgrimage gave them greater inner strength to cope with their illnesses and other problems of life.
- Places of pilgrimage have special connections with great figures or events in the Christian faith and so are full of holiness. Pilgrims hope that if they visit these places some of the holiness will rub off on them.

Where do Christians go to on pilgrimage?

There are four pilgrimage sites which are particularly important for Christians today.

Jerusalem

A major centre of Christian pilgrimage is Jerusalem in Israel, where the crucial events in the last week of Jesus' life took place; the events which are still celebrated in Christianity today. Pilgrims visit the following places:

Jewish tombs under the Church of the Holy Sepulchre.

- The **Cenacle**, thought to be the site of the Upper Room, which is important to pilgrims because it is where the Last Supper took place and the Last Supper is when Jesus instituted the Eucharist.
- The Church of All Nations on the Mount of Olives, which is important to pilgrims because it is where Jesus prayed to his Father to take the cup from him and where Jesus was arrested.
- The Convent of the Sisters of Zion, which is important to pilgrims because it is built on top of the pavement where Jesus was tried before Pontius Pilate and from which Pilate offered to release Jesus.
- The **Via Dolorosa**, or way of suffering, which is important to pilgrims because it is the route Jesus took as he was made to carry his cross to Golgotha, the place of crucifixion (pilgrims usually walk along the Via, praying at places where Jesus stopped and where Simon of Cyrene took over the cross).
- The Church of the Holy Sepulchre, which is perhaps the holiest place because it is believed to be the location of Golgotha, where Jesus was crucified (dying for the sins of the world) and Jesus' nearby tomb, where he was buried and rose from the dead, so guaranteeing eternal life to Christians.
- The Garden Tomb, which Protestants often visit rather than the Holy Sepulchre because some archaeologists believe it to be the true place of Golgotha.

Useful words

Cenacle – the Upper Room in Jerusalem where the Last Supper took place
Via Dolorosa – 'The Way of Tears', the route Jesus took from Pilate's court to Golgotha

Activity

Explain why Protestant Christians might go on pilgrimage to Jerusalem, but not to Walsingham or Lourdes.

Pilgrimage became very popular again in the nineteenth century among Roman Catholics, especially after the experiences of St Bernadette of Lourdes. On Thursday 11 February 1858, fourteen-year-old Bernadette Soubirous saw a beautiful young girl in a niche at a rocky outcrop near Lourdes in France. The apparition beckoned to her, but Bernadette did not move and the girl smiled at her before disappearing. Bernadette later described how she had seen a young girl of about her own age and height, clothed in a brilliant and unearthly white robe, with a blue girdle round her waist and a white veil on her head. This was the beginning of eighteen apparitions during the spring and early summer of 1858. During one of these, Bernadette asked the lady her name and she replied, 'I am the **immaculate conception**.' During another apparition, the lady led Bernadette to a grotto where a miraculous spring appeared. Since these miraculous appearances of the Virgin Mary, Lourdes has become a great place of pilgrimage for Catholics and many healing miracles are alleged to have taken place there.

Useful words

Immaculate conception – the Catholic belief that Mary was protected from original sin from the moment of her conception so that Jesus was not born with original sin

Walsingham

This village in Norfolk is known as 'the English Nazareth'. In 1061, the lady of the manor, Richeldis de Faverches, had a vision of the Virgin Mary and her home in Nazareth and Mary ordered Richeldis to build a copy of Mary's home. The house was eventually built and became a popular pilgrimage site when it became impossible for Christian pilgrims to get to the Holy Land because of Muslim conquests. In the shrine was a statue of Mary based on what Lady Richeldis saw in her vision and a phial which was supposed to contain milk from Mary's breasts. Many healings and visions are supposed to have happened at the shrine.

The shrine was destroyed at the time of the Reformation, but in 1921 the vicar of the parish had a new statue made based on an image on a seal he found in his church, and rebuilt the shrine. This is an Anglican shrine (only High Church Anglicans make a pilgrimage there); the Catholic Church had a fourteenth-century chapel restored which forms part of the Roman Catholic national shrine.

Modern pilgrims believe it is an important place of pilgrimage because:

- they can feel close to the Virgin Mary (Our Lady of Walsingham) when praying there
- it is a place where pilgrims claim their prayers have been answered
- it is a place where healings are claimed to have taken place
- it brings spiritual refreshment and today it is bringing Catholics and Anglicans closer together.

The Roman Catholic Walsingham pilgrimage walk. Pilgrims walk from the Slipper Chapel to Little Walsingham for an open-air Mass.

Iona

Iona is a small island just off the west coast of Scotland. St Columba, an Irish abbot, arrived there in 563CE and established a monastery to train missionaries to convert Scotland to Christianity. The monastery contained the relics of St Columba, but was destroyed by King Henry VIII during the Reformation.

In the 1930s, a Protestant minister from Glasgow, George Macleod, went there with some young ministers and construction workers to spend spiritual time together. They then returned to their work in the Glasgow area. The visits continued and during these 'pilgrimages' the abbey was restored as a centre for all Christians, whatever their denomination.

Iona is important for pilgrims because:

- it encourages clergy and ordinary Christians to spend time together and learn from each other
- it gives pilgrims an opportunity to discuss and learn about issues affecting Christians today
- it helps Christians from different Churches to come together and become more united
- it gives Christians time apart from the daily grind of life so they can think about God.

Taizé

The Taizé Community is an **ecumenical** monastic order in the south of France. It was founded in the village of Taizé by Roger Schütz, a Protestant who had helped to shelter Jews escaping from the Nazis during the Second World War. He founded the order to help get together different Christians and different races to bring lasting peace to Europe, especially through working with young people. The monastery now has more than 100 brothers, both Catholics and Protestants, from over 30 countries.

The community has become one of the world's most important sites of Christian pilgrimage. Over 100,000 young people from around the world make pilgrimages to Taizé each year for prayer, Bible study, sharing and communal work. Through the community's lifestyle, they are encouraged to live together, overcoming racial and religious differences.

Useful words

Ecumenical – promoting Christian unity

Activity

Look at the photos below. Why might a visit to either Graceland or Old Trafford be regarded as a pilgrimage?

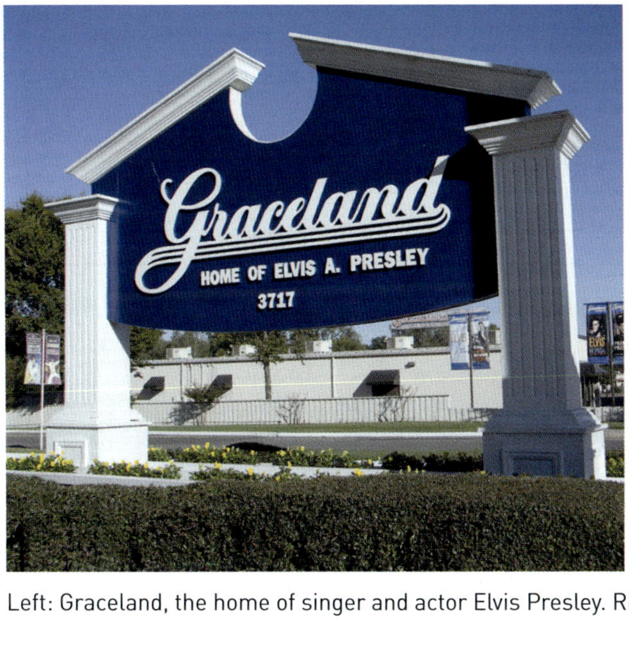

Left: Graceland, the home of singer and actor Elvis Presley. Right: Old Trafford, Manchester United football club's ground.

Activities

1. Explain why: a) Jerusalem, b) Walsingham, c) Iona and d) Taizé are important for Christians today.
2. Look at the second of the Ten Commandments on page 198. Do you think this commandment bans shrines of saints and pilgrimage to them?

Useful words

Revered – held in deep respect
Veneration – treating with deep respect

The pilgrims find their pilgrimage to Taizé important because:

- it gives young people an opportunity to meet and learn from other young people from different branches of Christianity
- it gives pilgrims an opportunity to meet and learn from young people of different races
- it encourages Christians to develop the spiritual gifts of kindness, simplicity and reconciliation
- it gives pilgrims an opportunity to learn about spirituality from the brothers of the community.

Conclusion

Most Protestant Christians have always been critical of pilgrimages. Martin Luther said:

> *All pilgrimages should be stopped. There is no good in them: no commandment enjoins them, no obedience attaches to them. Rather do these pilgrimages give countless occasions to commit sin and to despise God's commandments.* (To the Christian Nobility, *1520)*

Most Protestants tend to feel that emphasising special 'holy places' is wrong because believers can encounter God anywhere, because God is the same God everywhere. They are also opposed to any form of worshipping the Virgin Mary because they regard it as idolatry. They believe that as Mary had other children (Matthew 13:55–56) and James, the brother of Jesus, was the first Bishop of Jerusalem (according to the early church historian Eusebius), she cannot be **revered** as the Virgin Mary. They also regard any **veneration** of saints or relics as wrong because they believe only God should be venerated.

So Protestants will visit the holy places in Jerusalem and go to Iona and Taizé, but would not go to Walsingham or places like Lourdes.

Practice questions

c. Explain two reasons why pilgrimage is important for many Christians. In your answer you must refer to a source of wisdom and authority.

d. 'All Christians should go on pilgrimage to Jerusalem.' Evaluate this statement considering arguments for and against. In your response you should:
   - refer to Christian teachings
   - refer to different Christian points of view
   - reach a justified conclusion.

Summary

Pilgrimage has always been important for Christians as they believe it brings them closer to God. Christians go to Jerusalem to feel close to Jesus in the places he spent his final days. They visit places like Walsingham to feel close to the Virgin Mary and go on pilgrimage to places like Iona and Taizé to become more united with other Christians.

Topic 1.3.5 Christian religious celebrations

Thinking points

In this topic you need to:

- think about the nature, history, activities, significance and purpose of Christmas and Easter, including 1 Corinthians 15:12–34
- be able to evaluate the importance of these celebrations for Christians today.

Christian festivals are celebrated throughout the Church year (liturgical year) which begins with Advent and goes through Christmas, Epiphany, Lent, Easter and Pentecost to Trinity.

Christmas

Most Christians celebrate the birth of Jesus on 25 December, although many Orthodox Christians still use an old method of dating (the Julian calendar) in which 25 December is the equivalent of 7 January in the calendar used by most people (Gregorian calendar).

Advent

Christians prepare for the coming of Jesus during the season of **Advent**. Advent begins on the fourth Sunday before Christmas. During the four weeks of Advent, Christians remember the Old Testament prophecies about the coming of Jesus and think about the biblical references to the second coming of Jesus and the final judgement. They usually light a candle on an Advent wreath on each of the Sundays in Advent, lighting the final candle on Christmas Day.

Catholic Christians are expected to free themselves from sin before Christmas by receiving the sacrament of reconciliation. Towards the end of Advent, Anglican and **Nonconformist** Christians have carol services such as the Festival of Lessons and Carols held in Anglican cathedrals on Christmas Eve.

Useful words

Advent – season before Christmas remembering the first coming of Jesus and that he will come again

Nonconformist – a Protestant in England who is not a member of the Church of England

Lighting Advent candles in a Catholic church.

Activity

Look at the photo of the Advent wreath. Why do Christians celebrate Advent?

Christmas celebrations

The twelve days of Christmas (Christmas ends on 5 January, to be followed by Epiphany on 6 January) begin with:

- special services at midnight on Christmas Eve, when a **crib** is often set up and blessed
- services on the morning of Christmas Day which recall the Gospel accounts of Christmas and give Christians a chance to celebrate the coming of Jesus into the world
- gifts being exchanged to remember that Jesus was given presents by the wise men and as a sign of love for each other to reflect God's love in the gift of Jesus.
- On the Sunday after Christmas, Christians remember the family life of Jesus and Catholics have a special Mass for the Holy Family (Mary, Joseph and the baby Jesus).

Useful words

Crib – a nativity scene with baby Jesus in a manger (crib)
Incarnation – the belief that God took human form in Jesus

The significance of Christmas

Christmas is significant for Christians because:

- Christmas is the celebration of the **incarnation**, when Christians believe God became man as Jesus, and without the birth of Jesus Christ, there would be no Christianity.
- Christians believe that before the incarnation, it was only possible to have a partial relationship with God because of the effects of sin. However, through the incarnation (which led to the life, death and resurrection of Jesus) the power of sin has been cancelled so that it has become possible for humans to have a full relationship with God and go to heaven after death.
- Through celebrating the birth of Christ, Christians feel united with all other Christians when they celebrate as a worldwide community. The celebrations of Christmas remind Christians that all Christians, whatever their colour or ethnicity, share a common faith.
- Christmas shows the importance of the family. Jesus was born into a human family. At Christmas, Christians remember the humility and strength of Mary and Joseph, and in their worship remember to try and be spiritually like them.

Easter

Christians prepare for Easter during Holy Week.

Holy Week is the week before Easter Sunday. It begins with:

- Palm Sunday, which remembers the way Jesus was welcomed to Jerusalem by a crowd which five days later denied him. Christians celebrate it by processing near the church with palm leaves or branches, having special services with Bible readings of the events of Palm Sunday and Good Friday, and distributing palm crosses to the congregation.
- Holy (Maundy) Thursday remembers the Last Supper of Jesus with his apostles. Christians celebrate it with a special Eucharist when the priest or minister washes people's feet as Jesus washed the disciples' feet (in some Protestant Churches this is the only Eucharist of the year). There are readings about the Last Supper and the arrest

Activities

1. Do you think the way Christmas is celebrated in the UK makes people forget its meaning?
2. Do you think Christmas is still important for Christians?

of Jesus. In Anglican and Catholic churches the altar is stripped and all crosses are covered as Good Friday and Holy Saturday are days of mourning. In Catholic churches sufficient elements are consecrated for Good Friday and Holy Saturday as no Eucharists are celebrated on those days.

- Good Friday remembers the death of Jesus. Many Christians have a walk of witness in the local area carrying a cross. They then have a three-hour afternoon service marking the time Jesus was on the cross. Catholic churches have prayers at the **stations of the cross**.
- Holy Saturday is a day of reflection and prayer. No services are held on this day.

The significance of Holy Week

- Christians have an opportunity to renew and deepen their faith in Jesus through remembering the events of Holy Week. They are reminded that they need to serve one another and put themselves last as well as be public witnesses to their faith.
- It reminds them how Jesus faced **adulation** (on Palm Sunday), then rejection and crucifixion. This should inspire Christians to think about their role in the world, especially when they are asked to stand up for others in the cause of justice and peace.
- Palm Sunday reminds Christians that Jesus is the Messiah, the Son of God who is worthy of their praise and adoration.
- Holy Thursday reminds Christians of the origins and importance of the Eucharist. The foot washing reminds them of the need to serve each other.
- Holy Week reminds Christians of the suffering Jesus experienced, which will give them strength to cope with the suffering they may face.
- Holy Week reminds them of the **salvation** brought by Jesus. The death of Christ on the cross forgave the sins of the world and enabled people to have a full relationship with God. It was the death of Jesus that overcame sin, and during Holy Week Christians try to do things to make up for their sinfulness.

Foot washing in a church on Maundy Thursday.

Useful words

Stations of the cross – fourteen pictures representing stages of Christ's way to crucifixion
Adulation – extreme admiration
Salvation – the act of delivering from sin or saving from evil

For what I received I passed on to you as of first importance: that Christ died for our sins according to the Scriptures, that he was buried, that he was raised on the third day according to the Scriptures, and that he appeared to Cephas (Peter), and then to the Twelve. After that, he appeared to more than five hundred of the brothers and sisters at the same time, most of whom are still living, though some have fallen asleep. Then he appeared to James, then to all the apostles, and last of all he appeared to me also, as to one abnormally born.
(1 Corinthians 15:3–8)

Activity

Look at the photo of foot washing. Why do Christians re-enact this and what does it remind them they have to do?

Easter Day

Easter Day is the festival of joy as Christians celebrate the resurrection.

Some Christians (especially Catholics) celebrate with the Easter Vigil, which has:

- a ceremony of light to remember the darkness of the tomb and the joy and light of the resurrection
- Bible readings to remember how the resurrection of Jesus brought back the goodness of the world at creation
- a renewal of **baptismal vows** to remember the rebirth brought by Easter
- the Eucharist to remember that salvation now comes through the sacraments.

Some Christians have an open-air dawn Eucharist to celebrate what the first Christians found when they came to the tomb early in the morning.

All Christians have a joyful service to celebrate the resurrection of Jesus and the hope for eternal life which this brings to individual Christians. The tradition of Easter eggs comes from the fact that an egg seems to be dead, but out of it breaks new life.

Catholics have a second Mass later on Easter Day, which is the only occasion when Catholics are allowed to take communion twice in one day.

Useful words

Baptismal vows – the promises Christians (or their parents) make at their baptism

Two natures – the belief that Jesus was both human and divine

Creeds – statements of Christian belief

But if it is preached that Christ has been raised from the dead, how can some of you say that there is no resurrection of the dead? If there is no resurrection of the dead, then not even Christ has been raised. And if Christ has not been raised, our preaching is useless and so is your faith. More than that, we are then found to be false witnesses about God, for we have testified about God that he raised Christ from the dead. But he did not raise him if in fact the dead are not raised. (1 Corinthians 15:12–15)

The significance of Easter

Easter is extremely significant for Christians because:

- It celebrates the resurrection of Christ, which Christians believe proves the identity of Jesus. If Jesus rose from the dead he then must have been both human and divine, thus showing the **two natures** of Jesus as taught in the **creeds**.
- It is the final part of the work of Jesus: through his life, miracles, teachings and death, Jesus was trying to bring people back to God. The resurrection is the final part of this because through the resurrection, forgiveness of sins is assured and people can be restored to God.

The service of light outside a church, marking the beginning of Easter and the end of Lent.

Activity

Look at the quotations from 1 Corinthians 15 on pages 91 and 92 and put them into your own words. Why do think Christians think these quotations are important?

- It proves that death has been overcome and assures Christians that this life is not all there is. Easter celebrates the eternal life for those who follow Jesus.
- It gives Christians the assurance that Jesus is not dead; he is alive to help and guide his Church and to be with individual Christians.
- It celebrates Jesus' victory over death and evil, which is why new Christians are often baptised on Easter Sunday and why many Christians renew their baptismal vows and recommit themselves to the Christian life.
- It proves that the predictions Jesus made about his death and resurrection (for example in John 2:19–22) were true, and therefore Christians can believe the other things he said.

Activities

1. Do you think Easter is important for non-Christians?
2. Why is Easter important for Christians?

Practice questions

c Explain two reasons why Holy Week is significant for Christians. In your answer you must refer to a source of wisdom and authority.

d 'Christmas is more important than Easter.' Evaluate this statement considering arguments for and against. In your response you should:

- refer to Christian teachings
- reach a justified conclusion.

Summary

Advent is a four-week preparation for Christmas when Christians think about Jesus coming again to bring in the final judgement. Christmas celebrates the birth of Jesus and is important for Christians because without the birth of Jesus there would be no Christianity and no salvation from sin.

Holy Week is when Christians remember the last week of Jesus' life, especially the Last Supper on Maundy Thursday and the crucifixion on Good Friday. Easter Day celebrates Jesus rising from the dead. Easter is important because it celebrates the founding of the Eucharist, Jesus dying to save people from sin and rising from the dead to give Christians the hope of eternal life.

Topic 1.3.6 The future of the Church

Thinking points

In this topic you need to:

- think about Church growth; the history and purpose of missionary and evangelical work, including Mark 16:9–20 and John 20:21–22
- think about what the Church does locally, nationally and globally
- understand different Christian views about the importance of evangelical work
- be able to evaluate the importance of missionary and evangelical work.

The nature and purpose of missionary and evangelical work

A missionary is a person sent by a Church into an area to bring people into the Christian Church. Evangelical work is proclaiming the message of Christianity with the aim of converting people to Christianity. So the purpose of missionary work and evangelical work is to convert the world to Christianity.

Christians carry out missionary and evangelical work because this was the last commandment of Jesus to his disciples:

> *He said to them, 'Go into all the world and preach the gospel to all creation. Whoever believes and is baptised will be saved, but whoever does not believe will be condemned.'* (Mark 16:15–16)

> *Again Jesus said, 'Peace be with you! As the Father has sent me, I am sending you.' And with that he breathed on them and said, 'Receive the Holy Spirit.'* (John 20:21–22)

This is known by Christians as the '**Great Commission**' and so they believe it is something they must do.

Useful words

Great Commission – Jesus' last command to his disciples to go out and convert the world

Colonise – where one race or culture takes control of another

The history of missionary and evangelical work

The disciples of Jesus began this work immediately. The Acts of the Apostles in the New Testament record how St Peter organised conversions throughout Palestine and then St Philip converted an Ethiopian, which in turn led to Christianity spreading into Africa (the Ethiopian Church is one of the oldest Christian Churches). It records the great missionary journeys of St Paul, who founded Christian churches in Syria, Turkey and Greece before ending up in Rome, where there were already many Christians (tradition says that this Church was founded and led by St Peter – Catholics believe that St Peter was the first Bishop of Rome, the title of the Pope).

Tradition also says that St Thomas took Christianity to Iran and then to India in 52CE, and there were Christian churches in Egypt, Iraq, North Africa and the European parts of the Roman Empire, including Britain, by 100CE. Armenia and Georgia were Christian countries by 300CE and there were Christians in China by 600CE. St Cyril and his brother Methodius converted Russia and the Slavs of Eastern Europe in the ninth century. Cyril invented the Cyrillic alphabet so he could translate the Bible into Russian and the Slavonic languages.

When Europeans began to **colonise** America and Africa, Christian missionaries went with them, so conversion to Christianity went hand in hand with colonisation. These missionaries were very successful, and South and Central America became Catholic through the work of Spanish and Portuguese Catholics. North America and much of Africa south of the Sahara became Protestant through the work of British missionaries, although French and Belgian African colonies became Catholic.

Activities

1. Why do you think Christians call Matthew 28:19 the 'Great Commission'?
2. Explain how Christianity spread throughout the world.

Columban missionaries are Catholic missionaries who 'promote the message and values of the Gospel' in Asia and Latin America.

Activities

1. Look at the photo of the Columban missionary. Can you see any problems arising from what is going on in the photo?
2. Look at the Alpha advertisement on page 96. Would this make you want to join the course? What questions would you ask if you did?

Local missionary and evangelical work

This is covered in Topic 1.3.7 (page 98).

National missionary and evangelical work

Churches Together in England is a body uniting the Christian Churches in England. It organises Evangelism UK, which is dedicated to missionary and evangelical work in the whole of the UK, and it co-ordinates the work of the following groups:

- The **Alpha** course, now known simply as Alpha, aims to introduce non-churchgoers to the basics of the Christian faith through a series of talks and discussions. It describes itself as 'an opportunity to explore the meaning of life'. Alpha courses are run in churches throughout the UK by all the major Christian denominations.
- Hope is an organisation which aims at being a catalyst for missionary work in local church communities. It provides resources and ideas for **evangelisation** in local communities.
- Scripture Union works in partnership with individuals and churches to use the Bible to inspire children, young people and adults to come to know God. In the UK it uses social media such as YouTube and Facebook to bring the Christian message to those outside the Churches, as well as more traditional work in schools, youth camps and so on.
- Urban Saints runs youth and children's groups around the UK and organises events, holidays, mission trips and training courses about Christianity.
- Youth for Christ (YFC) provides resources for churches and schools, and runs residential events to bring the Christian message to young people outside the Church.

In 2010, Pope Benedict XVI created the 'Pontifical Council for the Promotion of New Evangelisation' to reinvigorate Christianity in Europe. Archbishop

Useful words

Alpha – the Christian course trying to convert non-churchgoers
Evangelisation – seeking to convert to Christianity

An advertisement for the Alpha course.

Useful words

Mission Metropolis – the Catholic mission to start the re-evangelisation of Europe from the cities

Re-evangelisation – trying to bring back Christianity to somewhere which was Christian but has left the faith

Global evangelism – preaching the Gospel to the whole world

Mission dioceses – an area of the country which requires spiritual and physical support from the Church for growth and development

Catechetical programmes – religious instruction given in preparation for Christian baptism or confirmation

Seminaries – educational institutions which prepare pupils for ordination as clergy

Fisichella was appointed the first President of the Council and established the **Mission Metropolis** in Lent 2012 to revive faith in Christianity in Europe by concentrating on the major cities of Barcelona, Brussels, Budapest, Cologne, Dublin, Lisbon, Liverpool, Paris, Turin, Vienna and Warsaw. The mission was centred on each cathedral and involved a continual reading of the Gospel, the local bishop teaching young people, families and those converting to Catholicism, the promotion of confession and a charitable initiative.

In England, the Archbishop of York, Dr John Sentamu, has called on the Church of England to begin an ambitious campaign aimed at the '**re-evangelisation** of England', on a par with the ministry of the northern saints such as Cuthbert, Hilda and Aidan who spread Christianity in Anglo-Saxon times.

Global missionary and evangelical work

Evangelical Protestants dedicated themselves to **global evangelism** at the Lausanne International Congress on World Evangelisation in Switzerland in 1974. Since then, these Churches have been trying to send missionaries to every ethnic group in the world. This has led to much more co-operation and friendliness among Churches and denominations in their effort to spread their Gospel message. In the process, Western mission efforts have become far more sensitive to the cultures of the people to whom they are taking their message. This has resulted in the Church of the 'Global South' (Africa, Asia and Latin America) becoming the driving force in missions. Latin American, African and Korean missionaries (especially from the Pentecostal Churches) can now be found all over the world.

The global missionary work of the Roman Catholic Church is organised by the Society for the Propagation of the Faith. This organisation is funded by offerings from Catholics on World Mission Sunday and throughout the rest of the year. The Society is in charge of the **mission dioceses** of the Catholic Church (which number about 1100) and works with them to provide **catechetical programmes** and **seminaries**, and to support the work of religious communities (monks and nuns), and the building of chapels, churches, orphanages and schools.

Modern Christian missions work to provide for material needs as well as spiritual needs. As Pope Francis has said:

> *It is not enough to offer someone a sandwich unless it is accompanied by the possibility of learning how to stand on one's own two feet. Charity that leaves the poor person as he is, is not sufficient. True mercy, the mercy God gives to us and teaches us, demands justice, it demands that the poor find the way to be poor no longer.*

In the 2001 Census it was found that 72 per cent of the population said they were Christian but by 2011 that figure had declined to 58.8 per cent with 33.3 per cent having no religion at all. In 2015, YouGov repeated the Census question and found only 49 per cent saying they were Christian, while 42 per cent said they had no religion.

In 1975, the average attendance at a Church of England service was 3 per cent of the population, in 2015 it was 1.5 per cent. In 1993, 1.28 million Catholics attended Mass, but by 2010 attendance at Mass had dropped to 0.88 million.

Different Christian views about the importance of missionary and evangelical work

Most conservative and evangelical Christians believe that missionary and evangelical work is very important because:

- The Great Commission of Jesus told Christians their duty was to preach the Gospel to all nations and bring the world to the Christian faith.
- They believe that they should share their faith with others out of love for them because being a Christian helps people to share God's love.
- They believe that non-Christians can only have their sins forgiven by becoming a Christian.
- They question whether people outside the faith can be assured a place in heaven.
- They are concerned about the decline in religion, especially in the UK, as the Archbishops of York and Canterbury said in a paper to the General Synod in 2015, 'The urgency of the challenge facing us is not in doubt ... Attendance at Church of England services has declined at an average of one per cent per annum over recent decades and, in addition, the age profile of our membership has become significantly older than that of the population.'

Many liberal Christians feel that missionary and evangelical work is no longer important because:

- They feel that trying to convert followers of other religions when living in a multifaith society is a type of prejudice and discrimination. Treating people differently because of their religion and trying to convert other religions is discriminating against those who do not have the same faith as you.
- They feel that trying to convert others means you think your religion is right and theirs is wrong, but it is impossible to regard all other religions as wrong unless you have studied all of them and compared them to decide which one is true, and very few, if any, Christians have done this.
- They feel that there are many problems connected with missionary work overseas, especially that people in less developed countries may resent missionaries, seeing them as a new form of colonisation.
- They feel that the most important commandment of Jesus was to love God and love your neighbour, and they think it is difficult to love your neighbour if you are telling them their religion is wrong.
- They see the problems that Christian missionary work is causing in Muslim countries.

Practice questions

c Explain two reasons why Christians carry out missionary work. In your answer you must refer to a source of wisdom and authority.

d 'All Christian should be missionaries.' Evaluate this statement considering arguments for and against. In your response you should:

- refer to Christian teachings
- refer to different Christian points of view
- reach a justified conclusion.

Activities

1. Do you think it is important for Christians to do missionary and evangelical work today?
2. How would you feel if a Christian tried to convert you?

Summary

Jesus told the disciples that they should try to convert the world to Christianity, and Christian missionaries have been trying to do this ever since. National missionary work involves Churches Together, which organises the Alpha Course, and the Catholic Church, which organises European missions through Mission Metropolis. Missions in Africa and Latin America are organised by the Church of the Global South. Some Christians think that missionary work is important because of Jesus' last command, but others think it is better to love their neighbours.

Topic 1.3.7 The importance of the local church

Thinking points

In this topic you need to:

- think about the role and importance of the local church in the local Christian community; how and why it helps the individual believer and the local area (parish activities, ecumenism, outreach work, the centre of Christian identity and worship, including 1 Peter 5:1–4)
- be able to evaluate the importance of the local church.

Useful words

Prayer groups – groups of Christians who join together to pray and increase their understanding of prayer
Sermons – talks on a religious subject (usually based on a Bible passage)
Parish – an area having its own church and clergy

The role and importance of the local church in the local Christian community

A local Christian church is important because it is the focal point of Christian identity and worship:

- The church is where people go to show their devotion to God in Sunday services such as the celebration of Mass.
- Special services are held for Christians to celebrate Christian festivals.
- It offers the sacraments to the people. A Catholic or High Anglican church will provide baptism, First Confession and Communion, regular confessions, confirmation and marriage. Other Anglican and most Protestant local churches will provide Holy Communion services and baptism.
- The local church provides marriage services for couples wanting a church wedding.
- It will provide discussion and **prayer groups**, as well as Bible readings and **sermons** in worship, to give people a chance to learn more about God and how they should behave as Christians.
- The church lets the people of the area share in worship with the Christians of the **parish**, helping them to grow in love of God and show their love of God.
- It gives Christians in the local area a sense of belonging, allowing them to live surrounded by people who not only share the same beliefs but also love them as brothers and sisters in Christ.

St Mary's Anglican church in Swinbrook, Oxfordshire (left) and Marychurch, a Roman Catholic church in Old Hatfield, Hertfordshire (right).

How the local church helps the local area

The parish church helps with local activities:

- supporting the local Christian schools (most areas have both Catholic and Church of England primary and secondary schools)
- allowing social facilities such as youth clubs, uniformed organisations, and mother and toddler groups to help fulfil people's need to socialise and make friends
- providing such things as lunch clubs for elderly people
- hosting discussion groups, such as Bible study groups, for Christians to deepen their faith.

The parish church might also be involved in outreach work by:

- supporting and putting people in contact with Christian organisations such as 'Good News Family Care', Catholic Marriage Care, the National Catholic Child Welfare Council and The Children's Society (Church of England), all of which provide support and advice for families that are experiencing difficulties
- priests or ministers giving help and advice to couples having family problems
- providing financial support if, for example, the family wage earner is ill or made redundant
- providing legal advice clinics in areas with substantial numbers of immigrants in which lawyers with appropriate language skills help immigrants to cope with the legal issues of settling in the UK
- holding services in languages other than English so that people can maintain their faith and worship until they learn English
- supporting causes such as Church Action on Poverty, a national ecumenical Christian social justice charity committed to tackling poverty in the UK; the group works in partnership with local churches and with people in poverty themselves to find solutions to poverty
- providing help for the needy through running food banks, helping with local hostels for the homeless, helping groups such as the Catholic St Vincent dePaul Society which help the poor, raising money and educating local people about the work of Christian Aid and CAFOD.

By its work, the church shows love for those in need as requested by Jesus in the Parable of the Sheep and the Goats.

The Churches Together logo.

Activities

1. Look at the photos of the two churches on page 98. Which one do you think looks more like a parish church?
2. Explain how a local church is a focal point of Christian identity and worship.
3. Explain how local churches help individual Christians in the area.
4. What influence do local churches have on you?
5. Do you know how local churches try to help people in your area?
6. Do you think the local church in your area is the centre of Christian identity and worship through living practices?
7. Read the passage from 1 Peter chapter 5 below. What effect might this passage have on local church leaders?

To the elders among you, I appeal as a fellow elder and a witness of Christ's sufferings who also will share in the glory to be revealed: Be shepherds of God's flock that is under your care, watching over them – not because you must, but because you are willing, as God wants you to be; not pursuing dishonest gain, but eager to serve; not lording it over those entrusted to you, but being examples to the flock. And when the Chief Shepherd appears, you will receive the crown of glory that will never fade away. (1 Peter 5:1–4)

The local church and ecumenism

Local churches come together with other Christian churches at a local level in all sorts of ways. Usually they form a local Churches Together group where local congregations commit to an ongoing relationship and work together. Such groups have joint activities – services, social gatherings and discussion groups – to learn about and from each other. After a few such meetings, they often plan efforts together, either working for Christian charities or striving to help people in the local area know about their nearby Christian churches and the facilities that they can provide. This is called **ecumenism**.

Useful words

Ecumenism – movement working for co-operation between the Churches and eventual Church unity

In locations where there is only the one church building, for example, in a village, a Churches Together group will involve all those who wish to worship locally in a shared use of the facility. In this way, people can worship without having to give up their denominational identity and yet will form a united community of Christians for more social functions.

How and why the local church helps the individual believer

A local church provides an individual believer with:

- the chance to worship
- the opportunity to partake in the sacraments
- a place where they can deepen their faith through sermons, discussion and Bible study groups and so on
- Christian fellowship with fellow Christians.

The church does this because it believes that it is part of the Body of Christ and that it must welcome, nurture and provide spiritual sustenance for fellow members of Christ's body.

Practice questions

c Explain two ways in which a local church is important for the local area.

d 'Each area should just have one Christian church, you don't need separate churches for each denomination.' Evaluate this statement considering arguments for and against. In your response you should:

- refer to Christian teachings
- reach a justified conclusion.

Summary

Local churches provide worship, the sacraments and opportunities to learn more about the faith. They are important to the local area because they also provide schools, social facilities and advice centres as well as running such things as food banks. They are also involved in working with other churches to bring about Church unity (ecumenism).

Topic 1.3.8 The worldwide Church

The Church in the world

Estimates from 2015 say there are about 2.4 billion Christians around the world, up from about 600 million in 1910. This makes Christianity the world's largest religion, with at least a third of the world's population being Christian. According to the 2012 Pew Research Centre survey, if current trends continue, Christianity will remain the world's largest religion by 2050, when the Christian population is expected to exceed 3 billion.

Every country in the world has at least a few Christians, with the possible exception of Sudan where Christians have been severely persecuted.

The Church has a world presence:

- The Catholic Church, being based in the independent state of Vatican City (known as the Holy See), is a member of the United Nations (UN) in a non-voting capacity. It has a permanent representative at the UN who can speak to the assembly.
- The other Christian Churches are represented at world level by the World Council of Churches, whose headquarters are at the Ecumenical Centre in Geneva, Switzerland, next to the UN building there.

The Church and reconciliation

One of the four aims of the World Council of Churches is to

> *engage in Christian service by serving human need, breaking down barriers between people, seeking justice and peace, and upholding the integrity of creation.*

Pope Francis and other Church leaders continually work for peace and **reconciliation** trying to bring people in conflict together. The visits of the Archbishop of Canterbury to Africa and the Middle East, and the visits of Pope Francis to Turkey, Kenya, Uganda and the Central African Republic in 2015 were all trying to bring peace and reconciliation to difficult areas.

Christians believe in reconciliation because:

- Most Christians believe that humanity had split from God through sin, but the forgiveness of sins brought by the death of God's son, Jesus, has allowed reconciliation between God and humans. Jesus died on the cross to bring forgiveness and reconciliation.
- Jesus said that if people do not forgive those who have sinned against them, God will not forgive their sins.
- St Paul said that Christians should try to live in peace with everyone. The only way to live in peace with everyone is to try to bring about reconciliation through forgiving those who wrong you.
- Christianity is based on the concept of forgiveness and reconciliation. All the Churches teach that Christians should be committed to forgiveness and reconciliation wherever there are conflicts between families or friends. Christians believe that the power of forgiveness and love can lead to reconciliation and the ending of conflict.

Thinking points

In this topic you need to:

- think about the role of the Church in the worldwide community; how and why it works for reconciliation; the problems faced by the persecuted Church
- consider Christian teachings about charity (1 Corinthians 13, Matthew 25:31–46); the work of Christian Aid and why it does this work
- be able to evaluate the role and importance of the Church in the world.

Useful words

Reconciliation – bringing together people who were opposed to each other

Activities

1. Explain why the Christian Church is important in the world.
2. Follow the news for a month and make notes on areas where the Church is working for reconciliation.

In September 2015, Pope Francis visited Cuba to bring reconciliation between Catholics and the communist leader of Cuba, Raúl Castro.

Problems faced by the persecuted Church

There are several countries in the world where it is no longer safe to be a Christian.

North Korea has 300,000 Christians but, like everyone else, Christians in North Korea must worship the nation's leader, and belonging to another religion makes you an enemy of the state. Thousands of Christians are imprisoned, and many have reportedly been tortured and executed. Believers meet secretly, risking arrest and death by doing so.

Most of the countries where Christians are persecuted are Muslim countries operating under a strict form of **Shari'ah law**, which makes converting to another religion a criminal offence. In Somalia, Islam is the state religion, and converting to another religion is illegal. The Islamist group al-Shabaab has stated that it wants to rid Somalia of all Christians, and people suspected of following the faith are likely to be killed on the spot. Many meet in secret, or do not meet at all, and cannot own Bibles.

As Islamic State (Isis) has taken control of large parts of Iraq, Christians and other minorities have been forced to convert, pay a punitive tax or be killed. An estimated 100,000 people fled their homes in Mosul, a city in a largely Christian region in northern Iraq, as Isis advanced on the region in late 2014. There have been public execution-style killings of Christians by Isis, some of them recorded and broadcast for propaganda purposes, and most churches have been demolished.

An estimated 700,000 Christians have fled Syria since the start of the civil war in 2011. In those parts of the country which have been claimed by Isis, Christians are often abducted and killed.

Useful words

Shari'ah law – Islamic law based on the Qur'an and the sayings of Muhammad

Activities

1. Look at the photo of Pope Francis and President Castro. Why do Christians believe in reconciliation?
2. What problems do Christians face when they are undergoing persecution?

Christian teachings about charity

Christianity teaches that God created humans to be **stewards** of the earth and that God wants Christians to love their neighbours. This means that riches must be used for helping others, especially the poor. Christians believe that all humans are equal in the eyes of God, and that all the good things of the earth have been given to humans by God to use to help each other.

These ideas about charity are based on St Paul's teachings about love in 1 Corinthians and Jesus' **Parable** of the Sheep and the Goats in Matthew's Gospel.

In 1 Corinthians 13, St Paul taught that love is greater than any other spiritual gift. He said that it does not matter how religious or good you look, or if you do things such as prophesying, speaking in tongues, being able to understand the greatest of mysteries, sacrificing everything; without love, then none of these things matter.

St Paul said that:

> *Love is patient, love is kind. It does not envy, it does not boast, it is not proud. It is not rude, it is not self-seeking, it is not easily angered, it keeps no record of wrongs. Love does not delight in evil but rejoices with the truth. It always protects, always trusts, always hopes, always perseveres.* (1 Corinthians 13:4–7)

St Paul ended his teachings about spiritual gifts with these words:

> *And now these three remain: faith, hope and love. But the greatest of these is love.* (1 Corinthians 13:13)

In Matthew 25:31–46, the Parable of the Sheep and the Goats, Jesus told a story about the end of the world when everyone will be brought before the Son of Man to be judged. Jesus said that:

- He would separate the people like a shepherd separates sheep from goats.
- The sheep would be those who fed Jesus when he was hungry, gave him drink when he was thirsty, took him in when he was a stranger, clothed him when he needed clothes, looked after him when he was sick and visited him when he was in prison.
- The people will say they never did this, but Jesus will say that whatever they did for someone suffering like this, they did for him, so they can go to heaven.
- Jesus identifies himself with those who suffer in this parable, showing his humanity.
- However, the goats will be told that they did not do any of these things for other people and so they did not do them for Jesus. Because they did not love others, they will go to hell.

Christians believe that the parable means that:

- Christians need to show love to everyone, especially those who are in need.
- By showing love for others you are showing love for God.

Useful words

Stewards – people appointed to look after something on behalf of someone else

Parable – a story told to illustrate a religious or moral issue

Activities

1. Why does the Parable of the Sheep and the Goats make Christians concerned about charity?
2. Do you think Christians are more concerned about charity and relieving poverty than non-religious people?

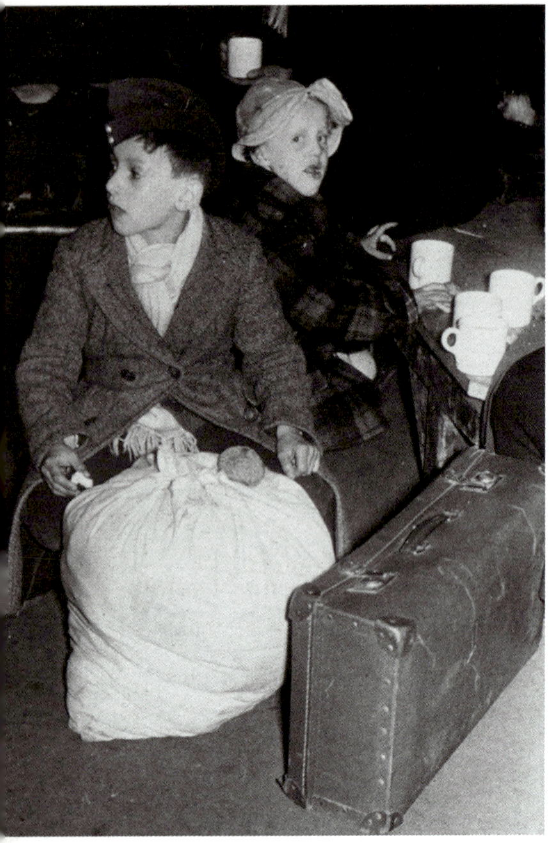

Child refugees during the Second World War in London.

- People will be judged by God according to the way they act, the way they treat others and the way they choose to spend their time.
- Love of others is what God wants: it means that everyone is cared for and no one suffers.
- Because of Jesus' resurrection he is not bound in time or place, so in the needy it is Christ himself appealing to us through the person in front of us.

This parable is important for Christian beliefs about charity because it:

- explains that by showing love for others Christians are showing love for God, and this is the most important commandment
- explains that loving others means caring for those people who are hungry, thirsty, strangers, short of clothes, sick or in prison
- shows that loving your neighbour is important and that it is doing what God wants
- shows Christians that there is a reward for showing love to those who are suffering: the reward is eternal life with God in heaven
- shows that those people who choose not to help those in need will be punished.

Christian Aid

There are many Christian agencies working for world development. The major one based in the UK is Christian Aid.

Christian Aid was founded by the British Council of Churches in 1944 to help relieve the suffering of people left homeless after the Second World War. It is now a leading UK and Irish overseas development agency that works across the globe in nearly 60 countries with people in need 'regardless of religion, ethnicity or nationality'. It aims to provide help where the need is greatest. Christian Aid works alongside 570 local partner organisations, in the belief that it is local groups that are best placed to find their own solutions to the problems they face.

Campaigning to end world poverty

Christian Aid speaks on behalf of poor communities to bring social justice. Christian Aid is campaigning to cancel the debt owed by some of the world's poorest countries. Many developing countries spend twice as much on debt repayments to rich creditors as they do on healthcare and education. Christian Aid also promotes **Fairtrade** products to bring better prices, decent working conditions, local sustainability, and fair terms of trade for farmers and workers in the developing world. Fifteen per cent of Christian Aid's spending in 2007 was on education, advocacy and campaigning. This includes organising marches, working with businesses and talking to governments about what they can do to make the world a fairer place in which to live.

Half of Christian Aid's spending is on development projects. Christian Aid works with over 600 local partner groups, which have more knowledge about the problems of a certain area and what can be done to solve them. They particularly work in four main areas of the world: Africa, Latin America, the Middle East and Asia.

Useful words

Fairtrade – a group aiming to help producers in developing countries achieve better trading conditions and to promote sustainability

A Christian Aid display stand at a village fête in Gloucestershire.

Some examples of Christian Aid's development projects are as follows:

- With a partner group, Centre Ecologique Albert Schweitzer, local workers living in Ouagadougou, the capital of Burkina Faso, have used solar technologies to create small businesses that make solar-powered fridges, water heaters and water pumps. The business behind this can be used to improve the standard of living of both the buyers and sellers of these machines.
- Christian Aid supports agricultural production and long-term food security in the Gaza Strip for unemployed daily wage earners who cannot get their goods to market because of Gaza's borders being closed for long periods of time.

Clearly, development projects will help to remove world poverty. More examples of this work can be found on the Christian Aid website (www.christianaid.org.uk).

Activity

Look at the Christian Aid photo above. How is Christian Aid trying to end world poverty?

Helping with disasters and emergencies

Christian Aid has a disaster fund to deal with natural disasters and refugees, which often have to take priority over development projects. Emergency aid includes sending water, food, antibiotics and shelters. These have been sent to victims of the 2004 Indian Ocean tsunami and flooding in India and Haiti, and to refugees in areas like Syria and the Democratic Republic of Congo. They also run appeals when disasters occur to try and raise more funding for these areas.

Why Christian Aid is trying to end world poverty

- According to the New Testament, riches must be used for helping others, especially the poor.
- Jesus told the Parable of the Sheep and the Goats where he said,

  When I was hungry, you fed me. When I was thirsty, you gave me drink. When I was naked, you clothed me. When I was sick or in prison, you visited me.

  The good people wanted to know when they had ever done this and Jesus said,

  When you did it for the least of my brothers, you did it for me.

  Christians want to help Jesus and so they help the poor and suffering.
- In the Sermon on the Mount (Matthew 5–7), Jesus taught that Christians should share their time and possessions to help those in need. So Christians should try to end world poverty.
- All the Churches teach that Christians have a duty to help the poor and suffering. For example, the House of Bishops of the Church of England stated in 2005 that

  our Christian calling demands us to speak out on behalf of those without a voice and to challenge unjust structures that keep people poor.
- The golden rule for Christians is to treat other people in the way you would like to be treated. Christian Aid believes that if Christians were suffering from world poverty, they would want rich Christians to try to end world poverty.

Practice questions

c Explain two reasons why Christians work to end world poverty. In your answer you must refer to a source of wisdom and authority.

d 'It's easy to be a Christian in today's world.' Evaluate this statement considering arguments for and against. In your response you should:

- refer to Christian teachings
- refer to different Christian points of view
- reach a justified conclusion.

Summary

Christianity is the world's largest religion and is at work throughout the world. It tries to bring an end to conflict because Christians believe that Jesus died to bring forgiveness and reconciliation. The Church is being persecuted in Muslim countries which operate Shari'ah (Islamic) law and in dictatorships like North Korea.

Christians help the poor because the teachings of Jesus say that they should love their neighbours. One way they do this is by supporting Christian Aid, which works for world development by promoting long-term development schemes, responding to emergencies and speaking out on behalf of poor communities.

How to answer questions

a) Outline three activities a Christian might do on pilgrimage. [3]

Pilgrims will pray at the shrine, in Jerusalem they walk down the Via Dolorosa, in Taizé they join in ecumenical services.

A high mark answer because three correct activities are clearly outlined.

b) Explain two reasons why the Lord's Prayer is important to Christians. [4]

The Lord's Prayer is important for Christians because it is the prayer that Jesus said Christians should use to avoid saying too much in prayer. It is also important because it contains adoration – 'hallowed be your name, your kingdom come, your will be done on earth as it is in heaven' – and confession – 'forgive us our trespasses, as we forgive those who trespass against us'.

A high mark answer because two correct reasons are given and each reason is developed.

c) Explain two reasons why worshippers in a Church community should evangelise in the local area. In your answer you must refer to a source of wisdom and authority. [5]

Christians should evangelise in the local area because the last commandment of Jesus to his disciples was: 'All authority in heaven and on earth has been given to me. Therefore go and make disciples of all nations' (Matthew 28:19).

Also evangelising could reverse the decline in church attendance which was highlighted as a massive problem by the Archbishops of York and Canterbury at the General Synod in 2015.

A high mark answer because two correct reasons are given and each reason is developed with a reference to Jesus and the Gospel of Matthew and the General Synod as sources of authority.

d) 'All Christians should give money to charity.' Evaluate this statement considering arguments for and against. In your response you should:

- **refer to Christian points of view**
- **refer to different Christian points of view**
- **reach a justified conclusion. [12 marks + 3 spelling, punctuation and grammar (SPaG) marks]**

Some Christians would agree with this because Christianity teaches that God created humans to be stewards of the earth and that God wants Christians to love their neighbours. This means that riches must be used for helping others. Also, Christians believe that all the good things of the earth have been given to humans by God to use to help each other. In the Parable of the Sheep and Goats, Jesus said that Christians should feed the hungry and clothe the naked and the best way to do this is to give money to charities like Christian Aid.

However, other Christians might say that it is better to help people physically rather than just give money, which is why many Christians run food banks. Jesus does not tell people to give money, and St Paul in 1 Corinthians says that even if you give all you have to the poor, it will be worthless if it is not done out of love. Then there is the issue of what the charities will do with the money. Catholics should not give to charities that sponsor contraception.

Despite the arguments against, I think people can't really call themselves Christians if they don't give to charity because the teaching and example of Jesus seem to be so clear. You can't imagine Jesus refusing to give money to charity!

[Continued]

A high mark answer because it gives three clear developed Christian reasons for thinking that Christians should give money. It then gives three Christian reasons for disagreeing and then reaches a fully justified conclusion.

SPaG

The answer would reach full marks for SPaG as spelling, punctuation and grammar are correct and a wide range of specialist vocabulary (stewards, love of neighbour, parable, Christian Aid, St Paul, 1 Corinthians) is used appropriately.

4 Matters of life and death

Area of study 1: Based on a study of Christianity

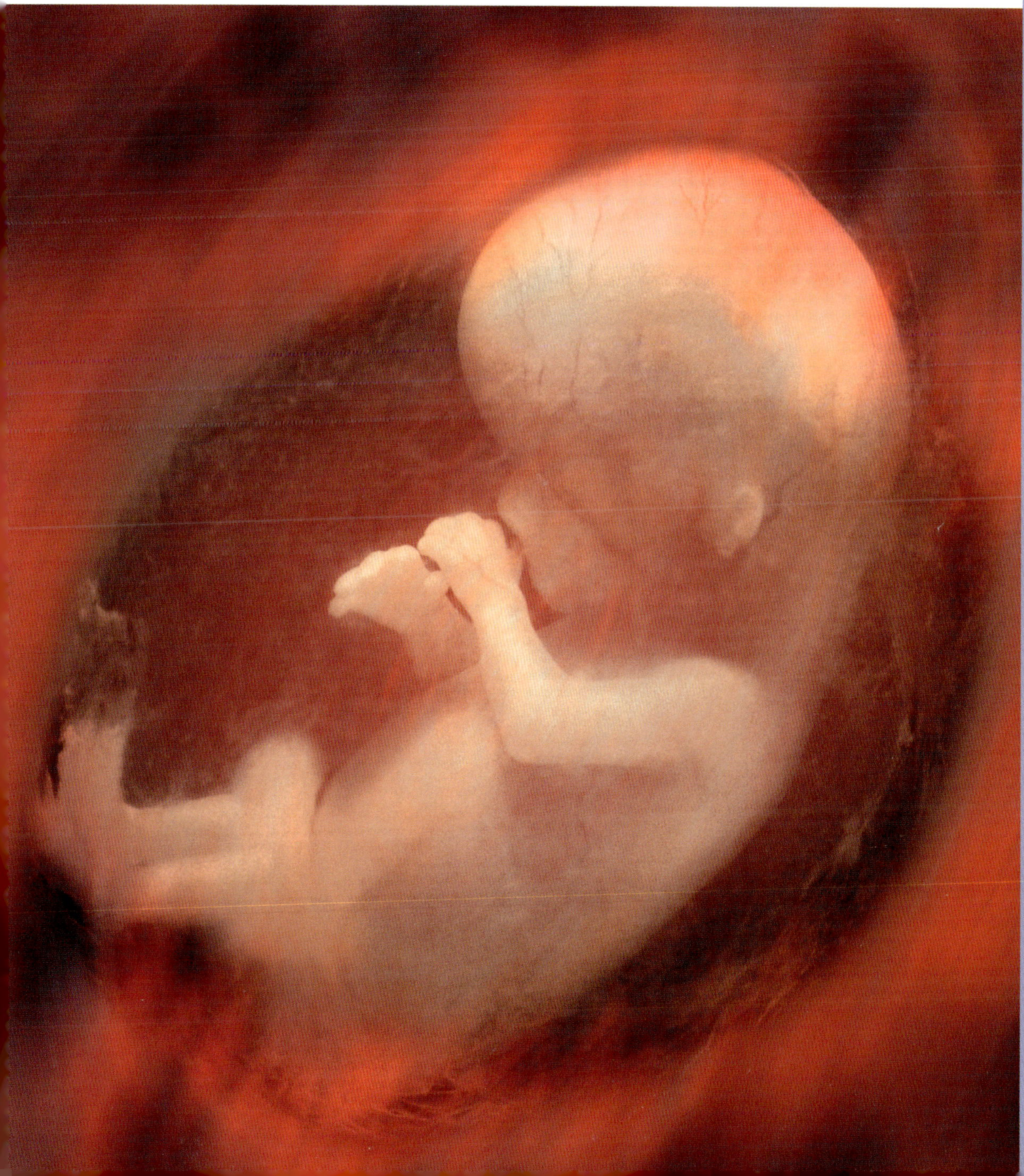

Topic 1.4.1 Origins and value of the universe

Thinking points

In this topic you need to:

- think about scientific explanations for the origins of the universe
- know about Christian responses to them, including the work of Georges Lemaître
- understand the value of the universe in Christian teaching
- think about responses to the view that the universe can be used as a commodity, including Genesis 1–2
- be able to explain and evaluate different Christian and non-religious attitudes to the origins and value of the universe.

Scientific explanations for the origins of the universe

The most accepted scientific theory for the origin of the universe is the Big Bang theory. It accounts for how the universe came into existence in the following way:

- Matter is eternal; it can neither be created nor destroyed, it can only be changed from one form in to another (scientists call this the law of thermodynamics).
- About 13.7 billion years ago, the matter of the universe became so compressed that it produced a huge explosion (the Big Bang).
- As the matter of the universe flew away from the explosion, the forces of gravity helped to join some of the matter into stars and, about 5 billion years ago, our solar system was formed.

Evidence for the Big Bang

The main evidence for the Big Bang is as follows:

- The redshift effect. Astrophysics tells us that the light from stars approaching us should be at the blue end of the light spectrum, whereas the light from stars going away from us should be at the red end. When astronomers study other galaxies they find they are at the red end of the spectrum. This redshift effect is evidence that the universe is still expanding from the point of the initial Big Bang.
- Radio telescopes have discovered background radiation throughout the universe which scientists believe is a remnant of the Big Bang.
- In March 2014, scientists detected ripples in deep space using a special telescope at the South Pole. These gravitational waves are claimed to have been triggered by the rapid expansion of the universe during the Big Bang.

These galaxies are at the red end of the light spectrum, showing that the universe is expanding.

The Higgs boson

One thing not explained by the Big Bang theory was why some particles came together to form planets and stars. In the 1960s a team of theoretical physicists led by Peter Higgs suggested that there must be an invisible field lying across the universe – they called this the Higgs field. This field would give particles mass, and this would allow them to form objects. They believed that this field would be made up of tiny particles called **Higgs boson** particles.

Since the 1960s scientists have been trying to find evidence that the Higgs boson exists. In 2012, in the Large Hadron Collider in Switzerland, they were able to re-create the conditions present immediately after the Big Bang and prove the existence of the Higgs field.

This discovery proved Higgs and his team right, and helped to explain exactly how the Big Bang created the universe.

Useful words

Higgs bosons – the particles that make up the Higgs field, which gives evidence for the Big Bang

The Large Hadron Collider can re-create the conditions when the universe began.

Activities

1. Make a diagram or poster to demonstrate what the Big Bang theory says.
2. Explain why scientists believe in the Big Bang.

Christian responses to the Big Bang theory

Some Christians simply ignore scientific explanations of the creation of the universe, but those who think about them have three types of response.

Useful words

Apparent Age – the idea that the world would have looked billions of years old when it was only a second old

Creationism – the belief that the universe, and humans, were created in the way the Bible says

Creationism

This view says that science is wrong and the Bible is right. It claims that all the evidence there is for the Big Bang and evolution can be explained by the effects of Noah's flood (which must have totally changed rock formations and created fossils, for example) and the **Apparent Age** theory.

The Apparent Age theory claims that if you accept the biblical account of creation in Genesis, then when Adam was made the earth was six days old, but to Adam it would have looked billions of years old. Trees would have been created with rings showing them to be hundreds of years old; the Grand Canyon would have looked 2 billion years old when it was one second old.

Therefore, these Christians believe that God created the universe in the way described in the Bible, which is why this response is often called **creationism**.

The intelligent design response

The 'intelligent design' argument developed from creationism. Christians who believe in this theory think that the universe is so complex that it can't have happened by chance. They believe that it must have been created by an intelligent designer – God.

They believe that the universe has different types of complexity:

- 'irreducible complexity' – the universe depends on many interacting parts and the removal of any one of those parts would mean that the whole system would stop working
- 'specified complexity' – the patterns in living things, for example in DNA.

They claim that these complexities mean that neither the Big Bang nor evolution could have happened by chance.

Noah's ark, the boat in which his family, and the animals used to escape the Flood, which creationists believe provides evidence for the Big Bang and evolution.

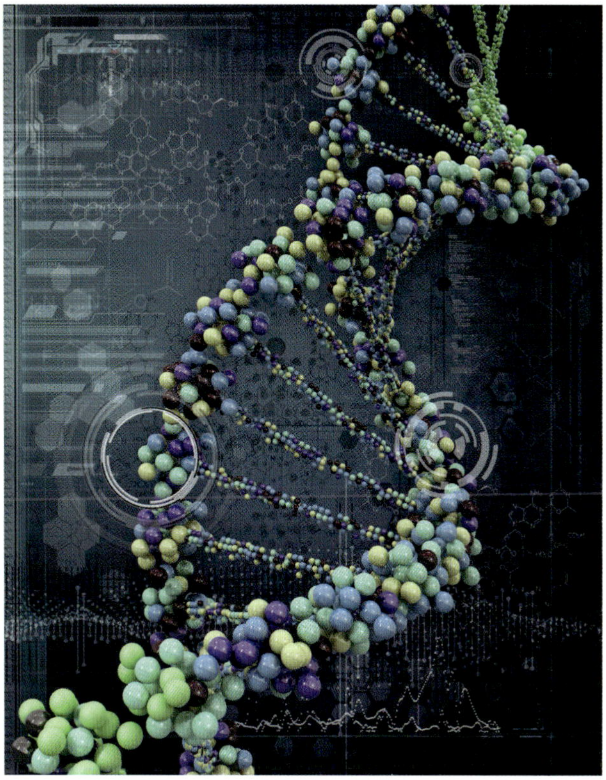

Intelligent design says that DNA is too complex to have arisen by chance.

The compatibility response

Many Christians believe that both the scientific and biblical explanations of creation are true.

They believe that the biblical stories of creation aren't meant to be read as literal accounts of exactly how God created the universe. They are simply meant to show us that God created everything. So they believe in the Big Bang, but believe that God set it off and controlled how the world has developed since.

Some Christians believe that the main points in the biblical creation story fit with science. The order of creation in Genesis broadly fits with the order science thinks the earth and life developed. They argue that Genesis 1:3 'God said, "Let there be light"', is a direct reference to the Big Bang.

These Christians see scientific discoveries as providing more evidence for God, for example:

- The Big Bang had to be at exactly the right microsecond. If the explosion had been too soon it would have been too small to form stars; if the explosion had been too late, everything would have flown away too quickly for stars to form.
- There had to be scientific laws such as gravity for the matter of the universe to form solar systems, and only God could have made the laws on which the universe is based.
- Stars are formed out of hydrogen and helium through nuclear reactions, producing carbon and oxygen, which are spread around the universe by exploding **supernovae**. The complexity of this system implies a creator organising things.
- Life on earth requires carbon to be able to bond with other atoms and water molecules. This could not have happened by chance, so God must have ensured that it was able to happen.

Activity

Outline how Christians respond to the Big Bang theory.

Useful words

Supernova – an explosion of a massive supergiant star

Activities

1. What do you think George Lemaître would have thought of Pope Francis's statement?
2. Do you think Genesis 1:28 justifies Christians in using the planet in any way they want?

The Big Bang, which today is held as the beginning of the world, does not contradict the intervention of the divine creator, but requires it. (Pope Francis speaking to the Pontifical Academy of Sciences, October 2014)

God blessed them and said to them, 'Be fruitful and increase in number; fill the earth and subdue it. Rule over the fish of the sea and the birds of the air and over every living thing that moves on the ground.' (Genesis 1:28)

Useful words

Commodity – something that humans need or want

The work of Georges Lemaître (1894–1966)

Lemaître was a Catholic priest and professor of physics who proposed what became known as the Big Bang theory of the origin of the universe. Lemaître called his theory 'the hypothesis of the primeval atom' or the 'cosmic egg'. Lemaître described the beginning of the universe as a burst of fireworks, comparing galaxies to the burning embers spreading out in a growing sphere from the centre of the burst. He believed this 'burst of fireworks' was the beginning of time, taking place on 'a day without yesterday'. In 1931, Lemaître proposed that the expansion of the universe was actually accelerating (the first scientist to do so), a claim which was only confirmed in the 1990s through observations with the Hubble Space Telescope.

In 1951, Pope Pius XII declared that Lemaître's theory gave a scientific proof for Catholic Christianity. However, Lemaître denied this and said his theory neither proved nor disproved religion and he persuaded the Pope to stop making proclamations about the scientific origins of the universe. Although Lemaître was a devout Roman Catholic, he was against mixing science with religion, but he believed these two fields of human experience did not conflict with each other.

The value of the universe in Christian teaching

Christianity teaches that God created the universe and everything in it, and that he made it in such a way that it has produced an environment on the earth which is perfectly suited for human life.

The creation accounts in Genesis 1 and 2 state that God made the universe, the earth, vegetation, animals and humans in six days. Some Christians regard these accounts as scientific fact. However, many Christians see them as an illustration of the teaching that the earth and everything in it was made by God in the way he intended it to be. As Genesis says, 'God saw what he had made and it was very good.'

This means that the universe has great value for Christians. God has made the universe, God has made it a good universe and God has placed humans in the universe to look after this most valuable creation.

Using the universe as a commodity

A few Christians believe that Genesis 1–2 means that the universe and all its vast resources are simply a **commodity** which humans can use, and misuse, as they wish, even though ideas like this have led to the growth of pollution, climate change and depletion of resources. However, most Christians believe that Genesis 1–2 means that, because God made the earth, the earth belongs to God, not to humans, and so it must be treated with respect, not as a commodity:

- As God has made everything, humans must respect the whole environment.
- The environment is a gift from God to humans and so must be treated with care.
- The Old Testament teaches that humans have a responsibility to treat animals humanely and to treat the land kindly by not growing crops every fiftieth year.

- In the Parable of the Talents or Minas (Luke 19:11–26), Jesus taught that God expects humans to pass on to the next generation more than they have been given. Many Christians believe that this means Christians have a responsibility to leave the earth a better place than they found it.
- The Bible also makes clear that there will be a judgement day at the end of the world when people will be judged on their beliefs and behaviour. Most Christians believe that part of this judgement will be based on how they have fulfilled their duty to preserve God's earth.

The Christian view that humans must not treat the universe as a commodity can be seen in these two statements:

*The universe as a whole is a product of God's creative and imaginative will. All its parts are interdependent. Men and women are to be stewards and creators, not exploiters, of its resources, material, animal and spiritual. Christians must support those working for **conservation** and the development of more appropriate sustainable life-styles. (A liberal Protestant view taken from 'Christian Faith Concerning the Environment', published by the Methodist Conference in 1991)*

Use of the mineral, vegetable and animal resources of the universe cannot be divorced from moral imperatives. Man's dominion over inanimate and other living beings granted by the Creator is not absolute; it is limited by concern for the quality of life of his neighbour, including generations to come; it requires a religious respect for the integrity of nature. (A statement from the Catechism of the Catholic Church)

Useful words

Conservation – protecting and preserving natural resources and the environment

Practice questions

c Explain two reasons why Christians should not use the world as a commodity. In your answer you must refer to a source of wisdom and authority.

d 'God created the universe.' Evaluate this statement considering arguments for and against. In your response you should:

- refer to Christian teachings
- reach a justified conclusion.

Summary

Science says the universe began when matter exploded (the Big Bang). The solar system came out of the explosion, and the nature of the earth allowed life to develop through evolution. Many Christians accept the scientific explanation, but believe that the Big Bang was how God created the universe. Some Christians believe that both science and the Bible are true because one of God's days could be billions of years long. Some Christians believe that the Bible is right and science is wrong. Most Christians believe that Genesis 1:28 means that Christians have a duty to look after the planet that God has put them in charge of.

Topic 1.4.2 Sanctity of life

Thinking points

In this topic you need to:

- think about why human life is holy
- know how life is shown as special in the Bible, including reference to being created in the image of God as shown in Genesis 1–3
- understand the importance of sanctity of life for Christians today
- be able to explain and evaluate different Christian and non-religious attitudes to the sanctity of life.

Useful words

Sanctified – made holy

Human life is sacred because from its beginning it involves the creative action of God and it remains forever in a special relationship with the Creator, who is its sole end. God alone is the Lord of life from its beginning until its end: no one can under any circumstance claim for himself the right directly to destroy an innocent human being. (Catholic Catechism 2258)

Why human life is holy

Sanctity of life means that life is holy or sacred. Christians believe that human life is holy because it is a gift from God. Regarding human life as sacred means human life is to be treated as holy and therefore valued and preserved.

Christians believe that because God creates life, humans do not have the right to treat life as they wish. Life belongs to its creator and so life and death decisions must be in the hands of God (the creator of life).

Christians believe that the life and death of Jesus show how sacred human life is. They believe that God **sanctified** human life by becoming human, and that the way Jesus suffered without any attempt to cut short his sufferings shows that life is not to be ended except when God decides to do so.

How life is shown as special in the Bible

The Bible teaches that human life is precious and special in several ways:

- Uniquely among all creatures, only man has the capacity for a relationship with God. Only man has a soul. Only man was made in God's likeness:

  So God created mankind in his own image, in the image of God he created them; male and female he created them. (Genesis 1:27)

- Human life is special because it comes directly from God:

  Then the Lord God formed a man from the dust of the ground and breathed into his nostrils the breath of life, and the man became a living being. (Genesis 2:7)

- The Bible makes the special nature of human life clear in the Ten Commandments where it says: 'You shall not murder' (Exodus 20:13).
- In the New Testament, St Paul describes the human body as a temple because God's spirit is in humans:

  Do you not know that your body is a temple of the Holy Spirit who is in you ...? (1 Corinthians 6:19)

The importance of sanctity of life for Christians today

The main issues where sanctity of life is particularly important for Christians today are abortion (see Topic 1.4.4, page 124) and euthanasia (see Topic 1.4.7, page 135). However, there are several other areas where this is important.

'So God created mankind in his own image'.

Killing in self-defence

If human life is sacred, what are Christians allowed to do if they are attacked? Does self-defence justify the taking of life? Most Christians would say that it is **legitimate** to take the life of someone attacking you if that is the only way to protect your own life. The sanctity of one's own life takes **precedence** over the sanctity of other people's lives. As the Catholic Catechism says:

> *Love toward oneself remains a* ***fundamental principle*** *of morality. Therefore it is legitimate to insist on respect for one's own right to life. Someone who defends his life is not guilty of murder even if he is forced to deal his aggressor a lethal blow.* (Catholic Catechism 2264)

Killing in war

Wars inevitably involve taking life. How does fighting in wars fit with belief in the sanctity of life? There are two very different Christian attitudes to this issue.

Some Christians believe that the sanctity of life means they should never fight in wars. **Pacifism** means refusing to fight in wars and there are many Christian pacifist groups, the largest being the Catholic group Pax Christi. The Quakers, Plymouth Brethren and Christadelphians are completely pacifist Christian Churches. As Jesus said:

> *You have heard that it was said, 'Love your neighbour and hate your enemy.' But I tell you: love your enemies and pray for those who persecute you.'* (Matthew 5:43–44)

Useful words

Legitimate – lawful
Precedence – priority in time, order of importance
Fundamental principle – the basic idea behind something
Pacifism – refusing to fight in wars

Activities

1. Why do Christians believe in the sanctity of human life?
2. Read the quotation from the Catholic Catechism. Which parts of it do you agree with?
3. How does the Bible show that human life is special?
4. Do you think it is justifiable to kill people: a) in self-defence, b) in a war, c) if they are murderers or terrorists?

Most Christians believe that they can fight in just wars because the need to protect the innocent from aggressors justifies breaking the sanctity of life beliefs. As the Catholic Catechism says:

> *Legitimate defence can be not only a right but a grave duty for one who is responsible for the lives of others. The defence of the common good requires that an unjust aggressor be rendered unable to cause harm. For this reason, those who legitimately hold authority also have the right to use arms to repel aggressors against the civil community entrusted to their responsibility.* (Catholic Catechism 2265)

Useful words

Capital punishment – the death penalty for a crime
Death penalty – execution ordered by a court of law

Capital punishment

If life is so sacred then is **capital punishment** allowed for Christians? Christians also have two views on this.

Many Christians believe that capital punishment is un-Christian, and that Christians should never use capital punishment. Christianity teaches that all life is sacred, which is why murder is condemned. If it is wrong to take life, then capital punishment must be wrong. Also, if abortion and euthanasia are wrong because of the sanctity of life, then so is capital punishment.

Other Christians believe that capital punishment can be used because the Bible gives the **death penalty** as the punishment for various offences, and the Roman Catholic Church and the Church of England have not cancelled their statements that capital punishment can be used by the state:

> *Assuming that the guilty party's identity and responsibility have been fully determined, the traditional teaching of the Church does not exclude recourse to the death penalty, if this is the only possible way of effectively defending human lives against the unjust aggressor. If, however, non-lethal means are sufficient to defend and protect people's safety from the aggressor, authority should limit itself to such means.* (Catholic Catechism 2267)

Practice questions

c Explain why Christians' belief in the sanctity of life causes problems for them.

d 'Christians should never take life.' Evaluate this statement considering arguments for and against. In your response you should:

- refer to Christian teachings
- reach a justified conclusion.

Summary

Christians believe that life is holy because it is created by God. The Bible shows that human life is special and that humans do not have the right to take life. This causes Christians to have problems with abortion, euthanasia and fighting in wars.

Topic 1.4.3 The origins and value of human life

Non-religious explanations about the origins and value of human life

The scientific explanation about the origins of human life is known as the theory of evolution and is associated with British naturalist and geologist Charles Darwin (1809–82). Darwin's visit to the isolated Galápagos Islands on HMS *Beagle* enabled him to observe the development of life forms that had been cut off from the rest of the world. His discoveries led to his famous book *On the Origin of Species* being published in 1859. Although the theory has been developed by subsequent scientific theories, it is still very similar to Darwin's original idea. The theory is that life on earth has evolved in the following way:

- After the earth formed about 4.5 billion years ago, the combination of gases on the earth's surface produced basic, single-celled life forms.
- Life forms reproduce and so become more numerous.
- Randomly occurring changes (mutations) in the genetic structure of these life forms means that the offspring have slight differences from their parents.
- As more offspring are produced than the environment can support, any offspring with changes better suited to living in the environment will be more likely to survive and reproduce. This has become known as survival of the fittest.
- This means that more offspring in the next generation will have the helpful difference.
- These differences gradually lead to changes within the population, and, over time, populations branch off and become new species.
- Over millions of years, new life forms were produced leading to vegetation, then invertebrate animals, then vertebrates and finally, about 2.5 million years ago, humans evolved.

Darwin called the process '**natural selection**' (meaning that each species has developed naturally without any need for divine intervention) and saw evidence that each species has developed from ancestors with similar features (at the time, Darwin was derided for suggesting that humans are descended from monkeys). The theory states that all living things are related, and so all life must be descended from a few forms, in a process that Darwin called 'descent with modification'.

Of course, the theory means that human life has no special value other than what humans choose to give to it.

Thinking points

In this topic you need to:

- think about Christian responses to scientific and non-religious explanations about the origins and value of human life, including evolution and survival of the fittest and Special Agenda IV
- understand the importance of the responses for Christians today
- be able to explain and evaluate Christian responses to non-religious explanations about the origins and valuc of human life.

Useful words

Natural selection – the idea that life evolved through mutations, making those life forms better suited to the environment survive, and the less well suited die out

Useful words

Fossil record – the evidence provided in fossils for evolution
Palaeontologists – scientists who study fossils
Geneticists – scientists in the study of heredity and genes

I think there's a common assumption that you cannot both be a rigorous, show-me-the-data scientist and a person who believes in a personal God. I would like to say that from my perspective that assumption is incorrect; that, in fact, these two areas are entirely compatible and not only can exist within the same person, but can exist in a very synthetic way, and not in a compartmentalized way. I have no reason to see a discordance between what I know as a scientist who spends all day studying the genome of humans and what I believe as somebody who pays a lot of attention to what the Bible has taught me about God and about Jesus Christ. Those are entirely compatible views. *(Francis Collins, Director of the Human Genome Project, www.pbs.org/wnet/religionandethics/transcripts/collins.html)*

Activities

1. Read the quotation from Francis Collins. Why would many people be surprised that the Director of the Human Genome project is a Christian?
2. Look at the photo of the dinosaur skeleton and explain how it might provide evidence for evolution.

The evidence for evolution

The main evidence for the theory of evolution is the **fossil record**. **Palaeontologists** have discovered that the older a fossil, the more simple its structure. Also, the fossil record provides examples of transitional species such as Archaeopteryx that had the characteristics of a reptile (such as a long, bony tail and conical teeth) and a bird (such as feathers and a wishbone). Then there are the fossils of species that have become extinct, such as dinosaurs. Natural selection explains why a branch no longer well suited to the environment will die out. Genetic studies also show clear connections between dinosaurs and crocodiles and birds.

More recent evidence for evolution is being discovered through investigations into DNA and genetics. **Geneticists** have discovered that about 50 per cent of human DNA is the same as that of a cabbage, probably indicating an ancestral connection between animal and vegetable life.

In January 2010, the Manchester Diocese of the Church of England in its Special Agenda IV responded to the scientific explanation by asking the Church of England to: 'affirm the compatibility of belief in God and an understanding of science; and urge the House of Bishops and all dioceses robustly to promote a better public understanding of the compatibility of science and Christian belief.'

The report points out that many people today feel that they have to choose between science and religion because:

- they have little or no awareness of what Christianity really is
- they are impressed by science and feel that science is something that really works and so its explanations must be true
- they feel that scientists like Richard Dawkins have proven that science is right and religion is wrong.

This skeleton of a dinosaur, which is half reptile and half bird, was found in China in July 2015.

Since this is how people feel, the report urged the Church to show people that:

- Science and religion go hand in hand rather than oppose each other.
- Science shows 'the amazing world God has created and the beauty and glory of God himself'.
- Science and religion working together can help humanity to understand more about the world.
- There are plenty of religious (Christian) scientists.
- The Church helps and supports Christians working in science.

Why evolution might cause issues for Christians

- Evolution challenges the authority of the Bible. If the theory of evolution is correct, then the Genesis creation stories must be wrong. They can just about accommodate the Big Bang theory, as we have seen, but not evolution. Genesis states that God specifically created vegetation, fish, reptiles, birds and humans, whereas, if evolution is correct, all of these were just a product of natural selection.
- Natural selection seems to provide an answer to the big questions of theology and philosophy as well as biology (as is claimed by scientists such as Richard Dawkins). The idea that life is a result of the process of evolution means that questions such as 'Why are we here?' 'What's life about?' 'Why is human nature what it is?' no longer need religion to answer them, they are all simply a product of natural selection.
- Christianity is still based on the concept of **original sin** and the **Fall of Man**, that Adam and Eve disobeyed God and so needed to be reconciled with God. The teaching of St Paul in passages such as Romans 5:12–19 claims that sin and death came into the world through Adam and that sin and death were only conquered through the death and resurrection of Jesus. However, if evolution is true, then there was no Adam and Eve, no Fall, and therefore no original sin and no need for the atoning death of Jesus. If evolution is true, then the whole Christian teaching on atonement and salvation is based on something that didn't happen.
- Christianity is based on the belief that God is good and that his creation is good, but natural selection operates on a principle of violence and suffering. Not only do species struggle to survive, but the food chain itself is based on violent cruelty as predators devour their prey in fierce and brutal ways and often seem to inflict suffering for no survival purpose at all (for example, well-fed domestic cats average about two kills a week, often playing with the victim and watching it struggle). This can be explained by evolution, but not by a good creator.
- Christianity is based on the intrinsic value of human life. Christians believe that humans have been made in the image of God and that they have a soul allowing them to have a relationship with God. From this, as we have seen, comes the belief in the sanctity of life.

Who trusted God was love
indeed
And love Creation's final law
Tho' Nature, red in tooth and
claw
With ravine, shriek'd against
his creed.
(From the poem
In Memoriam A.H.H., *1850,*
Alfred Lord Tennyson)

Activities

1. Do you think Special Agenda IV has had an effect on Christians?
2. Look at the poem above by Tennyson. What do you think he meant by 'nature red in tooth and claw' and why might this be regarded as evidence against God?

Useful words

Original sin – the sin of Adam and Eve disobeying God, which some Christians believe is passed on to all humans at birth

Fall of Man – the idea that when Adam disobeyed God by eating the forbidden fruit, sin came into the world

How Christians respond to evolution

- Creationist Christians reject evolution and claim that the fossil record does not provide evidence for evolution. They claim that the earth and the universe were created 10,000 years ago as the Bible says (these Christians are known as new-age creationists). They believe that fossils are the remains of animal life destroyed by Noah's flood (clearly, dinosaurs could not have been taken on to the ark as it was too small, according to the dimensions given in Genesis, so dinosaurs were killed off in the flood) and that there are no fossils showing changes from one species to another.
- Some Christians who believe in intelligent design and the Genesis date of creation think that God created each species separately and at the same time. God then allowed them to evolve within their own species which, they claim, is the only indication for evolution there is (for example, the evidence Darwin found on the Galápagos Islands was only of finches developing different beaks, not of finches developing into a whole new species). These Christians claim that evolution explains developments within species, but only God and Genesis can explain the creation of species.
- Some Christians who believe in intelligent design accept that the earth is millions of years old, but believe that life itself is too complex and specific to have evolved naturally. They believe that the evidence for evolution means that God must have intervened to allow new species to develop, that humans are so different and complex that their emergence must have required a direct intervention by an intelligent designer such as God.

This view was reiterated by Cardinal Christoph Schönborn of Vienna in an interview to the *New York Times* in 2005:

> *Evolution in the sense of common ancestry might be true, but evolution in the neo-Darwinian sense – an unguided, unplanned process ... is not.*

- Many Christians accept evolution as being a product of God's design of the universe. They believe that the way God made the universe was bound to result in evolution and the development of humans because of the laws of science and natural selection that he put in place. Christian philosophers such as Peter van Inwagen have even argued that God's design of evolution might actually have predisposed people to believe in God, since belief in God is an aid to human survival.
- Until Pope Benedict XVI began to discuss intelligent design, the Roman Catholic Church had never seen any conflict between Catholic beliefs and evolution. In 1950, Pope Pius XII proclaimed that there was no opposition between evolution and Catholic doctrine. On 27 October 2014, Pope Francis reaffirmed this view when he said:

> *When we read about Creation in Genesis, we run the risk of imagining God was a magician, with a magic wand able to do everything. But that is not so. He created human beings and let them develop according to the internal laws that he gave to each one so they would reach their fulfilment.*

The importance of Christian responses

The importance of the Christian responses can be seen in the section above, headed 'Why evolution might cause issues for Christians' (page 121). But the Christians' responses are also important, because if God is not responsible for the origins of human life then:

- humans have not been created by God, and if God did not create them, the purpose of life must be up to humans and not determined by God
- there can be no original sin and so there is no need for salvation from sin
- it is up to humans to decide what constitutes the value of human life, as human life cannot have sanctity since the sanctity of life depends on its being created by God
- all the biblical ideas about humans being the children of God must be wrong.

Activity

Which of the Christian responses to evolution would you be most likely to agree with and why?

Practice questions

c Explain two reasons why evolution raises issues for Christians. In your answer you must refer to a source of wisdom and authority.

d 'Humans have been created by God.' Evaluate this statement considering arguments for and against. In your response you should:

- refer to Christian teachings
- refer to non-religious points of view
- reach a justified conclusion.

Summary

Science says that human life originated through evolution: the idea that life developed because the genetic structure of life forms produces changes and any change that is better suited to living in the environment will survive and reproduce. Evolution causes issues for Christians because it denies Adam and Eve and is based on violence and struggle. Christians respond in different ways, from rejecting evolution to accepting it as part of God's design plan.

Topic 1.4.4 The issue of abortion

Thinking points

In this topic you need to:

- think about the nature of abortion
- understand different Christian teachings about abortion, including reference to *Humanae Vitae*
- understand atheist and Humanist arguments surrounding its use and Christian responses to them, including Situation Ethics
- be able to explain and evaluate different Christian and non-religious attitudes to abortion.

The nature of abortion

An abortion is the process of ending a pregnancy so it does not result in the birth of a baby. Abortion is also known as a termination or a termination of pregnancy. Depending on how many weeks the woman has been pregnant, the pregnancy is ended either by taking medication or by having a surgical procedure.

Abortions have been carried out since ancient times as women tried to avoid having a baby. In many countries, abortion is still illegal, but it appears that this makes little difference to the number of abortions. It is estimated that approximately 20 million unsafe abortions are performed annually around the world, mainly in countries where abortion is illegal, and tens of thousands of women die as a result. When abortion was legalised in South Africa in 1996, abortion-related deaths dropped by more than 90 per cent.

British law on abortion

The 1967 Abortion Act states that an abortion can only be carried out in a medically registered facility, and only if two doctors agree on the following:

- the mother's life is at risk
- there is a risk of injury to the mother's physical or mental health
- there is a risk that another child would put the mental or physical health of existing children at risk
- there is a substantial risk that the baby might be born seriously handicapped.

The 1990 Abortion Act states that abortions cannot take place after 24 weeks of pregnancy, unless the mother's life is gravely at risk or the **foetus** is likely to be born with severe mental or physical abnormalities. This is because advances in medical techniques mean that such foetuses have a chance of survival.

Activities

1. What is the British law on abortion?
2. Do you think making abortion illegal would stop women from trying to have one?

Useful words

Foetus – a developing human in the womb from the end of the second month after conception (until then it is an embryo)

Gestation – the process of a foetus developing inside the womb

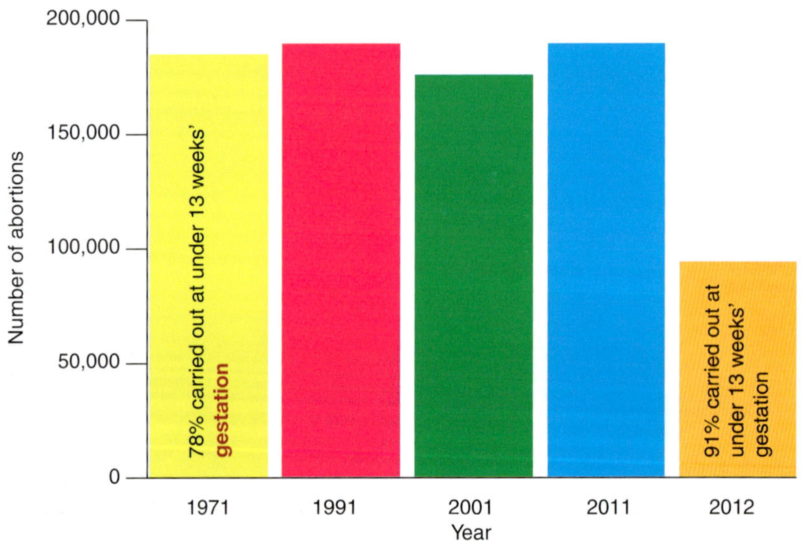

Number of abortions carried out in England and Wales 1971–2012 (source: Office for National Statistics).

Pro-choice is the name given to those who support a woman's right to abortion. They do not want women to risk their lives by having operations carried out by non-doctors in bad conditions.

Different Christian teachings about abortion

Christians have two differing attitudes to abortion.

1 The Catholic and Evangelical Pro-life attitude

The Catholic Church teaches that all abortion is wrong whatever the circumstances and so can never be permitted. This teaching is based on scripture, **Apostolic Tradition** and the Magisterium. The Church teaches that life begins at the moment of **conception**. This means that a woman does not have the right to do what she wants with her body after she has become pregnant because the new life has rights. The Church also teaches that because abortion is wrong, all medical staff should have the right to refuse to be involved in abortions. Catholics believe that abortion is wrong because:

- Life is holy and belongs to God, therefore only God has the right to end a pregnancy.
- Life begins at conception. Human life begins when an ovum is fertilised; abortion is therefore taking life.
- The Ten Commandments teach that it is wrong to take life; abortion is therefore wrong.
- Every person has a natural 'right to life'. A foetus is a human being and abortion destroys its right to life, so it follows that abortion is wrong.
- The Church points to evidence that some women who have abortions can suffer from traumas leading to guilt and sometimes mental illness.
- Catholics also believe that adoption is always a better solution to unwanted pregnancy than abortion as it preserves life and brings joy to a new family.

Catholics accept that there are difficult issues surrounding abortion, for example if doctors discover that a pregnant mother has cancer and chemotherapy would kill the foetus. In this situation, Catholic moral philosophers use the **doctrine of double effect**: the first effect is to save the mother's life, the second (double) effect is to end the life of the foetus. As the death of the foetus is secondary, and so not intended, an abortion has not occurred.

Useful words

Apostolic Tradition – the oral Gospel passed on by the Apostles to the Church
Conception – the fertilisation of the egg by the sperm
Infanticide – killing young children
Doctrine of double effect – the principle that it is acceptable to perform an action that has a side-effect as long as the intention was to achieve the good first effect

Human life must be respected and protected absolutely from the moment of conception. From the first moment of his existence, a human being must be recognised as having the rights of a person – among which is the inviolable right of every innocent being to life ... Abortion and ***infanticide*** *are abominable crimes ... The law must provide appropriate penal sanctions for every deliberate violation of the child's rights. (Catechism of the Catholic Church 2270–1, 2273)*

Activities

1. Why do some Christians agree with abortion and some do not?
2. Look at the Pro-Choice photo on page 125 and the Pro-Life photo opposite. Do you think Christians should demonstrate outside abortion clinics?
3. Look at the statement of the Catholic Church on page 125 and the statement of the Methodist Church on page 127. Which one do you agree with?

Life is an organisation dedicated to protecting the rights of unborn children. Why do you think Life is supported by many Catholics?

Another difficult situation is if a woman becomes pregnant as a result of rape. The Church teaches that one sinful act should not provoke another. With counselling, help and adoption, good can come out of evil in the form of a new life. The Bishops of England and Wales issued a statement saying that a rape victim may be given **contraception** to prevent implantation of the rapist's sperm as long as it could be established that conception had not taken place.

Evangelical Protestant Christians have exactly the same attitude to abortion as Catholics.

Useful words

Contraception – methods of preventing pregnancy occurring from sex

In conformity with these landmarks in the human and Christian vision of marriage, we must once again declare that the direct interruption of the generative process already begun, and, above all, directly willed and procured abortion, even if for therapeutic reasons, are to be absolutely excluded as licit means of regulating birth. (Humanae Vitae 14, Pope Paul VI's teaching on human life)

2 The liberal Protestant Pro-choice attitude

Other Christians (mainly liberal Protestants) believe that abortion is wrong, but it must be permitted in certain circumstances because:

- Jesus told Christians to love their neighbour as themselves, and abortion may be the most loving thing to do.
- They believe that life does not begin at conception.
- Christians should accept technological advances in medicine, therefore if doctors have developed tests to detect disease and suffering in a foetus, parents should be allowed abortions on the basis of such tests.
- Christianity is concerned with justice and if abortions were banned, an unjust situation would arise. Rich women would pay for abortions in another country, but the poor would use 'back-street' abortionists.

Atheist and Humanist attitudes to abortion

Most atheists and Humanists believe the following:

- A foetus cannot be considered as a separate life until it is capable of living outside the mother. Until that time, the foetus is part of the mother and its treatment should be determined by the mother. As life does not begin at conception, abortions before a certain point in the pregnancy are not taking life.

- A woman should have the right to do what she wants with her own body in the same way that men do. They would argue that an unwanted pregnancy is no different from an unwanted tumour. The problems caused to a woman by having an unwanted baby are a sufficient justification for her having an abortion.
- Abortion should be an automatic right for women who have been raped or subjected to incest or paedophilia.

Some Humanists argue that because foetuses born at 22–24 weeks can now survive, the time limit for abortions should be reduced to 18 or 20 weeks. However, others believe in '**abortion on demand**'. This is the idea that women should have the right to an abortion without having to meet the conditions of the 1967 Act because they are the ones who will have to carry and then bring up the baby.

For Humanists, the **quality of life** will always be more important than the preservation of life at all costs. The probable quality of life of the baby and the woman's rights should all be taken into account. Most Humanists put the interests of the woman first, since she would have to complete the pregnancy and probably care for the baby, whose happiness would largely depend on hers.

Christian responses to these atheist and Humanist views have been covered in the Christian attitudes above. There is little difference between the liberal Protestant Christian response and the Humanist attitude to abortion.

Situation Ethics and abortion

As we saw in Topic 1.2.6, Christians, Humanists and atheists often apply Situation Ethics to deal with ethical problems. They would look at the situation, decide on the pros and cons of the possible choices and then determine what would be the most loving thing to do. So, in the situation of a woman wanting an abortion they would look at the reasons, which could be, for example: if the woman has been raped, if the woman's life is at risk, if the foetus is so handicapped that it would have no quality of life, if the woman was living in poverty, if a baby would have a bad effect on the woman's physical or mental health, or if the effects of another child on the rest of the family would be negative, they would then decide if an abortion would be the most loving thing in that situation.

Practice questions

c Explain two reasons why Humanists agree with the British law on abortion.

d 'No Christian should ever have an abortion.' Evaluate this statement considering arguments for and against. In your response you should:

- refer to Christian teachings
- refer to other Christian points of view
- refer to non-religious points of view and ethical theories
- reach a justified conclusion.

Methodists would strongly prefer that through advances in medical science and social welfare, all abortions should become unnecessary. But termination as early as possible in the course of pregnancy may be the lesser of evils. If abortion were made a criminal offence again, the result would be 'one law for the rich and another for the poor', with increased risks of ill-health and death as a result of botched 'back-street' abortions. (Statement by the Methodist Church of England and Wales in What the Churches Say, *third edition)*

Useful words

Abortion on demand – the right to have an abortion whatever the woman's reasons

Quality of life – the idea that life must have some benefits for it to be worth living

Summary

Abortion is allowed in Britain if two doctors agree that there is medical reason. Abortion is not legal in Northern Ireland. Abortion is a controversial issue because people disagree about when life begins and whether abortion is murder.

Some Christians (Catholics and Evangelical Protestants) believe that abortion is always wrong because it is murder and against God's will. Some Christians believe that abortion is wrong but must be allowed in some circumstances as the lesser of two evils.

Topic 1.4.5 Death and the afterlife

Thinking points

In this topic you need to:

- think about Christian teachings and beliefs that support the existence of a life after death, including the resurrection of Jesus
- understand Christian and non-religious arguments for life after death such as remembered lives, paranormal, logic, reward, comfort and meeting loved ones who have passed on
- understand why people might hold these beliefs
- be able to explain Christian and non-religious beliefs in favour of an afterlife.

Why Christians believe in life after death

Christians believe that this life is not all there is. They believe that God will reward the good and punish the bad in some form of life after death. Although there are different views about what happens after death among Christians, all Christians believe in life after death because:

- The main Christian belief is that Jesus rose from the dead. All four Gospels record that Jesus was crucified and buried in a stone tomb. They also record that, on the Sunday morning, some of his women disciples went to the tomb and found it empty. Different Gospels then record different 'resurrection appearances' of Jesus. The rest of the New Testament is full of references to the resurrection of Jesus. If Jesus rose from the dead, then there must be life after death.
- St Paul teaches in 1 Corinthians 15 that people will have a resurrection like that of Jesus.
- St Paul says in Ephesians chapter 2 that God's great love has led him to give Christians eternal life in Christ by saving them from their sins.
- Jesus taught that he would come again at the end of the world for a final judgement, sending people to heaven or hell.
- The major creeds of the Church teach that Jesus rose from the dead and that there will be life after death.
- All the Christian Churches teach that there is life after death. Protestant, Catholic, Orthodox and Pentecostal Churches may have some differences about what they think life after death will be like, but they all teach their followers that there will be life after death.
- Many Christians believe that people are made up of a body and a soul (mind or personality). They believe in the **immortality of the soul**. They believe that when the body dies, the soul leaves the body to live with God.

Useful words

Immortality of the soul – the idea that the soul lives on after the death of the body

Activity

Why do Christians believe in life after death?

'But because of his great love for us, God, who is rich in mercy, made us alive with Christ even when we were dead in transgressions – it is by grace you have been saved. And God raised us up with Christ and seated us with him in the heavenly realms in Christ Jesus' (Ephesians 2:4–6).

Non-religious reasons for believing in an afterlife

Non-religious reasons for believing in life after death are often connected to evidence for the **paranormal**. This can refer to a wide range of things from ghosts to telekinesis (moving objects without touching them). However, there are three main parts of the paranormal that provide reasons for believing in life after death.

1 Near-death experiences

These are fairly recently recorded phenomena and happen when people are clinically dead for a period of time and then come back to life. In **near-death experiences** people often describe feeling peace and joy, a sensation of floating above the body, seeing a bright light, entering another world, meeting dead relatives and coming to a point of no return. In his research, Dr Sam Parnia of Southampton General Hospital found that four out of 63 patients who had survived a heart attack had near-death experiences. Similar research in the Netherlands by Dr Pim van Lommel, in the USA by Dr Raymond Moody and elsewhere in Britain by Dr Peter Fenwick and Dr Susan Blackmore produced similar results.

If near-death experiences are true, then there is a heaven and there is life after death, but this is not the same as resurrection, as described in the Gospels.

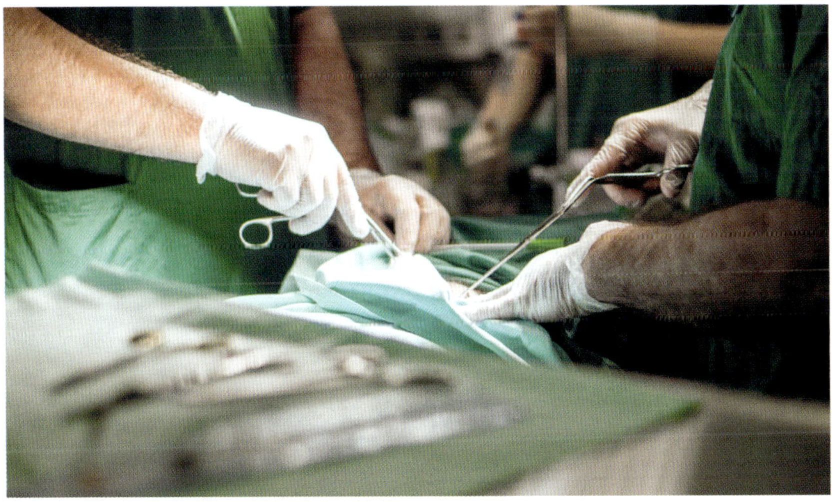

Some people have near-death experiences during heart surgery.

2 Evidence for a spirit world

Ghosts and ouija boards appear to give evidence of the spirits or souls of the dead surviving death but the clearest evidence seems to come from mediums.

A medium is a person who claims to have the gift of communicating between the material world in which we live and the spirit world inhabited by those who have died. They are sometimes called psychics, clairvoyants or spirit guides.

Mediums have always existed but they have become more well known in the twenty-first century thanks to cable television programmes such as *Psychic Witness*, *Psychic Investigations* and *Medium*.

If mediums can contact the dead in a spirit world then there must be a life after death.

Useful words

Paranormal – unexplained events that are thought to have spiritual causes, for example, ghosts, mediums

Near-death experiences – when people about to die have out-of-body feelings

Jeanette Mitchell-Meadows had a near-death experience when she was undergoing major spinal surgery. She felt herself leaving her body and following a bright light to what she thought was heaven. It was very peaceful, she heard music more clearly and tunefully than anything on earth and then she felt she met Jesus. She met her grandparents and her daughter, who had been killed in an accident about six months earlier. She did not want to leave, but was told God had things for her to do on earth. When she returned to her body she felt great pain.

Stephen O'Brien, a medium, told Marion Jones that he could see a peasant grandmother figure sitting on a rickety chair outside a wooden shack. She was nodding and looking very happy. Then she told Stephen that she was thanking Marion for helping her grandson and she was speaking the word Cruz. Stephen thought perhaps there was a South American connection. Marion realised that Cruz was the surname of a ten-year-old Mexican boy whose education and health she was sponsoring. She was sure that Stephen O'Brien had contacted the boy's grandmother in the spirit world and had information that he could not possibly have known.

Useful words

Remembered lives – memories of a previous existence

Reincarnation – the belief that, after death, souls are reborn in a new body

Activities

1. What do you think about near-death experiences?
2. Do you think mediums can contact the dead?
3. What do you think remembered lives prove?
4. Look at the photo of Balaji's tail. Do you think this is evidence for reincarnation?

3 The evidence of reincarnation (remembered lives)

Many non-religious people claim to have **remembered lives**; they can remember themselves in other lives. There have been many cases of children when they can first talk saying that they can remember another life. They talk about another house, other parents and families and about how they died. Sometimes these children become so unhappy that their parents arrange for them to go to the place where they say they lived before. In many cases they are able to identify their previous relatives. Usually the memories start to fade by the time the child is six or seven.

Hindus, Sikhs and Buddhists believe that life after death involves souls being reborn into another body (**reincarnation**). There are many stories of this in India, one of the most famous being reported in July 2002 at the National Conference of Forensic Science in India.

In 1996, Taranjit Singh was born to a poor peasant family and received no education. From the age of two he claimed he could remember a previous life and had been killed by a motor scooter on 10 September 1992. His parents took him to the village he said he came from and the local teacher confirmed the accident had happened and introduced him to his 'original parents', whom he recognised. A forensic scientist, Vikram Chauhan, checked the first boy's education and asked Taranjit to write the English and Punjabi alphabets (even though Taranjit had never been taught them). Not only could he write them, but when Mr Chauhan tested his handwriting against that of the dead boy, he found they were identical.

In 2003, crowds flocked to Indian temples to see a Muslim baby with a tail who was believed to be the reincarnation of a Hindu god. The eleven-month-old boy, named Balaji (another name for the monkey-faced Lord Hanuman) was reported to have a ten-centimetre long tail caused by genetic mutations during the development of the foetus. Iqbal Qureshi, the child's maternal grandfather, took Balaji from temple to temple where people offered money to see the boy. Mr Qureshi claimed the baby had nine spots on his body like Lord Hanuman.

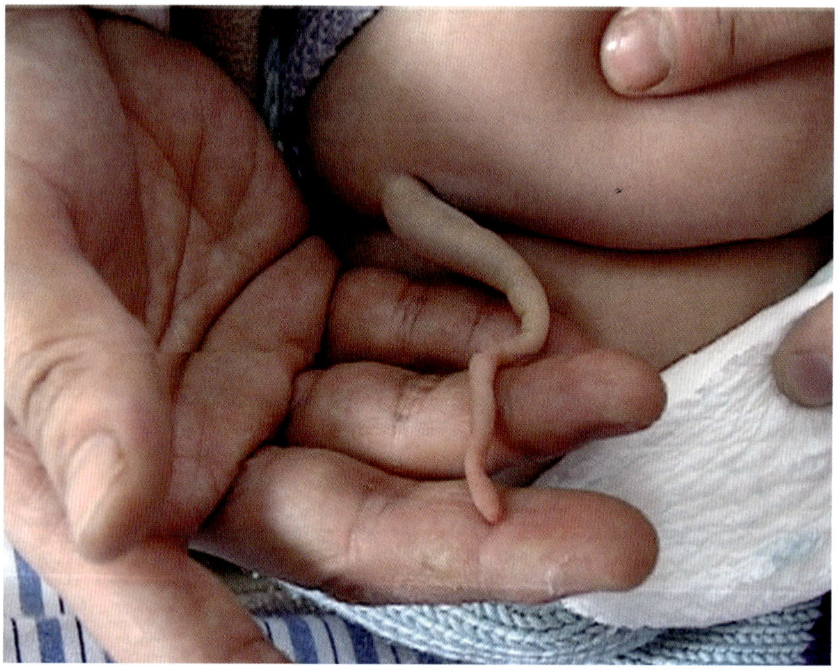

Arshid Ali Khan was born with a tail growing from his back and many believed he was the reincarnation of the Hindu monkey god Hanuman.

Other reasons why people believe in life after death

Other reasons why people might believe in life after death are:

- It gives their lives meaning and purpose. They feel that for life to end at death does not make sense. If the purpose of life is to live in such a way that you spend eternity in heaven, then that gives life meaning.
- It gives comfort when a loved one dies. When someone dies it is almost impossible to believe that they are gone forever. Belief in an afterlife gives the hope of meeting loved ones who have passed on and the comfort that they have not disappeared but are in a better place. Non-religious people often say that the dead have gone to be with the angels.
- It seems to be demanded by the nature of justice. It often appears that in this life, evil people prosper and the good suffer. The idea of an afterlife where evil people are punished and the good rewarded makes sense of people's belief in justice and fair play.

However, atheists and Humanists do not believe in life after death. Life after death would require some sort of divine being to organise what happens and to create a place where it could happen. As atheists and Humanists do not believe in any form of divine being they cannot believe in life after death.

Practice questions

c Explain two reasons why non-religious people believe in life after death.

d 'Only Christians have evidence for life after death.' Evaluate this statement considering arguments for and against. In your response you should:

- refer to Christian teachings
- refer to different Christian and non-religious points of view
- reach a justified conclusion.

Summary

Christians believe in life after death because Jesus rose from the dead, and the Bible and the Church say that there is life after death. Some people believe in life after death for non-religious reasons such as near-death experiences when people see things during heart attacks or medical operations, and the evidence of the spirit world, ghosts and mediums.

Topic 1.4.6 Non-religious arguments against life after death

Thinking points

In this topic you need to:

- think about arguments against life after death, including it being a source of comfort, lack of evidence, fraudulent accounts, social control and Humanist beliefs
- understand why Christians reject these arguments, including 1 Peter 3:18–22
- be able to explain and evaluate Christian and non-religious arguments about life after death.

Useful words

Fallible memories – memory can be mistaken
Bereaved – deprived of a close relation or friend through their death

Non-religious arguments against an afterlife

Humanists and atheists do not believe in life after death. They believe that just like animals and plants, humans cease to exist when they die and reject the arguments for life after death because:

- The different religions have different ideas about life after death. This is especially true of the difference between the ideas of Hindus, Buddhists and Sikhs, who all believe that people are reincarnated after death, and the ideas of Jews, Christians and Muslims, who all believe that people only have one life and after death there is judgement and heaven and hell.
- The religious evidence for life after death is based on holy books, but there is no way for a non-believer to decide which holy book is the true word of God.
- They think that the resurrection of Jesus is not based on sufficiently reliable evidence to prove the existence of an afterlife. They claim that the biblical accounts contain too many contradictions to be a proof.
- Evidence for near-death experiences is also unreliable. People have **fallible memories**, as has been shown by scientific research:

  We know that memories are extremely fallible. We are quite good at knowing that something happened, but we are very poor at knowing when it happened. It is quite possible that these experiences happened during the recovery or just before the cardiac arrest. To say that they happened when the brain was shut down, I think there is little evidence for that at all. (Dr Chris Freeman, consultant psychiatrist)

- They think that the evidence of mediums is suspect as most of it can be explained. One piece of evidence against the abilities of mediums is provided by Robert Thouless, President of the Society for Psychical Research. Thouless made a coded message before he died that required a key word to decode it. He told no-one the key word when he was alive and said that mediums should contact him after his death to get the key word, and prove there was life after death. At least 100 mediums have submitted keys to the cypher, but none was correct.
- They think that the evidence of remembered lives is unreliable as scientific investigations show that in only eleven of approximately 1111 reported rebirth cases had there been no contact between the two families before the investigation was begun, and of these, seven were seriously flawed in some respect.
- They think that life after death is simply a source of comfort to the **bereaved** with no factual evidence to support it.

Activity

Do you think that Christians can prove the resurrection of Jesus?

Does Buddhism offer an explanation for life after death?

People also have their own, more personal, reasons for not believing in life after death:

- They do not believe in God and if there is no God, and if there is nothing **non-material**, then there is no heaven to go to after death.
- Most beliefs in life after death assume that the mind or soul can survive without the body. However, scientific evidence shows that the human mind developed as the brain grew more complex, and so the mind cannot exist without the brain (for example, people who are brain dead have to be kept alive by a life-support machine).
- They believe that there is a problem as to where life after death could take place. Space exploration has shown there is no heaven above the sky and physics has shown there is no non-material world on earth. Where then could life after death take place?
- They argue that we can only recognise people by their bodies, so how would we recognise souls without bodies? If souls survive death, then they would be alone with no way of contacting other souls, which would not really be life after death.
- Philosopher and social theorist Karl Marx (1818–83) argued that belief in life after death was an invention of the ruling classes to be used as a means of social control. The rich could keep the working class happy with low wages and poor living conditions by promising them a reward and a better life in heaven after they had died.

You will eat, bye and bye,
In that glorious land above the sky;
Work and pray, live on hay,
You'll get pie in the sky when you die.

(The chorus of 'The Preacher and the Slave', a song written by the communist Joe Hill in 1911)

Useful words

Non-material – not physical

Activities

1. Which do you think is the most convincing argument against there being life after death?
2. What do you think of the song 'The Preacher and the Slave'?

For Christ also suffered once for sins, the righteous for the unrighteous, to bring you to God. He was put to death in the body but made alive in the Spirit. (1 Peter 3:18)

Why Christians reject these non-religious arguments

Christians reject non-religious arguments because they believe:

- Christianity is the one true religion, so the Bible and what it says can be relied on, therefore other religions and holy books saying different things about life after death do not matter.
- The biblical record of the resurrection can be relied on.
- The disciples must have known whether or not the resurrection happened and they would not have risked their lives as they did for something they knew was a lie.
- The arguments of philosophers such as René Descartes (1596–1650) show that the mind is separate from the body and so could survive without the body.
- Heaven is a spiritual dimension, outside but interacting with the material universe.
- Christianity has been at the forefront of reforms to improve the conditions of the working class, so Christian beliefs about life after death cannot be part of social control.

Activity

Explain why atheists and Humanists do not accept the evidence of the paranormal for life after death.

Practice questions

c Explain two reasons why Christians reject arguments against life after death. In your answer you must refer to a source of wisdom and authority.

d 'Life after death doesn't make sense in the modern world.' Evaluate this statement considering arguments for and against. In your response you should:

- refer to Christian teachings
- refer to non-religious points of view
- reach a justified conclusion.

Summary

Some people do not believe in life after death because they do not believe in God and so they don't see who could be responsible for it. They think there is no scientific evidence for it and they do not see where life after death could take place. Christians argue that these people ignore the evidence of the Bible.

Topic 1.4.7 Euthanasia

The nature of euthanasia

A dictionary definition of **euthanasia** is that it provides a gentle and easy death to someone suffering from a painful, terminal disease who has a poor **quality of life**. This can be done by:

- **assisted suicide**
- **voluntary euthanasia**
- **non-voluntary euthanasia**.

British law states that all these methods of euthanasia are illegal and can lead to a charge of murder. However, the law now agrees that withdrawing artificial nutrition and hydration or switching off a life-support machine is not classed as murder. In the same way, withholding treatment from patients with little or no chance of survival and ensuring a peaceful death for them is also not classed as murder. These two types of euthanasia (the withdrawal or withholding of treatment) are often called passive euthanasia, in contrast to positive euthanasia, which is the act of bringing someone's life to an end.

Christian attitudes to euthanasia

1 Acceptance of passive euthanasia

Most Christians, including Catholics, believe that assisted suicide, voluntary euthanasia and non-voluntary euthanasia are all wrong. However, they accept that modern medicine has introduced new issues. They believe that switching off life-support machines is not euthanasia if **brain death** has already been established by medical experts. They also believe that it is not wrong to allow death to occur by not giving extraordinary treatment (treatment that could cause distress to the patient and family and is only

The Dignitas House in Switzerland which provides assisted-suicide facilities for those who feel their illnesses are unbearable.

Thinking points

In this topic you need to:

- think about the nature of euthanasia, understand Christian teachings and different responses to euthanasia including support for hospice care and interpretations of Job 2:1–10
- understand non-religious (including atheist and Humanist) arguments surrounding its use (including ethical theories such as Situation Ethics) and Christian responses to them
- understand religious, non-religious and personal arguments surrounding its use and Christian responses to them, including support for hospice care
- be able to explain and evaluate different Christian and non-religious attitudes to euthanasia.

Useful words

Euthanasia – the painless killing of someone dying from a painful disease
Quality of life – the idea that life must have some benefits for it to be worth living
Assisted suicide – providing a seriously ill person with the means to kill themselves
Voluntary euthanasia – ending life painlessly when someone in great pain asks for death
Non-voluntary euthanasia – ending someone's life painlessly when they are unable to ask, but you have good reason for thinking they would want you to do so
Brain death – the brain is irreversibly damaged

His wife said to him, 'Are you still maintaining your integrity? Curse God and die!' He replied, 'You are talking like a foolish woman. Shall we accept good from God, and not trouble?' (Job 2:9–10)

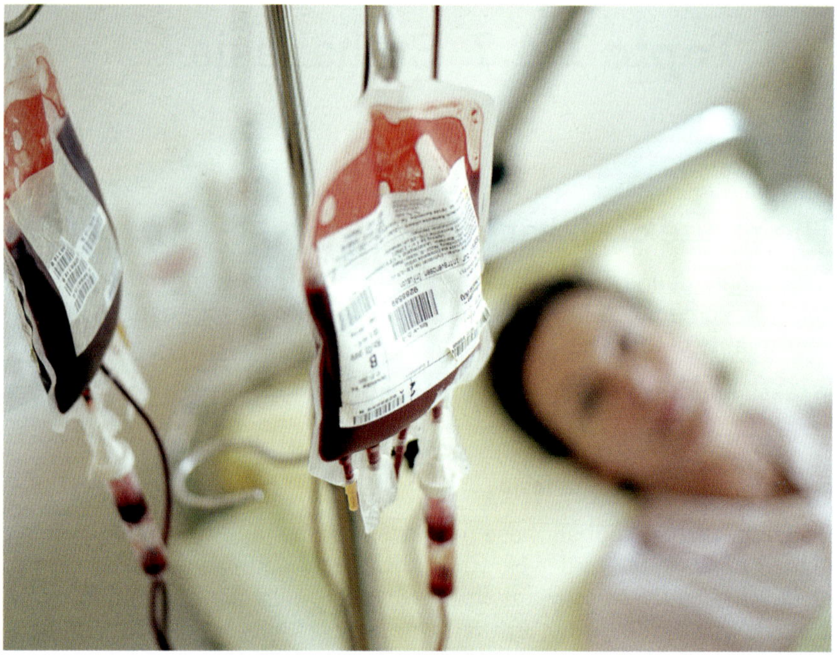

Hospitals deal with life and death situations all the time.

The use of painkillers to alleviate the suffering of the dying, even at the risk of shortening their days, can be morally in conformity with human dignity if death is not willed either as an end or a means, but only foreseen and tolerated as inevitable. (Catechism of the Catholic Church 2279)

Activities

1. Do you think it is right for people to be helped to end their lives when they have terminal illnesses?
2. Should the right to end someone's life rest with doctors or God?
3. Why are some Christians totally opposed to any form of ending people's lives early?
4. What do most Christians believe about euthanasia?
5. Look at the quotation above from Job. How do you think it is related to arguments about euthanasia for Christians?

likely to put off death for a short time), nor is it wrong to give dying people painkillers which may shorten their life. They have this attitude because:

- They believe that life is created by God and so is sacred to God (the sanctity of life). It is up to God, not humans, when people die. Euthanasia is to put oneself on a par with God, which is condemned in the Bible.
- They regard any form of euthanasia as a form of murder, and murder is forbidden in the Ten Commandments.
- They believe that it is up to medical experts to determine when death has occurred. If doctors confirm brain death, then that person has already died, so switching off the machine is accepting what God has already decided and it is not euthanasia.
- They believe that painkillers may be given to a dying person in great pain. This might shorten the person's life but the painkillers are given to remove the pain, and that is the intention; hastening the person's death is an unintended effect, and so giving the painkillers is not euthanasia. This is called the doctrine of double effect.
- They also believe that it is right not to give 'extraordinary treatment' to the dying as such treatment is likely to affect the dignity of dying:

Discontinuing medical procedures that are burdensome, dangerous, extraordinary, or disproportionate to the expected outcome can be legitimate; it is the refusal of 'over-zealous' treatment. (Catechism of the Catholic Church 2278)

2 All euthanasia is wrong

Some Christians (mainly Evangelical Protestants) believe that any form of euthanasia is wrong and they do not allow the switching off of life-support machines, the refusal of extraordinary treatment or the giving of large doses of painkillers. They have this attitude because:

- The Book of Job chapter 2 tells Christians to accept suffering as God's will:

  Shall we accept good from God and not trouble? (Job 2:10)

- They regard switching off a life-support machine, the refusal of extraordinary treatment and giving a large dose of painkillers as euthanasia. Life is being ended by humans, not God, and this is wrong.
- They regard any form of euthanasia as murder, and murder is banned by God in the Ten Commandments.
- They believe in the sanctity of life. Life is created by God and so it is sacred to God. It is up to God, not humans, when people die. Euthanasia is to put oneself on a par with God, which is condemned in the Bible.

3 Accept limited use of euthanasia

A few Christians accept a limited use of euthanasia. They agree with living wills in which people state what sort of treatment they wish to receive and how they want to die if they have a terminal illness. They believe this because:

- Modern medical science means that we can no longer be sure what God's wishes about someone's death actually are.
- The teaching of Jesus on loving your neighbour and helping people in trouble could be used to justify assisting suicide.
- Living wills give people a chance to be in control of what doctors are doing to them, which is a basic human right.

Atheist and Humanist attitudes to euthanasia

Atheist and Humanist arguments against euthanasia

Atheists and Humanists do not have an agreed position on euthanasia. Some want euthanasia to remain illegal because:

- There is always likely to be doubt as to whether it is what the person really wants. If there is money involved, relatives might request euthanasia for a rich relative to gain from their will.
- There is also the problem as to whether the disease is terminal. A cure might be found for the disease, or the patient may go into **remission**. Also, people thought of as being in irreversible comas have recovered after many years.
- Doctors would also face a big problem if they started to kill patients, even if the patient had requested it. It is the role of doctors to save lives, not end them. Would patients trust their doctors if they weren't sure about their dedication to saving life?
- People might change their mind about wanting euthanasia, but then it would be too late.
- Who would decide to allow the euthanasia to take place? What safeguards could there be that they were only killing people who really wanted and needed euthanasia?

Useful words

Remission – when a patient with a disease gets better

Some Humanists might use Situation Ethics to decide whether to permit euthanasia. They would look at the Humanist arguments for and against covered in these pages and then try to decide what would be the most loving thing to do. Their decision may well be affected by the intensity of pain the person was suffering and the quality of life they had.

Atheist and Humanist attitudes for euthanasia

Others believe that euthanasia should be legalised because:

- Advances in medicine have led to people being kept alive who would previously have died, but they judge their quality of life as poor. It is claimed that doctors and relatives should have the right to give such patients a painless death.
- The development of life-support machines has already brought in a form of euthanasia, as doctors and relatives can agree to switch off such machines if there is no chance of the patient regaining consciousness because they are said to be brain dead. It is claimed that the National Health Service (NHS) cannot afford to keep people alive for years on a life-support machine that could be used to save the life of someone who has a chance of recovery.
- Just as doctors can now switch off life-support machines, so judges have said that doctors can stop treatment.
- People now have the right to take their own lives (it used to be illegal and people could be put in jail if their suicide attempt failed!). If people have the right to kill themselves, then they should have the right to ask a doctor to assist their suicide if they are too weak to do it themselves.

St Joseph's Hospice in Hackney, London.

Christian responses to those who are dying

A major Christian response to the problems of the terminally ill has been the hospice movement.

The word 'hospice' was first used in the fourth century to describe how Christian monks and nuns welcomed travellers, the sick and those in many kinds of need. In the nineteenth century, it was used to describe the care of dying patients by Mme Jeanne Garnier in Lyon, France. However, it was the work of Dame Cicely Saunders (an Anglican nurse, then a doctor) in providing **palliative care** for the dying and founding St Christopher's Hospice in 1967 which led to the growth of the hospice movement.

Christians believe that instead of euthanasia, the terminally ill should be helped by hospices which aim to relieve and control the pain of the dying. The hospices should help patients, and their families and friends, to face up to death by allowing them to talk in a free and open way as well as care for the emotional needs of relatives before, during and after the patient's death.

After Saunders' pioneering work, UK hospices began to be founded as independent institutions with a Christian ethos. Hospices are now open to all people regardless of religion, although many still retain their Christian foundation names, such as St Oswald's in Newcastle. The NHS provides 32 per cent of the funding for adult hospices, although this varies by health authority. The balance of hospice funding comes from charitable donations. Christians are very involved in supporting the work of hospices both financially and as volunteer helpers.

In October 2015, the Economist Intelligence Unit described UK end-of-life care as the best in the world.

Two national charitable organisations, Marie Curie Cancer Care and the Sue Ryder Foundation, have also played an important role in providing specialised care for dying people and their families. Eleven Marie Curie Homes were developed in the 1950s and Sue Ryder Homes began to emerge in the 1970s.

Useful words

Palliative care – medical or nursing care that reduces pain and improves the quality of life of those who have terminal illnesses

Activity

Do you think Christians are right to support the hospice movement?

Practice questions

c Explain two reasons why Christians have different views about euthanasia. In your answer you must refer to a source of wisdom and authority

d 'People dying in agony should be offered euthanasia.' Evaluate this statement considering arguments for and against. In your response you should:

- refer to Christian teachings
- refer to non-religious points of view
- refer to different Christian points of view and ethical theories
- reach a justified conclusion.

Summary

Euthanasia is giving an easier death to those suffering intolerably. British law says that euthanasia is a crime, but withholding treatment from dying patients is not. All Christians are against euthanasia because they believe that life is sacred and belongs to God.

However, there are some different attitudes among Christians about switching off life-support machines, withdrawing treatment, and so on, because some think that these are not euthanasia.

Topic 1.4.8 The natural world

Thinking points

In this topic you need to:

- think about Christian responses to threats to the world, including pollution, global warming and the use of natural resources
- understand stewardship and humanity's role as stewards, including Sharing the Footprint
- know differing Christian responses to animal rights, including animal experimentation and the use of animals for food
- be able to explain and evaluate different Christian attitudes to the natural world.

Useful words

Stewardship – looking after something so it can be passed on to the next generation

Use of the mineral, vegetable and animal resources of the universe cannot be divorced from moral imperatives. Man's dominion over inanimate and other living beings granted by the Creator is not absolute; it is limited by concern for the quality of life of his neighbour, including generations to come; it requires a religious respect for the integrity of nature. (Catechism of the Catholic Church 2415)

Stewardship

It is a basic belief of Christianity that God gave humans the **stewardship** of the earth and its resources. Stewardship means looking after something so that it can be passed on to the next generation.

In the Genesis accounts of creation, God gave humans the right to rule over the earth. This gives humans control of animals and plants. However, the rest of the Bible makes clear that the right to rule gives humans many responsibilities. The Old Testament teaches that humans have a responsibility to treat animals humanely and to farm the land kindly by not growing crops every fiftieth year.

In the Parable of the Talents or Minas (Luke 19:11–26), Jesus taught that God expects humans to pass on to the next generation more than they have been given. Many Christians believe that this means Christians have a responsibility to leave the earth a better place than they found it. In many of his teachings, especially the Sermon on the Mount, Jesus taught that Christians have a responsibility to ensure a fair sharing of the earth's resources.

The Bible also makes clear that there will be a judgement day at the end of the world when people will be judged on their beliefs and behaviour. Most Christians believe that part of this judgement will be on how they have fulfilled their duty as stewards of God's earth.

The threat of pollution

The waste produced by humans in the form of sewage, refuse (rubbish put into bins) and litter (rubbish left on the streets and so on) is not only a form of pollution, but also a major threat to the future of the planet. As the world economy grows, so does its production of waste. For example, Europe produces more than 2.5 billion tonnes of solid waste a year, and every day the inhabitants of New York throw away approximately 26,000 tonnes. Traditional waste management strategies include reusing materials, recovering materials through recycling, incineration and landfills.

Human waste and other waterborne waste products from houses, streets and factories are transported through sewers to sewage works where the raw sewage has to undergo a series of treatments to make it safe for discharge into rivers or the sea. Solid sewage has to be pasteurised to make it safe to use as fertiliser on farmers' fields. Raw sewage, or sewage that has not been treated adequately, is one serious source of water pollution.

Apart from being unsightly and degrading, litter has helped to cause an increase in the UK's rat population to 70 million. Rats bring many diseases to humans such as the deadly Weil's disease, and the 2006 National Rodent Survey highlighted compost bins, discarded fast-food containers, bird feeders, litter and poor maintenance of sewerage pipes as some of the main causes of the rat boom. Litter also chokes many animals, it causes thousands of bike and car accidents when it is on roads, and it is estimated that a fire breaks out every twelve minutes because of litter.

This power station in Stockton-on-Tees runs on household waste. It therefore provides a solution to both the scarcity of oil and gas and waste disposal.

Christian responses

The responsibility to be God's stewards and to leave the earth a better place means that Christians should take an active role in dealing with the problems of pollution. They should try to reduce pollution by:

- recycling
- promoting the use of power from waste plants to produce electricity from human waste
- promoting the development of anaerobic digestion (the breakdown of organic material by microorganisms to produce biogas, which can be used as a fuel, and digestate, which can be used as a fertiliser) to deal with solid sewage and food waste
- encouraging people not to drop litter and reminding them that those who throw down, drop or deposit and leave litter in any place can be given an on-the-spot fine or face a court prosecution
- making sure to report any area that is badly littered to their local council, which has a responsibility to clear all the litter within a fixed period (six hours in places like a high street).

The threat of global warming

Global warming (now often termed **climate change**) refers to the fact that the earth is warmer than it has been for over 1000 years. Global average temperatures rose by about 0.8°C between 1901 and 2010 and by 0.5°C between 1979 and 2010. Many scientists believe that the earth has probably never warmed as rapidly as in the past 30 years – a period when natural influences on global temperatures, such as solar cycles and volcanoes, should have cooled us down. Most scientists believe that this is caused by the burning of **fossil fuels** in what is known as the '**greenhouse effect**'. Carbon dioxide from burned fossil fuels creates a barrier like the glass in a greenhouse and allows the sun's heat through, but then traps it, causing the temperature to rise. Without this barrier, the earth would be too cold for life, but as the barrier increases, so does the earth's temperature.

Activities

1. What do Christians believe about stewardship?
2. Why is pollution a threat to the earth?
3. Explain how Christians respond to the threat of pollution.
4. Do you think global warming is a problem?

Useful words

Global warming – the increase in the temperature of the earth's atmosphere (thought to be caused by the greenhouse effect)
Climate change – changes in global or regional climate patterns, attributed to the increased levels of carbon dioxide produced by the use of fossil fuels
Fossil fuels – natural fuels (coal, oil and gas) formed over millions of years through the breakdown of the remains of living organisms
Greenhouse effect – the carbon dioxide from burned fossil fuels creates a barrier in the same way as the glass in a greenhouse: it allows the sun's heat through, but then traps it, causing the temperature to rise

The UK Climate Impacts Programme assumes that if this trend continues, it will lead to average temperatures in the southeast of England rising by 1.3°C by 2020 and by 2°C by 2050. Rainfall would increase by 15–20 per cent in the north of England and Scotland by 2050. Other scientists have claimed that such rises in temperature will lead to a rise in the level of the sea (because of the ice caps melting), which means that some coastal areas could disappear. Other studies have predicted that southern Mediterranean countries, such as Spain, could become deserts.

Christian responses

Most of the world's scientists believe that climate change is mainly caused by the carbon emissions produced by human activity. Christians' responsibility to be good stewards and leave the earth a better place means that they should try to reduce carbon emissions by:

- using energy-efficient technologies (such as building insulation, more efficient light bulbs, energy-efficient electrical appliances and so on) to allow us to use less energy to get the same level of production, service and comfort
- using renewable energy sources such as solar, wind, geothermal, hydro and **bioenergy**, which could produce all the electricity we need without producing any carbon emissions
- building cheaper and more easily available methods of public transport, which could greatly reduce carbon emissions (the greenest forms of mass transport are electric trains and trams, the least green are planes and diesel buses)
- opposing tropical deforestation and working to reduce emissions from agriculture, which currently represent nearly 30 per cent of the world's heat-trapping emissions
- encouraging car manufacturers to use ethanol, biodiesel, electric batteries and hydrogen to power cars without carbon emissions.

Useful words

Bioenergy – renewable energy made from materials derived from biological sources such as wood waste, straw, manure and sugar cane
Renewable resources – resources which do not run out, for example hydroelectric power from water
Biofuels – fuels produced from plants

Threats caused by the use of natural resources

Natural resources are naturally occurring materials, such as oil and fertile land, which can be used by humans. They can be divided into two types: **renewable resources** and non-renewable resources.

Renewable resources

These are resources that can be used over and over again because they renew themselves. Examples of renewable resources are:

- wind power
- solar power
- water power
- fertile land producing food, oilseed rape and **biofuels** (which can provide fuel for vehicles)
- soft woods (which grow very quickly and can be used for paper, furniture and other uses).

Human use of such renewable resources causes no problems. However, using renewable resources to produce electricity is often more expensive.

Activity

How should Christians respond to the shortage of natural resources?

Non-renewable resources

These resources are finite: they disappear once they are used. Examples include:

- oil
- coal
- iron
- tin
- copper
- uranium
- natural gas
- hard woods.

Human use of **finite resources** causes major problems because as the resource is used, it becomes scarcer and less available.

Problems caused by human use of finite resources are most obvious in the case of oil. It is usually thought that a decline in the availability of oil would have the most effect on people's use of cars, but it is not only petrol and diesel that come from oil. All plastics and road surfaces, most candles, polishes and chemical foodstuffs come from oil. Clearly, if the oil begins to dry up, there will be major effects on people's lives. Similarly, all the metals used in everyday living, from car panels and railway tracks to pans and kitchen appliances, come from finite ores such as iron, aluminium and tin.

Useful words

Finite resources – resources which can only be used once, for example oil, metals

Environment – the surroundings in which plants and animals live and on which they depend for survival

Christian responses

Christians are taught not only that they should be stewards of God's earth, but also that stewardship means a fair sharing of the earth's resources. This means that Christians should respond to the threats caused by the use of resources by:

- promoting the use of renewable resources to produce electricity, for example by: nuclear power, wind power, sea power (using either the waves or the tides), hydroelectric power (using water in a dam) or solar power (using the sun's heat)
- encouraging car manufacturers to use water, sugar cane and electric batteries as ways of powering cars (there are already a few fuel-cell cars on the market powered by the hydrogen from water)
- promoting the use of recycling to enable the lifetime of many finite resources to be extended. For example, some cars are now made of almost 75 per cent recycled materials
- encouraging the work of scientists to produce chemicals from plants rather than oil to make such things as plastics.

The belief that, after death, they will be judged by God on their behaviour as stewards means that many Christians feel they have a duty to share in and support the work of groups which try to reduce pollution and global warming, and conserve resources. This is a way of living as God wants them to. Belief in stewardship also means that every Christian should be judging what they are doing in their life as an individual by the standards of Christian stewardship. It is only by being a good steward and conserving the **environment** and scarce resources that they can become a good Christian.

Solar panels on a church roof in Melbourne, Derbyshire.

Activities

1. Read the Christian Declaration on Nature. Do you think Christians are following its recommendations?
2. What do you think about utilitarianism?

Utilitarianism is an ethical principles connected with the philosopher John Stuart Mill who claimed that people should decide what is the right thing to do by working out which choice will bring about 'the greatest happiness of the greatest number of people'.

Participants of a pro-research rally in the USA defend the use of animals in medical research.

The Christian Declaration on Nature

At a conference of world religious leaders held at Assisi in 1986, the Christian delegates issued a declaration on the environment. It stated that Christians believe that God created everything to be good and created everything to live in harmony. God created humans in his likeness to have a unique dominion over his creation, but it is a dominion designed to protect, not destroy, God's creation. Anything humans do to damage creation is a sin and the declaration condemns the environmental damage caused by human activity: 'All human activity in the world must therefore lead to the mutual enrichment of man and creatures.'

The Declaration ends with these words:

> *Christians repudiate:*
> - *All forms of human activity – wars, discrimination, and destruction of cultures – which do not respect the authentic interests of the human race, in accordance with God's will and design, and do not enable men as individuals and as members of society to pursue and fulfil their total vocation within the harmony of the universe.*
> - *All ill-considered exploitation of nature which threatens to destroy it and, in turn, to make man the victim of degradation.*
>
> *In the name of Christ, who will repay everyone for good works, Christians call upon all men and women to pursue:*
> - *a synthesis between culture and faith*
> - *ecumenical dialogue on the goals of scientific research and on the environmental consequences of the use of its findings*
> - *the priority of moral values over technological advances*
> - *truth, justice and the peaceful coexistence of all peoples.*

Animal rights

Animal rights is the idea that non-human animals are entitled to certain kinds of consideration and that their most basic interests – such as the need to avoid suffering – should be given the same consideration as human beings. Those who support animal rights argue that animals should no longer be viewed as property or used as food, clothing, research subjects, entertainment or beasts of burden.

Christian responses

Most Christians support animal research because they believe that:

- Humans are unlike animals because only humans were made in the image of God.
- According to the Genesis creation stories, God put humankind in charge of animals to use for human benefit.
- Christians believe that only humans have souls and so they have more rights than animals.
- Animal testing has helped to develop vaccines against diseases like rabies, polio, measles, mumps, rubella and tuberculosis.
- Advances in treatments for fatal diseases rely on animal tests because other testing methods are not advanced enough.

Protesting against animal testing in Hertfordshire.

Some Christians oppose animal research because:

- They believe that all animals are made by God and so are just as intrinsically valuable as humans.
- Jesus said:

  Are not two sparrows sold for a penny? Yet not one of them will fall to the ground apart from the will of your Father. (Matthew 10:29–31)

  This seems to mean that even the smallest animal is valuable to God.
- They believe that animals have souls just like humans and that, for example, pet animals will go to heaven.
- They are opposed to giving scientists freedom to experiment on animals because they believe that many experiments are performed for curiosity's sake or for cosmetic purposes.

Most Christians support the use of animals for food because they believe that this is why God produced the food chain. They believe what Genesis says:

> *Then God said, 'I give you every seed-bearing plant on the face of the whole earth and every tree that has fruit with seed in it, they will be yours for food. And to all the beasts of the earth and all the birds of the air and all the creatures that move on the ground – everything that has the breath of life in it – I give every green plant for food'. (Genesis 1:29–30)*

and also

> *The fear and the dread of you will fall upon all the beasts of the earth and all the birds of the air, upon every creature that moves along the ground, and upon all the fish of the sea; they are given into your hands. Everything that lives and moves will be food for you. (Genesis 9:2–3)*

The Church recognises the need for animals to be used in certain research to improve medical understanding, veterinary or behavioural knowledge, and to test for the safety of chemicals, and understands that such testing is a requirement of law. It also, however, affirms that responsible stewardship of the natural world requires all animals to receive careful and sympathetic treatment, both during their lives and in the manner of their dying. (Statement from the Church of England)

God entrusted animals to the stewardship of those whom he created in his own image. Hence it is legitimate to use animals for food and clothing. They may be domesticated to help man in his work and leisure. Medical and scientific experiments on animals, if it remains within reasonable limits, is a morally acceptable practice since it contributes to caring for or saving human lives. (Catholic Catechism 2417)

Activities

1. What do you think about using animals for medical research?
2. Explain why Christians have different attitudes to animal rights.
3. Should we use animals for food?

Some Christians are vegetarians and are opposed to animals being used for food. They also oppose the hunting of animals and fishing. They believe this because:

- God is the creator of animals as well as humans.
- Humans have a duty to care for animals as part of their duty as stewards of God's creation.
- Christians should never be cruel, as Jesus said he was the good shepherd who would lay down his life for his sheep rather than let them be harmed, and it is impossible to slaughter animals for food or experiment on them without being cruel.
- Using animals for food is a waste of resources as it takes far more vegetation to raise animals for food than for humans to get the same nutrition from the vegetation.

Practice questions

c) Explain two reasons why Christians work to conserve the environment. In your answer you must refer to a source of wisdom and authority.

d) 'Animals can't have rights.' Evaluate this statement considering arguments for and against. In your response you should:
- refer to Christian teachings
- refer to other Christian points of view and ethical theories
- reach a justified conclusion.

Summary

There are many threats to the environment:

- Pollution damages buildings and can cause major health problems.
- The burning of fossil fuels causes global warming which could cause the ice caps to melt, leaving some towns and cities under water.
- Non-renewable resources such as oil, natural gas and metals cannot be replaced and so will disappear.

Christians believe that God gave humans the stewardship of the earth, so they have a duty to look after the environment and therefore Christians should:

- reduce carbon dioxide emissions by using renewable ways of producing electricity
- employ more energy efficiency
- use more efficient means of waste disposal: recycling, nuclear reprocessing and geological storage.

The Church of England is encouraging Christians to be better stewards through its Shrinking the Footprint campaign. Some Christians are in favour of animal rights and oppose the use of animals in research because animals are made by God. Other Christians disagree because the Bible says God gave humans control of animals.

How to answer questions

a) Outline three Christian beliefs about sanctity of life. [3]

Christians believe that human life is holy because it is a gift from God. They believe that human life is to be treated as holy and therefore valued and preserved. They believe that only God should make life and death decisions.

A high mark answer because three correct beliefs are clearly outlined.

b) Explain two reasons why some Christians do not accept euthanasia. [4]

Some Christians regard any form of euthanasia as murder, and murder is banned by God in the Ten Commandments. They also believe in the sanctity of life. Life is created by God and so it is sacred to God. It is up to God, not humans, when people should die. Euthanasia is to put oneself on a par with God, which is condemned in the Bible.

A high mark answer because two correct reasons are given and each reason is developed.

c) Explain two reasons why Christians believe in life after death. In your answer you must refer to a source of wisdom and authority. [5]

Christians believe in life after death because Jesus rose from the dead. All four Gospels record resurrection appearances of Jesus. Clearly, if Jesus rose from the dead, then there is life after death.

Also St Paul teaches in 1 Corinthians 15 that Christians will have a resurrection like that of Jesus, and will have a spiritual resurrection body given to them by God.

A high mark answer because two correct reasons are given and each reason is developed with a reference to the Gospels and 1 Corinthians, which are sources of authority for Christians.

d) 'Christians should be vegetarian.' Evaluate this statement considering arguments for and against. In your response you should:

- **refer to Christian points of view**
- **refer to different Christian points of view**
- **reach a justified conclusion. [12]**

Some Christians would agree with this because they believe that animals have been given life by God, and humans have been given the responsibility to care for them. They claim that Genesis 1:29 gave humans a vegetarian diet: 'every plant yielding seed that is on the face of all the earth, and every tree with seed in its fruit. You shall have them for food.' They also claim that Christians should never be cruel as Jesus said he was the good shepherd who would lay down his life for his sheep rather than let them be harmed, and it is impossible to slaughter animals for food without being cruel.

Other Christians support the use of animals for food because they believe that this is why God produced the food chain. They believe that God recommended meat eating for humans in Genesis 9:2–3, 'Everything that lives and moves will be food for you.' They also point to St Paul's words, 'eat anything sold in the meat market without raising questions of conscience' (1 Corinthians 10:25).

[Continued]

It seems to me that Christians can be justified in either being vegetarians or meat-eaters especially when you think of John Stuart Mill's ethical principle that we should seek the greatest happiness of the greatest number of people which could be used to justify either meat-eating or vegetarianism, and so it cannot be right to say that all Christians should be vegetarian, it must be up to the individual Christian.

A high mark answer because it gives three clear developed Christian reasons for thinking that Christians should be vegetarian. It then gives three reasons for Christians disagreeing and then reaches a fully justified conclusion which uses the ethical principle of utilitarianism.

1a Muslim beliefs

Area of study 2: Introduction (Islam)

For those of you studying the area based on Islam, it is important that you should understand some of the different groups within Islam. This will allow you to understand their beliefs and attitudes.

Islam should be one religion, but within 30 years of Muhammad's death, Islam split into two groups:

- Sunnis: Muslims who follow only the example of Muhammad.
- Shi'as: Muslims who follow the example of Ali, Muhammad's son-in-law, as well as Muhammad.

About 80–85 per cent of Muslims are Sunni, the rest are Shi'a. The first division arose because when Muhammad died, many Muslims believed that the leader should be Ali as he was Muhammad's first convert, closest relative and father of Muhammad's grandchildren. However, the majority of Muslims elected three of Muhammad's best companions as caliphs before eventually Ali was elected as the fourth caliph. After Ali's death, there was more conflict as some Muslims wanted Ali's sons, Hasan and Husayn (who were Muhammad's grandsons), to be caliph, but Hasan was poisoned and Husayn and his followers were massacred at Karbala. Those who followed Ali became Shi'as and those who followed the Umayyad caliphs became Sunnis.

Most Sunni Muslims are not aware of any differences within Sunni Islam and think all Sunnis have the same beliefs of following the Five Pillars and the holy law of Islam known as the Shari'ah. However, there are different groups in Sunni Islam:

- The Salafis (often connected with a Saudi Arabian group which began in the eighteenth century, the Wahhabis) teach that Islam should be based solely on Qur'an and hadith, Muhammad must not be worshipped and festivals connected with him should not be celebrated. They also teach that Muslims should not celebrate birthdays, listen to music, dance, or have their photos taken or displayed (a form of idolatry). They should not worship at the graves of saints or follow special holy men. The Taleban, al-Qaeda and Isis are developments from these groups.
- The most numerous Sunni group among British Muslims is the Barelvi, who originated in northern India as a reaction against Wahhabism. They revere the Prophet Muhammad, celebrate his birthday, do not ban music and dancing, and have close connections with Sufism.

Sufism is the name given to the Islamic mystical movement which tries to unite individual believers with Allah. Some Muslims regard the Sufis as very important because they encourage Muslims to look at their relationship with Allah and emphasise the value of religious experience. Others regard Sufis as non-Muslim because they seem to think that finding Allah is more important than following the Shari'ah and the Five Pillars.

Pilgrims mourning the death of Husayn at the Karbala Mosque.

The Shi'as have split into many different groups. Most Shi'as believe in the Twelve Imams as successors of Ali and that the twelfth Imam did not die, but went into hiding in a mosque in Baghdad and will return before the end of the world. Iran is a Twelver Shi'a country. Ismaili Shi'as believe that the seventh Imam should have been Isma'il and that his descendants are the true Imams. There are many offshoots of the Ismailis such as the Nizari Khojas, whose leader, the Aga Khan, is regarded as the Imam of the age, and the Druze, some of whom believe in reincarnation. Other Muslims have Christian names and some believe there is no need to follow the Five Pillars. Shi'as have their own Shari'ah based on the hadith of Ali as well as the Qur'an and the hadith of Muhammad.

It is important to be aware that the main religion in Britain is Christianity.

Topic 2.1a.1 The six beliefs of Islam

Thinking points

In this topic you need to:

- think about the nature, history and purpose of the six beliefs and their importance for Muslims
- be able to explain and evaluate how the beliefs are understood and expressed in Muslim communities.

The six beliefs of Islam

Sunni Muslims believe that there are six principal beliefs, commonly referred to as articles of faith, that a Muslim must believe to be accepted as a Muslim. These six beliefs are:

- belief in Allah
- belief in His angels
- belief in His holy books
- belief in His messengers
- belief in the Last Day
- belief in life after death.

The first five beliefs are based on Qur'anic verses such as:

> *Whoever disbelieveth in God and His angels and His scriptures and His messengers and the Last Day, he verily wandered far stray.* (4:136)

> *It is righteousness to believe in God and the Last Day and the Angels and the Book and the Messengers.* (2:177)

> *The men of faith. Each one believeth in God and His angels, His books and His apostles.* (2:285)

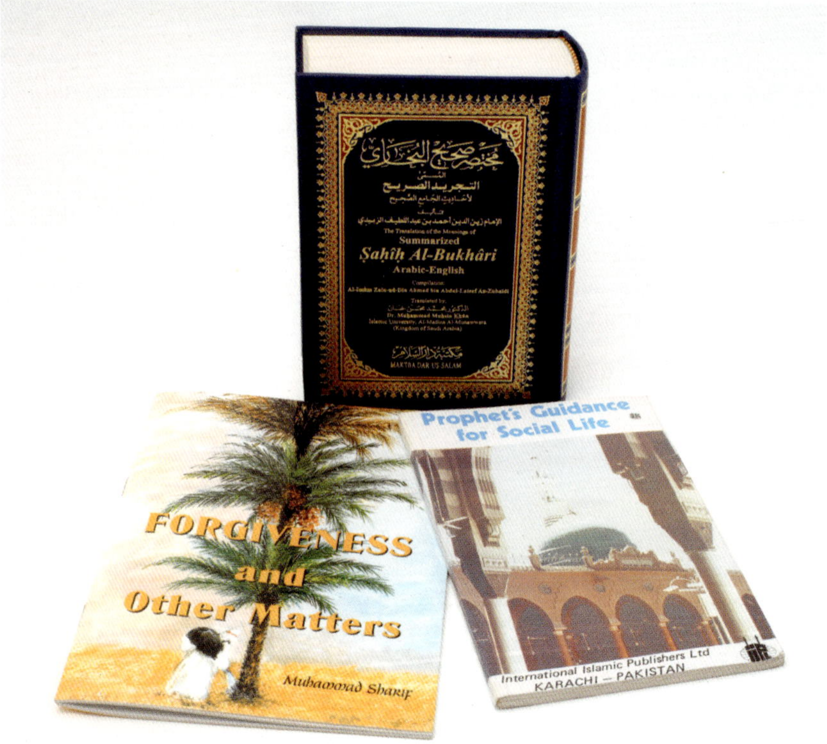

Hadith Sayings of Muhammad, *Social Guidance* and *Forgiveness*.

However, the full six beliefs are based on a **hadith** of the Prophet Muhammad recorded by Sahih Muslim:

> *A man came up to Muhammad and said; 'Prophet of Allah tell me what is* ***Iman*** *(faith)?' Upon this the Holy Prophet replied, 'You must believe in Allah, his angels, his holy books, his Messengers, in the Last Day and life after death.'* (Kitab al-iman 1:4)

Hadith are second in authority to the Qur'an for Sunni Muslims because Sunni Muslims believe:

- Muhammad was the final prophet so his words must be important.
- The best person to interpret the Qur'an must be Muhammad.
- If the Qur'an is not clear, a Muslim must follow hadith.
- Hadith are one of the bases of the **Shari'ah**.

History

There has always been some disagreement among Muslims about the sixth belief. Some believe that it simply refers to life after death, others believe that it refers to 'destiny', meaning Allah's control of the future of humans and their fate in the afterlife, an idea known as predestination (*al-Qadr*, see Topic 2.1a.7, page 175). Perhaps this is why Sunni Muslims now describe the six beliefs using these three categories:

- ***Tawhid*** (the oneness of Allah) – belief in Allah
- ***Risalah*** (the messengers of Allah) – belief in angels, holy books and messengers
- ***Akirah*** (the last things) – belief in the Last Day and life after death.

Importance

The six beliefs are very important for Sunni Muslims because:

- Believing in *Tawhid* shows that Muslims believe God is the only one, and if God is the only one, He must be the creator of everything, and so He must be all-powerful and in control of everything. It also means that God must be present everywhere in the universe He has created and so people can be in contact with God anywhere.
- Believing in *Tawhid* also shows that the God Muslims worship is the same God worshipped by Jews and Christians.
- Believing in angels shows that God can communicate with humans using His special beings.
- Believing in the prophets of God shows that Islam is both the first religion (it began with the Prophet Adam) and the last religion (the final prophet is Muhammad).
- Believing in the holy books of God demonstrates that God has sent books to show humans what to believe and how to live. This belief also shows that the holy books given to Jews and Christians were distorted, and so are no longer God's true word. Most importantly, it shows that the Qur'an is God's final word to humanity, which shows humanity what to believe and how to live.
- Believing in *Akirah* is important for Muslims because believing that all people will be judged by Allah on the Last Day is bound to have a major effect on how Muslims live their lives. Muslims believe they will be judged on the basis of how they have lived their lives and will be sent to heaven or hell as a result of that judgement.

Useful words

Hadith – sayings of the Prophet Muhammad
Iman – faith
Shari'ah – the holy law of Islam which covers all aspects of life
Tawhid – belief in Allah's unity
Risalah – belief in Allah's angels, prophets and holy books
Akirah – belief in the Last Day and life after death

Hadith are things that Muhammad is recorded as having said. There are several collections of hadith, but the ones which most Sunni Muslims accept as genuine are the Hadith of Bukhari and the Hadith of Sahih Muslim. These are regarded as genuine because they have a line of guarantors going back to a companion of the Prophet who heard Muhammad say them.

Activities

1. Why do you think hadith are important for Muslims?
2. What are the six beliefs based on?

The understanding of the six beliefs in Muslim communities today

Useful words

Piety – religious devotion

Activity

How are the six beliefs understood by Muslim communities today?

Most Sunni Muslim communities believe that the six beliefs mean that all people are created equal in the sight of Allah. No one is superior to another except because of their **piety** and righteousness. The beliefs also mean that Muslims are required to respect the dignity of mankind, regardless of religion, race, nationality or place of birth. People should not be judged on factors over which they had no choice such as gender, colour, ethnicity or disability.

The six beliefs mean that in Sunni Islam there are no priests, priesthood or holy men with special authority. The only intermediaries between God and humans are angels, and the only humans given special authority by God were the prophets. However, since belief in *Risalah* means that there can be no prophets after Muhammad, no humans can have God's special authority.

From the six beliefs, Muslims believe that people are born free of any sin and bear no responsibility for the faults and sins of other people. It is only after they reach the age of puberty and knowingly commit sins that people will be held responsible for their actions in this life. Salvation in Islam comes through believing the six beliefs and living in the way set out by Islam.

Shi'a Muslims have expressed the six beliefs as five roots. The five roots are covered in the next section.

Practice questions

c Explain two reasons why the six beliefs are important for Muslims. In your answer you must refer to a source of wisdom and authority.

d 'You can't be a Muslim if you don't believe in the six beliefs.' Evaluate this statement considering arguments for and against. In your answer you should:

- refer to Muslim points of view
- refer to different Muslim points of view
- reach a justified conclusion.

Summary

The six beliefs are the basis of Islam and are summarised by Sunni Muslims as:

- *Tawhid* – belief in only one God
- *Rislah* – belief in God's angels, messengers and holy books
- *Akirah* – belief in the Last Day and life after death.

Topic 2.1a.2 The five roots in Shi'a Islam

The five roots in Shi'a Islam

Shi'a Muslims have five roots of faith (known as **Usul ad-din**), which are the basis of Shi'a faith. The roots are:

- Belief in the oneness of Allah (*Tawhid*) and all Allah's characteristics that come from his oneness:

  Say, 'He is God, the One and Only, God the Eternal, the Absolute; He begetteth not nor is He begotten; and there is none like unto Him.' (Surah 112)

- Belief in Allah's justice (***Adalat***). Allah is described in the Qur'an as 'the All-just'. Justice means fairness and the maintenance of what is right. Muslims believe that Allah created the world in a just way. Shi'a Muslims believe the universe works according to laws established by Allah and the way it operates is fair and just.
- Belief in Allah's prophets from Adam to Muhammad (**Nubuwwah**).
- Belief in the successors of Muhammad (**imamah**) and belief that chosen descendants of the Prophet Muhammad were given special powers by Allah. The Imam is the one who determines what the Qur'an means and who determines what the law should be – the problem is to know what the Imam says! There is a Shi'a hadith which says,

  whosoever knows not the Imam of his age dies the death of a heathen.

  Some Shi'as believe that specially chosen descendants of the prophet are in touch with the **Hidden Imam** and pass on his messages; others believe that specially chosen leaders called **mujtahids** or **ayatollahs** interpret his messages.
- Belief in the Day of Judgement, with judgement being based on believing the five roots and following the Shi'a Shari'ah (which is based on hadith from Imam Ali as well the Prophet Muhammad).

History, purpose and importance

The five roots developed in order to sum up what one must believe to be a Shi'a Muslim. They are based on the Qur'an and the teachings of the Twelve Imams, especially when it became necessary to differentiate Shi'a beliefs from those of the Sunnis. At one point, some Shi'a scholars taught that only belief in the Oneness of Allah, the prophets of Allah and the Day of Judgement were essential beliefs for being a Muslim, and belief in the Imams and Allah's justice were what differentiated Shi'as from Sunnis. However, nowadays Shi'as regard belief in all five roots as essential.

The five roots are important because:

- They are the basis of Shi'a Islam; it is from the roots that the religion grows.
- They are the five principles of faith and show a person what they must believe to be a Muslim.

Thinking points

In this topic you need to:

- think about the nature, history and purpose of the five roots in Shi'a Islam, and their importance for different Shi'a communities today
- be able to explain and evaluate the importance of the five roots.

Useful words

Usul ad-din – the five roots of Shi'a Islam
Adalat – God's attribute of justice
Nubuwwah – prophets of God
Imamah – belief in the successors of the Prophet Muhammad. For Shi'as, Imam is a successor, but 'imam' with a small 'i' is a prayer leader for Sunnis
Hidden Imam – the twelfth Imam who disappeared and is believed to be in contact with the ayatollahs
Mujtahid – a Shi'a scholar with sufficient training and knowledge to interpret the Shari'ah
Ayatollah – the highest ranking religious leader in Twelver Shi'ism

Activities

1. What are the five roots based on?
2. What are the main differences and similarities between the six beliefs and the five roots?

Qom is one of the holiest cities in Iran and has the largest theology school in Iran.

- They come from the teachings of the Qur'an and the Twelve Imams, which means they are of utmost important to Shi'a Muslims.
- Shi'a Muslims believe that unless they understand and believe the five roots, they will not be able to perform the acts of worship necessary to live the Muslim life.
- They are the beliefs that Muslims must hold if their practices are to be correct and to ensure that they go to heaven.

Importance in different Shi'a communities

There are many different **sects** within Shi'a Islam (although the vast majority of Shi'as are Twelvers who believe in the Twelve Imams and all five roots) and their origins have led to the five roots having different levels of importance, in particular the fourth root about the successor of Muhammad.

The **Ismaili** Shi'as (Seveners) believe that the seventh imam, Isma'il, was the final Imam. The Nizari Khoja branch of Ismailis believe that the **Imamate** continued from Isma'il to the present day, that there is no Hidden Imam and that their current leader, the Aga Khan, is the Imam. The Druze (found mainly in Syria, Lebanon and Israel) believe in reincarnation as part of the afterlife and accept a **Fatimid caliph**, al-Hakim, as the final Imam.

The **Ahmadiyya**, who developed from Ismailis in Pakistan 150 years ago, accept the Sunni six beliefs rather than the Shi'a five roots, although they believe that their founder, Mirza Ahmad, received a special message.

Sunnis and the five roots

Sunnis accept four of the five roots since they are contained in the six beliefs. Root 1 is *Tawhid*, and Sunnis believe that the second root, God's justice, is part of God's oneness. Root 3 (belief in the prophets from Adam to Muhammad) is *Risalah* and Root 5 (belief in the Day of Judgement) is *Akirah*. However, Sunnis cannot accept Root 4 (belief in the successors of Muhammad) since they believe that Muhammad was the last of the prophets and there can be no messengers after him. Root 4 is the basis of conflicts between Shi'as and Sunnis.

Useful words

Sects – group with different religious beliefs from those of a larger group to which they belong
Ismaili – Shi'as who believe that the seventh Imam, Isma'il, was the final Imam
Imamate – the office of the Imam
Fatimid – an Ismaili caliphate that ruled North Africa from 909CE to 1171CE
Caliph – leader of the Islamic community
Ahmadiyya – a Muslim sect founded in Pakistan by Yirza Ahmad

Activity

Why are there different understandings of the five roots among Shi'a Muslims?

Summary

The five roots are the basic beliefs of Shi'a Muslims. They are belief in God's oneness, God's justice, God's messengers from Adam to Muhammad, the Last Judgement and Muhammad's successors. Sunni Muslims do not accept the root about Muhammad's successors and some Shi'a groups do not accept that there were twelve successors.

Practice questions

c Explain two reasons why the five roots are important for Shi'a Muslims. In your answer you must refer to a source of wisdom and authority.

d 'It doesn't matter what you believe as long as you worship God and live a good life.' Evaluate this statement considering arguments for and against. In your answer you should:

- refer to Muslim points of view
- refer to different Muslim points of view
- reach a justified conclusion.

Topic 2.1a.3 The nature of Allah

Allah

Muslims always refer to God as **Allah** because this is the word used for God in the Qur'an and is the word the Prophet Muhammad used for God.

Allah is the Arabic for God, but, unlike the English word God, Allah has no plural form. It is impossible to say Allahs in Arabic, so referring to God as Allah is confirming the absolutely fundamental Muslim belief about God: that Allah is the one and only God.

Muslim beliefs about the characteristics of God are found in the book he has given to the world, the Qur'an. Muslims believe that the Qur'an has total authority because they believe that the Qur'an:

- contains God's actual words to humanity
- was revealed to Muhammad in such a way that it can never be distorted
- is God's final word: there will never be another book from God
- tells humans all they need to know about God, religion and how to live their lives.

Muslims believe that God's nature is shown in the 99 names of God which can be found in the Qur'an. These names are the titles given to God within the Qur'an itself and include such titles as:

- the Creator
- the Tremendous
- the Bestower
- the All-knowing
- the Ever-providing
- the All-seeing
- the Judge.

Many Muslims like to remind themselves of God's nature by having a rosary of 33 beads (which they pass through their fingers three times) or 99 beads to remind themselves of what God is like and how great He is.

> *This is the Book, in it is guidance sure without doubt to those who fear Allah.* (Sura 2:2)

A *shahadah* inside the Taynal Mosque, Tripoli, Lebanon.

Thinking points

In this topic you need to:

- think about how the characteristics of Allah are revealed in the Qur'an: *Tawhid*, immanence, transcendence, omnipotence, beneficence and mercy, fairness and justice, *Adalat* in Shi'a Islam
- be able to explain and evaluate the importance of these characteristics for Muslims.

Useful words

Allah – the Arabic for God

Activity

Why do you think the Qur'an has total authority for Muslims?

The Qur'an

The main characteristics of God revealed in the Qur'an are considered below.

Oneness (*Tawhid*)

Tawhid is belief in Allah's oneness. This is the absolute basis of Islam, as the first part of the Muslim creed (***shahadah***, the first pillar) states, 'I bear witness that there is no god, but God'.

Allah's oneness means that he has no partners, no helpers and especially no equals. Muslims feel that the Christian belief in God as a Trinity, and especially the belief in Jesus as the Son of God, is an insult to Allah's oneness.

Belief in Allah's oneness means that Allah must be the creator of everything since he is the only God. It also means that Allah must be all-powerful and in control of everything and that Allah must be present in the universe He has created.

> *And verily, We have sent among every nation a Messenger proclaiming: 'Worship Allah Alone, and avoid all false deities'.*
> *(Surah 16:36)*

Omnipotence

Two of the **ninety-nine names** of Allah are: 'the Absolute' and 'the All-powerful' and it is a fundamental belief that Allah has complete power. He has created the universe and so must have complete power over it.

This belief in Allah's **omnipotence** can be seen in the name of the religion. Islam means submission to God's will and Muslims are those who have submitted their wills to God's will because God is so great.

Allah's omnipotence also implies his **omniscience**, as another of his names is 'the All-knowing'. The first **surah** of the Qur'an says that Allah is 'the Master of the Day of Judgement' and for Allah to be in charge of the Day of Judgement, he must know everything about what humans do in order to have the power and authority to judge them.

Beneficence and mercy

Every surah except Surah 9 begins with the ***bismillah***:

> *In the name of Allah, Most Gracious, Most Merciful,*

showing that a major characteristic of Allah is his beneficence. This means not only that Allah is good, but that he is kind and loving to his creation. Islam teaches that when God created humans, he did not leave them alone to get on with their lives as best they could, he sent prophets with his word to show humans how to live their lives in the best way so that they would go to heaven.

The Qur'an also teaches that Allah's mercy is such that if people are not perfect and fail in their attempts to live the perfect Muslim life, he will forgive them. He is 'the All-forgiving', which is why Muslims believe that trying to be a good Muslim by doing things like fasting in Ramadan (the pillar of ***sawm***, see page 164) and going on pilgrimage to Makkah (the pillar of ***hajj***, see page 273) can ensure that a Muslim's sins are forgiven by Allah.

Useful words

Shahadah – the Muslim creed and first pillar
Ninety-nine names – the titles or characteristics given to Allah in the Qur'an
Omnipotence – unlimited power
Omniscience – God's characteristic of being all-knowing
Surah – a chapter of the Qur'an (there are 114 surahs)
Bismillah – the words at the beginning of each surah, 'in the name of Allah, the Merciful, the Compassionate'
Sawm – fasting, the fourth pillar
Hajj – pilgrimage, the fifth pillar

Activities

1. Look at the illustration on page 157. Why do you think many Muslims prefer to translate this as, 'There is no deity except Allah'?
2. How do the words Islam and Muslim show Muslims' belief in God's omnipotence?

Justice (*Adalat*)

Allah is described in the Qur'an as 'the All-just'. Justice means fairness and the maintenance of what is right. Muslims believe that Allah created the world in a just way. They believe that the universe works according to laws established by Allah and the way it operates is fair and just. The composition of the earth provides food and liquid for humans which enables them to survive and prosper. Allah has designed everything to work well together and provide a fair life for people.

Muslims believe that Allah's justice is also shown in the way he has provided his holy law, the **Shari'ah**, to make sure that humans deal fairly and justly with each other. They believe that if everyone followed the Shari'ah, the world would have a just society.

Allah's justice is also shown in the way he deals with humans. At the end of the world all humans will be brought before the court of Allah to be judged by him and he will judge everyone justly. The good will be rewarded and the evil punished, which is the basis of justice.

> *In Allah's creation there is no extremism, immoderation or contradiction; the earth is most rightly and justly spaced apart from the sun. If the earth were closer to the sun, it would be a blazing furnace; if it were farther, it would be an ice grave. Distances between the sun and the earth, and between all of the heavenly objects are most rightly and justly designed.* ('Understanding God's Attributes', Dr Muhammad Ratib An-Nabulsi, www.onislam.net)

Transcendence

Transcendence refers to the aspect of God's nature and power which is totally beyond the material and so beyond human experience. This attribute can be seen in some of the 99 names of God to be found in the Qur'an. 'The Greatest', 'the Highest', 'the Glorious', 'the Supreme One', 'the Magnificent' all show how far beyond any human description God is.

Immanence

Although Islam believes that Allah is transcendent, is also teaches that Allah has the attribute of immanence, he is close to humans and can be contacted by humans:

> *We are nearer to man than his jugular vein.* (Surah 50:16)

This is Allah's attribute of immanence; Allah is within the universe he has created:

> *Whithersoever ye turn, there is the presence of God.* (Surah 2:115)

> *When My servants ask thee concerning Me, I am indeed close to them: I listen to the prayer of every suppliant when he calleth on Me.* (Surah 2:186)

Transcendence and immanence are a great mystery in Islam, and indeed in most religions. God is both far beyond humans and yet also closer to them than their own jugular veins.

Activity

Which characteristic of Allah is most important for Muslims and why do you think so?

Useful words

Shari'ah – the holy law of Islam

> *Thy Lord is self-sufficient, full of Mercy: if it were God's will, God could destroy you, and in your place appoint whom God will as your successors, even as God raised you up from the posterity of other people.* (Surah 6:133)

> *God! There is no god but He – the Loving, the Self-Subsisting, Eternal. No slumber can seize Him nor sleep. His are all things in the heavens and on earth.* (Surah 2:255)

> *God Most Gracious is firmly established on the throne of authority. To Him belongs what is in the heavens and on earth and all between them.* (Surah 20:5)

> *The most beloved of speech according to Allah is when the servant says, 'Subhanallahi wa bihamdihi' [How Transcendent is Allah and we praise him!].* (Muslim)

Why the characteristics of Allah are important for Muslims

Tawhid

Belief in *Tawhid* is important for Muslims because it means that:

- There is only one God who created everything that exists.
- If one God created everything, then Muslims must try to preserve the oneness of the world he has created.
- If the universe was made by and belongs to one God, then the Muslim community must itself be a unity (this is called the ***ummah***).
- There can only be one law for Muslims, Allah's law, which is known as the Shari'ah.
- Muslims must only worship Allah; the worst sin a Muslim can commit is the sin of ***shirk***, which is to associate others with Allah. This is why there can be no images or statues in the mosque and why Muslims decorate with calligraphy rather than representational art.

Useful words

Ummah – the Muslim community

Shirk – the sin of associating other things with God; it is the worst sin

Omnipotence

Belief in Allah's omnipotence is important for Muslims because:

- It means that Muslims believe Allah is in control of everything that happens.
- It means that Allah has a plan for the world and the power to make sure that that plan actually happens.
- Part of that plan is that God will bring the world to an end on the Last Day and God's omnipotence means that he has the power to do this:

Blessed be He in whose hands is dominion, and He over all things hath power. (Surah 67:1)

Benevolence

Belief in Allah's benevolence is important for Muslims because:

- If God is compassionate and merciful to sinners, Muslims should be merciful and forgiving to those who cause them offence.
- On the Day of Judgement, Muslims will be able to request Allah's mercy for their sins, but how can Muslims ask for Allah's forgiveness if they themselves are not prepared to forgive?

Justice

Belief in Allah's justice is important for Muslims because:

- The Qur'an teaches that God is a just God who will reward the good and punish the bad on the Last Day; therefore Muslims need to work for justice, so they are not sent to hell on the Last Day.
- Islamic teaching on the Last Day is concerned with the need for the good to be rewarded and the evil punished, which is the basis of justice.
- The fact that Allah is just means that Muslims must behave justly to other people and ensure that the world is governed in a fair way by following the Shari'ah.

Activities

1. Do you think it is possible for God to be both transcendent and immanent?
2. Do you think it is possible for humans to say what God is like?

- Allah's justice means that Muslims must work to make sure that all people have equal rights before the law and that Muslims should work for a fairer sharing of the earth's resources through the pillar of *zakah* (see page 269) and groups such as Muslim Aid and Islamic Relief.

Transcendence

Belief in transcendence is important for Muslims because:

- It shows that Allah is worthy of humanity's worship and praise since he is greater than anything.
- It shows that Allah is in control because nothing is as great as Allah.
- It shows that Allah is not restricted in any way – by time, space or matter. He is **self-subsistent** and eternal and so can be contacted by humans wherever they are and whenever they ask.

Immanence

Belief in Allah's immanence is important for Muslims because:

- It means that Allah is within the universe he has created and so science and learning can comprehend Allah.
- It means that, despite his greatness, Allah can be contacted by humans.
- It means that Allah is present for all the religious activities of a Muslim, especially such things as ***salah*** and *sawm*.

Conclusion

For Muslim theologians, all the characteristics of Allah can be summed up by *Tawhid*. Everything comes from Allah's oneness to express their faith in the oneness of Allah.

Practice questions

c Explain two reasons why God's justice is important for Muslims. In your answer you must refer to a source of wisdom and authority.

d 'No one knows what God is like.' Evaluate this statement considering arguments for and against. In your answer you should:
- refer to Muslim points of view
- reach a justified conclusion.

Useful words

Self-subsistent – without dependence on or support from anything else
Salah – ritual prayer, the second pillar

Summary

Muslims call God Allah because this is the word used in the Qur'an. The Qur'an says that the main characteristics of God are:

- oneness
- omnipotence (all-powerful)
- beneficence (love and compassion) and mercy
- justice (*adalat*)
- transcendence
- immanence.

God's oneness is the basis of Islam and is the first part of the Muslim creed.

Topic 2.1a.4 *Risalah* (prophets)

Thinking points

In this topic you need to:

- think about the nature and history of prophethood, especially the Qur'an's teachings about the prophets: Adam, Ibrahim, Isma'il, Musa, Dawud, Isa and Muhammad
- be able to explain what these beliefs teach Muslims, and evaluate their importance for Muslims.

Useful words

Khalifahs – Allah's stewards or vicegerents
Vicegerent – a person appointed to look after things on behalf of a ruler

The nature of the prophets

Muslims believe that Allah created humans to look after the earth for him (Allah's ***khalifahs*** or **vicegerents**) and humans need prophets to know how to do this. Muslims do not believe that Islam began with Muhammad; rather, it began with the creation of humans and so it is the original religion begun by Allah and his first prophet, Adam.

Islam teaches that the prophets were all ordinary human beings; what made them different was that they were chosen to receive Allah's messages. Muslims believe it is wrong to treat prophets in the same way Christians treat Jesus, because they are not divine. All the prophets except Isa were married and had children.

However, most Muslims believe that the prophets were sinless after they had been called by Allah to be his messenger. This is why they believe that prophets should be blessed whenever their name is mentioned: 'Peace be upon him' (p.b.u.h. or in Arabic *alayhi al-salām*, a.s.), although many Muslims use s.a.w. or s.a.a.w. ('May Allah honour him and grant him peace'; *ṣallā llāhu ʿalay-hi wa-sallam* in Arabic) when they mention Muhammad.

According to the Qur'an, each prophet was given Allah's word for their generation, so each prophet brought Islam in its perfect form. However, humans either ignored, distorted or forgot Allah's word so that Allah had to keep sending a new prophet until, Muslims believe, Muhammad was given the Qur'an in a form that could never be distorted.

Arabic calligraphy for the name of Muhammad and peace be upon him.

Activities

1. Which prophets were married?
2. Why did Allah have to keep sending new prophets?

The main prophets of Islam are:

Adam

According to the Qur'an, the first prophet of Islam was the first man, Adam. He was created by Allah to be Allah's vicegerent to look after the earth for Allah in the way Allah wanted. At first, Adam and his wife **Hawwa** (Eve), though she is not named in the Qur'an, lived in the Garden, and were told by Allah not to eat the fruit of a certain tree. However, Iblis tempted them by telling them that Allah did not want them to eat because he did not want them to become like the angels. Adam and Hawwa succumbed and ate the fruit and so had to leave the Garden.

Allah placed Adam and his wife on earth to live. They realised they had been wrong to follow Iblis' advice and asked Allah for forgiveness. Allah forgave them and gave Adam his guidance, and in Islam those who receive Allah's guidance are his prophets. The hadith record that as a sign of his thanks for Allah's forgiveness and guidance, Adam built a House for Allah in **Makkah** (Mecca) called the **Ka'aba**.

Useful words

Hawwa – the first woman, Adam's wife (Eve)
Makkah – the city in Arabia where Muhammad was born
Ka'aba – the shrine in Makkah which Muslims face to say prayers and which is the centre of *hajj*
Ishaq – Ibrahim's son Isaac, the father of the Jewish people

Ibrahim (Abraham)

Muslims regard Ibrahim as the greatest of the prophets before Isa. He was born into a polytheistic (worshipping many gods) family, which shows that the message of the previous prophets had been ignored or forgotten. However, Ibrahim rejected polytheism. He argued with his father and his father's people about the wrongness of false gods. He broke down the idols they worshipped to show that they had no power. When the people tried to burn Ibrahim, Allah saved him from the fire. So he condemned idolatry and showed the people the truth of Islam.

Abraham was not a Jew nor yet a Christian, but he was true in faith and bowed his will to God's, which is Islam. (Surah 3:67)

Say ye: 'We believe in Allah and the revelation given to us, and to Abraham, Ismail, Isaac, Jacob and the Tribes, and that given to Moses and Jesus, and that given to all prophets from their Lord: We make no difference between one and another of them: And we bow to Allah in Islam.' (Surah 2:136)

The Qur'an records that Ibrahim and his wife had no children into their old age, but then Allah granted them the gift of two sons, Isma'il and **Ishaq**. Muslims believe that Ishaq was the prophet for the Jews and Isma'il the prophet for the Arabs.

The Qur'an records that Ibrahim had a vision from Allah where he sacrificed his son. His son urged him to obey Allah's command in the vision, but as Ibrahim was about to sacrifice his son, Allah called out and stopped the sacrifice and rewarded them for being obedient to his will and doing right. Ibrahim and Isma'il are also recorded in the Qur'an as restoring the Ka'aba after it had been destroyed in Noah's flood. They established the Ka'aba as a place of assembly and pilgrimage for Muslims.

Ibrahim was given the holy book of Sahifah (The Scrolls of Ibrahim), the first of the holy books mentioned in the Qur'an. The Qur'an teaches that Ibrahim was specially chosen by Allah to deliver 'A message for the nations' (Surah 6:90), and that all the prophets between Ibrahim and Muhammad (Moses, David, Solomon, John the Baptist and Jesus) were descendants of Ibrahim. Muslims regard Ibrahim as a role model for how to live the Muslim life.

Abraham was indeed a model devoutly obedient to God, true in faith, and he joined not gods with God. (Surah 16:120)

Activity

Look at the quotation from Surah 2:136 above. What does it tell us about Muslim beliefs?

The holy Ka'aba. Muslims believe the blocks are the ones used by Ibrahim and Isma'il.

Isma'il: he was strictly true to what he promised, and he was an apostle and a prophet. (Surah 19:54)

Also mention in the Book (the story of) Moses: for he was specially chosen, and he was a messenger (and) a prophet. And we called him from the right side of Mount (Sinai), and made him draw near to Us, for mystic (converse). And, out of Our Mercy, We gave him his brother Aaron, (also) a prophet. (Surah 19:51–53)

Isma'il (Ishmael)

As discussed above, Isma'il was the eldest son of Ibrahim (in Muslim tradition his mother was Ibrahim's second wife Hagar) who helped his father in the rebuilding of the Ka'aba and establishing it as a place of pilgrimage. He was also the one who encouraged Ibrahim to sacrifice him to show his obedience to Allah. Isma'il is regarded as the prophet to the Arabs and is believed by Muslims to be the ancestor of Muhammad.

Musa (Moses)

Musa has more mentions in the Qur'an than any other prophet. The Qur'an records how Musa was born a Jew but brought up by Pharaoh's wife. He killed an Egyptian and fled to Midian, where God called him to go back to Egypt and lead the Jews out of slavery in Egypt and into God's promised land. Musa was chosen to receive the holy book of Tawrat (Torah), but the people rejected or distorted his message.

Dawud (David)

The Qur'an teaches that Dawud, the great king of Israel, was chosen as a prophet and was given the holy book of Zabur (Psalms) because of the distortion of the Tawrat. The Zabur was not written down until long after Dawud's death, so it was never written down properly. However, part of the Zabur is recorded in the Qur'an (this is the only quotation from the Bible in the Qur'an):

Before this we wrote in the Psalms, after the message given to Moses: 'My servants the righteous shall inherit the earth.' (Surah 21:105 and Psalm 37:29)

Activity

Look at the photo above. Why do you think the Ka'aba is important to Muslims?

Isa (Jesus)

Isa and his mother Maryam are major figures in the Qur'an. Surah 19 is called Maryam and is all about her and Isa. This surah records that Isa had a virgin birth. His mother never had sex and was 'the most virtuous of women' who conceived Isa by the power of Allah. The Qur'an records many miracles of Isa such as healing lepers, making the dumb speak and the lame walk, raising the dead and making clay birds fly. According to the Qur'an, the Jewish authorities wanted to have Isa executed and attempted to crucify him, but Allah prevented this from happening:

> *They said in boast, 'We killed Christ Jesus, the son of Mary, the Apostle of God'; but they killed him not nor crucified him, but so it was made to appear to them.* (Surah 4:157)

Muslims believe that Allah took Isa to heaven from the cross so that Isa never died.

Isa was given the holy book Injil (Gospel). However, the Qur'an makes it plain that he was only a prophet, an ordinary man, not the son of God:

> *Christ the son of Mary was no more than an Apostle: many were the apostles that passed away before him. His mother was a woman of truth. They both had to eat their daily bread.* (Surah 5:78)

Muhammad

There are many references in the Qur'an to the Messenger of Allah, the Apostle of Allah and Allah's prophet, which are clearly references to Muhammad. These references show that:

- Muhammad was called by Allah to bring his final message to humanity.
- His message must be followed and those who follow his message will be rewarded, but those who reject it will be punished.
- His life was a perfect example for people to follow.
- The message of the prophets was distorted or forgotten so Allah sent Muhammad with a message that could not be distorted and a holy book (the Qur'an) which could never be distorted.

However, there are only four references to Muhammad's name in the Qur'an plus one that refers to Ahmad which is assumed to refer to Muhammad:

> *Muhammad is no more than an Apostle: many were the Apostles that passed away before him.* (Surah 3:144)
>
> *Muhammad is not the father of any of your men, but he is the Apostle of God, and the Seal of the prophets.* (Surah 33:40)
>
> *Those who believe and work deeds of righteousness, and believe in the revelation sent down to Muhammad – for it is the truth from their Lord – He will remove from them their ills.* (Surah 47:2)
>
> *Muhammad is the Apostle of God; and those who are with him are strong against Unbelievers, but compassionate amongst each other.* (Surah 48:29)
>
> *Jesus the son of Mary said, 'O Children of Israel! I am the apostle of God sent to you confirming the Law which came before me, and giving glad tidings of an Apostle to come after me, whose name shall be Ahmad.'* (Surah 61:6)

Activities

1. Why might Christians disagree with what the Qur'an says about Isa?
2. Why do you think Muhammad is so important to Muslims?

So Muhammad is:

- The final prophet; there will never be another prophet.
- The final example of how humans should live.
- The seal of the prophets; he acts like the seal people used to prove origin and to show that the message hadn't been tampered with. As the seal, Muhammad is the final prophet with Allah's final message for humanity.

What the prophets teach Muslims

- Islam is the original religion. Allah taught Islam to his first prophet, Adam, and then taught the same religion to all the prophets through to the final prophet, Muhammad.
- Every prophet was called by Allah and given Allah's true message to give to the people of earth and so Muslims should follow the teachings of the prophets.
- Prophets were just ordinary human beings who were chosen by Allah to be his messengers. They were not angels, they were not divine. Even Isa was only human even though he had a virgin birth. This teaches Muslims that they should have nothing to do with religions which claim any sort of divine status for their leaders and that Muslims should beware of treating their prophets as if they were semi-divine.
- Because prophets were given their message from Allah in the form of a holy book, Muslims should follow the teachings of the holy book given by God to his final prophet, Muhammad – the Qur'an.
- People before Muhammad were able to ignore, forget or even distort Allah's message, so Muslims should treat the Qur'an respectfully and make sure they do not distort it. They must also read it regularly so that there is no chance of them ignoring or forgetting its message.
- Muhammad received Allah's message in a way that could not be distorted or forgotten, so his message is the final message from Allah, which means that Islam is both the first religion (God sent it to Adam) and the last religion (Muhammad was the final prophet).
- All the prophets lived lives whose example could be followed, but Muhammad's has to be the most important one. Muhammad was the final prophet, there will be no more prophets of God and so Muhammad's life provides a perfect example for Muslims. Good Muslims should follow the **Sunnah** of the Prophet Muhammad because his is the last example people have of how to live their lives.

Useful words

Sunnah – the example and way of life of the Prophet Muhammad

Summary

Muslims believe that God sent prophets with his message telling humans how to look after the world. Prophets were ordinary human beings who brought God's message in a perfect form, but the messages of Adam, Ibrahim, Ism'ail, Musa, Dawud and Isa were altered or forgotten so that God had to send his final message to Muhammad in a form that could never be altered or forgotten. This means there can be no more prophets after Muhammad.

Practice questions

c Explain two beliefs which the prophets teach Muslims.

d 'Prophets show how much God loves humanity.' Evaluate this statement considering arguments for and against. In your answer you should:

- refer to Muslim points of view
- reach a justified conclusion.

Topic 2.1a.5 Muslim holy books

The nature, history and purpose of Muslim holy books

Muslims believe that God sent prophets (*rasul*) with his message and the most important of these were given the message in the form of God's holy book.

There is some dispute about the exact nature of the holy books (***kitub***):

- Most Muslims believe that God made one holy book, the Qur'an, which is his eternal word, and each holy book given to a prophet was simply a copy of that 'heavenly original'. Unfortunately, over time these holy books became distorted by humans. Sometimes God sent a prophet to correct the distortions, but on four occasions he sent a new copy of the holy book until finally he sent the Qur'an to Muhammad in a form that could never be distorted.
- Some Muslim scholars believe that the earlier holy books were not the Qur'an as they only contained certain parts of the Qur'an. They contained God's message appropriate to the needs of the prophet's time. They believe that only Muhammad was given God's full eternal word in the undistortable Qur'an.

The purpose of holy books was so that Muslims would know what to believe and how to live. Muslims believe that God created humans to look after the world for him in the way he wanted – they were to be God's *khalifahs* or vicegerents. However, in order to do this, they needed to know what God's way of living was.

The history of holy books begins with Adam. God gave the Qur'an to his first Prophet, Adam, so that he could tell people what to believe and how to live. Unfortunately, according to Islam, humans subsequently distorted God's words and so God had to send other messengers.

Muslims believe that God sent his word three times to prophets of Judaism:

- Prophet Ibrahim (Abraham) was given the message in a book known as **Sahifa Ibrahim** (the Scrolls of Abraham).

  But We have already given the family of Abraham the Book and Wisdom, and conferred upon them a great kingdom. (Qur'an 4:54).

  However, this book became so distorted that all copies were lost.
- Prophet Musa (Moses) was given the message in the holy book known as **Tawrat** (Torah). Although Musa's message became distorted, some parts remained in the Torah of the Old Testament, which is why many elements of Judaism (including the food laws) are still very similar to Islam.

  It was We who revealed the to Moses: therein was guidance and light. By its standards have been judged the Jews by the prophets who bowed (as in Islam) to God's will by the Rabbis and the Doctors of Law: for to them was entrusted the protection of God's Book. (Surah 5:47)

Thinking points

In this topic you need to:

- think about the nature, history and purpose of Muslim holy books: the Qur'an, Tawrat (Torah), Zabur (Psalms), Injil (Gospel) and Sahifah (Scrolls)
- be able to explain why the holy books are important in Muslim life.

We have been commanded to believe in previously revealed Books only in the sense of admitting that, before the Qur'an, God also sent down books through His Prophets, that they were all from the same God, the God who sent the Qur'an, and the sending of the Qur'an ... confirms, restates and completes those divine instructions. ('Towards Understanding Islam', Abul Ala Mawdudi, Islamic Foundation, 1980)

Useful words

Kitub – holy books (singular *kitab*)
Sahifa Ibrahim – the holy book given to Ibrahim (Abraham)
Tawrat – the holy book given to Musa (Moses)

Activity

Look at the quotation above and put it into your own words.

Useful words

Zabur – the holy book given to Dawud (David)
Injil – the Gospel given to Isa (Jesus)
Apostles – Prophets or messengers: the titles given to those who brought God's message

And in their footsteps We sent Jesus the son of Mary, confirming the Law that had come before him: We sent him the Gospel: therein was guidance and light, and confirmation of the Law that had come before him: a guidance and an admonition to those who fear Allah. (Surah 5:46)

Activities

1. Which is the only other Muslim holy book actually quoted in the Qur'an?
2. Look at the picture of holy books below. Why is it difficult to find them in their original form?
3. What are the differences between the Injil of Islam and the Gospels in the Christian New Testament?

- Prophet Dawud (David) was given the message in the **Zabur** (Psalms), some of which, Muslims believe, have survived undistorted in the Psalms of the Old Testament. The Qur'an has a direct quotation from the Psalms of the Old Testament in Surah 21:105,

  Before this We wrote in the Psalms, after the message given to Moses, 'My servants the righteous shall inherit the earth',

  which quotes Psalm 37:29:

  We have sent thee inspiration as We sent it to Noah and the Messengers after him ... And to David We gave the Psalms. (Surah 4:163)

Injil

The final prophet before Muhammad was Isa (Jesus), who was given the holy book the **Injil** (Gospel). However, Muslims believe the holy book Injil was not the same as the New Testament or the four Gospels, it was the book given to Isa by God which he then preached to the Jewish people:

Muslims believe that the Gospels in the New Testament are human records of what people remembered of the true Gospel preached by Isa.

The main distortions of the Injil contained in the New Testament are that:

- Isa was the Son of God when he was really the prophet of God.
- Isa died on the cross when Muslims believe he was taken to heaven.
- Christians removed those parts of the Injil which foretold the coming of Muhammad.

Christ Jesus the son of Mary was no more than an Apostle of God, and His Word, which He bestoweth on Mary, and a Spirit proceeding from Him: so believe in God and His ***apostles****. Say not 'Trinity': desist: it will be better for you: for God is One God. Glory be to Him far exalted is He above having a son. (Surah 4:171)*

A selection of Islamic holy books.

The Qur'an

Muslims believe that God decided that his word needed revealing in a new way because:

- He had sent it five times and each time it had been distorted.
- People had ignored or disobeyed what God's word said.
- People no longer knew what the Qur'an was.

This meant that the Qur'an needed to be sent to a prophet who could not read and write and so would recite God's words. The prophet's only message would be the Qur'an in a form such that the Qur'an could be preserved in a book that could never be distorted.

Muslims believe that Muhammad was the ideal person to receive the revelation because he was highly intelligent; he could not read or write but he had an excellent memory and he had a perfect moral and religious character. This meant that God could give Muhammad his message as a dictation which Muhammad could learn by heart and recite to the people. So Muhammad recited the words God gave him:

> *Proclaim (recite) in the name of thy Lord and Cherisher who created.* (Surah 96:1)

Muhammad ensured that his followers memorised the revelations, although later he had secretaries who wrote down the revelations on whatever came to hand (bits of leather, pottery or paper). Muhammad checked that each written revelation was accurate, then put them into a chest kept by his wife Hafsa. In 631CE Muhammad sorted the revelations into 114 surahs based on their being revealed at the same time or being on a common theme.

History

When Muhammad died, his friend and first convert, **Abu Bak'r**, decided that it was essential for there to be an authorised version of the revelations. As Muhammad had used secretaries to write down the revelations and to help him in sorting out the revelations, Abu Bak'r decided to use the chief secretary, **Zayd ibn Thabit**, to make the authorised version.

The third Caliph, **Uthman** (644–56CE), ordered all the surviving secretaries of Muhammad to meet together to make an official version of the Qur'an based on Abu Bak'r's authorised version. When this was done, all other written versions were destroyed. Uthman organised the Qur'an by length of surah so that Surah 2 is the longest and Surah 114 the shortest. Surah 1 is a call to prayer used by Muslims in the five times a day prayer of *salah*.

Every surah apart from Surah 9 begins with the *bismillah*:

> *'In the name of God, the Merciful, the Compassionate', showing that what follows is the Word of God.*

Muslims believe that the way the Qur'an was revealed to Muhammad and then compiled by the caliphs guarantees that the Arabic Qur'an, as used by Muslims today, is the exact words of God revealed to Muhammad. They believe that the Arabic Qur'an is 'An earthly copy of a heavenly original' because:

- All Arabic Qur'ans today have the same surahs, words and letters.
- All old copies of the Qur'an have the same surahs, words and letters.

Activity

Why might non-Muslims have some doubts about whether the Qur'an came directly from God?

Since Uthman's time, all Qur'ans in existence have had:

- 114 Surahs
- 77,639 Arabic words.

Useful words

Abu Bak'r – Muhammad's friend and first Caliph, who ordered the first collection of the Qur'an
Zayd ibn Thabit – Muhammad's chief secretary, who organised Uthman's Qur'an
Uthman – the third caliph, who ordered the final official copy of the Qur'an

Divergent Muslim views about the importance of the holy books

Muslim beliefs about the holy books revealed before Muhammad received the Qur'an are very significant because they show that God has always made sure people knew what to believe and how to live. They also show that these books are no longer important because they have been distorted and so are no longer God's word. This means that the Jewish Tenakh and the Christian Bible are not holy books for the majority of Muslims.

Other Muslims believe that since the Qur'an refers to these books as holy books, parts of them must still show what God revealed. So they believe that they are still holy and if what they say fits in with what the Qur'an says then their teachings should be followed by Muslims.

Activities

1. Look at the lists of what the Qur'an tells Muslims to believe and do. Which of these would Christians agree with?
2. Do you think non-Muslims would find it hard not to eat pork, drink alcohol or gamble?

The importance of the Qur'an for Muslims today

The belief that the Qur'an used today is the exact Qur'an revealed to Muhammad, an earthly copy of a heavenly original, the very words of God himself, is hugely significant because it means that:

- Everything in the Qur'an must be true because God said it.
- Muslims must believe everything in the Qur'an because all of it is God's words.
- Muslims must follow everything that the Qur'an says if they want to do what God wants them to do.
- Nothing in the Qur'an can be altered because it is the eternal Word of God. There can be no greater authority, for Muslims, than the Qur'an.

The Qur'an tells Muslims what to believe:

- Belief in God as a unity who is omnipotent, omniscient and omnipresent is a fundamental teaching of the Qur'an.
- Belief in God's angels is clearly shown as Jibril revealed the Qur'an to Muhammad.
- Belief in God's messengers and holy books because they are a major theme of the Qur'an.
- Belief in the Last Day and life after death, which are referred to throughout the Qur'an.

The Qur'an sets out how Muslims should live, through:

- regular ritual prayer (*salah*), and assembling for worship on Friday
- fasting during the month of Ramadan (*sawm*) and celebrating the end of fasting with the festival of Id-ul-Fitr
- paying a religious tax to help orphans (*zakah*)
- going on pilgrimage to Makkah, to join in the pilgrimage around the world with the sacrificial festival of Id-ul-Adha
- not eating pork, not drinking alcohol or gambling, and not being involved in interest.

A copy of the Qur'an on a special stand in Dubai.

The importance of the Qur'an is shown in Muslims' daily lives. Muslims for whom Arabic is not their native language learn to read Arabic (even if they don't understand it) so they can read the Qur'an in Arabic, the language in which the Qur'an was revealed. They show they believe the Qur'an is holy by never touching it without first washing their hands (clean hands), always keeping it above all other books, never holding the Qur'an below their waist, and never eating, drinking or talking while reading it.

They also obey what the Qur'an says. A Muslim who performs the pillars does so because it is commanded in the Qur'an. A Muslim who follows the Shari'ah (Islamic law) does so out of respect for the Qur'an.

Practice questions

c Explain two reasons why there are Muslim holy books other than the Qur'an. In your answer you must refer to a source of wisdom and authority.

d 'The Qur'an is God's final word to humanity and so should be obeyed.' Evaluate this statement considering arguments for and against. In your answer you should:

- refer to Muslim points of view,
- refer to different Muslim points of view
- reach a justified conclusion.

Summary

Muslims believe that God sent messengers (prophets) with holy books (*kitub*) which contained God's message on how people should live and what they should believe. God sent the Salifah to Ibrahim, the Tawrat to Musa, the Zabur to Dawud and the Injil to Isa. However, people altered these and God had to send his final word, the Qur'an, in a form that can never be changed. So the Qur'an is the most important book a Muslim can have as it contains God's words on how to live and what to believe.

Topic 2.1a.6 *Malaikah* (angels)

Thinking points

In this topic you need to:

- think about the nature and importance of angels for Muslims and what the Qur'an teaches about Jibril, Mika'il and Izra'il
- be able to explain what these beliefs teach Muslims.

Useful words

Malaikah – angels
Shaytan – the devil

Activities

1. Why do you think Muslims believe God cannot communicate directly with humans?
2. What are the differences between angels and humans?

The nature of angels

Muslims believe that the unity and greatness of Allah mean that he is far too holy to communicate directly with humans.

The Qur'an teaches that Allah created the angels (***malaikah***) as immortal beings without free will. According to the Qur'an, angels are male and have wings. As they have no free will, they obey all of Allah's commands and so never commit sins. Because they are sinless, angels can have direct contact with Allah and pass his messages to humans; therefore Angels are the ones who can act as go-betweens between humans and Allah.

The Qur'an teaches that when he created Adam, Allah ordered the angels to bow down to him because Adam had been able to name Allah's creations while the angels (with no free will) had not. Muslims believe that Iblis (**Shaytan**) was an angel who refused to bow down to Adam and so was sent out of heaven and set up his own kingdom of hell. The Qur'an says that Iblis begged Allah to postpone his punishment for disobedience until the Last Day and this is why Iblis is able to tempt humans to go against Allah (Surah 7:11–18).

Muslims believe that Shaytan set up the kingdom of hell after being sent out of heaven by Allah.

Muslims believe that angels have many functions:

- They praise Allah in heaven.
- They are the guardians of the gates of hell.
- They record the good and bad deeds of humans (humans are often thought to have a recording angel on each shoulder, one writing down good deeds, the other bad deeds) to present to Allah on the Last Day as the basis for his judgement.

Allah created angels from intellect without sensuality, the beasts from sensuality without intellect, and mankind from both intellect and sensuality. So when a person's intellect overcomes his sensuality, he is better than the angels; but when his sensuality overcomes his intellect, he is worse than the beasts. (Hadith recorded by Bukhari)

Jibril (Gabriel)

Jibril is the chief of the angels whose main role, according to the Qur'an, is to deliver Allah's message to the prophets so that they could pass it on to humanity.

Muslims also believe that Jibril told the prophet Ibrahim about the birth of his sons, Ishaq (Isaac) and Isma'il (Ishmael). He also told the prophet Zechariah about the birth of **Yahya** (John the Baptist), and **Maryam** (Mary) about the birth of Isa (Jesus). According to the Qur'an, it was Jibril who told Maryam she would have a child even though she was still a virgin.

Jibril's most important role, however, was to reveal the Qur'an to Muhammad. In 610CE during the month of Ramadan, while Muhammad was meditating in a cave near Makkah, God sent the angel Jibril with the first revelation of the Qur'an.

Jibril continued to give Muhammad revelations for the next twenty years until the Qur'an was complete.

Muslim pilgrims at the entrance of Cave Hira, where the Angel Jibril appeared with the first revelation of the Qur'an.

Activities

1. Rewrite the hadith recorded by Bukhari in your own words.
2. Look at the photo of Cave Hira. Discuss what you think happened when Muhammad received his first revelation.

Say: 'Whoever is an enemy to Gabriel – for he brings down the revelation to they heart by God's will, a confirmation of what went before and guidance and glad tidings for those who believe.' (Surah 2:97)

Useful words

Jibril – the archangel Gabriel
Yahya – John the Baptist
Maryam – the Virgin Mary

There is a whole Surah – Surah 19 – about the role of Jibril in telling Zechariah about the birth of Yahya (John the Baptist), telling Maryam about the birth of Isa (Jesus) and helping Maryam after the birth (which happened in the desert) by causing a small stream to flow to give her water and providing dates from the palm tree she was leaning against.

Useful words

Mika'il – the angel Michael
Izra'il – the angel of death

Mika'il (Michael)

Mika'il is the second most important angel. Mika'il is believed to be the guardian of heaven, protecting it from evil and the Devil. He also ensures that humans are nourished by sending rain to the earth. There is only one reference to Mika'il in the Qur'an, which states:

> *Whoever is an enemy of God or his angels or his apostles or Jibril or Mika'il, verily God is an enemy of the unbelievers.* (Surah 2:98)

Izra'il

Izra'il is the angel of death. The Qur'an says that the angel of death (his name is not mentioned) takes the soul of people at death and returns it to Allah:

> *The Angel of Death put in charge of you, will take your souls: then shall ye be brought back to your Lord.* (Surah 32:11)

However, Izra'il only acts at Allah's command because it is Allah alone who decides when a person will die:

> *Nor can a soul die except by God's leave.* (Surah 3:145)

There are hadith which record that the prophets met Izra'il during their lives and that Izra'il watches over the dying.

Why angels are important for Muslims

Angels are important for Muslims because:

- Angels communicated the Qur'an to Muhammad so without them Muslims would not have God's instructions on how to live and what to believe.
- Angels called the prophets to serve God and proclaim God's message; without angels, Muhammad would not have been the perfect example for Muslims.
- Angels ensure that on the Day of Judgement God will have all the facts when judging people on their lives.
- Angels make sure that heaven is safe from evil.

Summary

Muslims believe that angels:

- communicate God's messages to humans as God is so holy
- record people's good and bad deeds for God to use on the Day of Judgement
- guard the gates of hell.

Jibril communicates God's messages to the prophets, Mika'il is the guardian of heaven and Izra'il is the angel of death.

Practice questions

c Explain two of the roles of angels in Islam. In your answer you must refer to a source of wisdom and authority.

d 'Without angels there would be no Islam.' Evaluate this statement considering arguments for and against. In your answer you should:

- refer to Muslim points of view
- reach a justified conclusion.

Topic 2.1a.7 *Al-Qadr* (fate)

What Muslims believe about *al-Qadr*

Al-Qadr means power or fate or **predestination**, and is taken to mean that everything in the universe is following a divine plan. This belief comes from such Qur'anic verses as:

> *The command of God is a* ***decree*** *determined* (Surah 33:38)

and

> *In all things the master-planning is God's.* (Surah 13:42)

It also comes from numerous references in the Qur'an to the way in which things happened in the lives of the prophets that they did not understand at the time, but which they later came to see were a part of Allah's plan for them. As **Yusuf** (Joseph) says at the end of Surah 12 (a whole surah about the life of Yusuf):

> *This is the fulfilment of my vision of old! God hath made it come true! He was indeed good to me when He took me out of prison and brought you out of the desert, even after Satan had sown enmity between me and my brothers. Verily my Lord understandeth best the mysteries of all He planneth to do.* (Surah 12:100)

From such verses, Muslims believe that Allah has a plan for the universe that he created, that he has the power to make that plan happen (Allah is omnipotent) and that he knows what will happen (he is omniscient) so that in the end everything will work out as Allah willed and as Allah wanted. This is why many Muslims will say '***insh Allah***', meaning 'if Allah wills', after statements such as 'See you next week' – things will only happen if Allah wants them to. However, belief in *al-Qadr* is not without its problems.

Al-Qadr and the Day of Judgement

The Muslim teachings on *Akirah* are that people will be brought before Allah at the end of the world for the final judgement. Allah will judge everyone on the basis of their beliefs and actions and reward or punish them accordingly. But surely people can only be punished for something they did of their own free will? People can only be punished for actions for which they are responsible and which they could have done differently if they had so chosen. On this understanding, belief in *al-Qadr* and Allah's final judgement seem to be mutually contradictory.

This has led to two different Muslim explanations:

- Many Shi'a Muslims follow the explanation of the eighth-century Muslim theologians called **Mu'tazilites** who suggested that Allah created humans with free will and made them his vicegerents responsible for the world. So it is up to humans what happens and individual humans are responsible if misusing their free will results in them disobeying God. Therefore, they can be judged by God on the Last Day because they are responsible for their actions.

Thinking points

In this topic you need to think about the nature and importance of predestination for Muslims; how *al-Qadr* and human freedom relate to the Day of Judgement and different understandings of predestination in Sunni and Shi'a Islam. By the end of this topic you should be able to explain and evaluate the implications of belief in *al-Qadr* for Muslims today.

Useful words

Predestination – the belief that everything that happens has already been decided
Decree – an official order from a high authority
Yusuf – the prophet Joseph (coat of many colours)
Insh Allah – if God wills
Mu'tazilites – eighth-century Muslim theologians regarded as non-Muslim by most Sunni Muslims today

Activities

1. Why do Muslims believe in *al-Qadr*?
2. How does belief in *al-Qadr* make it difficult to explain why there is evil and suffering in the world?

Useful words

Foreknowledge – knowing what is going to happen long before it does

The Prophet said, 'Allah says, "The vow, does not bring about for the son of Adam anything I have not decreed for him, but his vow may coincide with what has been decided for him, and by this way I cause a miser to spend of his wealth. So he gives Me (spends in charity) for the fulfilment of what has been decreed for him what he would not give Me before but for his vow."' (Sahih Bukhari 78:685)

- Sunni Muslims tend to follow the explanation of another eighth-century theologian, al'Ashari, who claimed that Allah knows what people will do before they do it, since he has the attribute of **foreknowledge**. Allah knows what people will do, but they do it of their own free will. This idea was explained more recently by a Sunni scholar:

> *By believing in* al-Qadr *we testify that Allah is the Absolute Controller of the affairs of His universe. It is He who decides what is good and what is bad ... We are unable to understand and interpret many of Allah's actions. It is meaningless to argue that human beings act without freedom and that we are forced to act in the way we do. We decide for ourselves what we will do, and what we will not, and we are responsible for our own actions. This freedom of action does not conflict with the foreknowledge of Allah.*

The implications of belief in *al-Qadr* for Muslims today

Belief in *al-Qadr* means that Allah has a master plan for the universe, and, since Allah is omnipotent, that means that nothing happens without Allah's permission. This means that:

- Although they may face present sufferings, Muslims do not need to worry about their long-term future because God is in control, so all will be well.
- Any sufferings Muslims undergo must be accepted because what they suffer must be part of God's plan and so will have an eventual good outcome.
- Muslims cannot sit back and let God take responsibility for things because Muslims have free will and so although God's plans will happen, Muslims have to make their own choices and be responsible for their own actions and destiny.

Muslims need to work out what God wants them to do (for most Muslims this simply means observing the Five Pillars and living according to the Shari'ah) so they can be sure their choices are what God wants to happen.

Activities

1. Why does belief in *al-Qadr* make it difficult to accept Muslim beliefs about the Day of Judgement?
2. Do you think it is possible to believe in *al-Qadr* and that humans are free to choose what they want to do?

Summary

Al-Qadr is the belief that God has a plan for the world and so everything that happens is part of this. The Qur'an says that nothing happens unless God wants it to happen. Sunni Muslims believe that people choose what to do but they only choose what God wants. Shi'as believe that people have free will which somehow fits with God's plans.

Practice questions

c. Explain two reasons why Muslims believe in *al-Qadr*. In your answer you must refer to a source of wisdom and authority.

d. 'Nothing happens unless God wants it to.' Evaluate this statement considering arguments for and against. In your answer you should:
   - refer to Muslim points of view
   - refer to different Muslim points of view
   - reach a justified conclusion.

Topic 2.1a.8 *Akirah* (Muslim beliefs about life after death)

Muslim beliefs about life after death

Muslims believe that when people die their body stays in the grave until the Last Day.

The Qur'an teaches that this world will be brought to an end by God on a day of his choosing (the Last Day). Before that, Isa (Jesus) will return, the angel **Israfil** will sound the trumpet and the dead will be raised. Everyone will stand before God on the plain of Arafat (near Makkah) to be judged by God and sent to either heaven or hell:

> *They say, 'What when we are reduced to bones and dust should we really be raised up to be a new creation?' Say, 'Nay be ye stones or iron, or created matter which in your minds is hardest to be raised up, yet shall ye be raised up'.* (Surah 17:49–51)

> *That Day shall all men be sorted out. Then those who have believed and worked righteous deeds shall be made happy in a mead of delight. And those who have rejected faith and falsely denied Our signs and the meeting of the Hereafter, such shall be brought to punishment.* (Surah 30:14–16)

Most Muslims believe that the final judgement on the Last Day will be based on a mixture of faith and action. There are many Qur'anic references to those doing evil deeds as well as those rejecting faith being sent to hell; consequently, the most common belief is that only good Muslims will pass the test of the final judgement.

However, many Muslim think that the verse:

> *Whoever does evil will be requited accordingly, nor will he find, besides God, any protector or helper* (Surah 4:123)

means that in the end God will **intercede** for Muslims who have tried their best to be good Muslims, but have committed sins. After all, one of the major teachings of the Qur'an is that God is 'the Merciful' and 'the Compassionate'. There is another Muslim belief, based on the hadith, that the Prophet Muhammad will intercede for his followers who have sinned and that God will accept his intercession.

Muslims prepare for the Last Day when they confess their sins at Arafat.

Thinking points

In this topic you need to:

- think about Muslim beliefs about life after death: judgement, paradise, and hell, and how they are shown in the Qur'an
- think about the similarities and differences between Christian and Muslim beliefs
- be able to explain and evaluate why life after death is important for Muslims and how it might affect their lives.

Useful words

Israfil – the angel who begins the Last Day by blowing his trumpet

Intercede – to use your influence to persuade someone in authority to forgive another person

Activities

1. Read either Surah 17 or Surah 52 and write down any teachings about life after death that are not mentioned in the passages on this page.
2. Look at the photo of Arafat. Muslims believe they will have to read the book of their life in front of everyone there. Why might this be a frightening idea?

Useful words

Al'Jannah – heaven
Jahannam – hell
Barzakh – the period between death and the Last Day

Activities

1. Write out two different Muslim views about hell.
2. Look at the photo of the Muslim cemetery below. What is the big difference between this and a Christian cemetery? Why do you think this is?

> *One day He will gather them together: it will be as if they had tarried but an hour of a day: they will recognise each other. (Surah 10:45)*

A relative prays in a Muslim cemetery in Algeria.

Muslim beliefs about paradise

All Muslims believe that heaven is paradise. The Qur'an describes heaven as ***al'Jannah*** (the Garden):

> *Gardens of perpetual bliss: they shall enter there, as well as the righteous among their fathers, their spouses, and their offspring. Angels shall enter from every gate (with the salutation): 'Peace be with you, that you persevered in patience! Now how excellent is the final home!' (Surah 13:23–24)*

The Qur'an also describes heaven as a place of delights:

> *They will not hear therein ill speech or commission of sin. But only the saying of: 'Peace! Peace!' (Surah 56:25–26)*

> *Allah hath promised to Believers, men and women, gardens under which rivers flow, to dwell therein, and beautiful mansions in gardens of everlasting bliss. But the greatest bliss is the good pleasure of Allah. That is the supreme felicity. (Surah 9:72)*

Muslim beliefs about hell

Hell is ***Jahannam*** and is portrayed in the Qur'an as a place of fire and torture. However, there are different Muslim attitudes about the nature of hell because of different statements in the Qur'an about hell. The general view is that people will stay in hell forever, but some Muslims believe that bad Muslims will only stay in hell for a short time to be punished for their sins. They believe this because Surah 15 says that there are seven classes of hell and Surah 6 says that people only stay in hell for as long as God wills. Some Muslims even believe that these verses mean that good followers of other religions will only stay in hell for a short time.

Between death and the Last Day

There are also differences about what happens between death and the Last Day. The belief that after death souls stay in the grave until the Last Day is challenged by the Qur'anic teaching that those who die when on *hajj* or fighting in a holy war will go straight to heaven after death. Some Muslims use these verses to claim that the afterlife is spiritual and that people's souls are judged immediately after death and then go to a spiritual heaven or hell.

Muslims also have different beliefs about what happens in the period between people dying and their body being raised on the Last Day (this period is known as ***Barzakh***). Some Muslim traditions say that after death, souls are visited by the angel of death and questioned about their faith. If they answer with true Muslim belief, they are shown their place in heaven, and look at it until they are raised on the Last Day. If they answer wrongly, they are beaten with clubs until the Last Day.

Other Muslim traditions say that after the death of the body, the soul hovers over the grave until the Last Day. Other Muslim traditions claim that the soul simply sleeps until the Last Day so that *Barzakh* will just seem like a moment between death and the Last Day, as stated in the Qur'an quotation in the margin.

Of course, all these traditions explain why Muslims are so careful with the body after death, why they insist on burial and not cremation, and why they are doubtful about autopsies and transplants.

Why life after death is important for Muslims

- The Qur'an teaches that there is life after death. Muslims believe that the Qur'an is the Word of God which contains everything God wants humans to know, therefore they must believe whatever the Qur'an says.
- Muhammad taught that there is life after death. Muslims believe that Muhammad is the last prophet God will ever send and the perfect example for Muslims. Therefore, they must believe whatever he taught.
- Islam has six fundamental beliefs (Allah, his angels, his holy books, his messengers, the Last Day and life after death) which all Muslims are expected to believe. Since Muhammad said that all Muslims must believe these, Muslims must believe in life after death.
- Muslims believe that this life is a test from God. The idea of a test involves the need for a judgement, and rewards for those who pass. Judgement and reward can only happen if there is life after death, therefore Muslims believe in life after death because it makes sense of this life being a test.
- Many Muslims believe in life after death because it gives their lives meaning and purpose. A life after death, in which people will be judged on how they lived this life, with the good rewarded and the evil punished, makes sense of this life. If the purpose of life is to live your life in such a way that you spend eternity in heaven, then that gives life meaning.

How Muslim beliefs about life after death affect the lives of Muslims

- Islam teaches that on the Last Day, all humans will be gathered before God on a vast plain and judged by God. The judgement will be made on the nature of people's lives. Those who have lived good Muslim lives will pass the judgement and go to paradise; everyone else will fail and go to hell. This affects Muslims' lives because they must try to live good Muslim lives if they are to go to paradise and avoid hell.
- Living a good Muslim life means observing the Five Pillars of Islam. So belief in life after death means that Muslims will pray five times a day, they will fast during Ramadan, they will pay their *zakah* and they will go on *hajj* at least once. So their beliefs about life after death will have a big effect on their lives.
- Living a good Muslim life also means following the holy law of Islam, the Shari'ah. This will affect Muslims' lives because they will have to eat *halal* food, observe Muslim dress laws, not drink alcohol, not gamble and not be involved in lending at or receiving interest.
- Muslims believe that resurrection means that nothing should be removed from the body after death. This means that funerals take place within 48 hours and the body is simply embalmed and buried. This affects Muslims' lives because they try to avoid post-mortems and autopsies and many Muslims have concerns about transplant surgery.

- Muslim beliefs about life after death give their lives meaning and purpose. Living your life with a purpose and believing that this life has meaning both affect the way you live. It may be why in surveys Muslims suffer less from depression and are less likely to die by suicide than atheists and agnostics.

Muslim and Christian beliefs about life after death

Similarities:

- Both believe this life is not all there is and that there will be life after death.
- Both believe there will be some form of judgement after death based on how people have lived on earth.
- Both believe in heaven as a place of paradise with God.
- Both believe that good people will go to heaven.
- Both believe that life after death is important because it makes sense of this life because it makes sure that the good are rewarded.

Similarities between Catholics and Conservative Protestants and Muslims:

- Both believe that the dead will be raised on the Last Day.
- Both believe that the Last Day will bring the world as we know it to an end.
- Both believe that people will be judged on what they have believed as well as how they have behaved.
- Both believe in hell as well as heaven and that bad people and people with the wrong beliefs will go to hell.

Differences:

- Christians do not believe the dead need to be buried quickly.
- Christians believe bodies can be cremated.
- Some Christians believe in immortality of the soul not resurrection of the body.
- Some Christians do not believe in the Last Day and believe judgement will take place as soon as people die.
- Catholic Christians believe that people not ready for heaven will go to purgatory to be cleansed of their sins before the Last Day.
- Some Christians do not believe in hell and believe that eventually everyone will go to heaven.

Summary

Muslims have different beliefs about what happens after people die; this period is known as *Barzakh*. Muslims all agree that on the Last Day the dead will be raised and judged by God. Good Muslims will go to paradise and evil people will go to hell, but there are some different ideas among Muslims about what happens to bad Muslims and good non-Muslims.

Practice questions

c Explain two different Muslim views about the final judgement. In your answer you must refer to a source of wisdom and authority.

d 'When you're dead, you're dead and that's the end of you.' Evaluate this statement considering arguments for and against. In your answer you should:

- refer to Muslim points of view
- refer to different Muslim points of view
- reach a justified conclusion.

How to answer questions

a) Describe two similarities between Muslim beliefs about life after death and the beliefs of the main religious tradition of Britain. [3]

Christianity is the main religious tradition of Britain. One similarity is that both Christians and Muslims believe this life is not all there is and that there will be life after death. Another similarity is that both Christians and Muslims believe there will be some form of judgement after death based on how people have lived on earth.

A high mark answer because Christianity is identified as the main religious tradition of Britain and two similarities are clearly described.

b) Explain two reasons why the five roots of Usul ad-din are important for Shi'a Muslims. [4]

The five roots are important for Shi'a Muslims because they come from the teachings of the Qur'an and the twelve imams, which means they have total authority.

Shi'a Muslims also believe that unless they understand and believe the five roots, they will not be able to perform the acts of worship necessary to live the Muslim life.

A high mark answer because two correct reasons are given and each reason is developed.

c) Explain two reasons why belief in *Akirah* is important for Muslims. In your answer you must refer to a source of wisdom and authority. [5]

The Qur'an teaches that there is life after death. Muslims believe that the Qur'an is the Word of God which contains everything God wants humans to know, therefore they must believe whatever the Qur'an says.

Muhammad taught that there is life after death. Muslims believe that Muhammad is the last prophet God will ever send and the perfect example for Muslims. Therefore, they must believe whatever he taught.

A high mark answer because two correct reasons are given and each reason is developed with a reference to the authority of the Qur'an and Muhammad.

d) 'Allah's omnipotence is His most important characteristic.' Evaluate this statement considering arguments for and against. In your response you should:

- **refer to Muslim points of view**
- **refer to different Muslim points of view**
- **reach a justified conclusion. [12 marks + 3 spelling, punctuation and grammar (SPaG) marks]**

Some Muslims might believe this because two of the 99 names of Allah are: 'The Absolute' and 'the All-powerful' and it is a fundamental belief of Islam that Allah has complete power. He has created the universe and so must have complete power over the universe he has created. Islam means submission to God's will and a Muslim is one who has submitted their will to God's will because God is so great. That phrase is repeated many times during *salah* prayers: '*Allahu akbar*' – 'God is great'.

[Continued]

However, most Muslims would think that God's most important characteristic is his oneness. The *shahadah* begins, 'I bear witness that there is no god, but God.' Belief in God's oneness means that God must be the Creator of everything and he must be the all-powerful who is in control of everything.

It seems to me that for Islam omnipotence is not the most important characteristic of God, his oneness is because this is the basic belief of Islam and all God's other characteristics come from his oneness.

A high mark answer because it gives three clear developed reasons for thinking that omnipotence must be God's greatest characteristic. It then gives three reasons for disagreeing and then reaches a fully justified conclusion.

The answer would reach full marks for SPaG as spelling, punctuation and grammar are correct and a wide range of specialist vocabulary (99 names, the Absolute, *salah*, *Allahu akbar*, *shahadah*) is used appropriately.

SPaG

A high mark answer because the answer spells, punctuates and uses the rules of grammar with consistent accuracy and effective control of meaning. A wide range of specialist terms is used adeptly and with precision.

1b Jewish beliefs

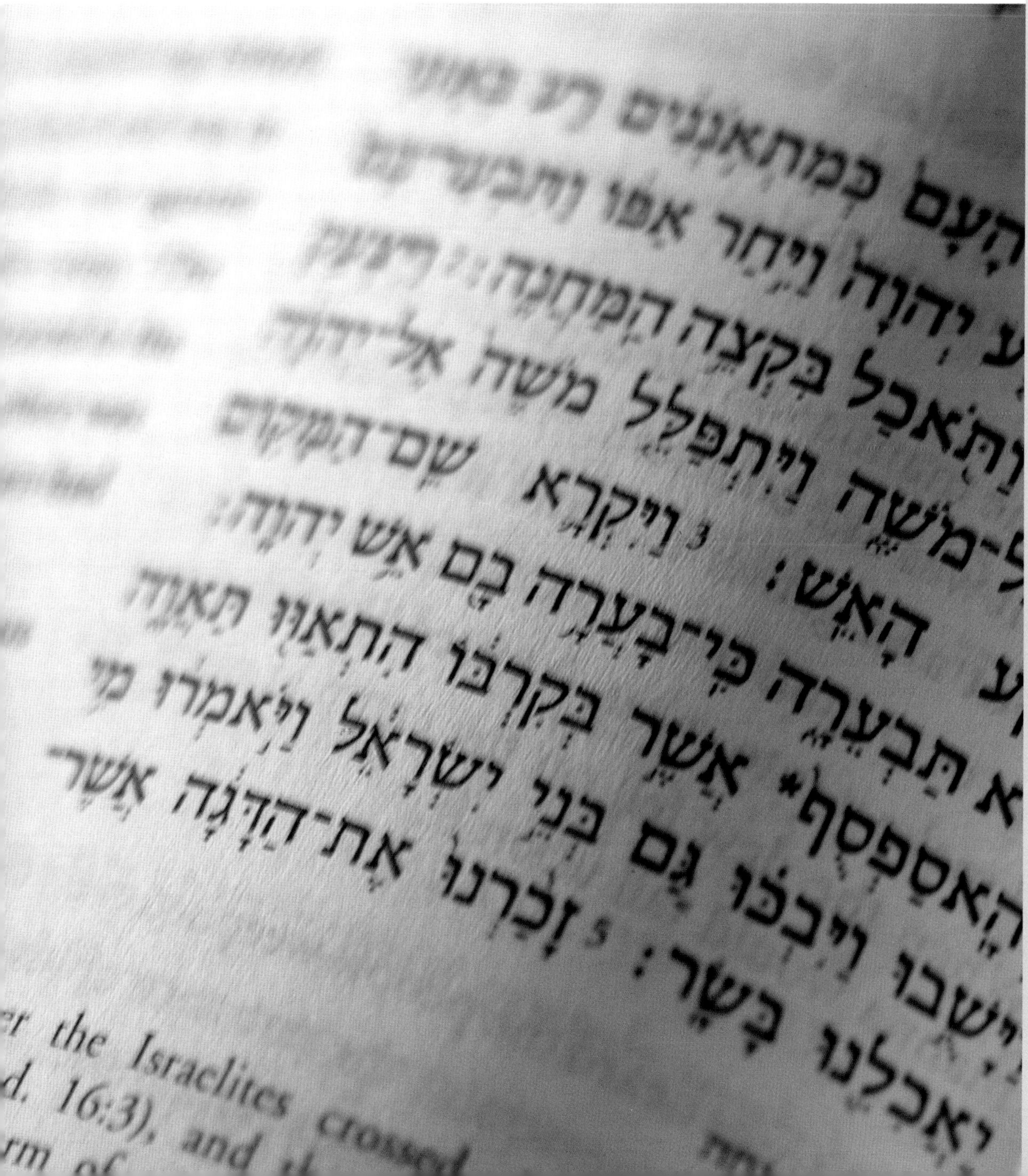

Area of study 2: Introduction (Judaism)

For those of you studying this area based on Judaism, it is important that you should understand some of the different groups within Judaism. This will allow you to understand Jewish beliefs and attitudes.

Five hundred years ago the major division in Judaism was between the Sephardic Jews and the Ashkenazi Jews. The Sephardi are the Jews from Spain, Portugal and the Middle East; the Ashkenazi are Jews from Germany and Eastern Europe whose separate language is Yiddish (a mix of German and Hebrew). However, the differences between these groups are mainly cultural, although the Sephardi have always believed in integrating within the community in which they live.

Hasidic Jews in London.

In modern Judaism, the main division is between Orthodox and Reform.

The Judaism most non-Jews think of as Judaism is Orthodox Judaism. The Orthodox regard the Torah as the infallible Word of God and therefore follow all of its commandments (*mitzvot*). But there are many differences within the Orthodox. The modern Orthodox teach that Jewish people should follow all the laws of the Torah (*halakhah*) but should otherwise integrate into modern life and the community in which they live.

However, there are other Orthodox groups such as the Hasidim who teach that Jewish people should maintain a separate culture and identity (as evidenced by their dress – a long black coat, white shirt, big black hat – and use of Yiddish). A development from the Hasidim is Lubavich or Chabad Judaism, which was led until 1994 by Rebbe Menachem Mendel. The Lubavich have many Hasidic practices, but believe that Judaism must relate to the modern world (they use the latest technology to spread their beliefs), and must be joyful (their worship involves music and dancing) and mystical (they are very connected to the *kabbalah*).

Reform Judaism resulted from nineteenth-century attempts to 'modernise' Judaism by bringing the findings of science and biblical criticism into Judaism. Reform Jews do not believe that the Torah is the Word of God, but rather that it was written by people inspired by God. They feel that it is the moral commands of the law which must be followed and believe that the ritual laws, such as keeping *kosher*, can be ignored. They are committed to working for social justice, which they call *Tikkun Olan* (the repair of the world), and have complete equality of the sexes including having women rabbis. Reform Judaism is the most popular group in American Judaism, but in British Judaism, the liberal and progressive synagogues are the ones closest to American Reform while the British Reform synagogues tend to be more traditional in observance of *Shabbat* and *kosher*.

It is important to be aware that the main religion in Britain is Christianity.

Topic 2.1b.1 The nature of the Almighty

Thinking points

In this topic you need to think about how the characteristics of God are shown in the scriptures:

- oneness
- creator
- law-giver
- judge.

By the end of this topic you should be able to evaluate the importance of these characteristics in Jewish life today.

Jewish scriptures

The Jewish scriptures are known as the **Tenakh**, from the three divisions of the Jewish scriptures:

- **Torah** (the five books of Moses, initial letter *Te* in Hebrew)
- **Nevi'im** (the Prophets, initial letter *Na*) and
- **Ketuvim** (the Writings, initial letter *Kh*).

The Tenakh has the same books as the Protestant Christian Old Testament, although in a different order, and some of the books in the Tenakh have been separated into two or three books by the Christians (the Tenakh has 24 books, the Old Testament has 39; but remember the Tenakh came first!).

The Torah is the holiest and most important part of the Tenakh for Jewish people because they believe that it came directly from God to Moses. The Torah has always been written on scrolls and every synagogue has a Torah scroll kept in a special place.

Useful words

Tenakh – the Jewish scriptures
Torah – the law book or books of Moses
Nevi'im – the books of the prophets
Ketuvim – the books of the writings
Shema – statement of God's oneness

God is one

It is the clear teaching of the Jewish scriptures that the most important characteristic of God is his oneness.

The Torah teaches that God is one:

> *The Lord is God in heaven above and on earth below. There is no other.* (Deuteronomy 4:39)

> *See now that I myself am He! There is no god besides me.* (Deuteronomy 32:39)

The most basic teaching of Judaism from the Torah is known as the ***shema*** and it begins with the words,

> *Hear, O Israel! The Lord our God, the Lord is one. Love the Lord your God with all your heart and with all your soul and with all your strength.* (Deuteronomy 6:4–5)

Judaism teaches strict monotheism (belief in only one God), just the same as Islam.

The *shema*

> *Hear, O Israel! The Lord our God, the Lord is one. Love the Lord your God with all your heart and with all your soul and with all your strength. These commandments that I give you today are to be upon your hearts. Impress them on your children. Talk about them when you sit at home and when you walk along the road, when you lie down and when you get up. 'Tie them as symbols on your hands and bind them on your foreheads. Write them on the doorframes of your houses and on your gates.'* (Deuteronomy 6:4–9)

Activities

1. What is the Tenakh?
2. What is the holiest part of the Tenakh and why?

The importance of belief in God's oneness

Belief in God's oneness can be seen in the following ways:

- Jewish people have a container holding the *shema* on their gates and doorframes of each room in the house other than bathrooms and toilets (this is known as a ***mezuzah***, even though technically a *mezuzah* is the parchment with the *shema* on it). Every time a Jew passes through a door with an affixed *mezuzah*, he or she should kiss their fingers and touch them to the *mezuzah*, expressing their love and respect for God and his commandments and reminding themselves of his oneness.
- Jewish men bind ***tefillin*** (leather boxes containing the *shema*) to their foreheads and arms when they pray every morning.
- Jewish people think of people, plants, animals, rock formations and so on as unified because they are the creation of the one God. In this way, belief in God's unity means that all of God's creation is an opportunity to come face to face with God.
- Judaism teaches the unity of creation and the need for people to try to bring unity to society.

Someone touching a *mezuzah* on a doorframe.

God the creator

The very first words of the Torah are:

> *In the beginning God created the heaven and the earth* (Genesis 1:1)

showing that another key characteristic of God is his creativity. God the creator is the one who can breathe life into inanimate objects – he is a life-giving force:

> *Then the Lord God formed a man from the dust of the ground and breathed into his nostrils the breath of life, and the man became a living being.* (Genesis 2:7)

As well as the Torah beginning by referring to God the creator, the concept of God the Creator is first of the **Thirteen Principles of Faith** set out by **Maimonides**, which are regarded as a summary of the Jewish faith: 'I believe with perfect faith that God is the Creator and Ruler of all things. He alone has made, does make, and will make all things'.

The Torah teaches that because God is the creator everything belongs to him: the universe and everything in it comes from God and therefore depends on God. However, the key teaching of the Torah is that God's creation is good. Genesis 1 states after each day of creation, 'and God saw that it was good', and at the completion of creation,

> *God saw all he had made and indeed it was very good.* (Genesis 1:31)

It also teaches that God gave humans control of the earth,

> *God blessed them and said to them, 'Be fruitful and increase in number; fill the earth and subdue it. Rule over the fish ... and the birds ... and over every living creature'.* (Genesis 1:28)

Useful words

Mezuzah – a container for the *shema* scroll put on doorposts
Tefillin – a container for the *shema* scroll to put on the arms and head
Thirteen Principles of Faith – a summary of Jewish beliefs written by Maimonides
Maimonides – medieval rabbi and philosopher (1135–1204) who wrote the Thirteen Principles

Activities

1. Why do you think the *shema* is so important for Jewish people?
2. How do Jewish people remind themselves of God's oneness every day?

Activity

Look at the picture opposite. Do you think Jewish people would think this is a good way of showing God creating?

The Torah teaches that God is the creator.

The importance of belief in God as Creator

Belief that God created the universe and that his creation is good is important for Jews because it means that:

- Creation is a gift from God and Jews must therefore look after the earth in the way in which God intended.
- Since God created the universe and all the things in it, life has a meaning and purpose given to it by God.
- God's work of creation did not stop at the end of Genesis 1. God the creator continues to be the creator. In their prayer every day, Jewish people praise God who 'in His goodness renews the work of creation each day continually'.
- God's creation is good and so should be respected, which is why Jewish people care for the environment.

God the law-giver

The Torah teaches that as well as being the Creator and the One, God is the great law-giver.

God did not simply create the universe and leave humanity to get on with things. The Torah teaches that God gave laws to help people look after the earth in the way he wanted.

Some of these laws were given to Noah as part of God's **covenant** with Noah; others were given to Abraham as part of God's covenant with him (see Topic 2.1b.5, page 200). God then gave all 613 commands (***mitzvot***) of the Jewish law to Moses for him to give to the people. The laws were to help the people keep their side of the agreement:

> *Take to heart all the words I have solemnly declared to you this day, so that you may command your children to obey carefully all the words of this law. They are not just idle words for you – they are your life. By them you will live long in the land.* (Deuteronomy 32:46–47)

Useful words

Covenant – a binding agreement between two parties; usually refers to God and Israel

Mitzvot – commandments/laws (the singular of *mitzvot* is *mitzvah*)

All 613 *mitzvot* are to be found in the Torah (the first five books – Genesis, Exodus, Leviticus, Numbers, Deuteronomy – which Orthodox Jews believe were given to Moses directly by God). By keeping the *mitzvot* Jewish people believe they are connecting with God in a deep and special way, and so can bring holiness into the world and prepare the world for the time when God's plan for the world will be fulfilled. By keeping the *mitzvot* they become God's people.

The importance of belief in God as law-giver

Believing that God is the law-giver is important in Judaism today because:

- God's laws (the *mitzvot*) form the ***halakhah***, which is the basis of how Jews live their lives today.
- Following God's laws gives meaning and purpose to Jewish people's lives today.
- The laws of the Torah are part of the covenant with Moses, which is the basis of Judaism.
- The fact that God is a law-giver means that he cares about his creation and so cares about humans, which gives Jews security and helps them in their relationship with creation.

I believe with perfect faith that the entire Torah that we now have is that which was given to Moses. (Principle 8 of the Thirteen Principles)

I believe with perfect faith that this Torah will not be changed, and that there will never be another given by God. (Principle 9 of the Thirteen Principles)

Useful words

Halakhah – the holy law of Judaism

God the judge

The law of the Torah as set out in the *mitzvot* is known in Judaism as the *halakhah*, which literally means 'the path that one walks'. This is the divine law of Judaism, and any divine law requires a divine judge. The Tenakh has many references to God acting as judge for his creation:

> *For the Lord is our judge, The Lord is our lawgiver, The Lord is our king; He will save us.* (Isaiah 33:22)

The Tenakh teaches that God as judge will ensure that the good are rewarded and the evil punished. The dictionary defines justice as 'the exercise of authority in the maintenance of right', and the Tenakh shows that this is what God the Judge does:

> *And He will judge the world in righteousness; He will execute judgement for the peoples with equity.* (Psalm 9:8)

God is a just judge who will treat everyone fairly, making sure that justice reigns. However, the time when God the judge will make justice reign is in the future:

> *Before the Lord, for He is coming to judge the earth.* (Psalm 98:9)

> *For the Lord will vindicate His people, and will have compassion on His servants.* (Deuteronomy 32:36)

The Tenakh seems to connect this time of justice and judgement with the coming of the Messianic Age (see Topic 2.1b.3, page 194):

> *He will not judge by what he sees with his eyes or decide by what he hears with his ears; but with righteousness he will judge the needy, with justice he will give decisions for the poor of the earth.* (Isaiah 11:3)

Activity

Read Principles 8 and 9 above. How do they show the importance of Torah law?

The scales of justice.

Principle 11 says, 'I believe with perfect faith that God rewards those who keep His commandments, and punishes those who transgress Him.'

The importance of belief in God as judge

The belief that God is judge is important for Jewish life today because it ensures that:

- The good are rewarded and the evil punished.
- The world is protected from the chaos that would come if there was no way of making sure that people keep God's laws.
- People know there will be punishments for those who do not keep God's laws.
- There will be rewards for those who do keep God's laws.

Activity

Look at the picture of the scales of justice. Why is it important that God is both law-giver and judge?

Summary

The fundamental Jewish belief about God is that God is one as the Torah teaches in the *shema*. The Torah also teaches from its very first verse that God is the creator of everything and that God's creation is good. The Torah says God is the law-giver and it contains all 613 of God's *mitzvot*. God's laws require a judge and the Tenakh shows God as the one who judges everyone.

Practice questions

c Explain two reasons why it is important for Jews that God is a law-giver. In your answer you must refer to a source of wisdom and authority.

d 'God's oneness is his most important characteristic.' Evaluate this statement considering arguments for and against. In your answer you should:

- refer to Jewish points of view
- reach a justified conclusion.

Topic 2.1b.2 *Shekhinah*

What *shekhinah* is

The Hebrew word *shekhinah* is deliberately difficult to define because it is a way of describing the Almighty's presence in the world.

If you think of the characteristics of God outlined in Topic 2.1b.1, you can begin to realise why *shekhinah* is difficult to define because any definition is going to be an attempt to use finite words to describe the infinite – something which could never be accurate.

Jewish scholars sometimes define *shekhinah* as 'the majestic presence or manifestation of God which has descended to dwell among men'. Others translate this 'majestic presence' more simply as 'the glory of God'.

The **rabbis** always used the term *shekhinah* when they were referring to any form of contact humans may have with God. Humans cannot have contact with God's immensity (the finite cannot comprehend the infinite), they can only have contact with God's presence – that part of God which 'has descended to dwell among men'.

How *shekhinah* is shown in the Torah

The Torah speaks of God's presence (*shekhinah*) going with Moses to guide him through the wilderness to the promised land:

> *My presence will go with you and I will give you rest.* (Exodus 33:14)

The divine presence is associated with clouds,

> *When Moses went up on the mountain, the cloud covered it, and the glory of the Lord settled on Mount Sinai.* (Exodus 24:15)

It is also associated with smoke and fire:

> *Mount Sinai was covered with smoke, because the Lord descended on it in fire.* (Exodus 19:18)

The Torah also speaks of God choosing a place 'as a dwelling for His name' (Deuteronomy 12:11) and calls it the **tabernacle**. God instructed Moses to have the Israelites build this for God's presence to be: 'I will dwell among the Israelites and be their God' (Exodus 29:45). So the Torah makes plain that the *shekhinah* is the presence of God closely connected with the tabernacle, holy and untouchable:

> *Then have them make a* ***sanctuary*** *for me, and I will dwell among them.* (Exodus 25:8)

Activity

State four things the Torah says about *shekhinah*.

Thinking points

In this topic you need to:

- explore what *shekhinah* is and how it is shown in Jewish scriptures, including how it is shown in the Torah and 2 Chronicles 7:1–3
- be aware of the different understandings of *shekhinah* for Jews today
- be able to explain why *shekhinah* is important for Judaism and why the different understandings of it are important for Jews today.

Useful words

Rabbis – ordained Jewish religious leaders or teachers
Tabernacle – the holy place containing the Ark of the Covenant
Sanctuary – the most holy part of a religious building (can also mean a place of safety)

When Moses came into contact with the divine presence when he received the commandments on Mount Sinai, his face shone and the people were afraid of how he looked. (Exodus 34:29–35)

Useful words

Temple – the centre of worship built by Solomon in Jerusalem and destroyed in 70CE
Mount Zion – the holy hill in Jerusalem where the Temple was
Talmud – writings explaining the Torah
Kabbalah – Jewish mysticism

The tabernacle became the **Temple** in Jerusalem when the Israelites reached the promised land, and when King Solomon dedicated the Temple the *shekhinah* came to dwell there:

> *When Solomon finished praying, fire came down from heaven and consumed the burnt offering and the sacrifices, and the glory of the Lord filled the temple. The priests could not enter the temple of the Lord because the glory of the Lord filled it. When all the Israelites saw the fire coming down and the glory of the Lord above the temple, they knelt on the pavement with their faces to the ground, and they worshipped and gave thanks to the Lord, saying, 'He is good; his love endures forever.'* (2 Chronicles 7:1–3)

The Nevi'im and Ketuvim make many references to the *shekhinah* being in Jerusalem and on **Mount Zion** (the hill in Jerusalem on which the Temple was built), for example:

> *The Lord Almighty who dwells on Mount Zion.* (Isaiah 8:18)

There are also many references to the prophets having visions of the presence of God, which are regarded as the presence of the *shekhinah*. For example, Isaiah said,

> *I saw the Lord seated on a throne, high and exalted and the train of his robe filled the temple.* (Isaiah 6:1)

In the **Talmud** (the writings explaining the Torah) and the writings of later rabbis, *shekhinah* begins to be used for the presence of God in the world.

Different understandings of *shekhinah* for Jews today

- Some Orthodox Jews base themselves on the teachings of Maimonides, who described the *shekhinah* as a light created to be a link between God and the world.
- Others regard the *shekhinah* as an expression for the various ways in which God is related to the world, especially such things as the dwelling of God in the midst of Israel and his personal presence.
- Others believe that *shekhinah* simply means God. They feel that *shekhinah* and God are interchangeable words.
- *Shekhinah* is held by some modern (especially Reform) Jews to represent the feminine attributes of the presence of God because *shekhinah* is a feminine word in Hebrew.
- In the ***kabbalah*** (Jewish mysticism which tries to define the nature of the universe and the nature and purpose of existence, and provide ways for people to gain their spiritual goal) *shekhinah* is called the tenth *sephira*, which is the gateway to higher consciousness, that brings followers into God's presence.
- Some Jews who have been influenced by Christian ideas claim that *shekhinah* is simply the Jewish word for the Holy Spirit – God's presence at work in the world.

Activities

1. Look at the painting of *shekhinah* on page 193. Do you think this is a good representation of Jewish belief?
2. What does 2 Chronicles 7:1–3 tell us about the *shekhinah*?

Why *shekhinah* is important for Judaism

- The idea of *shekhinah* shows that however close Jews may feel to God, God's presence is so holy and awesome that they must always maintain a deep sense of respect for God. This sense of respect is shown by Jews only referring to God's name in worship. Jews otherwise refer to God as the Almighty or, more often, ***Hashem*** (the name, the one whose name must be treated respectfully and not pronounced unnecessarily). When writing they will often use G–d to express this idea.
- The Tenakh references to the *shekhinah* being at the Temple, Mount Zion and Jerusalem are what makes those places so special for some Jews.
- The teaching that Moses was surrounded by the *shekhinah* when he received the Torah means that Moses received the *mitzvot* directly from God, so they are God's words.
- The *shekhinah* teaches that God's presence is in the world and that believers might therefore come across the *shekhinah* at any time.
- The *shekhinah* shows that the prophets of the Tenakh were truly inspired by God and so their message must be true.

'The Shekinah Glory Enters the Tabernacle', an illustration from 1908.

Useful words

Hashem – the Name, a word used to refer to God without mentioning his name

Immutable – unable to be changed and unchanging over time

Why the different understandings of *shekhinah* are important for Jews today

The fact that there are different understandings of the word *shekhinah* is important:

- The different meanings show that God is far beyond human thought. He is the eternal **immutable** and so there are many ways of understanding his presence.
- This allows Judaism to relate God to the ideas of the modern world such as feminism and the theological debates about whether God is masculine.
- It makes it easier for Jews and Christians to come together in their search for God.
- The concept of *shekhinah* in the *kabbalah* brought together different religions, making it easier to break down religious hatred; there are Christian, Sunni Muslim and Shi'a Muslim kabbalists.

Practice questions

c Explain two reasons why different understandings of *shekhinah* are important for Jews today.

d 'The concept of *shekhinah* is not important for understanding Judaism.' Evaluate this statement considering arguments for and against. In your answer you should:

- refer to Jewish points of view
- refer to different Jewish points of view
- reach a justified conclusion.

Summary

Shekinah refers to the presence of God on earth and is used in the Torah to describe God's presence in the Tabernacle, Temple and Jerusalem. It is difficult to understand and is interpreted in different ways by different rabbis, but it is the basis of the belief that God's name reflects his presence and is so holy that it should only be used in worship.

Topic 2.1b.3 Messiah

Thinking points

In this topic you need to think about:

- the nature and purpose of the Messiah
- how messiahship is shown in the scriptures
- the nature and significance of the Messianic Age
- the different understandings of the Messiah.

By the end of this topic you should be able to explain the importance of the Messiah for Jews today.

Useful words

Messianic Age – a time when all nations will live at peace and there will be justice in the world

Inspired – stimulated by God to do things

The nature and purpose of the Messiah

The word Messiah means 'anointed one' and was used to refer to the kings of Israel who were anointed.

When the Israelite kingdom was captured by the Babylonians and the monarchy ended (586BCE), Jewish people began to refer to the purpose of the Messiah as the one who will:

- rebuild the Temple in Jerusalem
- unite all the peoples of the world
- make all the peoples of the world aware of the presence of God
- bring in the **Messianic Age**, when all will live at peace
- establish God's kingdom.

Most Jews believe that the nature of the Messiah will be to be:

- a descendant of King David
- a human, not a divine being
- a man of great piety and close to God
- a man of great learning
- a man with great leadership qualities.

How messiahship is shown in the scriptures

There are no references to the Messiah in the Torah, but the Nevi'im say that:

- The Messiah will be a descendant of David:

  'The days are coming,' declares the Lord, 'when I will raise up for David a righteous Branch, a King who will reign wisely and do what is just and right in the land. In his days Judah will be saved and Israel will live in safety. This is the name by which he will be called: The Lord Our Righteous Saviour.' 'So then, the days are coming,' declares the Lord, 'when people will no longer say, "As surely as the Lord lives, who brought the Israelites up out of Egypt," but they will say, "As surely as the Lord lives, who brought the descendants of Israel up out of the land of the north and out of all the countries where he had banished them." Then they will live in their own land.' (Jeremiah 23:5–8)

- The Messiah will be **inspired** by God:

  The Spirit of the Lord will rest upon him. (Isaiah 11:2).

  The Messiah will rule wisely and justly and ensure the poor are treated fairly. (Isaiah 11:3–5)

- The Messiah will rebuild the Temple in Jerusalem.

The Messianic Age

The time when the Messiah comes is known as the Messianic Age or *Olam Ha-Ba* (the 'world to come') and the Nevi'im say that during this time:

- There will be peace among all nations (Isaiah 2:4; Micah 4:3).
- There will be justice and prosperity throughout the world (Isaiah 11:6–9).
- All the Jewish people will return from **exile** to Israel (Jeremiah 23:8; Hosea 3:4–5).
- The Temple will be rebuilt in Jerusalem (Ezekiel 37:26–27).
- The whole world will accept the Jewish God and Jewish religion (Isaiah 2:3; Zechariah 14:9).
- There will be no sin or evil as everyone will obey all the commandments (Zephaniah 3:13).

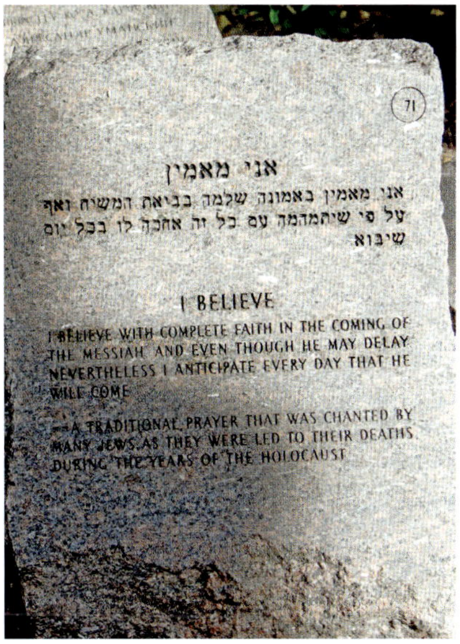

'I believe with complete faith in the coming of the Messiah and even though he may delay, nevertheless I anticipate every day that he will come.'

Different understandings of the Messiah

Belief in the Messiah is basic to Judaism as it is one of the Thirteen Principles,

> *I believe with perfect faith in the coming of the Messiah. However long it takes, I will await His coming every day (the twelfth of Maimonides' Thirteen Principles).*

However, exactly what this means is a matter of dispute:

- Some rabbis have taught that there are a finite number of souls destined to enter the world and live within human bodies. When all these souls have arrived on earth, the Messiah will come and bring in the Messianic Age.
- Other rabbis have taught that the Messiah will not come until all Jewish people observe all the *mitzvot* fully, with no Jew breaking a command.
- Some Kabbalistic Jews believe that the Messiah (Messiah ben David) will be preceded by Messiah ben Joseph, who will lead the Children of Israel to Jerusalem and re-establish Temple worship and set up his own dominion. Then the forces of evil will wage war against Messiah ben Joseph and kill him. After this, the Messiah ben David will appear, defeat the forces of evil, resurrect Messiah ben Joseph and bring in the Messianic Age.
- Some Jewish thinkers believe that the Messianic Age will be similar to the current age except that the Jewish people will have returned to Jerusalem and Temple worship will have been restored.
- Other Jewish thinkers believe that the coming of the Messiah will result in the resurrection of the dead and everyone being given a spiritual body to live in a spiritual world.

Useful words

Exile – when the Jewish people had to leave their homeland and live elsewhere

Sanctuary – God's holy place

> *My servant David will be king over them; and they will all have one shepherd. They will follow my laws and be careful to keep my decrees. They will live in the land I gave to my servant Jacob, the land where your fathers lived. They and their children and their children's children will live there for ever, and David my servant will be their Prince for ever. I will make a covenant of peace with them; it will be an everlasting covenant. I will establish them and increase their numbers, and I will put my* ***sanctuary*** *among them for ever. My dwelling place will be with them; I will be their God, and they will be my people. Then the nations will know that I the Lord make Israel holy when my sanctuary is among them for ever. (Ezekiel 37:24–28)*

Activities

1. Read the passage from Ezekiel 37 opposite. Make a list of the features of messiahship and the Messianic Age in this passage and a list of those features which are not in the passage.
2. Do you think the Messianic Age will ever happen?

Activity

Do you think all Jews have the same ideas about the Messiah?

- Most rabbis have followed the teaching of Maimonides that no one can know when the Messiah will come other than God himself.
- Many Reform Jews no longer believe in the idea of an individual Messiah who will make the world perfect. They think that was an idea which arose out of the need for Jewish people to have a hope of returning to their homeland after being driven out by the Babylonians and then by the Romans. These Reform Jews believe that it is up to individual Jewish people to change this world, bringing the nations together and establishing justice and peace just as the Tenakh predicts the Messianic Age will do.

The importance of ideas about the Messiah for Jews today

Belief in the coming of the Messiah is one the Thirteen Principles of the Faith and so it has to be important since these are regarded as the minimum requirements of Jewish belief.

The importance can also be seen in the fact that in the prayer which Jews recite three times a day, they pray for the coming of the Messiah, as well as the return of the exiles, reward to the righteous, the rebuilding of Jerusalem, the restoration of the line of King David and the restoration of the Temple service.

The way the idea of the Messianic Age (especially the Reform view) has attracted Jewish people to liberal and left-wing political causes shows another importance. Many think that the Messianic ideal of peace and justice for the poor is the reason why so many left-wing thinkers were Jewish (for example, Karl Marx and Leon Trotsky).

Summary

Jews believe that the Messiah will be sent by God to bring in the Messianic Age, when everyone will live in peace and worship the one true God. There are different ideas among Jews about when the Messiah will come and how the Messianic Age will be bought in.

Practice questions

c Explain two reasons why beliefs about the Messiah are important for Jews today. You must refer to a source of wisdom and authority in your answer.

d 'All Jews should have the same beliefs about the Messiah.' Evaluate this statement, considering arguments for and against. In your answer you should:

- refer to Jewish points of view
- refer to different Jewish points of view
- reach a justified conclusion.

Topic 2.1b.4 The covenant at Sinai

The nature and history of the covenant at Sinai

Moses is the great teacher of Judaism. The Jewish people were in captivity in Egypt, working as slaves for the Egyptian pharaoh (probably Rameses II), when Moses was called by God to lead his people out of Egypt to the Promised Land of Canaan. This is known as the **Exodus** and the most famous event was when God opened up the Red Sea to let the Israelites cross on dry land, but then brought back the waters to trap the Egyptian army.

Moses then spent 40 years wandering in the Sinai wilderness preparing the people to enter and possess the promised land, where they would set up their own country based on God's laws. It was during this time that God appeared to Moses on Mount Sinai to make the **covenant**.

A covenant is a binding agreement between two parties with certain conditions and promises. The Mosaic Covenant was an agreement between God and the Jewish people given to Moses. God gave Moses his laws on two tablets of stone. These were to be kept in the **Ark of the Covenant**, which had to be kept in the tabernacle. The agreement was that if the people kept God's laws, then

> *out of all the nations, you will be my treasured possession ... you will be for me a kingdom of priests and a holy nation.* (Exodus 19:5–6)

The importance of the Mosaic Covenant for Jews today

- The Mosaic Covenant has become the very basis of Judaism. Moses was given 613 *mitzvot* by God in the Torah which provide the way of life for Jewish people and which separate them from **Gentiles** (see Topic 2.1b.7, page 206).
- The covenant God made with Moses means that Jewish people have a duty to keep the *mitzvot* as part of their side of the covenant to make them God's people.
- The Tenakh teaches that by keeping the Mosaic Covenant, the Jewish people will fulfil their destiny of bringing the whole world to worship God:

  > *I will also make you a light for the Gentiles, that you may bring salvation to the whole earth.* (Isaiah 49:6)

- The laws given to Moses are so important for modern Jews that the divisions into Reform and Orthodox, Hasidic and Ultra-Orthodox and so on are all based on interpretations of how Jewish people should obey the Mosaic Covenant.

The role of Moses in the covenant

Moses was crucial to the covenant. He met the *shekhinah* on Mount Sinai and received the laws directly from God. God made the covenant with Moses and Moses then delivered it to the Jewish people, and explained it to them so that they then took the covenant on themselves.

Thinking points

In this topic you need to:

- think about the nature and history of the covenant at Sinai (the Ten Commandments), including Exodus 20:2–17
- understand the role of Moses in the covenant
- be able to explain and evaluate the importance of the covenant and the Ten Commandments for Jews today.

Useful words

Exodus – the Israelites' escape from slavery in Egypt
Covenant – an agreement between God and his people
Ark of the Covenant – the holy container for the tablets of the commandments
Gentiles – non-Jews

> *You are standing here in order to enter into covenant with the Lord your God, a covenant the Lord is entering into with you this day and sealing with an oath, to confirm you this day as his people that he may be your God as he promised you and as he swore to your fathers, Abraham, Isaac and Jacob. I am making this covenant, with its oath, not only with you who are standing here with us today in the presence of the Lord our God, but also with those who are not here today.* (Deuteronomy 29:12–15)

Activity

What is the Mosaic Covenant?

The Ten Commandments.

The Ten Commandments

Although Moses was given 613 commandments from God, Jews regard the Ten Commandments as special because they are commandments to be kept by all Jews, women as well as men, children as well as adults. This makes them different from the 613 *mitzvot* because some of the *mitzvot* are only to be kept by men, some are only to be kept by women and some are not to be kept by children. English-speaking Jews often refer to the Ten Commandments as the **Decalogue** (Exodus 20:2–17).

Useful words

Decalogue – the Ten Commandments
Shabbat – the Jewish holy day on Saturday, the seventh day of the week

Why the Decalogue is important in Jewish life today

The first commandment is important because Jewish people:

- Touch the *mezuzah* when they go in and out to remind themselves of the *shema*, which tells them they worship one God only.
- Pray three times a day (morning, afternoon, evening) to the one true God, when males wear the *tefillin* containing the *shema* to remind them that they believe in one God only.
- Say grace to the one God before and after food.
- Have frequent reference in daily prayers and synagogue worship to the fact that Jewish people worship one God only.

The second commandment is important because Jewish people prohibit having any form of statue in the synagogue or their home. Most Jewish people would not make or have in the home anything that might look like an idol. They would allow paintings as long as they were somehow incomplete (for example, only the top half, no face, no human with an animal head). There is much debate about what art is permitted in Judaism, showing how seriously the second commandment is taken.

The third commandment is important because Jewish people would not use God's name in any form of swearing and, indeed, most Jewish people say, 'the Almighty' rather than speaking the word God or Lord or so on, which will always be written as G-d, L-rd and so on. The name which God told Moses was his name (Jahweh) in Exodus is never pronounced and only appears as JHWH.

Activity

Look at the abbreviation above. Do you think Jewish people would use this in a mobile message?

The fourth commandment is very important in modern Jewish life. The commandment makes plain that the Sabbath is the seventh day of the week – Saturday – and on that day Orthodox Jews do no work. ***Shabbat*** begins at sunset on Friday and ends when the stars appear on Saturday. Orthodox Jews are very strict about what constitutes work. See Topic 2.1b.6 (page 204).

'[Moses] took the calf which they had made and burned it with fire, and ground it to powder, and scattered it over the surface of the water and made the sons of Israel drink it.'

The fifth commandment to honour parents is important as it helps Jewish people in their family life and parents in their task of bringing their children up to be good Jews. As part of keeping the commandment, Jewish people in the UK support Jewish Care, a charity which provides community centres and care homes for elderly or disabled relatives.

Jewish people find the last five commandments very important when they are making moral decisions as they give very clear moral guidance:

- do not kill
- do not commit adultery
- do not steal
- do not lie
- do not desire other people's things.

If Jewish people follow these commandments, they will have a good relationship with their neighbours. By not killing and not stealing, they will be rejecting violence. By not committing adultery or desiring other people's partners, they will promote marriage and family life.

Following the Ten Commandments means Jewish people will not lie or cheat people, nor will they covet or desire other people's possessions. Applying the Ten Commandments means Jewish people should act against all forms of greed and materialism.

Activities

1. Look at the painting above. Do you think it is breaking the second commandment?
2. How would the last six of the Ten Commandments help Jewish people to make moral decisions?

Practice questions

c Explain two ways in which Moses is important for the Jewish people. In your answer you must refer to a source of wisdom and authority.

d 'The Mosaic Covenant is not relevant for Jewish life today.' Evaluate this statement considering arguments for and against. In your answer you should:

- refer to Jewish points of view
- refer to different Jewish points of view
- reach a justified conclusion.

Summary

The covenant with Moses is the agreement between God and the Jewish people that the people would keep the 613 *mitzvot* God gave to Moses and God would make them his holy people. The Ten Commandments (Decalogue) are part of the covenant which God gave to Moses on Mount Sinai. The Ten Commandments sum up the worship and morality of the covenant.

Topic 2.1b.5 The covenant with Abraham

Thinking points

In this topic you need to:

- think about what the Abrahamic Covenant is, including the role of Abraham in Genesis 17:1–12, and how it has developed
- be able to explain and evaluate the importance of this covenant for Jews today.

Useful words

Canaan – ancient name for the land of Israel
Ishmael – Abraham's son through Hagar, ancestor of Arab people
Isaac – Abraham's son through Sarah, ancestor of Jewish people
Brit milah – covenant of circumcision

Activity

Read the passage from Genesis chapter 17 and make a list of what God's side of the agreement was and what Abraham's side was.

The nature and history of the Abrahamic Covenant

A thousand years before Moses, the Torah says that God called Abraham to leave his family in Iraq and travel to Canaan to worship the one true God. God said to him:

> *I will make you a great nation and I will bless you ... and all peoples on earth will be blessed through you.* (Genesis 12:2–3)

In a second appearance, God promised to give the land of **Canaan** to Abraham's descendants. Abraham had no children and so his wife, Sarah, offered him her maid, Hagar, to have a surrogate child who was named Ishmael, but Sarah found it difficult to accept **Ishmael**. Then God told Abraham that Sarah would have a child in her old age – **Isaac**. The couple found this difficult to believe, but it happened and their son Isaac became the heir to the promises. God promised that Ishmael would be the father of a great nation (both Jews and Muslims believe that Ishmael was the ancestor of the Arabs). However, it was with Abraham and Isaac that God made his covenant of circumcision (***brit milah***).

The Abrahamic Covenant

> *When Abram was ninety-nine years old, the Lord appeared to him and said, 'I am God Almighty; walk before me faithfully and be blameless. Then I will make my covenant between me and you and will greatly increase your numbers.' Abram fell facedown, and God said to him, 'As for me, this is my covenant with you: You will be the father of many nations. No longer will you be called Abram; your name will be Abraham, for I have made you a father of many nations. I will make you very fruitful; I will make nations of you, and kings will come from you. I will establish my covenant as an everlasting covenant between me and you and your descendants after you for the generations to come, to be your God and the God of your descendants after you. The whole land of Canaan, where you now reside as a foreigner, I will give as an everlasting possession to you and your descendants after you; and I will be their God.' Then God said to Abraham, 'As for you, you must keep my covenant, you and your descendants after you for the generations to come. This is my covenant with you and your descendants after you, the covenant you are to keep: Every male among you shall be circumcised. You are to undergo circumcision, and it will be the sign of the covenant between me and you. For the generations to come every male among you who is eight days old must be circumcised.'* (Genesis 17:1–12)

'"Look up at the heavens and count the stars – if indeed you can count them." Then he said to him, "So shall your offspring be"' (Genesis 15:5).

Genesis 17:13–27 goes on to say that Abraham and Sarah would have a son Isaac with whom God would establish an everlasting covenant for his descendants. Then Abraham circumcised himself and his son Ishmael and all the male members of his household.

The Torah has many references to the importance of circumcision, but gives no reason why this should have been such a major part of the covenant with Abraham. Two suggestions made by the rabbis are:

- It is appropriate that a bodily sign of Israel's commitment to God throughout the generations should be on that part of the male anatomy which will create the future generations.
- Man should not be satisfied with his imperfect condition. Circumcision makes a perfect male without the useless foreskin and Jewish men should try to perfect themselves and serve God with every part of their body.

However, some modern Jews feel that it is the Mosaic Covenant that is important for Jewish people, not the Abrahamic one. They do not circumcise their children because the Torah prohibits marking or altering the human body:

> *You shall not make any cuttings in your flesh on account of the dead or tattoo any marks upon you: I am the Lord.* (Leviticus 19:28)

They also insist that the Torah does not allow another person to be harmed (Exodus 21:18–27). Added to this, growing awareness of infant pain has brought the ethics of circumcision into question. They also refer to the statement in the *Encyclopedia Judaica*: 'Any child born of a Jewish mother is a Jew, whether circumcised or not.'

Activities

1. Look at the photo above. Has the prediction come true?
2. Who are the Children of Israel?
3. What is the difference between an Israelite and an Israeli?

History of the Abrahamic Covenant

The promise God made to Abraham was that he would be the father of a great nation. Abraham's grandson, Jacob, was renamed by God and his new name was Israel:

> *Your name is Jacob, but you will no longer be called Jacob, your name will be Israel ... A nation and a community of nations will come from your body. The land I gave to Abraham and Isaac I will also give to you, and I will give this land to your descendants after you.* (Genesis 35:10–12)

Jacob had twelve sons, the Children of Israel. These twelve were the ancestors of the twelve tribes of Israel, from which any Jewish person can claim descent. In the Torah, the Children of Israel are the heirs to the promises made to Abraham and are the ones who are part of the Mosaic Covenant: 'Moses said to the whole Israelite community,

> *This is what the Lord has commanded.'* (Exodus 35:4)

In later Jewish history, the Jewish kingdom split into two: the ten northern tribes formed the Kingdom of Israel, which was conquered by the Assyrians in 721BCE, and the two southern tribes formed the Kingdom of Judah, which was not conquered until 586BCE. It is from this kingdom that the words Judaism and Jew originate. However, it is the Children of Israel who are the Jewish people.

When the modern Jewish state was established, it was called Israel; nowadays an Israelite is used to refer to an ethnic Jew who follows the Jewish religion whereas an Israeli is a citizen of the state of Israel.

Why the Abrahamic Covenant is important for Jews today

The covenant is important for Jews today for the following reasons:

- Most Jewish baby boys are circumcised, usually at eight days old. This often entails a special *brit milah* ceremony when a ***mohel*** circumcises the boy, and the father promises to bring the boy up in the Jewish faith and thanks God for circumcision,

  by which our sons enter into the covenant of Abraham our father.

- Some Reform and Liberal Jews choose not to circumcise their sons, often because they are concerned about medical issues. However, the covenant is still important to them and some Reform rabbis have developed a welcoming ceremony that they call the ***brit shalom*** (covenant of peace), which claims the child as an heir of the Abrahamic covenant.
- The importance of the Abrahamic covenant can be seen in the increasing popularity of the ***brit chayim*** (covenant of life) ceremony for Jewish baby girls among Reform and Liberal Jews. This ceremony welcomes girls into the Jewish faith and claims them as heirs to the Abrahamic Covenant.
- The covenant gave rise to the idea that Jewish people had a right to live in the area that was the ancient Kingdom of Israel, which has led to the importance of the land of Israel to Jewish people. The state of Israel was established in 1947 as a place of security for all Jews, and Jewish people living anywhere in the world have the right to live in Israel and become a citizen. In 2015 there were 6.3 million Children of

Useful words

Mohel – expert circumciser
Brit shalom – covenant of peace (ceremony welcoming uncircumcised male babies)
Brit chayim – covenant of life ceremony for Reform girl babies

Activities

1. Do you think the Abrahamic Covenant is important for Jews today?
2. Look at the Pew Research Center data on page 203. Why do you think more American Christians than American Jews believe that God gave the Jewish people the land of Israel?

Israel living in Israel, making up 75 per cent of the population of Israel (worldwide there are 13.9 million Jews, of whom 5.7 million live in the USA).

There is a major debate in the Jewish communities outside Israel about the idea of the state of Israel being a fulfilment of God's promise to Abraham to give the Children of Israel the Promised Land. Ultra-Orthodox groups outside Israel teach that the return to the Promised Land will only come with the coming of the Messiah and that rather than supporting Israel, good Jews should be following all the *mitzvot* and praying for the coming of the Messiah.

Only 40 percent of American Jews believe the land that is now Israel was given to the Jewish people by God. However, 55 percent of American Christians believe this, and 64 percent of Protestant Christians in the USA believe it. (Pew Research Center, Survey of US Jews, 2013)

Practice questions

c Explain two reasons why male Jewish babies are circumcised. In your answer you must refer to a source of wisdom and authority.

d 'The covenant with Moses is more important than the covenant with Abraham.' Evaluate this statement considering arguments for and against. In your answer you should:

- refer to Jewish points of view
- reach a justified conclusion.

Summary

The Abrahamic Covenant is God's agreement with Abraham that God would make a great nation from Abraham's descendants and give them the Promised Land as their own if all their male children were circumcised and they worshipped God alone. The covenant is so important that many Reform and Liberal Jews have a ceremony for girls to welcome them into Abraham's covenant.

Topic 2.1b.6 Sanctity of life

Thinking points

In this topic you need to:

- think about the nature and importance of *pikuach nefesh* (saving a life)
- think about why human life is holy and how life is shown as special and as taking precedence over everything (Talmud *Yoma*)
- be able to explain and evaluate Jewish ideas about the sanctity of life and its importance for Jews today.

The nature and importance of *pikuach nefesh*

Judaism teaches that life is sacred – life is a gift from God. It follows that as God is the author of life, life itself is holy and must be valued and preserved. As the Torah says:

> *See now that I myself am He! There is no god beside me. I put to death, and I bring to life.* (Deuteronomy 32:39)

> *You shall not murder.* (Exodus 20:13)

> *If anyone takes the life of a human being, he must be put to death. Anyone who takes the life of someone's animal must make restitution – life for life.* (Leviticus 24:17–18)

Jewish people believe that God is in control of his creation and that whatever comes to life or dies is caused to do so by God. Humans have to respect all human life. It is up to God to say when life will begin or end. As the Tenakh says,

> *Naked I came from my mother's womb, and naked I shall depart. The Lord gave and the Lord has taken away; may the name of the Lord be blessed.* (Job 1:21)

The sacredness and importance of human life is shown in the concept of *pikuach nefesh*, which is the principle in Jewish law that the preservation of human life overrides almost all other religious considerations.

The **Talmud** explains this principle of *pikuach nefesh* using the verse,

> *Keep my decrees and laws, for the person who obeys them will live by them. I am the Lord* (Leviticus 18:5)

to which the rabbis added:

> *That he shall live by them, and not that he shall die by them.* (Babylonian Talmud, Yoma 85b)

When life is involved, all Sabbath laws may be suspended to safeguard the health of the individual. A Jew is not merely permitted but is actually required to disregard a law that conflicts with life or health.

> *It is a religious precept to* ***desecrate*** *the Sabbath for any person afflicted with an illness that may prove dangerous; he who is zealous is praiseworthy while he who asks questions sheds blood.* (Shulhan Arukh, Orah Hayyim 328:2)

Pikuach nefesh is also derived from the Torah verse,

> *Do not do anything that endangers your neighbour's life.* (Leviticus 19:16)

According to *pikuach nefesh*, a person must do everything in their power to save the life of another, so it is permissible to break the **Yom Kippur** fast, break the ***kashrut*** rules and so on. The Talmud contains several instances where the laws of the Sabbath are to be broken to save the life of another; these occasions include rescuing a child from the sea, breaking apart a

Useful words

Talmud – collection of Mishneh and other writing on the Jewish law
Desecrate – violate a sacred place or law
Yom Kippur – the Day of Atonement when religious Jews fast for the whole day
Kashrut – keeping Jewish food laws

Activities

1. How do the scriptures show the sanctity of life?
2. What is the principle of *pikuach nefesh* based on?

Hatzola is a voluntary medical emergency service that provides care to the Orthodox Jewish community of north London. A Jew reluctant to violate Sabbath rules when receiving medical attention may be more at ease and easily convinced of the medical urgency when the paramedic is a fellow Orthodox Jew.

wall that has collapsed on a child, breaking down a door about to close on an infant, and extinguishing a fire (*Yoma* 84b).

Clearly the concept of *pikuach nefesh* is based on the **sanctity of life** and shows how important the belief in sanctity of life is to Judaism.

Useful words

Sanctity of life – the belief that life is holy and belongs to God

Why the concept of *pikuach nefesh* is important for Jews today

Pikuach nefesh is particularly important in areas of medical ethics such as:

- Abortion: some Jews believe that abortion can never be allowed because of the belief in the sanctity of life, but *pikuach nefesh* means that if the mother's life is at risk, then it should be allowed.
- Contraception: Orthodox Judaism does not allow the use of condoms because the Torah teaches that the male seed is sacred, but the Jewish Aids Trust promotes the use of condoms to prevent HIV transmission because this *mitzvah* can be broken to save the lives of people who may become infected with HIV.
- Transplant surgery should not be allowed because there is a *mitzvah* which says dead bodies must not be interfered with, but *pikuach nefesh* means that this *mitzvah* can be broken to transplant on organ from a dead person to save the life of a living person.

Pikuach nefesh is also an important principle for Jews living in the complex world of today. It is a means of deciding when and where the *mitzvot* take priority.

Activities

1. Look at the photo above. How does this photo explain the concept of *pikuach nefesh*?
2. Can you think of a situation where *pikuach nefesh* could be used to justify breaking a *mitzvah*?

Practice questions

c Explain two reasons why Jews believe in the sanctity of life. In your answer you must refer to a source of wisdom and authority.

d 'Orthodox Jews should always obey the *mitzvot*.' Evaluate this statement considering arguments for and against. In your answer you should:

- refer to Jewish points of view
- refer to different Jewish points of view
- reach a justified conclusion.

Summary

Jewish people believe in the sanctity of life because they believe that life is a gift from God which makes life itself holy. This is taught in the Torah. The importance of the sanctity of life is seen in the teaching of *pikuach nefesh*, which says that a Jew must do everything in their power to save a life even if it involves breaking the *mitzvot*.

Topic 2.1b.7 Moral principles and the *mitzvot*

Thinking points

In this topic you will need to:

- think about the nature of the *mitzvot*, including the Mishneh Torah of Maimonides
- consider the relationship between keeping the *mitzvot* and free will
- understand the *mitzvot* between the Almighty and humans
- be able to explain why the *mitzvot* are important for Jewish life today.

Useful words

Mitzvot – commandments (plural)
Oral Torah – the unwritten Torah given to Moses by God
Halakhah – Jewish law from the Written and Oral Torah
Mishneh – the Oral Torah

The nature of the *mitzvot*

As we have seen, Moses received 613 ***mitzvot*** on Mount Sinai. These are recorded in the Torah and the Jewish people are to observe them as their part of the Mosaic Covenant.

However, the *mitzvot* in the Torah are stated very briefly, and needed some explanation. For example, the fourth of the Ten Commandments says that Jewish people should do no work on the Sabbath, but it does not explain what is meant by work. According to Jewish tradition, this explanation was given to Moses by God in the form of the '**Oral Torah**' which was passed on by priests, judges and later by rabbis. The Oral and Written Torah made up the ***halakhah*** (the Jewish law).

The Oral Torah was written down in the Talmud during the second century CE, but the **Mishneh** Torah compiled by Maimonides between 1170 and 1180 (especially the five books of the Sefer Madda) is regarded by many Jews as the major code of Jewish law. Maimonides intended to provide a complete statement of the oral law, so that a Jew who mastered first the Written Torah and then the Mishneh Torah would be in no need of any other book. Many rabbis believe that the Mishneh Torah gives the correct meaning of the Oral Torah and so no decisions on the *halakhah* can be accepted if they disagree with Maimonides.

Although the *mitzvot* cannot change because they were given to Moses by God, the understanding of them and the interpretation of them for life today are always changing. New discoveries and new social conditions mean that people's ways of living have changed and the *halakhah* has to be adapted. As an example, can automated machinery be used on *Shabbat*? So new commentaries on the *mitzvot* are continually being added.

For most Jewish people the *mitzvot* and *halakhah* are one and the same thing because by following the Jewish law (*halakhah*) they are keeping the *mitzvot*.

> *This day ... I have set before you life and death, blessings and curses. Now choose life so that you and your children may live. (Deuteronomy 30:19)*

Keeping the *mitzvot* and free will

The *mitzvot* are commandments and therefore not optional. Judaism teaches that each Jew must decide whether or not to follow the *mitzvot* of their own free will. The first book of the Torah (Genesis) teaches that God created humans in his own image:

> *So God created man in his own image, in the image of God he created him; male and female he created them. (Genesis 1:27)*

Judaism understands this to mean that God has created humans with free will, every person is free to choose whether to do good or evil. In particular, they are free to choose whether to obey the *mitzvot* or ignore them.

This is important because it means that following the *mitzvot* is not something originating from people's nature as human beings. Humans have no choice about breathing, it is just something that happens; but humans do have a choice about following the *mitzvot*, and because it is a choice, it is something about which they can be judged (see Topic 2.1b.1, page 186).

Activity

Look at the quotation from Deuteronomy above. What choice do you think is being referred to?

Why the *mitzvot* are important for understanding the relationship between humans and the Almighty

The *mitzvot* should be understood at a much deeper spiritual level than simply keeping them day by day.

The word *mitzvah* means commandment, but it is closely related to the Hebrew word for 'connection' and Jewish people believe that the *mitzvot* are a way for individuals to connect with God. By keeping the *mitzvot*, Jewish people communicate with God.

The *mitzvot* are God's way of reaching out to human beings and helping them to live in the correct way. By obeying the *mitzvot*, humans are reaching back to God and so becoming in a true way, 'the people of God'. This, of course, is the meaning of the Mosaic Covenant – God has agreed to be the Jewish people's God, and look after them, if they keep his *mitzvot*.

Activity

Do you think following the *mitzvot* will improve relationships between people?

The importance of the *mitzvot* for relationships between people

It is important for Jewish people to understand the *mitzvot* because it is only if a Jewish person really understands the *mitzvot* that he or she will keep them properly. Judaism teaches that through understanding the *mitzvot* will come better behaviour, and it is the aim of Judaism to help people behave in the best way possible. As the Talmud says, 'The *mitzvot* were given for the purpose of refining people'.

A *kosher* McDonald's restaurant in Buenos Aires, Argentina.

Useful words

Mitzvah – commandment (singular)
Chukim – *mitzvot* with no reason given for them
Kosher – food which a Jew is allowed to eat

American Jews consider the most essential elements of being Jewish to be: Remembering the Holocaust, leading an ethical and moral life, working for justice/equality, being intellectually curious. (Pew Research Center, Survey of US Jews, 2013)

Each ***mitzvah*** (this is the singular, *mitzvot* is plural) has something to teach. For example, the laws about borrowing and lending teach compassion for those less well-off than oneself; the laws on damages and compensation teach the need for personal responsibility; the laws on the punishment of criminals teach the need to respect human dignity. Consequently, it is important to understand these *mitzvot* in order to understand what they teach.

However, there are some *mitzvot* (known as ***chukim***) which have no reason given for them, for example the *mitzvot* on keeping ***kosher***. Jewish scholars say it is important to understand that these *mitzvot* were given by God as a test of faith and that observing these *mitzvot* strengthens a Jew's faith in the Almighty.

Why there are different views in Judaism about the importance of the *mitzvot*

The Orthodox view

The *mitzvot* are particularly important for Orthodox Jews because they cover the whole of life. No feature of life is unaffected by the *mitzvot*. For the Orthodox Jew there is a right and a wrong way of doing everything. For example, there are *mitzvot* which tell people how to organise the kitchen, how to dress, what to eat, how to grow crops, who they can marry, how to divorce, when they can work, which jobs they cannot do, paying wages and ownership of property and business.

The Liberal/Reform view

The *mitzvot* are not as important for Liberal Jews as they do not regard the *mitzvot* as coming to Moses directly from God, and so they believe that observing the *mitzvot* is a matter of personal choice. For example, some Liberal Jews keep *kashrut*, some just eat *kosher* food, others ignore the food laws altogether. This attitude to the *mitzvot* means that they are not considered as important to Liberal Jews as to the Orthodox.

Summary

The *mitzvot* are the 613 commands/laws Moses received from God on Sinai. They are the Written Torah which are explained by the Oral Torahs written in the Talmud and Mishneh Torah. These make up the Jewish law (*halakhah*). They affect the whole of a Jew's life, but only the Orthodox follow all of them because for Liberal/Reform Jews the *mitzvot* are optional.

Practice questions

c Explain two reasons why Jews need the *halakhah* as well as the Written Torah. In your answer you must refer to a source of wisdom and authority.

d 'The *mitzvot* are no longer relevant to modern life.' Evaluate this statement considering arguments for and against. In your answer you should:

- refer to Jewish points of view
- refer to different Jewish points of view
- reach a justified conclusion.

Topic 2.1b.8 Jewish beliefs about life after death

Scriptural teachings about life after death

There is clear evidence in the Torah of belief in existence after death. The Torah indicates in several places that the righteous will be reunited with their loved ones after death, while the wicked will be excluded from this reunion. The Torah speaks of the **patriarchs** being 'gathered to their people':

> *There on the mountain that you [Moses] have climbed, you will die and be gathered to your people.* (Deuteronomy 32:50)

Being gathered to your people after death is believed by Jews to mean that there will be an afterlife which will involve meeting with their dead family.

The Tenakh has many references to life after death. The Tenakh says that God will end the world, raise the dead and create a new world by rebuilding Jerusalem and the Temple. God will decide what happens to people in the afterlife on the basis of how they have lived their lives and what they have believed:

> *But your dead will live; their bodies will rise. You who dwell in the dust, wake up and shout for joy. Your dew is like the dew of the morning; the earth will give birth to her dead.* (Isaiah 26:19)

> *At that time Michael, the great prince who protects your people, will arise. And there will be a time of distress, such as has not happened from the beginning of nations until then. But at that time your people – everyone whose name shall be found written in the book – will be delivered. Multitudes who sleep in the dust of the earth will awake, some to everlasting life, others to shame and everlasting contempt.* (Daniel 12:1–13)

Different Jewish understandings of life after death

There is disagreement in Judaism about how the scriptural evidence for the afterlife should be interpreted.

Resurrection

The Thirteen Principles of Faith (written by Maimonides and described as 'Articles of the Jewish Creed' in the Jewish Daily Prayer Book) state,

> *I believe with perfect faith that there will be a resurrection of the dead at a time that will please the Creator, blessed be his name.*

However, there are disagreements about resurrection, making it unclear exactly who will be resurrected, when it will happen and what will take place:

- Some sources imply that the resurrection of the dead will occur during the Messianic Age.
- Others indicate that resurrection will follow the Messianic Age.
- According to some, only the righteous will be resurrected.

Thinking points

In this topic you need to:

- think about Jewish teachings about life after death; the nature of resurrection and judgement; heaven and hell
- consider different Jewish understandings about life after death, including interpretations of Ecclesiastes 12:7
- similarities and differences between Christian and Jewish beliefs
- be able to evaluate different Jewish understandings about life after death and explain why life after death may be important for Jews today.

Useful words

Patriarchs – the fathers of Judaism (Abraham, Isaac, Jacob, Moses)

> *And the dust returns to the ground it came from, and the spirit returns to God who gave it.* (Ecclesiastes 12:7)

> *Fear God and keep his commandments for this is the whole duty of man. For God will bring every deed into judgement, including every hidden thing whether it is good or evil.* (Ecclesiastes 12:13–14)

Activity

Read the quotations from Ecclesiastes chapter 12. What do you think they mean?

Activities

1. Explain three different Jewish interpretations of judgement.
2. Outline three different Jewish ideas about what happens after judgement.

Useful words

Gan Eden – heaven
Gehinnom – hell
Mishneh Torah – the code of law written by Maimonides
Tosefta – rabbinic opinions extra to the Mishneh

- Other rabbis say that everyone will be resurrected and – as implied in Daniel – a day of judgement will follow.
- Other rabbis have argued for the immortality of the soul, the idea that the soul lives on after death as a spiritual being in the spiritual 'world to come' (*olam haba*), meaning there will be no resurrection.

The 'world to come' (*olam haba*) is another unclear idea. According to Maimonides, the 'world to come' refers to a time even beyond the world of the resurrected. He believed that the resurrected will eventually die a second death, at which point the souls of the righteous will enjoy a spiritual, bodiless existence in the presence of God. In other sources, the 'world to come' refers to the world inhabited by the righteous immediately following death, that is heaven (***Gan Eden***). In this view, the 'world to come' exists now, in some parallel universe.

Judgement

There are differences about the nature of judgement:

- Some rabbis have taught that judgement will be based purely on behaviour, for example Rabbi Hanina is recorded in the Babylonian Talmud, tractate Baba Metzia 58b, as saying that,

  *all who go down to **Gehinnom** will go up again, except adulterers, those who put their fellows to shame in public, and those who call their fellows by an obnoxious name.*

- The great Jewish scholar Maimonides went so far as to say that all good people will go to heaven, as can be seen in this quotation from **Mishneh Torah**, Repentance 3:5,

  *Moses Maimonides, echoing the **Tosefta** to Sanhedrin, maintained that the pious of all the nations of the world have a portion in the world-to-come.*

- Others have suggested that judgement will be based on a combination of belief and behaviour, as can be seen in this quotation from the Talmud (Sanhedrin 10:1),

  All Israelites have a share in the world-to-come ... [However], these are they that have no share in the world-to-come: one who says there is no resurrection of the dead prescribed in the Torah, and that the Torah is not from Heaven, and an Epicurean.

- Many modern rabbis prefer to concentrate on this life rather than worrying about the details of an afterlife about which no one can be certain. However, Jewish thinkers seem to be agreed that God will judge people on the basis of how they have lived their lives as much as, if not more than, on what they have believed.

Heaven and hell

There is disagreement about what happens after judgement. Indeed, the notion of heaven and hell has lots of different understandings. The earliest reference to *Gan Eden* (heaven) and *Gehinnom* (hell) as a pair is the first-century rabbinic statement: 'There are two paths before me, one leading to *Gan Eden* and the other to *Gehinnom*.' However, who goes to which and what they are like is unclear:

- Many rabbis have taught that the souls of the totally righteous ascend to heaven (*Gan Eden*) whereas the souls of ordinary people go to a place of punishment known as *Gehinnom* (referred to in the Christian New Testament as *gehenna* or hell).

- Some rabbis have taught that *Gehinnom* is more like the Catholic **purgatory** and that souls are purified of their sins through punishment and fire.
- Other rabbis have taught that *Gehinnom* is a place where souls have a chance to review what they have done with their lives on earth and repent for their wrong actions. However, this period in *Gehinnom* will only last for twelve months, after which souls will rise to heaven to await the resurrection.
- Some rabbis teach that totally evil souls are eternally damned and so are punished in *Gehinnom* forever.
- Others teach that the souls of the truly wicked are destroyed by God and so cease to exist.

A Jewish cemetery in Southgate, London.

Useful words

Purgatory – a place where Catholic Christians believe souls go after death to be purified

Why belief in life after death is important for Jews today

Belief in life after death is important because:

- It is the teaching of the Tenakh. Jews believe that the first five books of the Tenakh (the Torah) are a direct communication from God which must be believed. The other books of the Tenakh are inspired by God. Therefore, Jews should believe what the Tenakh says.
- It is the teaching of the Talmud. The Talmud is a collection of the Oral Torah, discussions by rabbis about the laws of the Torah, which most Jews try to follow.
- It is one of the Thirteen Principles of Faith which are described in the Daily Prayer Book as 'Articles of the Jewish Creed'. As part of the creed, Jews would feel they should believe it.
- Many Jews find that belief in life after death gives their lives meaning and purpose. They feel that for life to end at death does not make sense. A life after death, in which people will be judged on how they live this life, with the good rewarded and the evil punished, makes sense of this life. If the purpose of life is to live your life in such a way that you spend eternity in heaven, then that gives life meaning.
- Believing that God will decide what happens to people on the basis of how they have lived their lives is important for Jewish people because it means they must try to live good Jewish lives if they are to have a good life after death. This is a reason for them to observe the Torah and *halakhah*, making their beliefs about life after death have a big effect on their lives.

Christian and Jewish beliefs about life after death

Major differences:

- Most Jews believe that the Messiah will come and bring in the Messianic Age at the Last Day, whereas Conservative Christians believe that Jesus will return, and Liberal Christians do not believe in the Last Day.
- Many Jews believe that at the end of the world the Jewish people will bring all the non-Jews to worship God.

Activity

Look at the photo of the cemetery above. Why do you think Jews call this the House of Life?

Activity

Explain why believing in life after death is important for Jewish people.

A major similarity about life after death between the two religions is that not all Jews believe the same things about life after death, and not all Christians believe the same things about life after death. This tends to mean that conservative Jews and conservative Christians have similar beliefs about life after death whereas liberal Jews and liberal Christians have different views from the conservatives in their religion but similar views to the liberals in the other religion! If you are asked a question about asking you to explain differences, you should choose a conservative Christian and a contrasting liberal Jewish belief.

Conservatives' beliefs:

- Some Jews and some Christians believe in resurrection of the body.
- Some Jews and some Christians believe that the dead will be raised on the Last Day.
- Some Jews and some Christians believe that the Last Day will bring the world as we know it to an end.
- Some Jews and some Christians believe that people will be judged on what they have believed as well as how they have behaved.
- Some Jews and some Christians believe in hell as well as heaven and that bad people and people with the wrong beliefs will go to hell.

Liberals' beliefs:

- Some Jews and some Christians believe in immortality of the soul not resurrection of the body.
- Some Jews and some Christians do not believe in the Last Day and believe judgement will take place as soon as people die.
- Some Jews and some Christians do not believe in hell and believe that eventually everyone will go to heaven.

Major similarities:

- Both Christians and Jews believe this life is not all there is and that there will be life after death.
- Both Christians and Jews believe there will be some form of judgement after death based on how people have lived on earth.
- Both Christians and Jews believe in heaven as a place of paradise with God.
- Both Christians and Jews believe that good people will go to heaven.
- Both Christians and Jews believe that life after death is important because it makes sense of this life because it makes sure that the good are rewarded.

Summary

Based on the teachings of the Tenakh, Jews believe that there will be life after death. Most Jews believe that the dead will be raised (resurrection) and judged by God, but there are lots of different Jewish ideas about life after death. Some Jews think judgement will be just about behaviour, others that it will also be about religion. Some think everyone will eventually go to heaven, others that the very evil will spend eternity in hell.

Practice questions

c Explain two reasons why believing in life after death is important for Jews. In your answer you must refer to a source of wisdom and authority.

d 'When you're dead, you're dead and that's the end of you.' Evaluate this statement considering arguments for and against. In your answer you should:

- refer to Jewish points of view
- refer to different Jewish points of view
- reach a justified conclusion.

How to answer questions

a) Describe two similarities between Jewish beliefs about life after death and the beliefs of the main religious tradition of Britain. [3]

Christianity is the main religious tradition of Britain. One similarity is that both Christians and Jews believe that this life is not all there is and that there will be life after death. Another similarity is that both Christians and Jews believe that there will be some form of judgement after death based on how people have lived on earth.

A high mark answer because Christianity is identified as the main religious tradition of Britain and two similarities are clearly described.

b) Explain two reasons why the covenant with Abraham is important for Jews today. [4]

The covenant with Abraham is important because it is the reason why Jewish boys are still circumcised at eight days old as a sign of their Jewishness. It is also important because many Jews believe that they have been given the state of Israel by God for keeping the covenant.

A high mark answer because two correct reasons are given and each reason is developed.

c) Explain two reasons why it is important for Jewish people to keep all the *mitzvot*. In your answer you must refer to a source of wisdom and authority. [5]

The covenant which God made with Moses on Sinai means that Jewish people have a duty to keep the *mitzvot* as part of their side of the covenant to make them God's people. The Tenakh teaches that by keeping the *mitzvot*, the Jewish people will fulfil their destiny of bringing the whole world to worship God – 'I will also make you a light for the Gentiles, that you may bring salvation to the whole earth' (Isaiah 49:6).

A high mark answer because two correct reasons are given and each reason is developed with a reference to the covenant, the Tenakh and Isaiah as sources of authority.

d) 'Only the Almighty should judge.' Evaluate this statement considering arguments for and against. In your response you should:

- **refer to Jewish points of view**
- **refer to different Jewish points of view**
- **reach a justified conclusion. [12 marks + 3 spelling, punctuation and grammar (SPaG) marks]**

Many Jews would agree with this because the Tenakh is full of references to God acting as judge, for example, 'For the Lord is our judge, The Lord is our lawgiver, The Lord is our king; He will save us' (Isaiah 33:22). The Tenakh teaches that God as judge will ensure that the good are rewarded and the evil punished. 'And He will judge the world in righteousness; He will execute judgement for the peoples with equity' (Psalm 9:8).

However, the time when God the judge will make justice reign is in the future and so many Jews would say that although God is the perfect judge and will ensure that justice is done in the future, society needs judges other than God in order to function. Judaism has the Bet Din to make judgements about the *halakhah* and Jews accept the need for English courts and judges to ensure that the law is upheld here and now.

[Continued]

It seems to me that if you believe in the Jewish God, you will believe he is the only perfect judge for what happens at the end of the world, but for life to function properly, we need judges and a legal system operating in society in the present.

A high mark answer because it gives three clear developed Jewish reasons for thinking that God should be the only God. It then gives three reasons for disagreeing and then reaches a fully justified conclusion.

The answer would reach full marks for SPaG as spelling, punctuation and grammar are correct and a wide range of specialist vocabulary (Tenakh, Isaiah, Psalm, Bet Din, *halakhah*, legal system) is used appropriately.

SPaG

A high mark answer because the answer spells, punctuates and uses the rules of grammar with consistent accuracy and effective control of meaning. A wide range of specialist terms is used adeptly and with precision.

2 Crime and punishment

Area of study 2: Based on a study of Islam or Judaism

Topic 2.2.1 Justice

Thinking points

In this topic you need to:

- think about the nature of justice
- think about non-religious attitudes about why justice is important

either

- understand why justice is important for Muslims, including Qur'an 4:135

or

- understand why justice is important for Jews, including Deuteronomy 19:19–20
- understand why justice is important for the victim
- be able to explain and evaluate different responses to why justice is important.

Useful words

Justice – due allocation of reward and punishment, the maintenance of right
Laws – rules made by Parliament and enforceable by the courts
Hadith – sayings of the Prophet Muhammad

The nature of justice

Justice means rewarding the good and punishing the bad and making sure that what is right is what happens in society.

The way to make sure there is justice in society is to have **laws** which organise the behaviour of individuals and to protect the weak from the strong. Interestingly, a second meaning of justice is 'the administration of the law' because it is through making sure that laws work properly that there can be justice in society.

Non-religious attitudes to justice

Atheists and Humanists believe that justice is important because justice makes sure that:

- people are rewarded for their labour: without laws about business deals and work, modern-day society could not operate (people would not work if they weren't sure they would be paid and people would not make things if others could just take them away) and the justice system (police, courts and prisons) makes sure laws are obeyed and enforced
- the weak are protected from the strong (imagine if there were no laws on stealing, murder and rape, life would be 'nasty, brutish and short' in Thomas Hobbes' words)
- an advanced civilisation, such as the UK's, keeps operating properly. Without laws and justice, civilisation as we know it cannot function.

Why justice is important for Muslims

Justice is important for Muslims because:

- The Qur'an describes God as just. Four of the 99 names of God given in the Qur'an are the Judge, the Utterly Just, the Truth and the Equitable. As God himself is just, then justice must be of the highest importance for Muslims.
- The Qur'an says that God wants people to treat each other fairly and to establish justice:

  God commands justice, the doing of good ... and He forbids all shameful deeds and injustice. (Surah 16:90)

  And act justly. Truly, God loves those who are just. (Surah 49:9)

- There are many **hadith** in which Muhammad is shown as acting justly and telling Muslims to treat everyone justly and equally. For example, it is reported that the Prophet Muhammad said:

  People, beware of injustice, for injustice shall be darkness on the Day of Judgement.

  Many a community ruined itself in the past as they only punished the poor and ignored the offences of the exalted. By Allah, if my daughter Fatima would have committed theft, her hand would have been severed. (Hadith recorded by Sahih Bukhari)

An Islamic Relief charity shop in Cardiff.

- Muslims believe that it is part of their role as **vicegerents** of God's creation to behave justly to other people and to ensure that the world is governed in a fair way. For Islam, the way to do this is to follow the Shari'ah. In Islam, the law of the land should be the law of God, the Shari'ah, and so Islam has always had a system of justice based on courts with strict rules about how everyone should be treated fairly. The Shari'ah is based on justice for everyone.
- Equality before the law is one of the basic principles of the Islamic justice system. Justice has to be given out with fairness even if it goes against one's own self, one's parents or nearest relatives and whether it goes against the rich or in favour of the poor (Surah 4:135). The administration of justice in Islam has to be without any favouritism or prejudice (Surah 5:8).
- Muslims believe that all people should have equal rights before the law and that Muslims should work for a fairer sharing of the earth's resources. The pillar of *zakah* and the work of groups such as Muslim Aid and Islamic Relief are all trying to bring justice into the world.
- As part of their belief in justice, Muslims refuse to be involved in the charging of interest on loans, credit cards and so on. They believe that interest is unjust because it takes money from the poor and gives it to the rich, whereas the just thing would be to take money from the rich and give it to the poor.
- Islamic teaching on the Last Day is concerned with the need for the good to be rewarded and the evil punished, which is the basis of justice.

Useful words

Vicegerent – someone working as God's steward or representative on earth

O ye who believe! Stand out firmly for justice, as witnesses to God, even as against yourselves or your parents, or your kin, and whether it be against rich or poor: for God can best protect both. Follow not the lusts of your hearts lest ye swerve, and if ye distort justice or decline to do justice, verily God is well acquainted with all that ye do. (Surah 4:135)

Activities

1. What do you think justice is?
2. Look at the quotation from the Qur'an. Put it into your own words and then explain why it might be important for an understanding of justice.

Why justice is important for Jews

Jews believe that justice is hugely important. God is just, and God created the world as a place of justice and so Jews must practise justice themselves. From the earliest times, Judaism has had a system of justice and courts based on the Torah. Jews have to live their lives according to the *mitzvot* (laws) of the Torah and so it has always been important for the courts to operate fairly and for everyone to be treated equally by the law.

As part of their belief in justice, Jews have been particularly involved in the struggle for equal rights and the changing of unjust laws. Many American Jews felt it was their duty to join the **civil rights** movement, led by Martin Luther King Jr, a Christian minister, which campaigned for equal rights for black Americans in the 1960s.

Most Jews also believe that they should work for a fairer sharing of the earth's resources because God's justice applies to the whole world, not simply the Jewish people. Consequently, Jews are involved in groups such as Oxfam as well as World Jewish Relief.

Jews believe that justice is important because:

- The Tenakh says that God is a God of justice:

  He is the Rock! His works are perfect, and all His ways are just; A faithful God who does no wrong, upright and just is He. (Deuteronomy 32:4)

- The Tenakh says that people should be treated fairly and not cheated:

  Do not defraud your neighbour; nor rob him; do not hold back the wages if a hired man. (Leviticus 19:13)

  Do not deprive the ***alien*** *or the fatherless of justice.* (Deuteronomy 24:17)

- The Torah teaches that the rich should share with the poor:

  If there is a poor man among your brothers in any of the towns of the land that the Lord your God is giving you, do not be hard-hearted or tight-fisted towards your brother. Rather be open-handed and freely lend him whatever he needs. (Deuteronomy 15:7–8)

- The Talmud states that Rabbi Eleazar used to give a coin to a poor man and then say his prayers because it is written, 'I in righteousness shall behold thy face' (Psalm 17:15). This means that he believed it was through giving to charity (*tzedakah*) that he came closest to God. This is the basis for the custom of the charity box in the synagogue. During the week, before the service begins, everyone has the opportunity of training himself to live properly by dropping in some coins for charity.

If a ***malicious*** *witness takes the stand to accuse someone of a crime, the two people involved in the dispute must stand in the presence of the Lord before the priests and the judges who are in office at the time. The judges must make a thorough investigation, and if the witness proves to be a liar, giving false testimony against a fellow Israelite, then do to the false witness as that witness intended to do to the other party. You must purge the evil from among you. The rest of the people will hear of this and be afraid, and never again will such an evil thing be done among you.* (Deuteronomy 19:16–20)

Useful words

Civil rights – the rights of citizens to political and social freedom and equality
Alien – a foreigner, especially one who is not a naturalised citizen of the country where he or she is living
Malicious – having or showing a desire to cause harm to someone

'Let justice roll on like a river, righteousness like a never-failing stream' (Amos 5:24)

Activities

1. What do you think of the non-religious attitude to justice?
2. Look at the quotation from Deuteronomy. Put it into your own words and then explain why it might be important for an understanding of justice.

Why justice is important for the victim

The most obvious cases of **victims** being concerned about justice are such offences as burglary and assaults of various kinds as these involve the violation of people's personal space. However, financial offences can be just as hurtful, for example, when a scammer manages to remove a person's life savings from their bank account. Then there are offences such as causing death by dangerous driving from which the **perpetrator** gains nothing, but which cause tremendous hurt to the victim.

Useful words

Victims – those who have suffered from a crime

Perpetrator – one who commits a crime

Driver Neil Urwin's tiredness caused an accident leading to the death of a cyclist. Mr Urwin suffered from sleep apnoea meaning that his night-time breathing was interrupted, causing him to wake, leading to daytime tiredness. He consulted a specialist doctor who told him that he was not fit to drive. The day after receiving this advice, Mr Urwin hit and killed Andy Charlton, a 43-year-old father of three. During the trial for causing death by dangerous driving, Mr Charlton's widow, Katy Charlton, spoke directly to Mr Urwin: 'Shame on you, if you had followed that advice and not driven that day Andy would still be alive. I like to imagine that you are a decent man who made a foolish decision, a decision you will live with for the rest of your life.' Mrs Charlton went on to describe the impact her husband's death had on her family: 'You will always be the one who suffers least.' Mr Urwin was found guilty by the court and jailed for two years. (Based on several news reports)

Victims think it is important that justice is done so that they feel the hurt that they have suffered is recognised by society and paid for by the perpetrator. Victims think that justice has been done if the perpetrator has been caught and given a sentence that's appropriate for the pain they have inflicted, and they are aware of the effect their crime has had on their victim.

Why Muslims believe justice is important for the victim

Muslims believe that justice is important for the victim because:

- Islam teaches that justice should always be given and as the victim is totally innocent, justice can only be given when the victim receives justice from the perpetrator.

Should you drive if you are too tired? (Photo posed by a model.)

Activities

1. What do you think would be the best way of making sure that victims of crime are given justice?
2. Look at the case study on Neil Urwin. Do you think the driver was a criminal? Would a case like this make you think about your behaviour when you pass your driving test?

Summary

In Islam, justice is rewarding the good and punishing the bad. It is important for Muslims because the Qur'an says that God is just and that God demands justice from people. It is part of Muslims' duty as vicegerents to establish justice. Justice is important for the victims of crime because it means their hurt has been acknowledged by society and the criminal has been hurt as well. Muslims think this is right because it is part of the Qur'an's teaching on justice.

In Judaism, justice is rewarding the good and punishing the bad. It is important for Jews because the Tenakh says that God is just and that God demands justice from people. The Torah says that Jews must work for justice. Justice is important for the victims of crime because it means their hurt has been acknowledged by society and the criminal has been hurt as well. Jews think this is right because it is part of the Tenakh's teaching on justice.

- Islam teaches that the victims of crime should be compensated based on this verse from the Qur'an: 'Never should a believer kill a believer; but if it so happens by mistake, compensation is due. If one kills a believer, it is ordained that he should free a believing slave and pay compensation to the deceased's family' (Surah 4:92). Muslims feel that making the criminal compensate their victim helps to give the victim justice.
- The fact that God commands Muslims to be just means that the unjust must be punished so that their victims are given justice: 'God commands justice, the doing of good and liberality to kith and kin, and He forbids all shameful deeds and injustice' (Surah 16:90).

Why Jews believe justice is important for the victim

Jewish people believe that justice is important for the victim because:

- Judaism teaches that justice should always be given and as the victim is totally innocent, justice can only be given when the victim receives justice from the perpetrator.
- The teaching of the Torah is that victims of crime should be compensated for any injury they have suffered, which is the way the Torah suggests for giving justice to the victims of crime: 'But if there is serious injury, you are to take life for life, eye for eye, tooth for tooth, hand for hand, foot for foot, burn for burn, wound for wound, bruise for bruise' (Exodus 21:24–25).
- In the Tenakh, God commands his people to be just. This means that the unjust must be punished so that their victims are given justice: 'When justice is done, it brings joy to the righteous but terror to evildoers' (Proverbs 21:15). 'For the Lord loves the just and will not forsake his faithful ones. They will be protected for ever, but the offspring of the wicked will be cut off' (Psalm 37:28).

Practice questions

c. Explain two reasons why justice is important for either Muslims or Jews. In your answer you must refer to a source of wisdom and authority.

d. 'It is more important that the justice system protects society from crime than that it gives justice to the victims of crime.' Evaluate this statement considering arguments for and against. In your answer you should:
   - refer to Muslim or Jewish points of view
   - refer to non-religious points of view
   - reach a justified conclusion.

Topic 2.2.2 Crime

The nature of crime

A crime is an act against the law, and laws are rules dictating how members of society are expected to behave. In the UK, laws are made either by Parliament or by judges as a result of the decisions they reach in the cases that they hear in court (known as common law). The law is upheld by courts and the police to ensure that all members of society obey the law.

Crime in the UK is classified under various headings such as:

- *Violent crime*, which ranges from minor assaults, such as pushing and shoving, that result in no physical harm, to murder. It includes offences where the victim was intentionally stabbed, punched, kicked, pushed or jostled, as well as offences where the victim was threatened with violence, whether or not there was any injury.
- **Cybercrime**, which is crime committed using the internet and involves such crimes as hacking people's bank accounts to steal money from them.

The causes of crime

There are many different reasons for people committing crimes. The main ones put forward by experts are described below.

Poverty

It is generally agreed that poverty is likely to lead people to crime. Many of the people convicted of shoplifting food were stealing it to feed themselves or their families. For example, in a survey of 45 food parcel recipients by a Coventry food bank, just under half answered yes to the question, 'Have you ever needed to steal to feed you or your family?'

Thinking points

In this topic, you need to:

- think about the nature, causes and problem of crime

either

- consider Muslim attitudes to crime, including Surah 16:90–92, and what action is taken by Muslim individuals and Muslim groups to end these causes, including the Muslim Chaplains' Association and the work of Mosaic

or

- consider Jewish attitudes to crime, including Deuteronomy 11, and what action is taken by Jewish individuals and Jewish groups to end these causes, including Jewish Care and the work of synagogues
- then be able to explain and evaluate different religious and non-religious attitudes to crime.

Useful words

Cybercrime – criminal activities carried out by means of computers or the internet

Activity

Look at the crime scene photo. Which type of crime are you most worried about? Give reasons for your answer.

Activities

1. Which type of crime are you most worried about? Give reasons for your answer.
2. What advice would you give to a mother with three young children who has no money and nothing to feed her children with?
3. Explain why people commit crimes.
4. Look at the statistics opposite. What might people find surprising about these statistics?

Useful words

Acquisitive crime – crimes such as stealing and burglary where the criminal wants to acquire someone else's property
Self-esteem – a person's opinion of how good or important they are
Madrasah – religious school or college

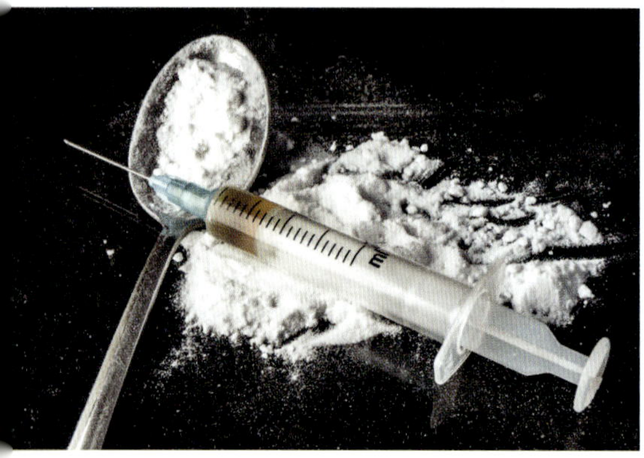

Drug abuse can result in crime.

God commands justice, the doing of good, and liberality to kith and kin, and He forbids all shameful deeds, and injustice and rebellion: He instructs you that that ye may receive admonition. (Surah 16:90)

Upbringing

There seems to be clear evidence that upbringing and family background have a major effect on the likelihood of people committing crimes.

In a survey of the prison population from 2011:

- Twenty-four per cent stated that they had been in care at some point during their childhood (only one per cent of children are in care).
- Twenty-nine per cent of prisoners had experienced abuse and 41 per cent had observed violence in the home as a child.
- Thirty-seven per cent of prisoners reported having family members who had been in prison, a young offenders' institution or borstal.

Drugs

Some research studies in the UK have found that a lot of **acquisitive crime** (stealing) is committed by users of heroin and crack cocaine trying to pay for their drugs. Some surveys show that a high proportion of people arrested for a range of offences test positive for drug use. It has been suggested that between a third and a half of all acquisitive crime is related to illegal drug use.

However, for other crimes, alcohol is more of an influence. Drunkenness is associated with a majority of murders, manslaughters and stabbings, and half of domestic assaults.

Low self-esteem

Much sociological research and thinking believes that there is a link between low **self-esteem** and criminal offending. Criminals in prison for drug offences and those with extensive criminal histories were found to have significantly lower self-esteem than the average.

Muslim attitudes to crime

Muslims are against crime because misdeeds are breaking the laws of God. They try to remove the cause of criminality and alleviate the problems of crime:

- Islam tries to deal with the issue of poverty in both a religious and a political way. Religiously, it tries to remove poverty by banning the use of interest (the poverty of many poor people is made worse by the high interest rates they are charged, which can lead them to be so desperate that they turn to crime); encouraging Muslims to share their wealth and let people off their debts; banning gambling, which can drive people into poverty; using *zakah* to help poor Muslims in the UK; and supporting charities such as Muslim Aid and Islamic Relief. Politically, Islam encourages its followers to think carefully about voting and to support policies aimed at removing poverty.
- Islam tries to deal with the problems of upbringing by helping people to fulfil their duties as Muslim parents. Islam teaches that children are a gift from God and that, on the Last Day, Muslim parents will be judged by God on how well they have brought up their children. So parents are expected to teach their children the difference between right and wrong, introduce them to the faith through observing *salah* and Ramadan at home, and make sure they go to the ***madrasah*** and celebrate the festivals. Islam also encourages families to stay together and many mosques provide family advice and support if parents have problems.

- Alcohol and drugs should not be a problem for Muslim families because they are prohibited for Muslims (*haram*) as the Qur'an says that intoxicants are a means by which Satan tries to keep people from God and from saying their prayers. Muslims are taught that Muhammad said several times that Muslims must not drink alcohol, and must also have nothing to do with the production or sale of alcohol.
- Islam's teachings should mean that no Muslim has problems with self-esteem. To know that you are the ***khalifah*** of God, given the task of looking after the world in the way God wants, should mean never having a problem with low self-esteem. However, being aware that the way you do this is being monitored by God, and that if you do not do it well you will be punished on the Day of Judgement, should mean never having too high an opinion of yourself.

Useful words

Khalifahs – Allah's stewards or vicegerents

The Muslim Chaplains' Association

The Muslim Chaplains' Association is an organisation which supports Muslim prison chaplains in their work towards the resettlement of prisoners and prevention of reoffending on release. Muslim Chaplains have been leading worship and providing pastoral care in prisons on a voluntary basis since the 1970s and as employees of the prison service since 1999. The Association organises regular meetings of chaplains to share good practices and to discuss the challenges facing both the Muslim prisoners and the UK community as a whole.

Mosaic

Mosaic, founded by Prince Charles in 2007, provides a mentoring programme, mainly (but not exclusively) for Muslim prisoners to provide support in the six months prior to release and for at least six months post-release. Volunteers mentor Muslim prisoners to help them prepare for life outside prison, help them to find work and somewhere to live, and visit them regularly when they leave prison, providing support if problems arise. The reoffending rate of those Muslim prisoners supported by Mosaic is up to twenty per cent lower than the national average.

Activities

1. How do Muslims try to stop crimes happening?
2. What does Surah 16 say about Muslim attitudes to crime?

Jewish attitudes to crime

Jews are against crime because misdeeds are breaking the laws of God. They try to remove the cause of criminality and alleviate the problems of crime:

- Judaism tries to deal with the issue of poverty in both a religious and a political way. Religiously, it teaches that Jews should give one tenth of their income to the poor as *tzedaka*; this is often used to help the poor in the UK and to fund charities such as Jewish Care and Jewish Relief. It also bans the use of interest (the poverty of many poor people is made worse by the high interest rates they are charged, which can lead them to be so desperate that they turn to crime). Politically, Judaism encourages its followers to think carefully about voting and to support policies aimed at removing poverty. As Maimonides said,

  The best form of charity makes sure that the poor will never need charity again.

See I am setting before you today a blessing and a curse – the blessing if you obey the commands of the Lord your God that I am giving you today; the curse if you disobey the commands of the Lord your God. (Deuteronomy 11:26–28)

- Judaism tries to deal with the problems of upbringing by helping parents to fulfil their duties as Jewish parents. Judaism teaches that the family was created by God as the basic unit of society and as the only place in which children should be brought up. Judaism teaches that the family is the place where children learn the difference between right and wrong and where children are introduced to the faith through ***brit milah***, observing ***Shabbat*** at home, being taken to synagogue, celebrating festivals and so on. If children are brought up in a strong Jewish family following the Torah and ***halakhah*** they are not likely to commit crimes.
- Alcohol and drugs should not be a problem for Jewish families because they are taught moderation at home. The command of the Torah to be holy means that Jewish people avoid drugs altogether and must be moderate in their use of alcohol. Drunkenness is condemned in the Tenakh and anyone under the influence of alcohol may not perform religious, legal or political functions and is forbidden to pray until sober.
- Judaism's teachings should mean that no Jewish person has problems with self-esteem. To know that you have been made in the image of God, and have been given the task of looking after the world in the way God wants, should mean never having a problem with low self-esteem. However, the self-reflection required during Rosh Hashanah, the Ten Days of Awe and Yom Kippur means that a Jew should always be aware of her or his shortcomings and so should not have problems with high self-esteem.
- The number of Jews in British prisons is very small, so provision for worship and counselling is provided by local synagogues. This is organised by a rabbi who is an advisor to the prison service. Help and support for Jewish prisoners on their release is provided by the social work section of Jewish Care.

Useful words

Brit milah – ceremony of circumcision for baby boys
Shabbat – the Jewish holy day on Saturday, the seventh day of the week
Halakhah – Jewish law from the written and Oral Torah

Summary

In Islam, a crime is an act against the law. The main causes of crime are: poverty, upbringing, drugs and low self-esteem. Muslims are against crime because crimes break the laws of God. They try to remove the causes of criminality by trying to remove poverty, helping parents to bring up their children to obey the law, banning alcohol and drugs, and improving self-esteem through religion. They try to stop criminals from reoffending through groups like Mosaic and the Muslim Chaplains' Association.

In Judaism, a crime is an act against the law. The main causes of crime are: poverty, upbringing, drugs and low self-esteem. Jews are against crime because crimes break the laws of God. They try to remove the causes of criminality by trying to remove poverty, helping parents to bring up their children to obey the law, encouraging a moderate use of alcohol, banning drugs and improving self-esteem through religion. They try to stop criminals from reoffending through rabbis visiting prisons and Jewish Care helping released prisoners.

Activities

1. How do Jews try to stop crimes happening?
2. What does Deuteronomy 11 say about Jewish attitudes to crime?

Practice questions

c. Explain two ways in which either Muslims or Jews try to stop people committing crimes.

d. 'Religion could do a lot more to prevent crime.' Evaluate this statement considering arguments for and against. In your answer you should:
   - refer to Muslim or Jewish points of view
   - refer to non-religious points of view
   - reach a justified conclusion.

Topic 2.2.3a Muslim attitudes to good, evil and suffering

The nature of good actions

In Islam, good actions are known as '***halal***', meaning 'that which is permitted'.

Although Muslims scholars are agreed that since God has created the universe everything must be *halal* except when God has specifically said it is not, they have subdivided good actions into:

- ***Fard***: actions which must be performed for a person to be regarded as good. These include observing the Five Pillars and obeying the laws of the Shari'ah, for example only eating *halal* food. Performing these actions will be rewarded and not performing them will be punished.
- ***Mandub***: actions which a Muslim will be rewarded for doing, but will not be punished if they do not do them, for example praying *du'a* prayers.
- ***Mubah***: actions which are permitted because nothing is said about them in the Qur'an or hadith, for example watching television. Such actions will be neither rewarded nor punished.

Islam teaches that those who perform good actions will be rewarded on the Day of Judgement by God sending them to paradise for eternity (see Topic 2.1a.8, page 177).

Burglary is an example of a moral evil.

Thinking points

In this topic you need to:

- think about the nature of good actions and how they are rewarded
- understand the nature of evil actions
- understand why people suffer and Surah 76
- non-religious attitudes about why people suffer
- be able to explain and evaluate Muslim attitudes to evil and suffering.

Useful words

Halal – that which is permitted
Fard – actions which must be performed for a person to be regarded as good
Mandub – actions which a Muslim will be rewarded for doing, but will not be punished if they do not do them
Mubah – actions which are permitted because nothing is said about them in the Qur'an or hadith

Activity

What are the differences between *fard* and *mubah* actions?

The floods that struck many parts of Britain in 2014 and caused much suffering are a natural evil.

Useful words

Haram – that which is forbidden
Moral evil – actions done by humans which cause suffering
Natural evil – things which cause suffering but have nothing to do with humans
Free will – the idea that human beings are free to make their own choices
Omnipotent – the belief that God is all-powerful
Omnibenevolent – the belief that God is all-good

The nature of evil actions

Evil actions are called '***haram***', meaning 'that which is forbidden'.

Basically, any action that is forbidden in the Qur'an, the hadith or the Shari'ah (for example, drinking alcohol, gambling, lending or borrowing money at interest) is *haram* and so is regarded as evil by Muslims and will be punished by God at the final judgement (see Topic 2.1a.8, page 177).

Evil is often divided into **moral evil** and **natural evil**:

- Moral evil is evil that is caused by humans misusing their **free will** (the human faculty of making choices). When faced with a moral decision, it is always possible to choose to do something good or something evil. When humans choose to do evil, it is described as moral evil. Rape, murder and burglary are clear examples of moral evil.
- Natural evil is suffering that has not been caused by humans. Earthquakes, floods, volcanoes, drought, tsunamis, hurricanes, tornadoes, cancers and so on are not actually caused by humans, but they result in massive amounts of human suffering.

Non-religious attitudes to evil and suffering

Many non-religious people, atheists and Humanists cannot believe that a good God would have designed a world that had natural evils. They cannot believe in a God who has created diseases such as cancer, which cause people to die in a most horrible way. They cannot believe that a good God would cause children to suffer from fatal diseases and conditions when they have had no chance to live. Non-religious people find it easier to believe that the bad things that happen are a result of the earth evolving by accident from the Big Bang. Natural evil makes non-religious people question or reject God's existence.

Non-religious people cannot believe in a God who allows humans to cause so much moral evil and suffering when he could stop it if he wanted to.

Non-religious philosophers express the problem of evil and suffering in this way:

- If God is **omnipotent** (all-powerful), he must be able to remove evil and suffering from the world.
- If God is **omnibenevolent** (all-good), he must want to remove evil and suffering from the world because they cause so much unhappiness.
- It follows that, if God exists, there should be no evil or suffering in the world.
- As there is evil and suffering in the world, either God is not omnipotent, or God is not omnibenevolent, or God does not exist.

So, atheists and Humanists believe that evil and suffering are either the fault of humans misusing their free will or the fault of the accidental nature of the universe. Some believe that a lot of suffering is caused by religion, as we will study in Section 4 on peace and conflict (page 325).

The Muslim answer to why people suffer

The verse in the margin from the Qur'an expresses the view that because God is so much greater than humans, they cannot understand his motives and therefore must just accept what God does. The Qur'an says that God is good and only wants good and so there must be good reasons for evil and suffering, but humans are not able to understand these reasons.

Humans can, and will, be questioned about their evil actions because they have been born with a natural instinct to understand the difference between right and wrong and have been given free will to choose between right and wrong. According to the Qur'an, when God created Adam, he ordered the angels to bow down to him. But one angel, Iblis, refused and was sent out of paradise. However, he was allowed to try to tempt humans to choose wrong rather than right until the Day of Judgement.

This means that for Muslims, life is a period of testing and temptations. Evil and suffering test people's belief in Islam, and a true Muslim will remain faithful through the trials of this life. If they keep true to the faith, they will be rewarded with eternity in paradise at the final judgement.

Islam teaches the endurance of suffering with hope and faith. The faithful should not ask why there is evil and suffering. Instead, they should accept it as God's will, knowing that God never asks more of them than they can endure. However, Islam also teaches the faithful to work actively to remove evil and suffering from the world. Muslims respond to evil and suffering by helping those who suffer, either practically or by prayer, because helping the suffering and fighting evil will be rewarded by God on the Last Day.

It is We who have sent down the Qur'an to thee by stages. Therefore be patient with constancy to the command of thy Lord, and hearken not to the sinner or the ingrate among them. (Surah 76:23–24)

Activities

1. Look at the photos on pages 225 and 226. Why might these cause non-religious people to doubt God's existence?
2. Read the quotation from Surah 21. What do you think it means?

Practice questions

c Explain two reasons why evil and suffering cause problems for Muslims.

d 'Evil and suffering are not a problem if you believe in God.' Evaluate this statement considering arguments for and against. In your answer you should:

- refer to Muslim points of view
- refer to different Muslim or non-religious points of view
- reach a justified conclusion.

Summary

Good actions are *halal* (permitted) or *fard* (what you must do to be good). Evil actions are *haram* (forbidden). Moral evil is a result of human action; natural evil refers to nature. Evil and suffering cause problems because a good all-powerful God shouldn't allow them. Muslims believe God allows evil and suffering to test people's faith and those who keep the faith and help the suffering will be rewarded.

Topic 2.2.3b Jewish attitudes to good, evil and suffering

Thinking points

In this topic you need to:

- think about the nature of good actions and how they are rewarded, including Exodus 33
- understand the nature of evil actions and how they are punished, including why people suffer
- non-religious attitudes about why people suffer
- be able to explain and evaluate different Jewish attitudes to punishment, evil and suffering.

Useful words

Mitzvot – commandments (plural)

And the Lord said, 'I will cause all my goodness to pass in front of you, and I will proclaim my name, the Lord, in your presence. I will have mercy on whom I will have mercy, and I will have compassion on whom I will have compassion.' (Exodus 33:19)

Activity

Read the quotation from Exodus 33. What do you think it means?

The nature of good actions

The basis of good actions in Judaism is the ***mitzvot***. To obey a *mitzvah* is to perform a good action.

There are 613 *mitzvot*, of which 248 are positive commands, so doing them is a good action, but 365 are negative commands, so doing them is an evil action. To take the Ten Commandments as an example: to honour your parents is a good action, but to steal is an evil action. Essentially, in Judaism good actions are ones which follow God's will for humans.

The Torah makes clear that good actions will be rewarded by God.

The rewards for good actions will come after death (see Topic 2.1b.8, page 209).

Robbery is a moral evil.

A tornado, which might cause enormous destruction and suffering, is a natural evil.

The nature of evil actions

Evil actions are ones which go against the *mitzvot* by either ignoring the positive commands or breaking the negative commands. Essentially, in Judaism evil actions are ones which go against God's will for humans.

The punishment for evil actions will come after death (see Topic 2.1b.8, page 209).

Evil is often divided into **moral evil** and **natural evil**:

- Moral evil is evil that is caused by humans misusing their **free will** (the human faculty of making choices). When faced with a moral decision, it is always possible to choose to do something good or something evil. When humans choose to do evil, it is described as moral evil. Rape, murder and burglary are clear examples of moral evil.
- Natural evil is suffering that has not been caused by humans. Earthquakes, floods, volcanoes, drought, tsunamis, hurricanes, tornadoes, cancers and so on are not actually caused by humans, but they result in massive amounts of human suffering.

Useful words

Moral evil – actions done by humans which cause suffering
Natural evil – things which cause suffering but have nothing to do with humans
Free will – the idea that human beings are free to make their own choices

Non-religious attitudes to evil and suffering

Many non-religious people, atheists and Humanists cannot believe that a good God would have designed a world that had natural evils. Even more tellingly, they cannot believe in a God who has created diseases such as cancer, which cause people to die in a most horrible way. They cannot believe that a good God would cause children to suffer from fatal diseases and conditions when they have had no chance to live. Non-religious people find it easier to believe that the bad things that happen are a result of the earth evolving by accident from the Big Bang. Natural evil makes non-religious people question or reject God's existence.

Non-religious people cannot believe in a God who allows humans to cause so much moral evil and suffering when he could stop it if he wanted to.

- If God is **omnipotent** (all-powerful), he must be able to remove evil and suffering from the world.
- If God is **omnibenevolent** (all-good), he must want to remove evil and suffering from the world because they cause so much unhappiness.
- It follows that, if God exists, there should be no evil or suffering in the world.
- As there is evil and suffering in the world, either God is not omnipotent, or God is not omnibenevolent, or God does not exist.

So, atheists and Humanists believe that evil and suffering are either the fault of humans misusing their free will or the fault of the accidental nature of the universe. Some believe that a lot of suffering is caused by religion, as we will study in Section 4 on peace and conflict (page 325).

Useful words

Omnipotent – the belief that God is all-powerful
Omnibenevolent – the belief that God is all-good

The Jewish answer to why people suffer

Judaism has several responses to the problem of evil and suffering.

- The Tenakh teaches that there is no point in worrying about the problem because humans cannot understand God's reasons for doing things. God must have a reason for evil and suffering, but humans cannot know what it is because they are not God. This is based on the Book of Job in the Old Testament.
- The Book of Psalms in the Tenakh shows that suffering is intended to be a part of life. Many of the Psalms tell of good religious people suffering, but the Psalms show that life is more than suffering. The other side of suffering is joy and in the Psalms suffering and joy go side by side. For example, Psalm 88 is full of grief,

  You have taken from me my closest friends ... I am confined and cannot escape, my eyes are dim with grief

  but the next Psalm (89) begins with the words,

  I will sing of the Lord's great love forever.

  This idea of sadness and joy going together and being part of God's plan helps some Jews. They are also helped by the way the Psalms show that God knows and cares for people's suffering and that he will comfort and help his suffering people:

  The righteous cry out and the Lord hears them; he delivers them from all their troubles. The Lord is close to the broken-hearted and saves those who are crushed in spirit. (Psalm 34:17–18)

Job was a sinless man who worshipped God faithfully. However, Satan argued with God that Job only worshipped him because God had given him a good life and that if his good life were to be removed, he would stop worshipping God. God did not believe this and so allowed Satan to remove Job's good life and afflict him with terrible diseases. Job asked God why this was happening to him and demanded that God should speak to him directly. However, when Job came face to face with God and was presented with his greatness and holiness, he realised that because God is so great that humans have no right to question him. God must have reasons for allowing evil and suffering, but as mere mortals, humans cannot understand them.

- Another response is to believe that there is a purpose in evil and suffering. The Torah teaches that God made humans with free will, and if free will is to mean anything then there must be evil so that humans have a genuine choice between good and evil. The existence of evil and suffering therefore helps people to develop their souls as they make their choices. **Yom Kippur** and the **Days of Awe** give people a chance throughout their lives to apologise to God (and the people they have harmed) for the wrong choices they have made, so that after death they can be rewarded by God.
- Another response is one that claims that suffering is not really that bad and can even be regarded as in some way beneficial. The suffering servant model referred to by the prophet Isaiah in the Tenakh suggests that the Jewish people suffer in order to make up for the wickedness of humanity. Jewish theologians have developed this as a response to the unique problems raised by the suffering of the Jews during the **Shoah** (which literally means catastrophe but is used by Jews to describe the Holocaust). The Jews suffered during the Shoah to bring the world back to God.
- Another response is that suffering is a test of an individual's spirit and commitment to God. In the Bible, God tested Abraham when he commanded Abraham to sacrifice his son, Isaac. The Talmud offers this explanation of the incident:

> *If you go to the marketplace, you will see the potter hitting his clay pots with a stick to show how strong and solid they are. But the wise potter only hits the strongest pots never the flawed ones. So, too God sends such tests and afflictions only to people God knows are capable of handling them, so that they and others can learn the extent of their spiritual strength.*

Most Jews will combine two or three of the responses to help them come to terms with the evil and suffering in the world. However, Judaism also teaches the faithful to work actively to remove evil and suffering from the world. All Jewish people should respond to evil and suffering by helping those who suffer, either practically or by prayer, because helping the suffering and fighting evil will be rewarded by God after death.

Practice questions

c Explain two reasons why evil and suffering cause problems for Jews.

d 'Evil and suffering are not a problem if you believe in God.' Evaluate this statement considering arguments for and against. In your answer you should:
- refer to Jewish points of view
- refer to different Jewish or non-religious points of view
- reach a justified conclusion.

Activities

1. Look at the photos on pages 228 and 229. Why might these cause non-religious people to doubt God's existence?
2. Which Jewish response to the problem of evil and suffering do you think is the best?

Useful words

Yom Kippur – the Day of Atonement
Days of Awe – the ten days between Rosh Hashanah and Yom Kippur when Jews consider their deeds of the past year and resolve to do better in the coming year
Shoah – the Holocaust

Summary

Good actions are those commanded by the *mitvot* and will be rewarded after death. Evil actions are those which break the *mitzvot* and will be punished. Moral evil is a result of human action; natural evil refers to nature. Evil and suffering cause problems because a good all-powerful God shouldn't allow them. Some Jews believe that God has a reason for suffering, but humans cannot understand it. Others believe that it helps people to develop their souls.

Topic 2.2.4 Attitudes to punishment

Thinking points

In this topic you need to:

- think about the nature of punishment

either

- understand why punishment is important for Muslims and consider Qur'anic teachings about punishment

or

- understand why punishment is important for Jews and consider Jewish teachings about punishment
- know why punishment can be regarded as justice
- understand why punishment might be needed in society
- be able to explain and evaluate different religious and non-religious attitudes to punishment.

Useful words

Probation – the release of a person from prison on the condition that they are monitored by a probation officer and don't break certain rules

Compensation – paying someone back for a wrong done to them

The nature of punishment

Punishment is a penalty inflicted on an offender for breaking the law. Punishment can take many forms, but the types of punishment imposed by UK courts are:

- **Imprisonment:** courts can take away the offender's freedom and send them to prison for a fixed period of time.
- **Suspended sentence:** courts can impose a term of imprisonment and then order that the sentence shall not take effect for a fixed period of one to three years unless the offender commits an offence again within that time.
- **Community Service Order:** an alternative to imprisonment where the offender is required to do unpaid work in the community, run by the **probation** service (failure to do the community service will result in imprisonment).
- **Probation:** offenders are placed under the supervision of a probation officer and required to be of good behaviour and to remain in contact with their probation officer for a fixed period. If they reoffend while on probation, or break the conditions of the probation order, they may be resentenced for the original offence.
- **Fine:** this is a monetary penalty which may be paid in instalments. Failure to pay a fine will result in imprisonment.
- **Compensation Order:** the court may order the offender to pay the victim **compensation** for personal injury, loss or damage to property and so on.
- **Restitution Order:** this forces the offender to return anything they gained by committing the crime.
- **Hospital Order:** people with mental health problems can be detained in a secure hospital. Where the crime is serious, and where doctors cannot predict when the offender may be fit for release, the period of detention is left open.

A prison.

Muslim teachings about punishment

Islam teaches that criminals should be punished for their crimes and the Qur'an sets down specific punishments for certain crimes. Islam also teaches that Muslims should not commit crimes because any crime is a sin against God. Those who commit crimes will not only be punished by the law, but also face the judgement of God on the Last Day.

The punishments set down in the Qur'an are known as ***hadd*** (or *hudud*) **punishments**. These are punishments fixed in the Qur'an and hadith for crimes considered to be against the rights of God. The six crimes for which punishments are fixed are:

- theft (**amputation** of the hand)
- illicit sexual relations (death by stoning or 100 lashes)
- making unproven accusations of illicit sex (80 lashes)
- drinking intoxicants (80 lashes)
- apostasy (death or banishment)
- highway robbery (death).

Strict requirements for evidence (including eyewitnesses) have severely limited the application of the *hadd* penalties.

Most Muslim countries operate a legal and punishment system similar to that of Europe. Until recently Saudi Arabia was the only country applying the *hadd* punishments, but now the Taliban, Isis and other areas under **Salafi** control tend to apply these punishments because they are set down in the Qur'an or Sunnah.

> *As to the thief, male or female, cut off his or her hands: a punishment by way of example, from God, for their crime. (Surah 5:41)*
>
> *The recompense for an injury is an injury equal thereto in degree: but if a person forgives and makes retribution, his reward is due from God: for God loveth not those who do wrong.* (Surah 42:40)

The Qur'an declares in Surah 2:178 that if the victim and perpetrator agree to an amount of compensation that can then take the place of punishment. Surah 5:44–46 states that justice and punishment should be given equitably to Muslims and non-Muslims, although it would be preferable for non-Muslims to use their own legal systems. This could be linked to the principles of Situation Ethics that the punishments given should be adjusted to the situation after the crime.

Useful words

***Hadd* punishments** – the punishments set down by the Qur'an

Amputation – cutting off a limb

Salafi – ultra-conservative reform movement in Sunni Islam

Activities

1. Which of the punishments available to British courts would be the best one for a 21-year-old man convicted of stealing £500 from a shopkeeper after threatening him with a baseball bat?
2. Why do you think punishment is important?
3. What are the *hadd* punishments and why do you think there is still crime in countries which have *hadd* punishments?
4. Explain why punishment is important for Muslims.

Activities

1. How do Jews interpret 'an eye for an eye'? Do you think this is a good form of punishment?
2. Explain why punishment is important for Jews.

Useful words

Capital punishment – the death penalty for a crime
Retributive justice – justice done by making the criminal pay for their crime
Proportional – in the right relation to

Jewish teachings about punishment

Jews believe that society has a right to punish those who break its laws. The Torah sets down certain punishments for certain offences, such as whipping and stoning to death. There are also passages in the Torah which seem to allow:

- Retribution: using punishment as revenge.

> *If anyone injures his neighbour whatever he has done must be done to him: fracture for fracture, eye for eye, tooth for tooth. As he has injured the other so he must be injured.* (Leviticus 24:19–20)

- Imprisonment:

> *While the Israelites were in the desert, a man was found gathering wood on the Sabbath day. Those who found him gathering wood brought him to Moses and Aaron and the whole assembly, and they kept him in custody because it was not clear what should be done to him.* (Numbers 15:34)

- **Capital punishment**:

> *If anyone kills a person, the murderer shall be put to death on the evidence of witnesses. But no person shall be put to death on the testimony of one witness.* (Numbers 35:30)

However, Jews believe that these punishments are not part of the *mitzvot*. No Jewish country would impose punishments of whipping or stoning today. Rather, Jews would look at the principles behind the laws. The idea of an eye for an eye and a tooth for a tooth is actually a restriction on punishment. It shows that if someone knocks your tooth out, you only have the right to one of their teeth, not to knock all of them out or even to chop off their head. Jews also believe that compensation is better than retribution, so that the value of a tooth or the value of an eye should form the basis of the punishment.

Why punishment can be regarded as justice

Some people, especially victims of crimes, regard punishment as a form of justice. **Retributive justice** is a theory of justice which considers that punishment proportionate to the crime is the best way of carrying out justice. When someone breaks the law, justice demands that they should be punished for what they have done. This is not revenge and is not like 'an eye for an eye and a tooth for a tooth'.

In contrast to revenge, punishment as justice is not personal and does not require the punishment to be the same as the crime. Rather, punishment as justice requires the punishment to be **proportional** to the crime, in other words the severity of the punishment must reflect the severity of the crime (the death penalty for shoplifting would not be justice, for example). On this view, punishment is a way of making the criminal atone for the crime they have committed and so justice is done.

Punishment can also be seen as justice because part of justice is making sure that the good are rewarded and the lawbreakers are punished. Furthermore, justice requires the law-abiding to be protected from the lawbreakers and punishment is a way of doing this.

Why punishment might be needed in society

Human beings live in groups, and any group needs rules to organise the behaviour of individuals and to protect the weak from the strong. Imagine what the roads would be like if there were no laws: people would be able to drive on whichever side of the road they liked, people would be able to drive at any speed they wanted and there could be no traffic lights because drivers would not need to obey them. Imagine what it would be like if there were no business laws: people could take the money for selling a house and then not move out, people could be sacked for no reason and given no compensation. Imagine what life would be like if there were no laws on stealing, murder, rape and so on.

If society needs laws, it also needs punishment in order to make sure that all members of society obey those laws and that the rest of society is protected from those people who want to break the laws.

Practice questions

c Explain two reasons why punishment is important for either Muslims or Jews. In your answer you must refer to a source of wisdom and authority.

d 'Punishment is better dealt with by the state than by religion.' Evaluate this statement considering arguments for and against. In your answer you should:

- refer to Muslim or Jewish points of view
- refer to different Muslim or Jewish points of view or Situation Ethics
- reach a justified conclusion.

Summary

Punishment is a penalty inflicted on those who break the law and can range from fines to death. Punishment can be regarded as justice because it rewards the good and punishes the bad. It is needed to make society work properly. Islam teaches that people should not commit crimes, but if they do, they must be punished.

The punishments given in the Qur'an are called *hadd* punishments and include things like cutting off a thief's hand. Most Muslims no longer agree with the *hadd* punishments.

Judaism teaches that people should not commit crimes, but if they do, they must be punished. The punishments in the Tenakh are not *mitzvot* and so Judaism approves of the types of punishment used in modern societies.

Topic 2.2.5 The aims of punishment

Thinking points

In this topic you need to:

- think about Muslim or Jewish attitudes towards each of the aims of punishment: protection, retribution, deterrence and reformation
- consider Qur'anic teachings about punishment, including Surah 4:26–32, or Jewish teachings, including Genesis 9:1–6
- be able to explain and evaluate different Muslim or Jewish attitudes
- explain why punishment can be regarded as justice
- explain why punishment is needed in society.

The aims of punishment

The main aim of punishment is to try to make sure that everyone obeys the law, but there are some other aims:

- To protect law-abiding members of society from the lawbreakers.
- To deter law-abiding citizens from committing crimes.
- To reform and rehabilitate criminals so that they do not break the law in the future.
- To make criminals pay for their actions and give the victims of crime a sense of retribution.

Based on these aims, experts have come up with various theories about what punishment should be and these are considered below.

Activity

For what type of criminal would community service be a good idea?

British singer–songwriter Boy George sweeping the street in New York as part of a community service order imposed on him by a US court.

Retribution and its benefits

Retribution is the theory that criminals should pay for their crimes. Many people think this should be the main reason for punishment because:

- It makes criminals pay for their crimes in proportion to the severity of the crimes they have committed. In the past, retributive punishments would have killed those who committed murder and taken the eyes out of those who blinded someone.
- It makes criminals suffer for what they have done wrong. Criminals make their victims suffer, so the criminals should also suffer.
- It actually punishes the criminal. The dictionary definition of punish is 'to make an offender suffer for what they have done' and this is exactly what retribution does.

Deterrence and its benefits

Deterrence is the theory that punishment should put people off committing crime. Many people think deterrence should be the main reason for punishment because the aim of punishment is to stop people from committing crimes. The idea of deterrent punishment is that punishment should be so severe no one will dare to commit crimes. For example:

- If someone knows they will have their hand cut off if they are caught stealing, then they will not steal.
- If people know they will be executed if they are found guilty, they will not murder.

Reformation and its benefits

Reformation is the theory that criminals should be taught not to commit crime again. Many people think reform should be the main reason for punishment because:

- They believe the only way to stop crime is to reform the criminals so that they become honest law-abiding citizens who will not want to commit crimes again.
- They believe that most criminals commit crimes because of how they have been brought up and because they do not know how to live without crime.
- Reformative punishments often involve giving criminals education and qualifications so that they can find a proper job and no longer feel the need to be a criminal (rehabilitation of offenders).

Protection and its benefits

Protection is the theory that punishment should protect society from criminals and their activities. Many people think this should be the main reason for punishment, so, for example, they might think:

- Capital punishment is a good punishment for murderers and terrorists because if they are dead they cannot threaten people.
- Long prison sentences are a good punishment for violent people or persistent burglars as they keep them out of society so that people and their property are protected.
- Community service can be a good punishment for hooligans and vandals because it keeps them off the streets.

*God doth wish to make clear to you and to show you the **ordinances** of those before you; and He doth wish to you in mercy and God is All-knowing, All-wise. (Surah 4:26)*

Whoever sheds human blood, by humans shall their blood be shed; for in the image of God has God made mankind. (Genesis 9:6)

Useful words

Ordinance – law

Activities

1. What do you think either Surah 4:26 or Genesis 9:6 means as far as punishment is concerned?
2. What are the weaknesses of retribution punishment?
3. What are the weaknesses of deterrent punishment?
4. What are the weaknesses of protection punishment?
5. What are the weaknesses of reformative punishment?

A prison cell at the Portland Young Offender Institution, Portland, Dorset.

Activity

Do you think prison is a good way of reforming female criminals – especially mothers?

Muslim attitudes to the aims of punishment

Muslim attitudes to punishment are based on retribution, deterrence and reform. The theory is that such punishments will deter most people from committing crimes because they will be frightened of the punishment. They also make the criminal pay for their crime (retribution) and will reform the criminal because no thief who has had one hand cut off will ever steal again in case they get the other hand cut off.

Imprisonment is used in Muslim countries to protect society from anti-social criminals. It is also possible in Islam for a criminal to pay compensation to the victim, or the victim's family, for certain crimes. This is done as a form of retribution.

Muslims have these views on punishment because:

- The Qur'an sets down lashes or amputation for certain crimes, and the Qur'an is the Word of God which must be followed.
- Whipping and amputation allow the offender to remain in society with their families where, it is believed, they are less likely to reoffend than those who have been sent to prison.
- The idea of deterrence requires very severe punishment to deter; amputation is much more likely to deter thieves than six months in prison.
- The strict punishments are only given as a last resort. Islamic courts investigate all the background to the case and, for example, would not amputate the hand of someone who stole to feed their family.

Jewish attitudes to the aims of punishment

Jews see the basic reasons for punishment as deterrence, protection and retribution. The aim of punishment is to protect society from the actions of the anti-social, and, if there is sufficient deterrence, there will be very little crime. Nevertheless, Jews would also see reform as a major part of the punishment process as this is likely to prevent crimes in the future.

Jews have these ideas about punishment because:

- The Torah says that criminals should be punished.
- The Torah gives deterrence, protection and retribution as the reasons for punishment.
- Society would be likely to collapse if criminals did not face punishment.
- Rabbis have always been involved in the Jewish court system and the punishment of offenders (the Bet Din must have at least three rabbis).

Summary

The aims of punishment are to protect society, punish criminals for their crimes (retribution), deter people from committing crimes and reform criminals. Muslims agree with all these aims because of the teachings of the Qur'an. Jews agree with all these aims because of the teaching of the Torah and the rabbis.

Practice questions

c Explain two reasons why punishment is important for either Muslims or Jews. In your answer you must refer to a source of wisdom and authority.

d 'Religious people should be concerned with reforming criminals, not punishing them.' Evaluate this statement considering arguments for and against. In your answer you should:

- refer to Muslim or Jewish points of view
- refer to different Muslim or Jewish points of view
- reach a justified conclusion.

Topic 2.2.6 Forgiveness

The nature of forgiveness

Forgiveness is a conscious, deliberate decision on the part of a victim to release the feelings of resentment or vengeance they have towards the person or group who has harmed them, regardless of whether they deserve such forgiveness. It is often connected with an increased ability to wish the offender well.

Forgiveness does not mean forgetting, nor does it mean condoning or excusing offences. Forgiveness can be the first step to reconciliation with the person who committed the harm, but it does not release them from legal accountability for their actions.

Muslim beliefs about forgiveness

The Qur'an teaches that God is compassionate and merciful to sinners. Indeed, every **surah** except one begins with the ***bismillah*** ('In the name of God the Merciful, the Compassionate'). Other verses in the Qur'an confirm this:

> *But if ye forgive and overlook and cover up their faults, verily God is Oft-forgiving, Most-merciful.* (Surah 64:14)

Consequently, Muslims believe that they too should be forgiving, because:

- On the Day of Judgement God will deal with everyone as they deserve, but Muslims will be able to request his mercy. However, how can Muslims ask for God's forgiveness if they are not prepared to forgive?
- The Qur'an says that Muslims should forgive other people's sins against them and Muslims should obey the Qur'an as they believe it is the Word of God.
- There are many hadith from the Prophet Muhammad about forgiving people who have offended others and bringing **reconciliation** to conflicts, and Muslims believe they should follow the example of the Prophet.

> *Be forgiving and control yourself in the face of provocation; give justice to the person who was unfair and unjust to you; give to the one who did not help you when you were in need, and keep fellowship with the one who did not care about you.* (Hadith)

Activities

1. What do you think the passage from Surah 64:14 adds to the idea of forgiveness?
2. Read the hadith above. Do you think you could carry out Muhammad's advice in your life?
3. Look at the photo on the right. Why might the words make Muslims work for forgiveness and reconciliation?

Thinking points

In this topic you need to:

- think about Muslim beliefs about the nature of forgiveness, including Surah 64:14, *or* think about Jewish beliefs about the nature of forgiveness, including Psalm 130:7
- understand how offenders are forgiven by the community and why this is needed
- understand the nature of restorative justice and why is it important for criminals, including either Muslim or Jewish attitudes
- be able to explain and evaluate different religious and non-religious attitudes to forgiveness.

Useful words

Surah – a chapter of the Qur'an (there are 114 surahs)

Bismillah – the words which begin the surahs ('In the Name of God the Compassionate, the Merciful')

Reconciliation – bringing together people who were opposed to each other

This quotation on a mosque is from the Qur'an and says 'In the name of God, the Merciful, the Compassionate'.

Activities

1. Read the quotations from Isaiah 55 and Psalm 130. What do these tell us about Jewish beliefs about God?
2. Look at the photo of a synagogue on Yom Kippur below. Why might the Yom Kippur service encourage Jewish people to seek reconciliation?

Useful words

Transgressions – breaking laws (especially God's laws)

Jewish teachings on forgiveness

The Tenakh teaches that God is a god who forgives:

If my people who are called by my name humble themselves, and pray and seek my face and turn from their wicked ways, then I will hear from heaven and will forgive their sin and heal their land. (2 Chronicles 7:14)

Whoever conceals his ***transgressions*** *will not prosper, but he who confesses and forsakes them will obtain mercy.* (Proverbs 28:13)

So, Judaism teaches that Jews should forgive those who wrong them, and try to bring about reconciliation, because:

- In the ten days between Rosh Hashanah and Yom Kippur, Jews are expected to seek out anyone they have wronged and ask their forgiveness, so ending the conflict and becoming reconciled with them. They do this because on Yom Kippur, they are going to ask God to forgive them for all the wrongs they have done to God in the past year.
- Judaism teaches that God forgives those who turn to him in true repentance and the sign of true repentance is to seek forgiveness for your own sins and be prepared to forgive others their sins.
- The Tenakh encourages people to forgive those who wrong them and try to bring reconciliation, and Jewish people should follow the teachings of the Tenakh.
- The rabbis encourage Jewish people to forgive those who wrong them and become reconciled with them.
- The Prayer Book teaches that Jewish people should always try to forgive those who have wronged them when on their deathbed, before they ask God to forgive their sins.

Seek the Lord while he may be found; call on him while he is near. Let the wicked forsake their ways and the unrighteous their thoughts. Let them turn to the Lord, and he will have mercy on them, and to our God, for he will freely pardon. (Isaiah 55:6–7)

If you, Lord, kept a record of sins, Lord, who could stand? But with you there is forgiveness, so that we can, with reverence, serve you ... Israel, put your hope in the Lord, for with the Lord is unfailing love and with him is full redemption. (Psalm 130)

A synagogue at Yom Kippur, when Jews ask God to forgive the sins they committed in the past year.

Why offenders need to be forgiven by the community

The prison system costs British taxpayers £11 billion each year. At any time, there are around 65,000 people in prison, and 60 per cent of prisoners reoffend within a year of being released back into society. Many people who are let out of prison find themselves distanced from friends and family, many have lost their homes and most have no job.

This means that the community needs to forgive offenders and help them to **reintegrate** into law-abiding society so that they are part of society and will not need to return to a life of crime.

Useful words

Reintegrate – for someone to fit back in to society
Rehabilitation – restoring to normal, productive life

How offenders are forgiven by the community

The UK government tries to help offenders through the Rehabilitation of Offenders Act 1974 (as amended in 2012), which makes sure that people do not have a lifelong blot on their records because of a relatively minor offence in their past. After a **rehabilitation** period, ex-offenders do not need to declare their convictions when applying for a job, obtaining insurance and so on.

Some business owners are helping to bring offenders back into the community:

- Timpson, the key-cutting and shoe repair business, has been running a rehabilitation scheme for twelve years and currently has 400 ex-offenders working at all levels of the business, including ten shop managers. The company goes into prisons and offers training workshops and, in many cases, starts employing prisoners on day-release schemes during the six months before the sentence is completed. In the twelve years since the scheme started, only three people have reoffended; the rest now contribute to society and pay taxes.
- The Joint, a restaurant in Brixton, south London, works in partnership with the Bad Boys' Bakery, established by celebrity chef Gordon Ramsay at Brixton prison, to provide paid employment for those who have completed their training in the Bad Boys' Bakery.
- Business in the Community (BITC) launched a campaign in 2013 asking employers to drop the tickbox that requires job applicants to reveal whether they have criminal convictions. It found that employment reduces reoffending rates by 33–50 per cent, but that many candidates were being disregarded by employers because of their criminal records.

A large number of charities work to help ex-offenders to become law-abiding members of society:

- The Apex Charitable Trust seeks to help people with criminal records to obtain appropriate jobs or self-employment by providing them with the skills they need in the labour market and by working with employers to break down the barriers to their employment.
- Nacro offers information and advice to ex-offenders, serving prisoners, their families and friends through a helpline.
- Trailblazers aims to reduce reoffending in young people by helping them change their attitude, thinking and behaviour through intensive mentoring, advice, advocacy and targeted specialist support.

Activities

1. Why does the community need to reintegrate offenders into society?
2. How does British society try to forgive offenders?

Activity

Do you think restorative justice is a good idea?

Restorative justice gives victims of crime the chance to explain to the offender how they have been affected by a crime and to ask any questions they may have about the incident. Offenders thus have the chance to understand the impact of their crime and take action to repair the harm caused. One of the obvious benefits of restorative justice is the extremely high levels of satisfaction among victims who take part. Restorative justice can provide a way for victims to get access to meaningful support and make positive and constructive steps towards getting on with their lives. Eighty per cent of offenders also said that restorative justice had helped them to get a sense of closure and take steps to resolve the problems caused by the offence. (Victim Support Report 2010)

Why restorative justice is important for criminals

Restorative justice is important for criminals because:

- It makes them realise the effects of their crime.
- It brings them face to face with their victims.
- It makes them realise that actions can have terrible consequences even when these were not intended.
- It helps them to determine to turn their backs on crime.

Muslim attitudes to restorative justice

Muslims are in favour of restorative justice because it is the only way of bringing peace and reconciliation between the criminal and the victim and that is what the Qur'an encourages. In Islam, all Muslims are brothers and sisters and should work to help each other:

> *The believers are but a single brotherhood: so make peace and reconciliation between your two contending brothers.* (Surah 49:10)

The Qur'an also says that on the Last Day those who have not been brought face to face with the evil they have done and repented of it (criminals who have not gone through the restorative justice process) will say:

> *Ah! Would that I had sent forth good deeds for this my former life.* (Surah 89:24)

Jewish attitudes to restorative justice

Jews are in favour of restorative justice because it is the only way of bringing peace and reconciliation between the criminal and the victim and that is what the Tenakh, Talmud and Mishneh encourage.

Restorative justice is helping the criminal to follow the advice of the Psalms and the Prophets:

> *Turn from evil and do good; then you will dwell in the land forever. For the Lord loves the just and will not forsake his faithful ones. Wrongdoers will be completely destroyed; the offspring of the wicked will perish. The righteous will inherit the land and dwell in it forever.* (Psalm 37:27–29)

> *Learn to do good; seek justice, correct oppression; bring justice to the fatherless, plead the widow's cause.* (Isaiah 1:17)

Practice questions

c Explain two reasons why either Muslims or Jews support restorative justice.

d 'Criminals are more likely to be forgiven and reintegrated into society by religious people.' Evaluate this statement considering arguments for and against. In your answer you should:

- refer to Muslim or Jewish points of view
- reach a justified conclusion.

Summary

Muslims try to forgive those who wrong them and try to resolve conflicts because this is the teaching of the Qur'an. Muslims are also taught to forgive if they expect God to forgive them.

Jews believe they should forgive those who wrong them because it is taught in the Tenakh. They also believe it is their duty to resolve conflicts as every year they have Yom Kippur when they must forgive people and resolve any personal conflicts.

The UK has laws to help offenders become good members of society and businesses and charities help them to find jobs. Restorative justice makes criminals face the effects of their crimes by facing their victims.

Topic 2.2.7 Treatment of criminals

Thinking points

In this topic you need to:

- think about use of torture, human rights, fair trial and trial by jury
- understand Muslim or Jewish attitudes towards the treatment of criminals
- understand atheist and Humanist attitudes towards the treatment of criminals
- be able to explain and evaluate different religious and non-religious attitudes to the treatment of criminals.

Some people would use ethical principles such as Situation Ethics to justify the use of torture in certain situations (but they would need to be very clear), for example, if a terrorist had planted a bomb that was going to kill many innocent victims, they would say it was justifiable to torture the terrorist until he or she revealed where the bomb was, so that it could be disarmed. They would claim that this was the most loving thing to do in that situation.

Human rights

The Universal Declaration of Human Rights was proclaimed by the **United Nations** General Assembly in Paris on 10 December 1948. It set out, for the first time, fundamental human rights to be universally protected. All the member states of the United Nations agreed to 'strive by teaching and education to promote respect for these rights and freedoms and by progressive measures, national and international, to secure their universal and effective recognition and observance'.

In 1998, the British government passed the Human Rights Act to give UK citizens the fundamental rights and freedoms contained in the European Union (EU) Charter of Fundamental Rights which all EU member states must accept.

As far as crime and punishment is concerned, these rights include the following:

- freedom from torture and degraded treatment – this means that no one can be tortured in the UK or by anyone acting on behalf of UK authorities, for example British soldiers
- the right to liberty – this means that people are free to do anything that is not against the law and cannot be imprisoned without being charged and brought before the courts
- the right to a fair trial – this means that trials are held in public, judgments are made by impartial people, and the accused must know what they are accused of, have access to **legal representation** and be able to argue their case and question the prosecution
- the right not to be punished for something that was not a crime when you did it
- freedom of thought, conscience and religion – this means that no one can be prosecuted for their ideas and beliefs
- **freedom of expression** – this means people can say what they think and publish their ideas, but only as long as they do not break other laws (respect for privacy, national security, racial and religious tolerance and so on)
- the right to participate in free elections – this includes the right to vote, the right to stand as a candidate and the right to a secret ballot.

Activities

1. Are there any rights in the UK Human Rights Act that you think should not be rights?
2. Are there any rights that you would add to the UK Human Rights Act?
3. Do you think torture can ever be justified?

Muslim attitudes to the treatment of criminals

There are two different attitudes to the treatment of criminals in Islam:

- The most common attitude comes from Muslims who live in Islamic states which have adopted Western-type legal systems or who live in non-Muslim states. Such Muslims believe that criminals should be treated fairly and that punishment should aim at both reforming criminals and bringing in restorative justice. Both the Muslim Prison Chaplains' Association and Muslim Aid work with Muslim prisoners to achieve these ends.
- Muslims in countries with Shari'ah justice systems have a somewhat different attitude as they believe that criminals should be punished according to the ***hadd* punishments** set out in the Qur'an.

Islam and the use of torture

All Muslims are opposed to the use of torture:

- The Cairo Declaration on Human Rights in Islam, in 1990, stated that no one should be subjected to arbitrary arrest, torture, maltreatment or indignity, and there are several hadith of the Prophet Muhammad which condemn the use of torture:

  Verily, Allah will torture those who torture people in this world (Sahih Muslim); *Do not torture the creation of Allah the Exalted.* (Al-Adab Al-Mufrad)

- The vast majority of Muslim countries have signed the United Nations Convention Against Torture, which states:

  Each State Party shall take effective legislative, administrative, judicial or other measures to prevent acts of torture in any territory under its jurisdiction. No exceptional circumstances whatsoever, whether a state of war or a threat of war, internal political instability or any other public emergency, may be invoked as a justification of torture.

However, torture is usually defined as, 'the action or practice of inflicting severe pain on someone as a punishment or in order to force them to do or say something'. Some non-Muslims interpret this as meaning that the Shari'ah punishments such as flogging, stoning, amputation and so on could be regarded as torture. Furthermore, some Muslims would say that it is permitted to torture criminals who are hiding a secret which will harm the innocent (for example, the location of a bomb) because of verses such as:

Most Muslims believe that the Qur'anic verse: 'and they feed, for the love of Allah, the indigent, the orphan, and the captive' (Surah 76:8) means that Muslims have been ordered by God to treat captives (prisoners) fairly and humanely, respecting their rights.

Islam and fair trial and trial by jury

The United Nations Declaration of Human Rights states: 'Everyone is entitled in full equality to a fair and public hearing by an independent and impartial tribunal, in the determination of ... any criminal charge against him.'

Muslim Aid

Muslim Aid provides male and female prisoners with a **mentor** while they are serving their sentences in prisons in London. Each prisoner completes an assessment with the community chaplaincy (or other agencies) which is used to determine their need, level of risk and suitability. They are then linked with a mentor who prepares them for their release and helps them after their release. Muslim Aid also runs visitor centre support, where volunteers provide support to family and friends of prisoners, from general mentoring to assistance in translation and filling in forms.

Useful words

United Nations (UN) – an international organisation, founded in 1945, to increase co-operation between member countries

Legal representation – a lawyer who makes sure an accused person is treated fairly and has their case put to best effect

Freedom of expression – the freedom to express your opinions in public (especially about politics and religion)

Mentor – an experienced and trusted adviser

***Hadd* punishments** – the punishments for crime set down in the Qur'an such as cutting a hand off for theft

Activity

Why are there different attitudes to torture in Islam?

Islamic states which have adopted Western-type legal systems provide fair trials where the accused is tried in open court with a defence lawyer. They mainly operate a jury system of trial, where twelve ordinary members of the public decide whether the accused is guilty. The case against the accused is presented by a prosecuting lawyer and the accused is represented by a defence lawyer. A judge makes sure that everything is done fairly and legally and decides on what punishment should be given if the accused is found guilty.

However, Muslim countries operating Shari'ah legal systems do not use jury or prosecutors and sometimes not even defence lawyers. Crimes against God's law (including drinking alcohol, lending with interest, committing adultery) are prosecuted by the state as *hadd* crimes, and all other criminal matters are treated as disputes between individuals, with an Islamic judge deciding the outcome based on the Shari'ah.

Islam and human rights

Muslims have some problems with the United Nations Declaration of Human Rights, especially in the areas of gay rights, the right of consensual sex outside marriage, freedom of speech and religion (especially the right to change your religion) and the issue of women's rights. As a result, Muslim countries signed an alternative agreement, the Cairo Declaration of Human Rights in Islam, in 1990. This Declaration states that:

> *All men are equal in terms of basic human dignity and basic obligations and responsibilities, without any discrimination on the basis of race, colour, language, belief, sex, religion, political affiliation, social status or other considerations. True religion is the guarantee for enhancing such dignity along the path to human integrity.*

The Declaration also states that:

> *... all rights and freedoms stipulated [in the Cairo Declaration] are subject to Islamic Shari'ah.*

This means that the Declaration does not tackle any of the contentious areas. In Muslim countries there are often no gay rights, no right of consensual sex outside marriage, no freedom of religion and no equal rights for women.

Jewish attitudes to the treatment of criminals

Throughout Jewish history, freeing someone held captive, including someone held in prison, has been a major *mitzvah*. As a result, Judaism teaches that criminals should be treated fairly and Jewish rabbis provide a prison chaplaincy service for Jewish prisoners even though there are very few Jews in UK prisons (Jews make up 0.47 per cent of people in England and Wales, while Jewish inmates constitute 0.38 per cent of the prison population). Jewish people are also dedicated to helping organisations working for fair treatment and helping prisoners after their release so that they do not reoffend.

The Talmud teaches that the aim of punishment is 'the return of the wicked to the ways of righteousness'. With this in mind, the Talmud is concerned that overly harsh punishment could drive an individual out of the community and into a lifetime of bad behaviour. Consequently, punishment should be aimed at achieving restorative justice where the victim's needs are met and the offender is reintegrated into society.

Judaism and fair trial and trial by jury

The United Nations Declaration of Human Rights states: 'Everyone is entitled in full equality to a fair and public hearing by an independent and impartial tribunal, in the determination of ... any criminal charge against him.'

Judaism teaches that all accused people are entitled to a fair trial, and most Jews would agree with trial by jury. A jury consisting of twelve ordinary members of the public decides whether the accused is guilty. The case against the accused is presented by a prosecuting lawyer and the accused is represented by a defence lawyer. A judge makes sure that everything is done fairly and legally and decides on what punishment should be given if the accused is found guilty.

In the state of Israel (the only Jewish state), there are no jury trials; instead, all trials are conducted before either one judge or a three-judge panel. Nevertheless, anyone facing police questioning has the right to consult a lawyer beforehand, and a police officer must warn a suspect that he or she does not have to say anything self-incriminating, and that anything said might be used against them in court. Everyone accused of a criminal offence has the right to be represented by a lawyer and if they cannot afford one, one will be provided by the public defender's office. Trials must be held in public and everyone has the same rights regardless of gender, faith or ethnicity.

'The best way to take control over a people and control them utterly is to take a little of their freedom at a time, to erode rights by a thousand tiny and almost imperceptible reductions. In this way, the people will not see those rights and freedoms being removed until past the point at which these changes cannot be reversed': Adolf Hitler, *Mein Kampf*.

Judaism and human rights

Jewish people have always been supporters of human rights, perhaps because they have suffered so much from their human rights being denied. In 1974, the McGill International Colloquium on Judaism and Human Rights declared that

> *Human rights are an integral part of the faith and tradition of Judaism. The beliefs that man was created in the divine image, that the human family is one, and that every person is obliged to deal justly with every other person are basic sources of the Jewish commitment to human rights ... We accordingly reaffirm our long-standing dedication to the advancement and protection of fundamental rights and freedoms for all persons.*

Judaism also supports human rights because of the teachings of the Tenakh. The Tenakh tells Jews that they should stand up for those who cannot speak for themselves, protect the rights of the poor and needy, and make sure the justice system is fair.

> *Open your mouth for the mute, for the rights of all who are destitute. Open your mouth, judge righteously, defend the rights of the poor and needy. (Proverbs 31:8–9)*

> *One witness is not enough to convict anyone accused of any crime or offence they may have committed. A matter must be established by the testimony of two or three witnesses. (Deuteronomy 19:15)*

Activities

1. Why are there different attitudes to torture in Judaism?
2. Look at the picture of Hitler's book above. Do you think Hitler's *Mein Kampf* statement shows why human rights are important?

Activities

1. Look at the photo. Do you think prisoners should be given good-quality accommodation?
2. Look at the statement by the British Humanist Association on page 249 and try to put it into your own words.

Judaism and the use of torture

All Jewish people are opposed to the use of torture because:

- They agree with the United Nations Declaration of Human Rights.
- Israel has signed the United Nations Convention Against Torture, which states:

  Each State Party shall take effective legislative, administrative, judicial or other measures to prevent acts of torture in any territory under its jurisdiction. No exceptional circumstances whatsoever, whether a state of war or a threat of war, internal political instability or any other public emergency, may be invoked as a justification of torture.

- The Tenakh says that God opposes hurting the afflicted:

  Defend the cause of the weak and fatherless; maintain the rights of the poor and oppressed. (Psalm 82:3)

  Learn to do right! Seek justice, encourage the oppressed; defend the cause of the fatherless. (Isaiah 1:17).

- The Torah says that people were made in the image of God, so people should not be tortured:

  And God created the person in God's image; in the image of God, God created him, male and female, God created them.

Jewish law presents some conflicting principles that affect how Jews view torture. In the case of a *rodef* (a pursuer), Jewish law teaches that in order to save innocent lives Jews should do anything they can, even killing the pursuer:

When one pursues another with intent to kill every Jew is commanded to save the intended victim, even at the cost of the pursuer's life. (Mishneh Torah, Rotzeach 1:6)

It is arguable that a suspect who possesses information that could lead to the prevention of a terrorist attack is a *rodef*, and therefore the community has the responsibility to use whatever means are at its disposal to extract that information.

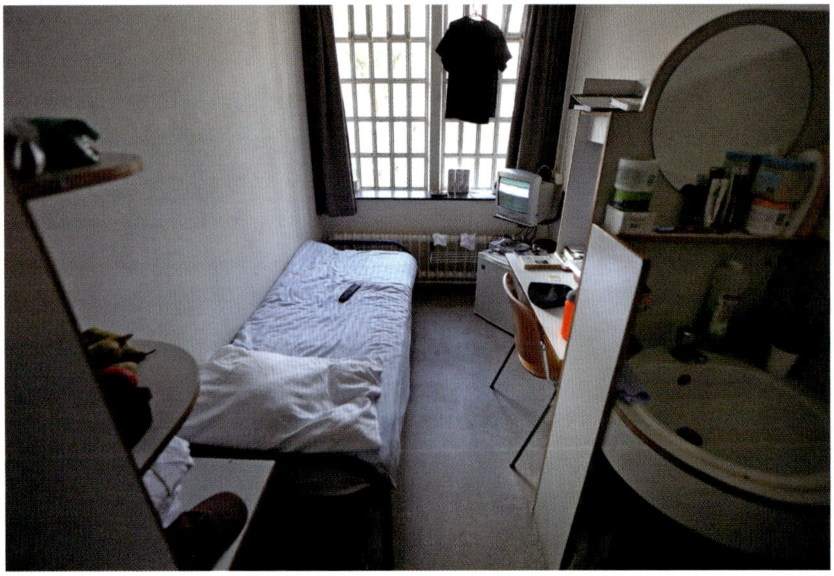

A modern prison cell.

Humanist and atheist attitudes to the treatment of criminals

Humanists believe that criminals should be treated justly and by this they mean that:

- Criminals should have a fair trial.
- Criminals should be allowed legal help to defend themselves.
- They should be treated **humanely** while in custody.
- Any punishment should be proportionate to the crime.
- Juvenile criminals should not be treated as if they are adults and their punishment should recognise their particular needs.
- Criminals should never be subjected to torture.

Humanists believe that treating criminals humanely also helps to ensure that innocent suspects are treated fairly. Humanists, who believe in approaching moral problems rationally and in using evidence to help them to understand society and to make moral decisions, have to think about the purpose and usefulness of punishment.

Humanists have always been in favour of human rights and are supporters of the United Nations Declaration of Human Rights and the UK's commitment to the European Convention on Human Rights.

> *The BHA [British Humanist Association] is firmly committed to the protection and promotion of human rights, as exemplified in documents such as the Universal Declaration of Human Rights. These rights represent shared values rooted in our common humanity and our shared human needs, transcending particular cultural and religious traditions. This regard for human rights and for the equal dignity of all human beings underpins many of our policies. (British Humanist Association, www.humanism.org.uk)*

Most atheists would agree with the Humanist attitudes, but some atheists think that convicted criminals should not be able to use human rights legislation for such things as stopping them from being deported as it would split them from their spouse and children or to allow them to vote while in prison. Such atheists are also likely to approve of government agencies using torture to prevent terrorist attacks.

Practice questions

c Explain two reasons good treatment of criminals is important for either Muslims or Jews. In your answer you must refer to a source of wisdom and authority.

d 'Religion ensures the best treatment for prisoners.' Evaluate this statement considering arguments for and against. In your answer you should:

- refer to Muslim or Jewish points of view
- refer to different Muslim or Jewish points of view or ethical theories
- reach a justified conclusion.

Useful words

Humane – treating with kindness and compassion

Summary

Human rights mean that there should be no torture, anyone accused of a crime should have a right to a fair trial and people in prison should be treated fairly.

Most Muslims agree with this and Muslim Aid and Muslim prison chaplains help prisoners. However, some Muslims agree with the *hadd* punishments (which infringe human rights) and would approve of torture in certain cases.

Jews approve of these rights and work for the fair treatment of prisoners and for their reform. The Talmud and the rabbis teach this and respect for human rights.

Humanists are totally in favour of human rights and the fair treatment of prisoners.

Topic 2.2.8 The death penalty

Thinking points

In this topic you need to:

- think about the nature and purpose of capital punishment
- understand Muslim attitudes and teachings about capital punishment, including Sahih Muslim 16:4152, or Jewish attitudes and teachings, including Exodus 21:12–25 and Mishneh Makkot 1:10
- understand Humanist and atheist attitudes towards the use of capital punishment
- be able to explain and evaluate religious and non-religious attitudes to capital punishment.

The nature and purpose of capital punishment

Capital punishment is punishment which takes away the criminal's life. This is often called execution or the **death penalty**. A crime which can be punished by the death penalty is called a **capital offence**.

In the past, offences such as sheep stealing were capital offences but gradually the number of capital offences was reduced until only murder was a capital offence. There are several methods of capital punishment still in use around the world, such as **lethal injection**, electrocution, hanging, firing squad, stoning and decapitation (cutting off the head).

Of the world's countries, 102 have abolished the death penalty for all crimes; seven have abolished it but retain it for exceptional or special circumstances (such as crimes committed in wartime). Fifty countries retain the death penalty but have not used it for at least ten years; 37 retain it in both law and practice. Belarus is the only European country to retain the death penalty. The USA, Japan and Singapore are the only industrialised countries to retain it.

The UK abolished the death penalty as a form of punishment in 1970. There have been debates in Parliament since 1970 on the reintroduction of capital punishment, which have all been defeated.

Those countries which retain capital punishment believe that its purpose is to deter people from committing murder, to protect society from dangerous people and to act as **retribution** for those who have taken a life.

Useful words

Death penalty – death as the punishment for a crime
Capital offence – a crime which can be punished by death
Lethal injection – executing a criminal by injecting them with sufficient poison to kill them
Retribution – the idea that punishment should make criminals pay for what they have done wrong

Executions and murders in the USA and the UK in 2014

Number of executions in 2014	Murder rate
USA: 35	4.5 per 100,000 people
UK: 0	1.0 per 100,000 people

Activities

1. What is the purpose of capital punishment?
2. Are you surprised at which countries no longer use capital punishment?
3. How do you think Situation Ethics could be used either for or against capital punishment?

Imam Samudra (centre) was sentenced to death by a court in Indonesia and executed by firing squad in 2008 for his part in a series of bombings in Bali in 2002.

Muslim attitudes and teachings about capital punishment

Islam allows capital punishment for three offences: murder, adultery and **apostasy**. Such crimes must be clearly proven and established by the correct processes of law laid down by the Shari'ah.

Most Muslims agree with capital punishment because:

- It is a punishment set down by God in the Qur'an and Muslims believe that the Qur'an is the Word of God:

  The punishment of those who wage war against God and His Apostle, and strive with might and main for mischief through the land is: execution, or crucifixion. (Surah 5:36)

  Take not life, which God hath made sacred, except by way of justice and the law. (Surah 6:151)

- Muhammad made several statements agreeing with capital punishment for murder, adultery and apostasy (see the hadith below), and Muslims believe that Muhammad is the seal of the prophets whose words should be obeyed.
- Muhammad sentenced people to death for murder when he was ruler of Madinah and Muslims believe that Muhammad is the final prophet whose example should be followed.
- The Shari'ah says that capital punishment is the punishment for murder, adultery and apostasy, and Muslims are expected to follow the holy law of Islam.

Some Muslims do not agree with capital punishment because:

- They feel that capital punishment is recommended by the Qur'an, but is not compulsory.
- The Shari'ah says that in certain circumstances, the family of a murder victim can accept money from the murderer rather than requiring the death sentence.
- They feel that since capital punishment does not reduce crimes and since there is a possibility of the wrong person being convicted and then executed, capital punishment is not justice and so is banned by Surah 6:151 (see above).

Useful words

Apostasy – giving up or denying your religious faith

Activities

1. Explain why many Muslims are in favour of capital punishment.
2. Look at the hadith below. Do you think these three cases deserve capital punishment?

Abdullah (b. Mas'ud) reported Allah's Messenger (Peace be upon him) as saying: It is not permissible to take the life of a Muslim who bears testimony to the fact that there is no god but Allah, and I am the Messenger of Allah, but in one of three cases: the married adulterer, a life for life, and the deserter of his Din (the faith of Islam), abandoning the community of Islam. (Hadith 16 from Sahih Muslim)

Activities

1. Explain why some Jews are in favour of capital punishment.
2. Look at the Torah quotation (Exodus 21) below. Why does this justify capital punishment for some Jews?

Jewish attitudes and teachings about capital punishment

Most Jews believe that capital punishment is acceptable, but should be used only as a last resort and with severe restrictions. Murderers who will not pose a threat to society should not be executed as they have a potential to reform. However, those who are likely to murder again should be executed to protect society. Jews believe this because:

- The Torah says that capital punishment should be used for certain offences.
- The Talmud says that capital punishment is allowed but only if the murderer has been warned of the consequences of their action and there are two independent witnesses to the murder.
- The basis of the Jewish theory of punishment is the protection of society, and so capital punishment should be used if a convicted criminal is a threat to society or if capital punishment will deter people from becoming a danger to society.
- Such Jews would also use the non-religious arguments in favour of capital punishment.

Some Jews do not believe in capital punishment because:

- Mishneh 10:1 says, 'A sanhedrin that executes once in seven years, is called murderous' (a sanhedrin is a Jewish court). This indicates that Jewish courts should not use capital punishment.
- They feel that since capital punishment does not reduce crimes and since there is a possibility of the wrong person being convicted and then executed, capital punishment is not justice and the Tenakh commands Jews always to seek justice.

Anyone who strikes a man and kills him shall surely be put to death. However, if he does not do it intentionally, but God lets it happen, he is to flee to a place I will designate. But if a man schemes and kills another man deliberately, take him away from my altar and put him to death. (Exodus 21:12–14)

Useful words

Indeterminate life sentence – being imprisoned for the rest of one's life with no chance of ever being released

Dr Harold Shipman (right) murdered an unknown number of his patients and was given an **indeterminate life sentence** (no chance of ever leaving prison). He killed himself in prison.

Humanist attitudes to capital punishment

In 1989, the worldwide group for Humanists (the International and Ethical Union, IHEU) called for the abolition of capital punishment across the world on the grounds that the death penalty denies the right to life as recognised by Article 3 of the Universal Declaration of Human Rights. Humanists also reject capital punishment on the grounds that:

- No court system can be sure that the correct verdict is always given. People are convicted for offences which it is later proved they did not commit. Such innocent people can be released and compensated if they have been given life imprisonment, but not if they have been executed.
- The statistics of countries with the death penalty and those without the death penalty show that, if anything, those countries which do not use the death penalty have a lower murder rate, showing that capital punishment does not act as a deterrent.
- Many murderers do not expect to be caught and so do not think about the punishment.

- Murderers who know they are going to be killed if caught are more likely to kill more people to avoid being caught.
- Terrorists who are executed are occasionally hailed as **martyrs** and encourage more of their followers to become terrorists.
- Human life is the most important thing there is, so no one has the right to take it. Executing murderers demonstrates that society does not regard human life as important.
- Murderers often regard life imprisonment as worse than death as they try to kill themselves when in prison for life.

Some atheists agree with the Humanist attitude to capital punishment and other atheists believe that murder, and often terrorism, should be punished by the death penalty because:

- If people know they will lose their life if they murder someone, it will act as a deterrent and there will be fewer murders.
- Murderers and terrorists are a great threat to society, and the best way to protect society from them is to take away their lives so they cannot reoffend.
- Human life is the most important thing there is and the value of human life can only be shown by giving those who take human life the worst possible punishment, which is the death penalty.
- Retribution and/or compensation are major parts of punishment and the only retribution or compensation for taking a life is for the criminal's life to be taken.

Practice questions

c Explain two reasons why punishment is important for either Muslims or Jews. In your answer you must refer to a source of wisdom and authority.

d 'Punishment is better dealt with by the state than by religion.' Evaluate this statement considering arguments for and against. In your answer you should:

- refer to Muslim or Jewish points of view
- refer to different Muslim or Jewish or non-religious points of view
- reach a justified conclusion.

Summary

Capital punishment is punishment which takes the life of the criminal. Some atheists think it is a good idea because it takes a life for a life and deters people from murdering others. All Humanists and some atheists think it is a bad punishment because there is evidence that it does not deter and mistakes during trials can lead to innocent people being killed for crimes they did not commit.

Most Muslims agree with capital punishment because it is the punishment for certain crimes in the Qur'an. Some Muslims do not agree with capital punishment, because it is not compulsory in the Shari'ah, and for non-religious reasons.

Most Jews agree with capital punishment because it is approved by the Torah, and they think it will deter criminals. Some Jews think capital punishment is wrong because of what the Mishneh says.

Useful words

Martyr – someone who is killed because of their beliefs

Activity

Look at the table on page 250 and the photo of Dr Harold Shipman on page 252. Do you agree with the message these give about capital punishment?

How to answer questions

a) Outline three Muslim responses to the causes of crime. [3]

Islam tries to deal with the cause of poverty by using *zakah* to help poor families. It tries to deal with the cause of poor upbringing by helping parents to fulfil their duties as Muslim parents. It deals with the cause of alcohol and drugs by banning their use in Muslim society.

A high mark answer because three correct responses are clearly outlined.

b) Explain two reasons why Muslims think good actions are rewarded. [4]

Muslims believe that good actions will be rewarded because they believe that God is just and so he will reward the good and punish the bad. The Qur'an tells Muslims that God will reward the good on the Day of Judgement by sending them to paradise.

A high mark answer because two correct reasons are given and each reason is developed.

c) Explain two reasons why Muslims believe it is important to forgive people. In your answer you must refer to a source of wisdom and authority. [5]

Muslims believe that they should be forgiving, because the Qur'an says that on the Day of Judgement God will deal with everyone as they deserve, but Muslims will be able to request his mercy. However, how can Muslims ask for God's forgiveness if they are not prepared to forgive? Also there are many hadith from the Prophet Muhammad about forgiving people who have offended others and Muslims believe they should follow the example of the Prophet.

A high mark answer because two correct reasons are given and each reason is developed with a reference to the Qur'an and hadith which are sources of authority for Muslims.

d) 'The use of torture is always wrong.' Evaluate this statement considering arguments for and against. In your response you should:

- **refer to Muslim points of view**
- **refer to different Muslim points of view**
- **reach a justified conclusion. [12]**

Many Muslims would agree with this because the Cairo Declaration on Human Rights in Islam says that no one should be subjected to torture. Also, there are several hadith of the Prophet Muhammad which condemn the use of torture: 'Verily, Allah will torture those who torture people in this world'. Furthermore, the vast majority of Muslim countries have signed the United Nations Convention Against Torture.

However, some Muslims would say that the Qur'an permits torturing criminals who are hiding a secret which will harm the innocent (for example, the location of a bomb). They believe that, although torture is wrong, it is a lesser evil than allowing harm to come to innocent people who could be saved by torturing the wicked. They may also feel that the *hadd* punishments like flogging and stoning are a form of torture, but they are set down as punishments in the Qur'an.

Most of me agrees that torture is always wrong, and I can see why most Muslims think so. But I can see why some Muslims feel it can be justified. If my child had been kidnapped and I could save it by torturing a kidnapper, I would be very tempted to do so.

A high mark answer because it gives three clear developed reasons for thinking that torture is always wrong. It then gives three reasons for disagreeing and then reaches a fully justified conclusion.

3a Living the Muslim life

Area of study 2: Based on a study of Islam or Judaism

Topic 2.3a.1 The Ten Obligatory Acts

Thinking points

In this topic you need to:

- think about the nature, history and purpose of the Ten Obligatory Acts and why the acts are important for Shi'a Muslims
- be able to evaluate the importance of the Ten Obligatory Acts for Shi'a Muslims today.

Useful words

Shahadah – the confession and witness of faith, the first pillar
Salah – ritual prayers to be said five times a day, the second pillar
Zakah – charity tax, the third pillar
Sawm – fasting, the fourth pillar
Ramadan – ninth month of the Islamic year; the month of fasting
Hajj – pilgrimage to Makkah, the fifth pillar
Khums – an additional charity tax for Shi'a Muslims

The Five Pillars of Islam in graphic form.

What are the Ten Obligatory Acts?

Sunni Muslims often refer to their faith as 'the House of Islam', by which they mean their home. A house needs foundations, and for the House of Islam this is the Qur'an. This is the word of Allah and so is the foundation of Muslim faith and worship. In the Middle East, houses are supported on pillars, and Sunni Muslims believe that the House of Islam is supported on five pillars:

1. ***Shahadah*** – declaration of faith.
2. ***Salah*** – ritual prayer.
3. ***Zakah*** – compulsory giving to the poor.
4. ***Sawm*** – fasting during **Ramadan**.
5. ***Hajj*** – annual pilgrimage to Makkah.

For Sunni Muslims, performing the Five Pillars is the practical expression of being a Muslim, and observing all five shows that a Muslim is a good Muslim.

Shi'a Islam teaches that there are Ten Obligatory Acts that Muslims must perform to show that they are good Shi'a Muslims who truly believe the Five Pillars. These acts are as follows:

1. *Salah* – the ritual prayer performed at set times, five times a day (covered in Topic 2.3a.3, page 260). Shi'as have some slightly different practices, such as using a tablet of wood or holy soil rather than a prayer mat, as they were mentioned in a Shi'a hadith. Some Shi'as combine the second and third prayers, and the fourth and fifth prayers.
2. *Sawm* – fasting during the month of Ramadan (covered in Topic 2.3a.4, page 264).
3. *Zakah* – the obligatory charity tax (covered in Topic 2.3a.5, page 269).
4. *Hajj* – the annual pilgrimage to Makkah (covered in Topic 2.3a.6, page 273).
5. ***Khums*** – this is a special type of *zakah* where a fifth of certain types of income must go to charity. This is a special Shi'a act (covered in Topic 2.3a.5, page 269).
6. *Jihad* – the struggle to be a good Muslim (covered in Topic 2.3a.7, page 278).
7. *Amr-bil-ma'ruf* (always doing that which is good). Shi'a Muslims are obliged always to seek out that which is good. For example, a Shi'a should never walk past someone in trouble, they should help them.
8. *Nahi anil munkar* (always avoiding that which is evil). Although a Shi'a should always seek out that which is good, they should keep well away from that which is evil and tell off anyone doing, or about to do, evil.
9. *Tawalla* (loving the relatives of the Prophet). This is closely connected with the Shi'a belief in the Imams: if the Prophet nominated his descendants to be Imams, then his relatives must also be special. Those who can trace their ancestry back to Muhammad receive special treatment from Shi'a Muslims.
10. *Tabarra* – hating those who hate Allah and his chosen ones.

History

The Ten Obligatory Acts were developed by the Twelve Imams of Shi'a Islam (all of whom were descendants of the Prophet Muhammad). They perhaps developed at a point before Sunni Muslims had accepted the *shahadah* as the first pillar, which is why it is not one of the Ten Obligatory Acts but is regarded by Shi'as as essential for becoming a Muslim (see Topic 2.3a.2, page 258).

The acts were presumably developed to differentiate Shi'a Muslims from the Sunnis. The last six acts are not in the Five Pillars, but Sunnis would also agree that doing that which is good and avoiding evil are essential features of being a Muslim, and there was much debate in Sunni Islam as to whether *jihad* should be included as the sixth pillar. Sunnis have their own addition to *zakah* known as *sadaqah*, which is a voluntary tax to the poor that could be compared to the Shi'a obligatory act of *khums*.

Importance

Shi'a Muslims believe that fulfilling the Ten Obligatory Acts is important because:

- The Acts were established by Muhammad, Ali and the Imams.
- Allah will punish those who do not fulfil the acts.
- By observing the four practical pillars, a Muslim is following the example of the Prophet Muhammad, and following his example is the way to lead a good Muslim life.
- By fulfilling the acts a Shi'a Muslim feels confident that on the Day of Judgement, Allah will allow him or her into heaven.
- The obligatory acts are a major way of differentiating Shi'a from Sunni Muslims.

Advertisement for a *hajj* tour in a mosque in the UK.

The believers, men and women, are protectors of one another: they enjoin what is just, and forbid what is evil: they observe regular prayers, practise regular charity, and obey God and His Apostle. (Surah 9:71)

Practice questions

c Explain two reasons why the Ten Obligatory Acts are important for Shi'a Muslims. In your answer you must refer to a source of wisdom and authority.

d 'The Ten Obligatory Acts should be performed by all Muslims.' Evaluate this statement considering arguments for and against. In your answer you should:

- refer to Muslim points of view
- refer to different Muslim points of view
- reach a justified conclusion.

Summary

The Ten Obligatory Acts are: the four practical pillars (*salah*, *sawm*, *zakah* and *hajj*) plus *khums*, *jihad*, doing good, avoiding evil, following the relatives of the prophet and hating those who hate Allah and his chosen ones. They are only obligatory for Shi'a Muslims because the last two refer to the Shi'a Imams who are rejected by Sunni Muslims.

Activities

1. Which pillar is not in the Ten Obligatory Acts?
2. Which of the Ten Obligatory Acts are not pillars?
3. Look at the quotation from Surah 9:71. Which of the Obligatory Acts does it say Muslims should observe?
4. Who established the Ten Obligatory Acts?
5. Which of the Ten Obligatory Acts would cause problems for Sunni Muslims?
6. Look at the advertisement for the *hajj*. How might this unite the Sunni and Shi'a communities?

Topic 2.3a.2 *Shahadah*

Thinking points

In this topic you need to:

- think about the nature of *shahadah* as one of the Five Pillars, why reciting *shahadah* is important for Muslims and its place in Muslim practice today
- be able to explain and evaluate the significance of the *shahadah* for Sunni and Shi'a Muslims today.

Useful words

Minaret – the tower beside the mosque from which the call to prayer is announced
Muezzin – the prayer caller who announces the call to prayer five times a day
Ibadah – worship
Iman – faith

There is no god but He: that is the witness of God, His angels and those endued with knowledge standing firm on justice. There is no god but He, the Exalted in Power, the Wise. (Surah 3:18)

Activities

1. When is the *shahadah* said?
2. Look at the photo. Why is the *shahadah* often called the Muslim creed?
3. What is the difference between the *shahadah* and the other four pillars?

What the *shahadah* is

The *shahadah* in Arabic is

> *La Ilaha Illallah, Muhammadur Rasulullah,*

which means,

> *There is no god but God. Muhammad is the prophet of God.*

Shahadah means 'to observe, witness, testify', and the word sometimes comes at the beginning so that it becomes a statement of belief: 'I bear witness that there is no god but God and that Muhammad is the prophet of God'.

The *shahadah* is often called the Muslim creed because it contains all that Muslims must believe to call themselves Muslims.

The words of the *shahadah* are repeated many times a day by Muslims in the prayer ritual of *salah*. They are announced five times a day from the **minaret** of the mosque as the **muezzin** calls Muslims to prayer. They are the first words a baby hears, as his or her father should whisper them into the baby's ears. They should be the last words a Muslim utters if they know they are dying.

The *shahadah* text above a doorway in the Topkapi Palace, Istanbul, Turkey.

The *shahadah* as one of the Five Pillars

Some scholars believe that, although it is now the first pillar, *shahadah* was the last of the pillars and was not generally accepted as a pillar until about 50 years after the death of Muhammad. The four active pillars are prescribed in the Qur'an but the first pillar simply sums up the teachings of the Qur'an. The active pillars are ways of ***ibadah*** (worship), but you cannot worship without the faith (***iman***) on which the worship is based. Hence, *shahadah* is the first and the most important pillar, as if one does not believe that, he is not a Muslim, but if one does not believe one of the others he may still be a Muslim.

The *shahadah* has two simple beliefs: the unity of God and the prophethood of Muhammad. From these two beliefs come all the other beliefs. If you believe in God's unity then you believe in the oneness of creation and humanity, the **vicegerency** of humans, angels, prophets and holy books. If you believe that Muhammad is the prophet of God, then you accept the Qur'an as the Word of God and the *sunnah* of Muhammad as the path to follow in your life.

This is the central pillar even though it is the only 'non-action' pillar. Iman [faith] provides the central pillar that sustains the whole structure. (Kurshid Ahmad, Islam – Its Meaning and Message, Islamic Foundation)

The importance of *shahadah* for Muslims today

The *shahadah* is important because:

- There are no ceremonies such as baptism or Bar Mitzvah to make you a Muslim; this is where the *shahadah* is of crucial importance because if someone converts, all they have to do is recite the *shahadah* in front of Muslim witnesses and then they are a Muslim.
- The *shahadah* shows that Muslims reject **polytheism** – there is no god but God.
- The *shahadah* shows that Islam rejects Christian beliefs about Jesus being the Son of God – Muhammad is nothing more than a prophet.
- The *shahadah* sums up the beliefs of Islam.
- Good Muslims recite it at least five times a day.

Useful words

Vicegerency – looking after something on behalf of someone else

Polytheism – worshipping many gods

The *shahadah* in Shi'a Islam

In just the same way as Sunni Muslims, the Shi'a teach that reciting the *shahadah* in Arabic is all that is required for a person to become a Muslim. However, there are two important differences between Shi'as and Sunnis about the *shahadah*:

- Shi'as agree with the Sunnis that the oneness of God and divine guidance through his messenger Muhammad are essential to Islam. However, the Shi'as believe that for the spiritual and moral guidance of the community, God instructed Muhammad to designate Ali as the leader of the community, and so most Shi'as also add 'Ali is the vicegerent of God' at the end of the *shahadah* to show their belief that Ali is the leader of the believers along with God and Muhammad.
- *Shahadah* is not one of the Ten Obligatory Acts for Shi'as, whereas it is the first pillar for Sunnis.

Activities

1. Explain why is the *shahadah* important for Muslims today.
2. Are there any differences between Sunnis and Shi'as about the *shahadah*?

Practice questions

c Explain two reasons why the *shahadah* is important for Muslims today. In your answer you must refer to a source of wisdom and authority

d 'The *shahadah* is the most important of the Five Pillars.' Evaluate this statement considering arguments for and against. In your answer you should:

- refer to Muslim points of view
- refer to different Muslim points of view
- reach a justified conclusion.

Summary

The *shahadah* is the first pillar and says that Allah is the only God and Muhammad is his prophet. It is important because is sums up Muslim beliefs and is all that people have to say to be a Muslim. It is not an Obligatory Act for Shi'as but it is a pillar for Sunnis.

Topic 2.3a.3 *Salah*

Thinking points

In this topic, you need to think about the nature, history, significance and purpose of *salah* for Sunni and Shi'a Muslims; how *salah* is performed (ablution, times, directions, movements and recitations) in the home and mosque; *jummah* prayer; and similarities and differences between Christian and Muslim worship. By the end of this topic you should be able to explain and evaluate the importance of *salah* for Muslims.

When ye prepare for prayer, wash your faces and your hands to the elbows, rub your head and your feet up to the ankles. If ye are in a state of impurity, bathe your whole body. (Surah 5:7)

Useful words

Prostrated – to put oneself flat on the ground so as to be lying face downwards, especially in respect of submission
Fajr – dawn prayer
Zuhr – midday prayers
As'r – afternoon prayer
Maghrib – sunset prayers
Isha – night prayer
Muezzin – the prayer caller
Adhan – the call to prayer
Minaret – the tower from which the prayer call comes
Wudu – the ritual washing before prayers

Activity

What must happen before a Muslim performs *salah*?

The history of *salah*

Salah is the five times a day ritual prayer of Islam. *Salah* as it is known today began with Muhammad (although Muslims would argue that *salah* began with Adam as it was part of the message given by God to the prophets).

According to the Muslim biographies, Muhammad began a system of morning and evening prayers during which Muslims faced Jerusalem and **prostrated** themselves as a sign of their submission to God. A hadith collected by al-Bukhari says that al-Bara' bin 'Azib narrated:

> *Allah's Messenger offered his prayers facing Bayt Al-Maqdis [Jerusalem] for sixteen or seventeen months.*

When Muhammad set up the Muslim community in Madinah in 622CE, the direction of prayer was changed from Jerusalem to Makkah and an afternoon prayer was added.

By 628CE the ritual prayer of *salah* was established at five times a day, with Muhammad indicating how to perform the ritual on the basis of revelations as recorded in the Qur'an:

> *Set up regular prayers; for such prayers are enjoined on believers at stated times.* (Surah 4:103)

> *Establish regular prayers at the sun's decline till the darkness of the night, and the morning prayer and reading: for the prayer and reading in the morning carry their testimony. And pray in the small watches of the morning an additional prayer.* (Surah 17:78)

> *Turn thy face in the direction of the Sacred Mosque; that is indeed the truth.* (Surah 2:149)

How *salah* is performed

- *Salah* should take place five times a day:
  - ***Fajr*** – between dawn and sunrise
  - ***Zuhr*** – after midday until afternoon
  - ***As'r*** – between late afternoon and sunset
  - ***Maghrib*** – between sunset and the end of daylight, and
  - ***Isha*** – between sunset and dawn.
- The time for prayer is announced by the **muezzin** making the ***adhan*** (call to prayer) from the **minaret** of the mosque.
- Muslims must prepare for *salah* by removing their shoes and then performing ***wudu*** (washing hands, arms to the elbow, face, nostrils, ears and head, and washing the feet three times). *Salah* is a sacred moment when a Muslim makes direct contact with God and so must be as pure as possible.
- Muslims must then find a clean place.

- To pray, Muslims must then face the direction of Makkah (***qibla***).
- A set prayer ritual must be carried out: repeat the call to prayer, make a prayer of intention, stand with hands to ears and recite Surah 1, kneel on the floor and touch the forehead to the ground as a sign of submission to God, raise the top half of the body and give God the glory, prostrate again, then stand up and say '*Allahu akbar*' (God is great). This ritual is called a ***raka*** and each prayer time has a set number of *rakat*.
- During each *salah* the prayer must repeat the *shahadah*, and request God's blessing on the people around them and Muhammad and all the prophets.
- *Salah* ends by saying 'the peace and mercy of Allah be upon you' over each shoulder.
- *Salah* must be said in Arabic, with all the people praying performing the same actions and facing the same direction.

Salah in the home

Many Muslims say their prayers at home as a family, with the whole family joining in. They often have a special room which they keep ritually clean and never enter when wearing shoes. They will perform their *wudu* in the bathroom and have prayer mats which are kept facing Makkah (the direction of the Ka'aba can be found using a *qibla* compass).

Many Muslims think that family *salah* is a good way of binding the family and even use the Christian saying 'the family that prays together stays together'. It is also often easier for women and girls to pray at home.

Salah in the mosque

Although *salah* can be said anywhere, it is thought preferable for it to be performed in the mosque because of this verse in the Qur'an:

> *bow down your heads with those who bow down in worship.*
> *(Surah 2:43)*

It is from the mosque that the muezzin makes the call to prayer:

> *God is great. I bear witness that there is no god but God and that Muhammad is the prophet of God. Rush to prayer. Rush to success. God is great. There is no god but God.*

Each mosque also has a prayer board with six clocks showing the times of the five daily prayers and ***jummah*** prayers on Friday. The prayer times vary from week to week (except near the equator) as they are based on the times of sunrise and sunset.

All mosques have communal *wudu* facilities and a prayer hall which can never be entered by anyone wearing shoes. The carpet in the hall will have lines directed to the prayer wall where the ***mihrab*** (*qibla* alcove) indicates the direction of the Ka'aba.

The worshippers stand in lines behind the **imam** (prayer leader), who leads them through the ritual.

Most mosques have a special area for women to perform *salah* (usually a gallery) as men and women must be separated. There is a tradition in the Indian subcontinent (India, Pakistan and Bangladesh) for women to pray at home.

Useful words

Qibla – direction of the Ka'aba in Makkah
Raka – the set actions in the prayer ritual (plural *rakat*)
Jummah – Friday midday prayers
Mihrab – alcove in mosques showing the direction of Makkah
Imam – prayer leader

Activities

1. Does the Qur'an tell Muslims all they need to know about *salah*?
2. Look at the photo of *salah* below. What can be learned from this about the nature and meaning of *salah*?
3. Why do you think many women prefer to pray at home?

Muslim sisters praying in their home.

A mosque clock in Manchester showing the time of prayers.

Jummah prayer

> *O ye who believe! When the call is proclaimed to prayer on Friday, hasten earnestly to the remembrance of God, and leave off business: that is best for you if ye but knew! And when the Prayer is finished, then ye may disperse through the land and seek the bounty of God.* (Surah 62:10)

This verse is the basis of the custom of Muslims attending mosque for *Zuhr* prayers on a Friday (many Muslim countries have a Friday to Saturday weekend). These prayers are now called *jummah* prayers and should be attended by at least 40 adult males, and so they are performed in mosques designated ***jami* mosques** where it can be expected there will be 40 adult males.

The imam leads the first two *rakat* and then preaches a sermon (***khutba***), often giving advice on how to live a good Muslim life (usually related to the country they are in), after which he leads the worshippers in the final *rakat*.

Muslims living in a non-Muslim country would only need an hour or so off from work on Friday to attend *jummah* prayers.

Useful words

***Jami* mosques** – mosques appointed for Friday prayers
Khutba – sermon

Why *salah* is important to Muslims today

- It puts them in direct contact with God five times a day.
- It reminds them every day that they have submitted themselves to God.
- It unites them with their fellow Muslims as they stand in lines performing the same actions and saying the same words.
- It is a discipline which forces Muslims to take their religion seriously.
- It reminds Muslims of the fundamentals of Islam: submission and peace.
- It is a way of having their sins forgiven, as a hadith says: 'the five prayers remove sins as water removes dirt'.
- It is commanded by the Qur'an in such verses as:

  But celebrate the praises of the Lord, and be of those who prostrate themselves in adoration. (Surah 15:98)

  Establish regular prayer, for prayer restrains from shameful and unjust deeds; and remembrance of God is the greatest thing in life. (Surah 29:45)

Activities

1. Why do you think *jummah* prayers are important?
2. Look at the prayer board above. Why do you think Muslims need to consult a board like this every week?

Shi'as and *salah*

Salah has the same importance for Shi'as as for Sunnis and *salah* is one of the Ten Obligatory Acts. The differences in practice have been covered in Topic 2.3a.1, page 256.

Christian and Muslim worship

Salah is Muslim worship and *du'a* is Muslim personal prayer. There are no differences between *du'a* and Christian personal prayer.

Differences:

- Muslims must perform *wudu* before worship, but Christians do not, although some Christians sprinkle themselves with holy water as they enter the church.
- Muslims must face Makkah for *salah* whereas Christians can worship facing any direction (although most Catholic, Orthodox and Anglican churches face the east).
- Muslims worship in Arabic, whereas Christians worship in their native language.
- Men and women worship separately in Islam, whereas the sexes worship together in Christianity.
- The Muslim special day for worship is Friday, whereas the Christian special day is Sunday.
- Muslims should perform *salah* five times a day at set times, whereas Christians are only required to go to church on Sunday, but are expected to pray every morning and evening.
- Muslims perform a set ritual to perform *salah*, but only Christian liturgical worship has set rituals; Pentecostals and other Protestants have no set rituals.
- Christian worship usually has musical accompaniment and often has hymns, Muslim worship does not.
- Christian worship often has visual stimuli (crosses, stained-glass windows, statues of Mary and the saints) Muslim worship does not.

Similarities:

- Weekly worship includes a sermon in both faiths.
- Worship involves the whole congregation saying a prayer together (even non-liturgical Christian worship includes saying the Lord's Prayer).
- Both worships involve praying for the needs of others.

Practice questions

c Explain two reasons why *jummah* prayers are important for Muslims. In your answer you must refer to a source of wisdom and authority.

d '*Salah* is the most important of the Five Pillars.' Evaluate this statement considering arguments for and against. In your answer you should:

- refer to Muslim points of view
- refer to different Muslim points of view
- reach a justified conclusion.

Summary

Salah should take place five times a day and can be performed wherever a Muslim is as long as they can find a clean place, face the direction of the Ka'aba and wash themselves according to the rules of *wudu*. There is a set ritual and the prayers must be said in Arabic. There is a special *salah* on Friday midday (*jummah* prayers) which must be said in the mosque. *Salah* is important because it gives direct contact with God five times a day.

Topic 2.3a.4 *Sawm*

Thinking points

In this topic you need to:

- think about the nature, history and purpose of *sawm*; and the nature and importance of *sawm* during Ramadan (Surah 2:183–185)
- consider the nature and significance of the Night of Power and why it is important for Muslims
- be able to explain and evaluate the importance of *sawm* and Ramadan for Muslims.

Useful words

Iftar – the meal breaking the fast at night
Suhur – the meal just before fasting starts at dawn

The nature of *sawm*

Sawm is the fourth pillar and means fasting. The Qur'an makes plain that Muslims must practise fasting. Muslims can fast voluntarily at any time (except the *ids*, when fasting is banned), but the month of Ramadan soon became a compulsory month of fasting.

The obligation to fast begins on the first day of Ramadan (the ninth month of the Islamic year), which occurs when the new moon is seen and lasts until the sighting of the next new moon.

Sawm means no food, drink, smoking, lying, gossiping, swearing, getting angry or sex from dawn to dusk. Families have two special meals a day, the ***iftar*** to break the fast at night and the ***suhur*** just before dawn to give strength to face the day's fast.

All Muslims above the age of puberty should fast, although there are special exemptions for those on journeys (often taken to cover doing exams), the elderly, the sick, breastfeeding mothers and menstruating women. However, the fast days should either be made up later or be compensated for by feeding a poor person.

> *O ye who believe! Fasting is prescribed to you as it was prescribed to those before you that ye may learn self-restraint for a fixed number of days; but if any of you is ill or on a journey, the prescribed number of days should be made up from days later. For those who can do it with hardship is a ransom, the feeding of one that is indigent. But he that will give more, of his own free will, it is better for him. And it is better for you that ye fast, if ye only knew. Ramadan is the month in which was sent down the Qur'an as a guide to mankind, also clear signs for guidance and judgement. So everyone of you who is present at his home in that month should spend it in fasting. But if anyone is ill or on a journey, the prescribed days should be made up by days later. God intends every facility for you. He does not want to put you to difficulties. He wants you to complete the prescribed period, and to glorify Him in that He has guided you; and perchance ye shall be grateful. (Surah 2:183–185)*

As part of the Ramadan fast, extra prayers are said and one thirtieth of the Qur'an is read each day so that at the end of Ramadan the whole Qur'an has been read. All Muslims try to attend mosque on the 27th of Ramadan (*Laylat al-Qad'r* – the Night of Power) to celebrate the night when Muhammad received the first revelation of the Qur'an.

Activities

1. What must Muslims do during Ramadan?
2. Why is *Laylat al-Qad'r* important for Muslims?

There are often social gatherings at *iftar* when traditional foods are consumed. This ASDA supermarket is making these foods easily available to its Muslim clients.

The history of *sawm*

Muslims believe that fasting has always been part of Islam:

> *Fasting is prescribed to you as it was prescribed to those before you.*
> (Surah 2:183)

This can be seen in the religions of Judaism and Christianity, which both have fasting (for example, Yom Kippur for Jews and Lent for Christians) as part of the message they were given which was distorted, but not forgotten.

Ramadan had been a traditional holy month in Arabia. It was a truce month (no fighting was allowed) and holy men fasted. It fell at a fixed time of the year and by making the Muslim calendar a lunar one, Muhammad made sure that Ramadan was no longer connected with Makkan polytheism and a particular season of the year. Ramadan moves back eleven days each year so that over a period of 32 years it moves through all the seasons (which causes major problems in northern latitudes when Ramadan falls in May, June and July).

The biographies record that Muhammad observed his first Ramadan in 625CE after the instruction in Surah 2 had been revealed to him.

Why *sawm* during Ramadan is important for Muslims

Sawm is important because:

- Keeping the fast is fulfilling the fourth pillar of Islam.
- The Qur'an is the greatest gift God has for humanity and keeping the fast in Ramadan is a way of thanking God for the Qur'an.
- Fasting brings Muslims closer to God so they can concentrate on God rather than the ordinary things of life.
- Fasting promotes the self-control which any Muslim needs to practise their faith properly.
- Many Muslims see Ramadan as an annual training programme to recharge their spiritual batteries so they can carry out their duties to God for the rest of the year.

Fasting in the Arctic Circle

The Islam Society of Northern Finland claims there are two schools of thought about the problem. Egyptian lawyers say that if the fast lasts more than 18 hours, then Muslims can follow the Makkan time or the nearest Muslim country time. Saudi Arabian lawyers say that whether the hours of fasting are long or short, Muslims have to follow the local time. The Society recommends that Muslims in northern Finland observe either Makkah's fasting hours or Turkish time because Turkey is the nearest Muslim country to Finland.

Activities

1. Why can Ramadan be a problem for Muslims living in the Arctic Circle?
2. What do you think about the advice given to such Muslims above?

Dusk at the Sultan Omar Ali Saifuddin Mosque in Brunei.

- Fasting in Ramadan unites and strengthens the Muslim community.
- Ramadan brings Muslim families together and strengthens their bonds.

Useful words

Laylat al-Qadr – the Night of Power (destiny)
Destiny – what has been set out to happen
Sirah – a biography of the prophet Muhammad
Jibril – the angel Gabriel

Laylat al-Qadr

Laylat al-Qadr can be translated as either the 'Night of Power and Excellence' or the 'Night of **Destiny**'. It was the night when Muhammad received the first revelation of the Qur'an.

The biographies of Muhammad (known as ***Sirah***) tell us that in the year before 610CE, Muhammad had become very dissatisfied with the polytheistic religion of Makkah and had begun to go to the nearby Mount Nur to fast, pray and meditate in Cave Hira. Muhammad decided to spend the whole month of Ramadan in contemplation. Towards the end of the month he was visited by the angel **Jibril**, who told him to 'recite', and Muhammad frighteningly replied that he had nothing to recite. This happened twice and then the angel said:

> *Proclaim in the name of thy Lord and Cherisher, who created, created man out of a clot of congealed blood. Proclaim! And thy Lord is Most Bountiful, He who taught the use of the pen, taught man that which he knew not.* (Surah 96:1–5)

This was the first revelation Muhammad received and the rest of the Qur'an came over the next 23 years. There is no indication in the Qur'an as to which date in Ramadan the revelation occurred, although it is generally agreed that the revelation occurred in the last ten days of the month.

Activity

Look at the photo of *al-Qadr* above. What do you think it means and do you think it is true?

As a result, those who can afford to, devote their time in **remembrance of Allah** (often retired people) and stay in the mosque for the final ten days of Ramadan. They fast during the day and occupy themselves with the remembrance of Allah, performing voluntary prayers and studying the Qur'an day and night. However, most Sunni Muslims celebrate the night on the 27th of Ramadan and attend mosque for special prayers and read the Qur'an.

Useful words

Remembrance of Allah – thinking about God in a meditative way

Muslim beliefs about the Night of Power

- Praying on that night is the best prayer (better than 1000 months of prayers).
- Praying in the mosque on the Night of Power can bring forgiveness of all a person's sins.
- There is a tradition that reciting Surahs 29 and 30 during the 23rd night of Ramadan will ensure admission into paradise.
- Praying on the Night of Power brings religious insight ('Therein come down the angels and the Spirit by Allah's permission').
- Meditating and retreating to the mosque for the last ten days of Ramadan can bring a special closeness to and relationship with Allah.

Many Muslims believe that *Laylat al-Qadr* is the night when Allah determines everyone's destiny (one meaning of *Qadr*) for the coming year:

> *During Lailatul-Qadr, the angels, the spirit, and the trusted scribes all descend to the lower heavens and write down whatever Allah decrees that year, and if Allah wishes to advance something or postpone it or add thereto, He orders the angel to erase it and replace it with whatever He decrees.* (Imam Abu Abdullah al-Sadiq)

According to this view, destiny includes life and death, sustenance, abundance of crops or famine, and everything good or bad. A Shi'a hadith claims that, 'Allah the Glorified and Exalted determines in this night each and every event to occur during the next year to any and all of His creation.'

Why the Night of Power is important for Muslims today

- It remembers and celebrates the revelation of the Qur'an, the final and unalterable Word of God.
- It remembers and celebrates the calling of Muhammad to be the last and final messenger of God to the world.
- Some Muslims believe this was the day Muhammad made his night journey to heaven (*al Mi'raj*) when God gave him the details of *salah*.
- It is also believed that this was the night when Moses died, when Joshua died and when Jesus was taken to heaven.
- Those who believe it is the Night of Destiny believe it is hugely important because God will decide everything to happen in the coming year.

Activity

Do you think your future has been decided or is your destiny in your own hands?

- It is particularly important for Shi'a Muslims because there is a hadith from Ali which says that this is the night when God decreed that Ali and his descendants would be the Imams:

Imam Ali ibn Abu Talib said, 'The Messenger of Allah asked me once, "O Ali! Do you know the implication of Lailatul-Qadr?" I said, "No, indeed, O Messenger of Allah!" He said, "Allah, the Praised One, the Most Glorified, decreed in it what will take place till the Day of Judgement, and among what He, the most Exalted, the Most Great, decreed was your own Imamate and the Imamate of your offspring till the Day of Resurrection."'

Practice questions

c Explain two reasons why Muslims fast in Ramadan. In your answer you must refer to a source of wisdom and authority.

d 'One night in Ramadan is no more important than another.' Evaluate this statement considering arguments for and against. In your answer you should:

- refer to Muslim points of view
- reach a justified conclusion.

Summary

Sawm is the fourth pillar. It means fasting and is used to refer to the month-long fast during Ramadan. Adult Muslims do not eat or drink during daylight hours and say extra prayers. It is commanded in the Qur'an and Muslims believe it is a way of thanking God for the Qur'an, which was given in Ramadan on the Night of Power. On this night special prayers are said. Muslims believe that fasting in Ramadan forgives sins.

Topic 2.3a.5 *Zakah* and *khums*

Zakah

Zakah is the third pillar of Islam and is an annual tax on wealth. It is often known as the charity tax.

The Qur'an does not specify exactly how much *zakah* should be paid:

> *O ye who believe spend out of the bounties We have provided for you.* (Surah 2:254)

> *They ask thee what they should spend in charity. Say, 'Whatever ye spend, that is good'.* (Surah 2:215)

Consequently, Sunni Muslims follow the Shari'ah based on the *sunnah* of the Prophet to know what to give.

Clearly, poor people should not have to pay *zakah* and the Shari'ah sets down a ***nisab*** which sets out the minimum people need to have before they have to pay *zakah*. If what you have left over has been in your possession for a lunar year and is more than the UK *nisab* (£2220 for 2015) then you must pay 2½ per cent of that amount as *zakah* (more details can be found at http://zakatcalculator.co.uk).

Many Muslims pay their *zakah* direct to Muslim charities such as Islamic Relief and Muslim Aid. Every mosque also has a *zakah* committee which collects *zakah* and distributes it according to the wishes of the mosque committee.

Special *zakahs* are paid on Id-ul-Fitr (currently £4 per family member) and on Id-ul-Adha, when a donation is often given to charity rather than sharing meat with the poor.

Thinking points

In this topic you need to:

- think about the nature, history, purpose and benefits of both *zakah* and *khums*
- be able to explain why *zakah* is important for Sunni Muslims and why *khums* is important for Shi'a Muslims.

Useful words

Nisab – the amount of income or wealth a Muslim needs to have before they are liable for *zakah*

Activity

Explain why *zakah* is important for Sunni Muslims.

Muslims paying *zakah* at a mosque in Singapore.

Useful words

Alms – charitable giving to the poor
Sadaqah – voluntary giving to the poor

The purpose of *zakah*

Surah 9:60 says,

> ***Alms*** *are for the poor and the needy, and those employed to administer the funds; for those whose hearts have been recently reconciled to the truth; for those in bondage and debt; in the cause of God and for the wayfarer.*

On the basis of this verse, *zakah* is used for orphans, widows, poor people, homeless people and tax collectors, and for religious purposes. Many Muslims give their *zakah* to charities helping the poor in less developed countries as they think this is the spirit of *zakah*.

Why Muslims give *zakah*

- It is the third pillar of Islam, which all Muslims must fulfil.
- Paying *zakah* is a sign of a Muslim's submission to God and worship of God.
- *Zakah* means purification. Islam teaches that wealth can be evil and cut people off from God, but if Muslims pays *zakah* they purify the wealth that they keep.
- There are Muslim teachings that connect *salah* and *zakah*; both are associated with purifying. Some scholars teach that God is more likely to accept prayers if the person praying pays *zakah*.

Sadaqah

Islam also has the idea of voluntary giving to charity. This is known as ***sadaqah*** because it is voluntary, whereas *zakah* is compulsory. *Zakah* aims to reduce the gap between the rich and the poor and so Muslims should give voluntary *sadaqah* above *zakah* to help the poor:

> *Seest thou one who denies the judgement to come? Then such is the man who repulses the orphan and encourages not the feeding of the indigent. (Surah 107:1–3)*

> *Those who in charity spend of their goods by night and by day, in secret and in public, have their reward with their Lord. (Surah 2:274)*

> *Protect your property by giving zakat, and help your relatives to recover from disease by giving charity. (Hadith)*

> *He who eats and drinks whilst his brother goes hungry is not one of us. (Hadith quoted by al-Bukhari)*

Khums

Shi'a Muslims also have a special *khums* tax.

Khums (one fifth of a gain) is based on this verse:

> *Know that whatever of a thing you acquire, a fifth of it is for Allah, for the Messenger, for the near relative, and the orphans and the needy and the wayfarer. (Surah 8:41)*

Activity

What are the similarities and differences between *zakah* and *khums*?

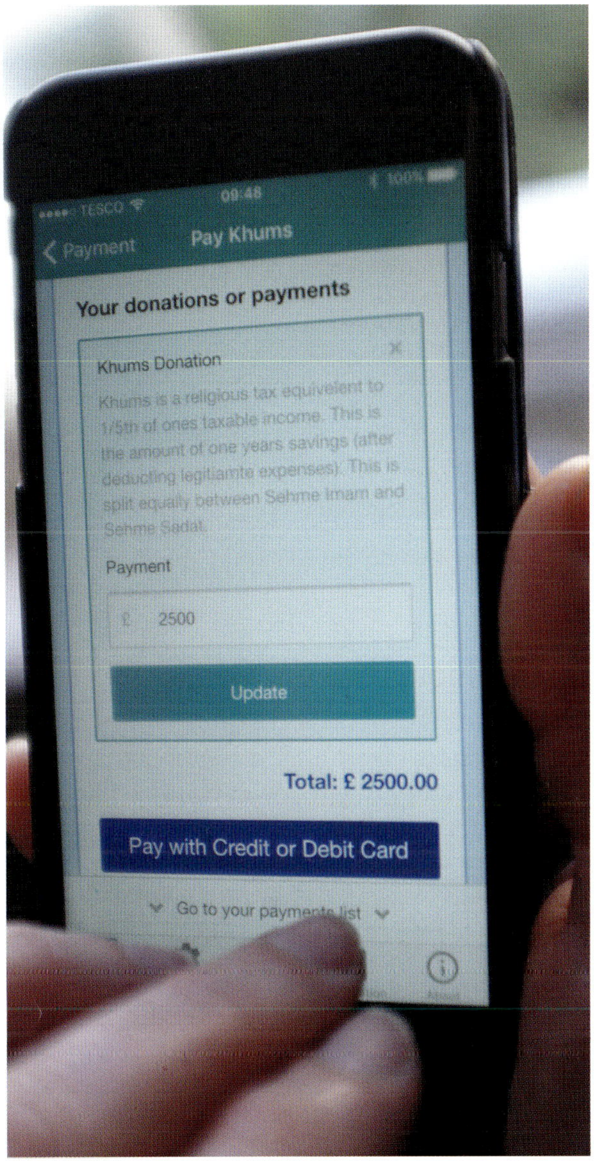

A business proprietor calculating her *khums* payment using a smartphone app.

(Sunni translations of the Qur'an read 'out of all the booty that ye may acquire a fifth share is assigned to God, and to the Apostle, and to near relatives, orphans, the needy, and to the wayfarer' and so Sunni Muslims teach that *khums* applies only to proceeds from war.)

Khums, in the Shi'a tradition, is applied to the business profit, or surplus, of a business income. It is payable at the beginning of the financial year. Shi'a lawyers say that twenty per cent of surplus of income (the difference between assets and outgoings), any proceeds from mines and minerals (this would include most jewellery), precious stones obtained from the sea by diving, treasures and proceeds from land sold to non-Muslims must be paid as *khums*.

Of the *khums* money, 50 per cent goes to religious causes and poor descendants of the Prophet, and 50 per cent goes to the poor, the orphans and the homeless. This means that ten per cent of income goes to religious lawyers and scholars. This has been a major source of income and financial independence for religious leaders in Shi'a areas.

Shi'as pay *zakah* if they are farmers or have gold or silver coins. They also pay *sadaqah* to the poor and needy.

Activities

1. Look at the photo above. How do you know this phone app is for a Shi'a Muslim?
2. Why do you think Shi'as feel it is important that religious leaders are properly cared for and are independent of state control or influence?
3. What do you think are the benefits of *khums* to: a) the community, b) those receiving *khums*, c) those giving *khums*?

The purpose of *khums*

- To ensure that the descendants of the Prophet are properly cared for.
- To make sure that religious leaders are properly cared for and are independent of state control or influence.
- To provide and support religious institutions such as school, colleges and mosques.
- To provide security for the poor, the homeless and orphans.

Why Shi'as pay *khums*

- It is commanded by the Qur'an.
- It is a way of supporting the descendants of the Prophet, who are given special reverence by Shi'a Muslims.
- It is commanded by Shi'a religious lawyers.
- It is a way of supporting and spreading Shi'a Islam.
- It helps the poor and needy.

The benefits of receiving *zakah* and *khums*

Rewards go not only to those who give *zakah* and *khums*, but also to the people who receive *zakah* and *khums*. Apart from receiving the benefit of money to relieve their poverty, they also receive the spiritual benefits of:

- knowing they have helped a fellow Muslim to purify their money
- knowing they have helped a fellow Muslim to have their sins forgiven
- knowing they have been part of God's plan to redistribute wealth from the rich to the poor.

Practice questions

c Explain two reasons why paying *zakah* is important for Muslims. In your answer you must refer to a source of wisdom and authority

d '*Zakah* and *khums* alone will never solve the problems of poverty.' Evaluate this statement considering arguments for and against. In your answer you should:

- refer to Muslim points of view
- refer to different Muslim points of view
- reach a justified conclusion.

Summary

Zakah is the third pillar and is an annual tax of 2½ per cent on wealth, which is paid to help the poor as commanded in the Qur'an. Special *zakahs* are paid on the *ids* and Muslims make voluntary donations called *sadaqah*. Shi'a Muslims pay a special *khums* tax of twenty per cent of business surplus which is how Shi'as interpret Surah 8:41, but Sunnis think it is twenty per cent of profits from war.

Topic 2.3a.6 *Hajj*

The nature of *hajj*

Hajj is the fifth of the Five Pillars and is the only one that is not compulsory. *Hajj* starts on the eighth day of the month of **Dhu al-Hijjah** and lasts until the thirteenth. Although all Muslims should try to go on *hajj*, they are only allowed to go if:

- They have sufficient money to provide for their dependants while they are away from home.
- They are physically and mentally fit and prepared for the physical demands of *hajj*.

While on *hajj* men must wear the ***ihram*** (two pieces of unsewn cloth, one around the waist and one over the shoulder); women wear a white garment covering the whole body except for the face and feet (no veils on *hajj*).

Hajj is now highly organised by the Saudi government, which is responsible for the holy sites and has carried out extensive building works so the area can cope with over 2 million pilgrims on *hajj*. Pilgrims are divided into groups (often called a caravan) with a group guide who will be a Saudi.

Most events take place in the Great Mosque of Makkah, which contains:

- the **Ka'aba**
- the **Zamzam well**
- the **Ma'sa**

On the first day of *hajj* pilgrims circuit the Ka'aba seven times while saying the ***talbiya*** prayer (this is called a ***tawaf***). Then they do seven circuits of the Ma'sa and return to the main courtyard for midday prayer, after which a sermon is preached outlining the events of *hajj* and giving advice to the pilgrims.

The next day the pilgrims are given water from the Zamzam well and then walk ten kilometres to **Mina**, where they stay until night prayers, and then walk overnight the eight kilometres to **Arafat**.

The next day is the Waquf of Arafat, when pilgrims stand on the plain in front of the hill of Arafat and confess their sins (it is believed that any sins confessed here are immediately forgiven). Then the pilgrims jog to Muzdalifah for a torchlight ***waquf*** before walking back to Mina. On the way to Mina they should collect 49 stones ready for the next day. Any pilgrims who miss the Waquf of Arafat must repeat *hajj*.

On the 10th of Dhu al-Hijjah the pilgrims throw stones at the stoning pillars (the pillars represent Satan and remind the pilgrims of Satan tempting Ibrahim to disobey God). Then the pilgrims offer a sacrifice to God remembering how God provided a sacrifice for Ibrahim after he obeyed God by being prepared to sacrifice his son. There are slaughterhouses around Mina and groups of pilgrims usually get together to buy an animal and appoint a slaughterer to make the sacrifice for them. Pilgrims should then eat some of the meat and give the rest to the poor. Nowadays, the Saudi government puts the meat on to refrigerator ships and sends it to poor

Thinking points

In this topic you need to:

- think about the nature, role, origins and significance of *hajj*, including Surah 2:124–130 and 22:25–30
- understand how *hajj* is performed and why *hajj* is important for Muslims
- be able to explain and evaluate the benefits and challenges from attending *hajj*.

Useful words

Dhu al-Hijjah – the twelfth month of the Islamic calendar, when *hajj* takes place
Ihram – pilgrim dress
Ka'aba – (or Ka'ba) the House of God in Makkah containing the black stone
Zamzam well – the well in the courtyard of the Great Mosque given by God for Hagar and Ismail
Ma'sa – the covered passageway between the hills Marwa and Safa, which pilgrims run between
Talbiya – the *hajj* prayer which pilgrims say constantly
Tawaf – seven circuits of the Ka'aba
Mina – the place ten kilometres from Makkah where pilgrims throw stones at Satan and make the sacrifice
Arafat – the plain and hill eighteen kilometres from Makkah where the central part of *hajj* takes place
Waquf – a standing prayer during *hajj*

Using an online travel agent to search for *hajj* travel packages from the UK.

Useful words

Hajji – one who has completed the *hajj*

Activities

1. What is pilgrim dress?
2. What happens at Arafat?
3. What happens at Mina?
4. Look at the quotations from the Qur'an opposite. What features of *hajj* are based on these verses?
5. Look at the photo above. How have websites like this changed the *hajj*?

countries. This is the part of *hajj* that all Muslims throughout the world join in as the festival of Id-ul-Adha.

For the next two days, pilgrims stone the pillars and then on the 12th of Dhu al-Hijjah the *hajj* regulations are over and pilgrims can dress ordinarily and have their hair cut. The next day, pilgrims walk to Makkah and perform a final *tawaf* and circuit of the Ma'sa. *Hajj* is then completed, although many Muslims go on to visit Madinah and the Mosque of Muhammad.

Anyone who completes *hajj* is known as a ***hajji*** and often colours their hair or beard with henna as a sign of their status. *Hajjis* receive special respect from the Muslim community, although there are many more of them nowadays thanks to the growth of package holidays.

> *Here I am O my God. Here I am. No partner hast thou, here am I. Truly the praise and the grace are thine and the empire. No partner hast thou, here am I. (The talbiya prayer which is said throughout* hajj*)*

The history of *hajj*

Hajj celebrates many historic events, from the founding of the Ka'aba by Adam to rebuilding by Ibrahim, and Ibrahim's relationship with his son Ismail and with God.

> *And remember that Abraham was tried by his Lord with certain commands, which he fulfilled: He said: 'I will make thee an Imam to the Nations.' He pleaded: 'And also (Imams) from my offspring!' He answered: 'But My Promise is not within the reach of evil-doers. Remember We made the House a place of assembly for men and a place of safety; and take ye the station of Abraham as a place of prayer; and We covenanted with Abraham and Isma'il, that they should sanctify My House for those who compass it round, or use it as a retreat, or bow, or prostrate themselves (therein in prayer). And remember Abraham said: 'My Lord, make this a City of Peace, and feed its people with fruits, such of them as believe in Allah and the Last Day.' He said: '(Yea), and such as reject Faith, for a while will I grant them their pleasure, but will soon drive them to the torment of Fire, an evil destination (indeed)! And remember Abraham and Isma'il raised the foundations of the House (With this prayer): 'Our Lord! Accept (this service) from us: For Thou art the All-Hearing, the All-Knowing'. (Surah 2:124–127)*

There were pilgrimages when Makkah was a non-Muslim state, but in 628CE Muhammad was given a vision from God of going on pilgrimage and the events of *hajj* were revealed to him in what is now Surah 22. Thereafter, Makkah became Muslim and Muhammad went on pilgrimage five times. On his final *hajj* in 632CE, Muhammad set out the pattern for all subsequent *hajj* and preached his final sermon at Arafat just a few weeks before he died.

> *Oh people listen carefully! All the believers are brothers ... none is higher than the other unless he is higher in obedience to Allah. No Arab is superior to a non-Arab except in piety. (From Muhammad's final sermon)*

Behold We gave the site to Abraham, of the Sacred House, saying: 'Associate not anything in worship with Me; and sanctify My House for those who compass it round, or stand up, or bow, or prostrate themselves therein in prayer.' And proclaim the Pilgrimage among men: they will come to thee on foot and (mounted) on every kind of camel, lean on account of journeys through deep and distant mountain highways; That they may witness the benefits (provided) for them, and celebrate the name of Allah, through the Days appointed, over the cattle which He has provided for them (for sacrifice): then eat ye thereof and feed the distressed ones in want. Then let them complete the rites prescribed for them, perform their vows, and (again) ***circumambulate*** *the Ancient House. (Surah 22:27–29)*

Activity

Look at the quotation from Muhammad's last sermon on page 274. Do you think this is shown during *hajj*?

Useful words

Circumambulate – walk round, make a circuit

The purpose of *hajj*

The main reasons for going on *hajj* are as follows:

- to fulfil the final pillar of the Five Pillars and so live a full Muslim life
- to follow the example of Muhammad in performing the actions he carried out in the places he did them
- to visit the holiest sites of Islam and feel part of their holiness
- to remember the ancient nature of Islam which began with Adam on Arafat and with Ibrahim and Ismail in Makkah and Mina
- for Muslims to prepare themselves for the Day of Judgement when they will next appear at Arafat (see Topic 2.1a.8, page 177) and to make sure that the sins they have committed will not count against them on that day
- to stone the devil within themselves at Mina and to show God they are prepared to sacrifice for him.

The benefits of *hajj*

- The pilgrim has fulfilled the requirements of the fifth pillar.
- The pilgrim has followed the example and actions of the Prophet.
- The pilgrim has taken part in the holiest event in the Muslim calendar and has come as close to God as is possible in this life – the contact with God which lasts for a short time in *salah* lasts for a week during *hajj*.
- The pilgrim has shown their devotion to God by taking part in a very expensive and physically demanding event.
- If a pilgrim dies on *hajj*, they will go straight to heaven without having to wait in the grave or face Judgement Day.
- The pilgrim has been made aware of the power of God to unite different races and languages into a common language, a common ritual and a common brotherhood (*ummah*) in Islam – many races, colours and languages come on *hajj*, but they all use the same words and perform the same actions, showing the unifying force of Islam.
- The pilgrim receives the respect and status of becoming a *hajji*.

The Ka'aba at the centre of the Great Mosque during *hajj*.

Activity

What happens in the Great Mosque during *hajj*?

The challenges of *hajj*

We have already seen, the two biggest challenges of *hajj* are the financial cost, even with a package trip, and the physical effort of walking, running and standing in one of the hottest places in the world (Makkah's average daytime temperature is more than 40°C for nine months of the year and *hajj* is based on a lunar calendar and so moves round the year). However, there are other challenges:

- Coping with the huge crowds (over 1800 people were crushed to death in a stampede at the 2015 *hajj*).
- Coping with the language problems (many of the people killed in 2015 would not have been able to understand the Arabic of the Saudi controllers).
- Coping with the hypocrisy of the rich and powerful getting preferential treatment on the holy *hajj* where everyone is supposed to be equal.

This obscenity reaches its peak around the Ka'ba itself when one of the heads of state performs the tawaf. The Ka'ba suffers the indignity of being surrounded by uniformed soldiers carrying arms and wearing boots. An area around the Ka'ba is cleared to allow the rulers of these nation states protection ... in the House of Allah!'
(Z. Khan, Hajj in Focus, *Open Press, 1986)*

The significance of *hajj*

Hajj has great significance for Muslims because a pilgrim:

- has fulfilled the fifth pillar as set down in Surah 22 and so can die happy
- has followed the example and actions of the Prophet in the very places the Prophet himself performed them
- has shown great devotion to God by fulfilling this expensive, dangerous (many pilgrims die or are injured during *hajj*) and time-consuming pillar
- has taken part in the holiest event in Islam and has come as close to God as is possible in this life; the sacred presence experienced momentarily during *salah* is believed to be present for the whole duration of *hajj*
- is made aware of the power of God to unite different races and languages into a common language, a common ritual and a common brotherhood in Islam
- can be called *hajji* when they return home; this is a title of honour and means they will be highly regarded in the community
- has their sins forgiven so they now live life as a perfect Muslim.

Practice questions

c Explain two reasons why *hajj* is important for Muslims. In your answer you must refer to a source of wisdom and authority.

d '*Hajj* has more benefits than drawbacks.' Evaluate this statement considering arguments for and against. In your answer you should:

- refer to Muslim points of view
- reach a justified conclusion.

Summary

Hajj is the fifth pillar and is the annual pilgrimage to Makkah which copies the ones Muhammad made. All Muslims should try to perform *hajj* once in their life, but they can only go if it will not cause their family financial hardship. Pilgrims perform special ceremonies at the Ka'aba in Makkah and on the plain of Arafat. The highlight is the sacrifice at the village of Mina which all Muslims join in as Id-ul-Adha.

Topic 2.3a.7 *Jihad*

Thinking points

In this topic you need to:

- think about the origins, meaning and significance of *jihad*
- understand the difference between lesser and greater *jihad*
- consider the conditions for the declaration of lesser *jihad*, including Surah 2:190–194, 22:39
- think about the different understandings of *jihad*
- be able to explain the importance of *jihad* in the life of Muslims today.

What is *jihad*?

The word *jihad* means 'to strive, to apply oneself, to struggle, to persevere'. However, it has come to be connected with struggling 'in the way of religion' or striving in the cause of God.

The origins of *jihad*

The belief in *jihad* is based on what the Qur'an says about *jihad* (which is translated as strive or striving, not fighting):

> *Those who believe, and suffer exile and strive with might and main in God's cause with their goods and their persons, have the highest rank in the sight of God. These are the people who will achieve salvation.* (Surah 9:20)

> *And strive in His cause as ye ought to strive.* (Surah 22:78)

> *Listen not to the unbelievers, but strive against them.* (Surah 25:52)

> *That ye believe in God and His Apostle, and that ye strive your utmost in the cause of God, with your property and your persons; that will be best for you if ye but knew!* (Surah 61:11)

An advertisement for the #MyJihad campaign in an underground train station in the USA. The advertising campaign aims to reclaim *jihad* from Muslim and anti-Muslim extremists.

Activity

What does the Qur'an say about *jihad*?

It seems clear from these verses that *jihad* means to strive with one's self and one's money in the cause of God. It is determining exactly what is meant by the cause of God which has led to there being two ideas about *jihad*: greater *jihad* and lesser *jihad*.

Greater *jihad*

Most Muslims believe that the greater *jihad* is the struggle to make oneself a perfect Muslim. This certainly requires 'striving with might and main', whether living in a Muslim or non-Muslim society:

- There is the struggle to perform all of the Five Pillars properly.
- There is the struggle to follow the Shari'ah exactly.
- There is the struggle to both discover and follow the perfect example of the Prophet Muhammad.
- There is the struggle to be 'pleasing to Allah' so that one will be allowed into paradise.

Most Muslim lawyers teach that the greater *jihad* is striving to uphold all of God's commandments and striving to avoid all of God's prohibitions. It is concerned with establishing right and removing evil from oneself before one can embark on removing evil from the world. It is the greater *jihad* which stops a Muslim from being a hypocrite – something which is condemned in the Qur'an – 'Why say ye that which ye do not? Grievously odious is it in the sight of God that ye say that which ye do not' (Surah 61:2).

By their greater *jihad* Muslims make sure that they practise Islam rather than just talking about how good it is.

Activities

1. What is the greater *jihad*?
2. What is the lesser *jihad*?

Lesser *jihad*

Having removed the evil from themselves, Muslims can then begin the work of the lesser *jihad* and remove the evil from society.

Muslim scholars teach that Muslim societies should be the first target of the lesser *jihad*. Those Muslims who have completed the greater *jihad* should target such injustices as:

- underdevelopment
- unfair trading
- lack of education
- lack of a welfare state
- the gap between rich and poor.

Muslims aim to produce a perfect Muslim society before they are in a position to target non-Muslim societies and bring them into Islam.

Islam teaches that it is Islamic teaching and God's law which can bring world peace. The Islamic **ummah** is the 'abode of peace' and the world outside Islam is the 'abode of war'. The aim of the lesser *jihad* is to bring the whole world into Islam and so into the abode of peace.

Useful words

Ummah – the Muslim community (brotherhood of Islam)

Useful words

Muslim Law Schools – the four schools which interpret the Shari'ah for Sunni Muslims

Jihadi – one fighting in a Holy War

Activity

What would make it difficult for a war to be called a Muslim Holy War?

Different understandings of *jihad* in Islam

Some Muslims feel that the lesser *jihad* prescribes a Holy War against non-Muslims to bring them into Islam. However, the **Muslim Law Schools** say that a Holy War can only be fought in the following conditions:

- in self-defence:

> *Fight in the cause of God those who fight you, but do not transgress the limits; for God loveth not the transgressor.* (Surah 2:190)

> *To those against whom war is made, permission is given to fight because they are wronged; – and verily God is most powerful, for their aid.* (Surah 22:39)

- if it is led by a religious leader well known for piety and chosen by the whole community
- if all the soldiers are good faithful Muslims well versed in the Qur'an
- if there is a good chance of the war being successful
- as long as the war does not harm the innocent (women, children or the elderly)
- after the enemies have been invited to join Islam peaceably.

Other Muslims feel that they are entitled to wage a Holy War against non-Muslims and they even call themselves ***jihadi***. They believe that because Muhammad was forced to fight to defend Islam when attacked by Makkah (and there are verses in the Qur'an about this) they have the right to fight for the faith, especially as the Qur'an says that those who die fighting a Holy War will go straight to paradise:

> *Think not of those who are slain in God's way as dead. Nay they live finding their sustenance in the presence of their Lord.* (Surah 3:169)

> *Those who kill innocent people in the name of Islam or in the name of God, and who think of themselves as martyrs, should think twice. Their act is categorically condemned by God ... in the Quran. These people are disobeying God's commandments and instead upholding the fabricated claims of their teachers/leaders!* (True Islam, www.quran-islam.org)

The importance of *jihad* in the life of Muslims

Jihad is important in the life of a Muslim because being a good Muslim involves a great deal of struggle, especially for Muslims living in a non-Muslim country.

A Muslim living in a non-Muslim country faces a considerable struggle to avoid being involved in the payment of interest, which is banned in the Qur'an. For example, a good Muslim should not use a credit card, even if they pay off their bill every month and so never pay interest themselves, as they are relying on other people paying interest to finance the credit card system (there is argument in Islam as to whether such bank accounts as the Lloyds Bank Islamic current account can be used when the bank itself is involved in interest even though the Islamic account is not).

Muslims in non-Muslim countries can also struggle to ensure that they keep to the ***halal*** (permitted) and avoid the ***haram*** (banned). This can be a particular struggle in regard to food: the Qur'an says that Muslims must not eat pork and that they should only eat meat slaughtered in the *halal* way, by slitting the throat and draining the blood. Some Muslims become vegetarian to make sure they avoid the *haram*. Alcohol and gambling are also *haram* and Muslims can often struggle to avoid these in their daily life.

Keeping the Five Pillars is also a struggle, especially if living in a non-Muslim country. Praying five times a day and performing *wudu* before each prayer can be a major problem, especially when working for a non-Muslim employer. Fasting during Ramadan is difficult when working with people who are eating (and even worse drinking) during daylight hours. It is even more of a struggle for Muslims living well north or south of the equator when Ramadan falls in midsummer.

So *jihad* is important because everyday life is a *jihad* to be a good Muslim.

Useful words

Halal – that which is permitted
Haram – that which is not permitted

Activity

Look at the picture on page 278. Do you think it is hard to conquer yourself?

Practice questions

c Explain two reasons why there are different understandings of *jihad* among Muslims. In your answer you must refer to a source of wisdom and authority.

d '*Jihad* is about making yourself a good Muslim, not fighting wars.' Evaluate this statement considering arguments for and against. In your answer you should:

- refer to Muslim points of view
- refer to different Muslim points of view
- reach a justified conclusion.

Summary

Jihad is struggling for religion. Muslims divide *jihad* into greater and lesser. Most Muslims believe that the greater *jihad* is the struggle to make oneself a perfect Muslim and only then can the lesser *jihad* of making the world Muslim begin. Most Muslims believe that lesser *jihad* should be peaceful, but some Muslims think that lesser *jihad* involves war against non-Muslims and some even think that this is the greater *jihad*.

Topic 2.3a.8 Celebrations and commemorations

Thinking points

In this topic you need to:

- think about the nature, meaning and significance of the celebration/ commemoration of the festivals of Id-ul-Adha and Id-ul-Fitr in Sunni and Shi'a Islam, and Id-ul-Ghadeer and Ashura in Shi'a and Sunni Islam
- be able to explain and evaluate the importance of these celebrations/ commemorations for Muslims today.

Useful words

Al-Hijra – 1 Muharram, Islamic New Year's Day
Mawlid al-Nabi – the birthday of the Prophet Muhammad
Lailat al-Miraj – the Prophet's night journey to Jerusalem and then to heaven
Shirk – the sin of associating other things with God; it is the worst sin
Hajj – pilgrimage to Makkah, the fifth pillar
Zakah – charity tax, the third pillar

The nature and importance of festivals and commemorations

Many Muslims and scholars believe that Islam is the only major world religion which does not have any real festivals. Most religions have festivals which are important in themselves, such as Christmas and Easter in Christianity and Diwali in Hinduism. But Islam has only two official festivals: Id-ul-Adha and Id-ul-Fitr, and they are not festivals in themselves, they are simply a part of the celebration of the pillar of *hajj* and the pillar of *sawm*.

There is much discussion among Muslims lawyers and scholars about the nature of festivals. Some believe that festivals should be celebrated in a similar fashion to other religions, connecting the celebration to parties and gifts. Others believe that in Islam there only two festivals and they are about worshippers coming close to God, not celebrating.

Many Sunni Muslims celebrate:

- **Al-Hijra** (1 Muharram), which is the Islamic New Year's Day and commemorates the Hijra in 622CE when the Prophet Muhammad moved from Makkah to Madinah.
- **Mawlid al-Nabi**, which celebrates the birthday of the Prophet Muhammad.
- **Lailat al-Miraj**, which celebrates the night journey when Muhammad was taken up to heaven and shown how to perform *salah*.

However, Salafi-type Muslims regard these celebrations as very wrong because they are dangerously close to worshipping Muhammad, which is the great sin of ***shirk***.

Shi'a Muslims have many more festivals (the two greatest ones are explored below), but Sunni Muslims regard all of these as wrong because they verge on idolatry.

The festival of Id-ul-Adha

On Id-ul-Adha, Muslims dress in their best clothes and go to the mosque for a special congregational prayer during which there is a special *khutba* (sermon) when the people are reminded of the origins of the festival and united with the pilgrims in Makkah performing ***hajj***. At the conclusion of the prayers and sermon, Muslims embrace and exchange greetings with one other (they wish each other 'Eid Mubarak'), give gifts to children and visit one another.

Families in rural communities sacrifice an animal and give a third to the poor, a third to relatives and a third to the close family. In urban communities, a special ***zakah*** is given to the poor and a special meal is held (although some families club together and buy an animal to be slaughtered by the *halal* butcher so that they take part in the sacrifice of *hajj*).

Activity

How and why do Muslims celebrate Id-ul-Adha?

This festival originates in God testing Ibrahim by telling him to sacrifice his son Ismail. When God saw that Ibrahim was prepared to obey him, God sent an animal sacrifice instead:

> *Then when the son reached the age of serious work with him, he said, 'O my son, I see in vision that I offer thee in sacrifice.' ... So when they had both submitted their wills to God. We called out to him, 'O Abraha! Thou hast already fulfilled thy vision ...' And we ransomed him with a momentous sacrifice ... Thus indeed do We reward those who do right for he (Ibrahim) was one of Our believing servants.* (Surah 37:102–111)

It receives its meaning from the way it was incorporated into the *hajj* so that during Id-ul-Adha Muslims feel that they are:

- following in the footsteps of both prophet Ibrahim and Prophet Muhammad
- sharing in the *hajj*
- symbolically sacrificing themselves to God
- sharing the good things of life with the poor
- uniting the family, as the *id* is a great family celebration.

The festival of Id-ul-Fitr

Id-ul-Fitr is celebrated on the 1st of Shawwal, which is signalled by the sighting of the new moon in the same way as the beginning of Ramadan. It is the festival of breaking the fast. It is a joyful day when cards and gifts are exchanged and new clothes are bought for children. Special services are held in the mosque or in the open air if there are likely to be too many people. There are special prayers thanking God for the benefits of Ramadan and a *khutba* reminding Muslims of the meaning of Ramadan. Some Muslim families visit the cemetery to remember their dead relatives. A special meal is shared – the first daylight meal for a month.

The festival originates in the month-long fast of Ramadan and the need to celebrate not only the end of the fast, but also the successful completion of the fast. The first Id-ul-Fitr was celebrated by the Prophet Muhammad and so Muslims feel they are copying the Prophet and becoming close to him while they celebrate.

Id-ul-Fitr gains its meaning from the pillar of ***sawm*** and the Qur'anic instruction to fast during the month of Ramadan. Muslims celebrate Id-ul-Fitr because it means:

- Ramadan has ended and they have completed a great religious feat and will gain many benefits.
- They have completed the fourth pillar of Islam.
- Their sins have been forgiven.
- They have become close to God.
- The fast is over and they can eat and drink in daylight again.

Shi'a Muslims go on *hajj* and fast during Ramadan so they celebrate Id-ul-Adha and Id-ul-Fitr just like Sunnis, although there may be some cultural differences in the way they celebrate.

Activity

How and why do Muslims celebrate Id-ul-Fitr?

The religious duties of the first ten days of Ramadan gain the mercy of God, those of the second ten merit his pardon, while those of the last ten save those who do them from the punishment of hell. (Part of the *Id-ul-Fitr* khutba)

Useful words

Sawm – fasting, the fourth pillar

The Pool of Khum today.

The commemoration of Id-ul-Ghadeer

For Shi'a Muslims the 18th of **Dhu al-Hijjah** is the Id-ul-Ghadeer, when they celebrate the occasion of Muhammad appointing Ali as his successor. They celebrate by fasting, ritual bathing and having a special service when a sermon is preached on the event and special prayers called *du'a nudba* are said. Food is given to poor Muslims after the service.

The commemoration has its origins in an event towards the end of Muhammad's life which Shi'as claim is referred to in Surah 5:3, but Sunnis dispute this. Shi'as claim that on his way back to Madinah from his final pilgrimage, Muhammad met Ali (who was returning from missionary work in Yemen) at the Pool (Ghadeer) of Khum, about halfway between Makkah and Madinah. Muhammad ordered a tent to be set up in which Ali could sit to receive the allegiance oath of Muslims. Thousands of Muslims saluted and congratulated Ali as **Amir al-Mu'minin**, commander of the faithful.

This event is very important to Shi'a Muslims because it means that:

- Ali should have been the first Caliph.
- Shi'a beliefs about the importance of Ali are correct.
- Shi'as are the true followers of Muhammad because they have followed his request to regard Ali as Muhammad's true successor.

Sunni Muslims reject this view and argue that it would have made no sense for Muhammad to have done this at **Ghadeer Khum**, when few Muslims were there, when he could have done it in his final sermon at the end of *hajj* in Makkah. They claim the Shi'as have misinterpreted Muhammad defending Ali at Ghadeer after Ali had been slandered.

Useful words

Dhu al-Hijjah – twelfth and final month of the Islamic calendar
Amir al-Mu'minin – commander of the faithful, a title given by Shi'as to Ali and his descendants
Ghadeer Khum – the Pool of Khum halfway between Makkah and Madinah
Muharram – the first month of the Islamic calendar
Husayn – Muhammad's grandson and the third imam of Shi'a Islam
Yazid – the sixth caliph of Sunni Islam
Karbala – site of the battle where Husayn was killed by Caliph Yazid (100 km southwest of Baghdad)

The commemoration of Ashura

Ashura is very much a remembrance rather than a celebration. On the 10th of **Muharram** 680CE, Muhammad's grandson, **Husayn**, who is regarded as the third imam by Shi'as, was killed (Shi'as say murdered) by **Yazid**, the leader of an Umayyad army, at the Battle of **Karbala**. This is remembered by Shi'a Muslims every year on Ashura Day.

On this day, Shi'a Muslims wear mourning attire, refrain from music, fast and treat it as a time for self-reflection as they commit themselves to the mourning of Husayn. Participants congregate in public processions for ceremonial chest beating as a display of their devotion to Husayn, in remembrance of his suffering. Many Shi'as also whip themselves and cut themselves as a sign of their devotion, although this has been banned in Iran and the Lebanon, where Shi'as often donate blood on Ashura as a sign of their identification with Husayn's martyrdom. In some Shi'a areas passion plays are performed, re-enacting the events of the martyrdom at Karbala.

The remembrance began as a ten-day commemoration, but can last for up to a month, and mosques, and some people, provide free meals on certain nights of the month. People also donate food and Middle Eastern sweets to the mosque. These meals are viewed as being special and holy, as they have been consecrated in the name of Husayn, and eating them is considered an act of communion with God and Husayn.

Husayn's grave at Karbala became a pilgrimage site among Shi'as only a few years after his death. A tradition of pilgrimage to the Imam Husayn Shrine and the other Karbala martyrs quickly developed, and from these came the public rites of remembrance now known as Ashura.

Activity

Look at the photo of Ghadeer Khum above. Why is this place important for Shi'a Muslims?

Meanings of Ashura

Shi'as regard Husayn's martyrdom as a symbol of the struggle against injustice, tyranny and oppression. They believe the Battle of Karbala was a fight between the forces of good represented by Husayn and the forces of evil represented by Yazid. Shi'as also believe the Battle of Karbala was fought to keep the Muslim religion free from corruption and they believe that Yazid was directing Islam to a wrong, evil path.

Ashura is important to Shi'as because:

- It gives Shi'as a chance to remember the great betrayal of Islam by the Sunnis.
- It allows Shi'as to show their devotion to the imams.
- It gives Shi'as a chance to grieve for the imam.
- It is a time when Shi'as can show they stand for the forces of good and are opposed to the forces of evil.
- Many Shi'as believe that taking part in Ashura washes away their sins; a popular Shi'a saying has it that, 'a single tear shed for Husayn washes away a hundred sins'.

Clearly, Sunni Muslims do not accept the Shi'a view of Ashura since Yazid was the leader of the Sunnis.

Dozens of people were killed and hundreds injured (including both Shi'a and Sunni commemorators) during the Ashura procession on 28 December 2009 when a massive bomb exploded at the procession in Karachi, Pakistan. Thirty Shi'a pilgrims participating in Ashura processions were killed by a series of bomb attacks in Hilla and Baghdad, Iraq on 5 December 2011. A suicide attack on 6 December 2011 killed 63 people and critically wounded 160 at a shrine in Kabul, Afghanistan where a crowd of hundreds had gathered for the day of Ashura observation. (Compiled from news reports)

People on their way to the Husayn Mosque in Karbala, Iraq.

Activities

1. Look at the photo of the shrine at Karbala above. Why is this place important for Shi'a Muslims?
2. Look at the reports above about troubles at Ashura commemorations. Why do you think these events cause problems between Shi'as and Sunnis?

Practice questions

c. Explain two reasons why Muslims celebrate Id-ul-Fitr. In your answer you must refer to a source of wisdom and authority.

d. 'Religious celebrations cause nothing but trouble.' Evaluate this statement considering arguments for and against. In your answer you should:
   - refer to Muslim points of view
   - refer to different Muslim points of view
   - reach a justified conclusion.

Summary

All Muslims celebrate Id-ul-Adha to join in the *hajj* sacrifice at Mina so that all Muslims are part of the *hajj*. They also celebrate Id-ul-Fitr at the end of the month-long fast of Ramadan, rejoicing in the benefits *sawm* brings to Muslims. Only Shi'a Muslims celebrate Id-ul-Ghadeer as this remembers Muhammad choosing Ali as his successor, which Sunnis do not think happened. Also only Shi'as celebrate Ashura since that remembers the Sunni army killing Ali's grandson in battle.

How to answer questions

a) Describe two differences between Muslim forms of worship and forms of worship in the main religious tradition of Britain. [3]

The main religious tradition of Britain is Christianity. One difference is that Muslims must perform *wudu* before worship, but Christians do not, though some sprinkle themselves with holy water as they enter church. Another difference is that Muslims must face Makkah for *salah* whereas Christians can worship facing any direction (although most Catholic, Orthodox and Anglican churches face the east).

A high mark answer because Christianity is identified as the main religious tradition and two differences are clearly described.

b) Explain two reasons why the festival of Id-ul-Adha is celebrated by Muslims. [4]

Muslims celebrate the festival of Id-ul-Adha to remember the testing of Ibrahim when God told him to sacrifice his son Ismail and Ibrahim was rewarded for his obedience. They also celebrate it as a way of joining in the annual *hajj* as the festival occurs at the same time as the pilgrims are sacrificing animals in Mina.

A high mark answer because two correct reasons are given and each reason is developed.

c) Explain two reasons why *khums* is important for Shi'a Muslims. In your answer you must refer to a source of wisdom and authority. [5]

Khums is important for Shi'a Muslims as they believe it is commanded by the Qur'an: 'Know that whatever of a thing you acquire, a fifth of it is for Allah, for the Messenger, for the near relative, and the orphans and the needy and the wayfarer' (Surah 8:41).

It is commanded by Shi'a lawyers and is a way of supporting the descendants of the Prophet who are given special reverence by Shi'a Muslims.

A high mark answer because two correct reasons are given and each reason is developed with a reference to the Qur'an, Shi'a lawyers and descendants of the prophet as sources of authority.

d) 'Hajj is essential for all Muslims.' Evaluate this statement considering arguments for and against. In your response you should:

- **refer to Muslim points of view**
- **refer to different Muslim points of view**
- **reach a justified conclusion. [12]**

Many Muslims would agree with this because *hajj* is the final pillar and so fulfilling it completes a Muslim's life. It also provides Muslims with the opportunity to follow the example of Muhammad in doing the actions that he performed in the places where he performed them, the holiest sites of Islam. It is also essential because it gives Muslims a chance to prepare themselves for the Day of Judgement at Arafat and to make sure that the sins they have committed will not count against them on that day.

However, Islam does teach that *hajj* is not compulsory since Muslims are only allowed to go on *hajj* if they have sufficient money to provide for their dependants while they are away from home, and they are physically and mentally fit enough for the physical demands of *hajj*. Also, some Muslims might not want to risk travelling through war zones to get there.

I think it is essential for most Muslims to go on *hajj* because it is the fifth pillar, but I do not think it is essential for all Muslims because the Qur'an itself excuses certain groups of Muslims from going.

A high mark answer because it gives three clear developed Muslim reasons for thinking that *hajj* is essential. It then gives two Muslim reasons for disagreeing and then reaches a fully justified conclusion.

3b Living the Jewish life

Area of study 2: Based on a study of Islam or Judaism

Topic 2.3b.1 Public acts of worship

Thinking points

In this topic you need to:

- think about the nature, features and purpose of public worship, including synagogue services
- be able to explain and evaluate the importance of synagogue services for the Jewish community and the individual.

Useful words

Homage – acknowledgement of superiority
Reverence – an act showing religious respect
Deity – god
Minyan – the required number of adult male Jews needed for certain prayers to be said in the synagogue
Shabbat – the Sabbath (from sunset on Friday to sunset on Saturday)
Rabbis – spiritual leaders of a Jewish community
Kiddush – a prayer said over wine to sanctify *Shabbat*
Sefer Torah – the scroll of the Torah
Ark – large cupboard at the front of the synagogue where the Torah scrolls are kept
Bimah – raised platform in front of the Ark from which the scriptures are read
Sidra – the portion of the Torah read at *Shabbat* morning service

Activity

What is public worship?

The nature of public worship

Worship is either **homage** or **reverence** paid to a **deity**. Jewish public worship is where this worship happens in a synagogue with a congregation of Jewish worshippers (the Orthodox would say with at least ten adult male Jewish worshippers forming a ***minyan***).

The purpose of public worship

Public worship in Judaism has several purposes. Worshipping with others in the synagogue:

- Gives a Jewish person a sense of belonging to a whole community of Jewish believers.
- Gives an opportunity to feel the strength of the faith.
- Gives an opportunity to make friends with others in the faith.
- Provides the opportunity to take part in those prayers which can only be said in a congregation (***Shabbat*** prayers and festival prayers in particular).
- Is important because the **rabbis** taught that there is more merit in praying with a group than there is in praying alone.
- Fulfils the requirement to worship publicly in the Temple. The rabbis take,

  How can I repay the Lord for all his goodness to me? I will lift up the cup of salvation and call on the name of the Lord. I will fulfil my vows to the Lord in the presence of all his people ... I will sacrifice a thank-offering to you and call on the name of the Lord. I will fulfil my vows to the Lord in the presence of all his people, in the courts of the house of the Lord. (Psalm 116:12–19)

  to mean that Jewish people are required to worship God in public as well as in the home.

Features of Jewish public worship

Each Friday after the welcoming of *Shabbat*, synagogues should hold *Shabbat* evening prayers when *Shabbat* is greeted like a bride coming to meet her husband – the Jewish people. After the service ends the rabbi takes a cup of wine and recites **Kiddush** to thank God for giving *Shabbat* to the Jewish people.

On *Shabbat* morning (Saturday), families go to synagogue for the morning prayer, which is the main service of the week. The high point of the service is when the **Sefer Torah** is taken out of the **Ark** and carried to the ***bimah*** for the rabbi to read the ***sidra*** (over the course of a year the whole Torah will be read). In an Orthodox synagogue, men are called from the congregation to recite a blessing at certain points of the reading, and at the end a man is called to read from one of the books of the prophets. After the Sefer Torah has been put back in the Ark, the rabbi gives a sermon.

On *Shabbat* afternoon, synagogues have afternoon prayers, when the Sefer Torah is again taken out of the Ark and a short part of the following week's *sidra* is read.

Public worship also takes place for various festivals. In preparation for **Rosh Hashanah**, Jews should worship in the synagogue each day of the month of **Ellul** for the blowing of the ***shofar***. **Yom Kippur** is the holiest day of the Jewish year and there are five prayer services in the synagogue during this day. The great festival of **Simchat Torah** must be celebrated in the synagogue to parade the sacred Sefer Torah around the congregation. The rabbinic festivals such as **Purim** also have special worship services in the synagogue.

Orthodox and Liberal/Reform synagogues have differences in their services. In Liberal synagogues:

- prayers are said mainly in English, not Hebrew
- women attend all the services and sit with the men
- the rabbi may well be a woman
- there are some different prayers.

The importance of synagogue worship

Worship is important for Jewish people because the Torah tells them

> *to love the Lord your God, and to serve him with all your heart and with all your soul.* (Deuteronomy 11:13)

Worship in the synagogue is important for the Jewish community because:

- To worship God with all your heart and all your soul requires people to be able to worship in community with other people who share the same beliefs and values.
- It is needed for the Jewish community to enhance *Shabbat* properly.
- It provides the community with the opportunity to share in family celebrations such as *brit milah*, Bar Mitzvah and weddings.
- It is required for the community to celebrate the great festivals such as Pesach, Rosh Hashanah, Yom Kippur and Simchat Torah.

Worship in the synagogue is important for a Jewish individual because:

- Worshipping with others in the synagogue gives a sense of belonging to a whole community of Jewish believers and an opportunity to feel the strength of the faith and make friends with others in the faith.
- It gives order and purpose to people's religious life.
- It also gives an individual the opportunity to reflect on the serious side of life, especially when worship gives an opportunity to think about the meaning of life at times such as Rosh Hashanah and Yom Kippur and at sad times like death.
- It gives an opportunity to listen to the reading of the Torah and the rest of the Tenakh.
- It also has sermons from the rabbi, which provide the individual with the opportunity to discover more about what it means to be a Jew, and how to live as a Jew in the twenty-first century.

Worship at the Western Wall of the Temple in Jerusalem, the holiest site for Jewish people.

Useful words

Rosh Hashanah – Jewish New Year
Ellul – the final month of the Jewish year
Shofar – ram's horn
Yom Kippur – Jewish holy day, also known as the Day of Atonement
Simchat Torah – the festival celebrating the giving of the Torah
Purim – Jewish holy day to celebrate the saving of the Jewish people from Haman, who was trying to kill all the Jews in Persia

Activities

1. Outline the main features of synagogue worship.
2. Why does Judaism regard public worship as important?

Activity

Look at the photos of worship on page 290 and here. Can you identify which is Orthodox and which is Liberal/Reform?

A synagogue in Paris, France.

Why Jewish people worship in different ways

- Liberal/Reform Jews allow the use of musical instruments in worship (banned on *Shabbat* by the Orthodox because it involves work) because of their belief that *Shabbat* rules can be interpreted to fit in with modern life.
- Orthodox women place much more importance on private worship as they do not attend daily prayers in the synagogue.
- Orthodox synagogues keep men and women separated because of the teachings of rabbis, whereas Liberal/Reform synagogues allow mixed seating.
- Liberal/Reform Jews often do not wear *tefillin* and *tallit* for worship, many of them do not keep *kosher*, and they have complete equality of the sexes, including having women rabbis. They do not believe that the Torah is the Word of God, but rather that it was written by people inspired by God. They feel it is the moral commands of the law which must be followed and believe the ritual laws can be ignored.
- There are slight variations in the words of the services. For example, Jews of Ashkenazi ancestry, Jews of Sephardic ancestry and Hasidic Jews have slightly different prayers because of their origins.

Summary

Jewish public worship takes place in the synagogue every day, but most Jews worship there on the evening and morning of *Shabbat* each week and on all the festivals. Public worship strengthens the Jewish community and gives individual Jews a sense of belonging and an opportunity to learn more about the faith. Orthodox Jews worship differently from Liberal/Reform Jews.

Practice questions

c Explain two reasons why Jewish people worship in different ways. In your answer you must refer to a source of wisdom and authority.

d 'You can worship God just as well at home as in the synagogue.' Evaluate this statement considering arguments for and against. In your answer you should:

- refer to Jewish points of view
- refer to different Jewish or non-religious points of view
- reach a justified conclusion.

Topic 2.3b.2 The Tenakh and Talmud

The purpose and history of the Tenakh

The Tenakh is the Jewish Bible. Its name comes from the initial letters (in Hebrew) of:

- **Torah** (the Five Books of Moses)
- **Nevi'im** (the books of the Prophets)
- **Ketuvim** (holy writings).

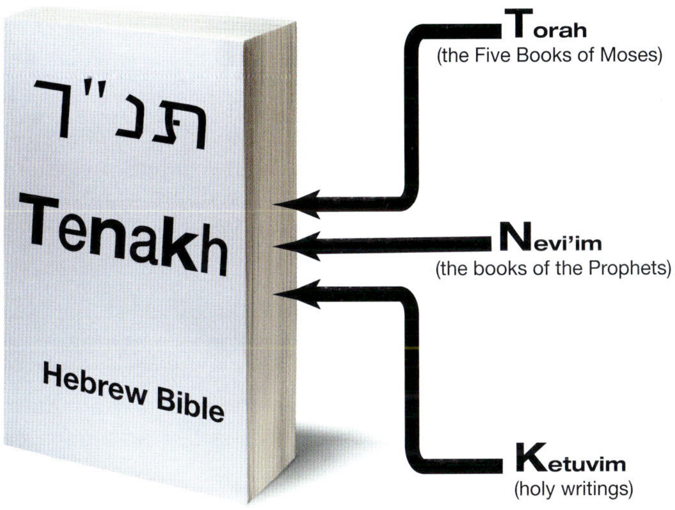

What the Tenakh consists of.

Torah

The Five Books of Moses contain the laws and moral ideas of Judaism set in the context of the history of the Jewish people (Israelites) from the creation of the world through the Exodus to the death of Moses. They contain the stories of the **patriarchs**, the Egyptian slavery, the Exodus, the long journey to the Promised Land, God's covenants with Abraham and Moses, and, of course, the giving of the Law to Moses.

They are regarded as the holiest part of the Tenakh because they contain the 613 *mitzvot* which are the basis of Jewish life. Their purpose is to tell the Jews who they are and how they must live to fulfil their part of the covenant and truly be God's chosen people.

Nevi'im

The first prophet books (Joshua, Judges, 1 & 2 Samuel, 1 & 2 Kings) are history books telling the story of Israel from the death of Moses, through the establishment of the monarchy by Saul and David, to the end of the kingdom and the exile of the Jewish people to Babylon. However, their main purpose is to teach the Jewish people how the covenant God made with Moses worked its way out through the Jewish people.

The other fifteen books are prophet books, starting with the huge works of Isaiah, Jeremiah and Ezekiel. Their purpose is to teach faith in the one God and to proclaim God's message of justice and compassion.

Thinking points

In this topic you need to:

- think about the purpose and history of the Tenakh and Talmud and the nature and purpose of Jewish food laws, including reference to Deuteronomy chapter 14
- be able to explain and evaluate the importance of the Tenakh and Talmud for daily life and the divergent implications of *kashrut* for Jewish people today.

Useful words

Torah – the Five Books of Moses
Nevi'im – the books of the Prophets
Ketuvim – holy writings
Patriarchs – the fathers of Israel (Abraham, Isaac, Jacob and Moses)

Rabban Gamaliel the son of Rabbi Judah the Prince said: Great is study of the Torah when combined with a worldly occupation, for toil in them both puts sin out of mind. All study of the Torah which is not supplemented by work is destined to prove futile and causes sin. (Pirkei Avot 2:2)

Activity

Why do you think most Jews regard the Torah as the most important part of the Tenakh?

Ketuvim

The writings are about many things. There are history books (1 & 2 Chronicles, Ezra, Nehemiah, Esther), poetry books (Psalms, Lamentations, Song of Songs), philosophical books (Job, Proverbs, Ecclesiastes) and Daniel, which is a mix of history and prophecy. Their purpose is to show how the way the Jews behaved towards God affected their history, to express the ups and downs of living as God's people, to express thoughts on the ultimate questions of suffering and death, and to give advice on how to live a moral life.

The purpose and history of the Talmud

According to Jewish tradition, when God gave Moses the Torah, he also gave him the Oral Torah to explain how the laws were to be obeyed. The Written Torah and the Oral Torah together make up the ***halakhah***. As time went on, people wanted explanations of these and also wanted to know how they applied to new situations. Decisions were given by priests, judges and later rabbis and added to the *halakhah*.

After the Temple was destroyed by the Romans and many Jews started to leave the Holy Land, Rabbi Judah the Prince saw that different versions of the *halakhah* were likely to develop in different countries and so he organised the writing down of the Oral Torah. This is known as the **Mishneh** and was completed in about 200CE.

From this time, the Mishneh was studied by rabbis and their students in academies in Israel and Babylon and their discussions on controversial points in the Mishneh were written down and filed into archives. In about 500CE, two Babylonian rabbis sorted out these archives and wrote down each paragraph of the Mishneh with the discussions that had gone on around it.

Useful words

Halakhah – Jewish law
Mishneh – commentaries on the Torah written about 200CE
Haftarot – portions of the Nevi'im read after the Torah in services

Anyone whose good deeds are more than his wisdom, his wisdom will endure. Anyone whose wisdom is more than his good deeds, his wisdom will not endure. (Saying from a first-century CE rabbi)

Rabban Yochanan ben Zakkai received the Torah from Hillel and from Shammai. He used to say: If you have learnt much Torah do not claim for yourself moral excellence, for to this end you were created. (Pirkei Avot 2:9)

Why the Tenakh and Talmud are important to Jews today

The Tenakh is important because:

- The Psalms are an essential part of daily prayers and of much synagogue worship.
- The Torah is particularly important in synagogue worship and daily living.
- Portions of the Nevi'im are read at the end of the Torah readings in synagogue. These readings are known as the ***haftarot***.
- Portions of the Ketuvim form an important part of the festivals of Yom Kippur (Book of Jonah) and Purim (Book of Esther).
- Jewish people study and meditate on the books of the Tenakh to help their understanding of, and their relationship with, God.

The Talmud is important because:

- It explains the meaning of the 613 *mitzvot*.
- It explains how the *mitzvot* should be applied in the daily lives of Jews.
- It is so important that commentaries relating the Talmud to life in the twenty-first century are still being written (for example, *Understanding the Talmud* by Rabbi Yitzchok Feigenbaum, 2012).

Activities

1. Look at the saying by the first-century rabbi above. What do you think it means?
2. Explain why the Talmud is important for Jewish people.
3. Read the two quotations from Pirkei Avot (above and page 291). What do you think they mean for the study of the Torah?

- It is the basis of the *halakhah*, which is the foundation of Orthodox Jewish life today.
- It is the main subject studied in the *yeshivot* (Jewish academies for post-A-level Jewish studies).

The nature and purpose of Jewish food laws

The purpose of Jewish food laws is to obey these *mitzvot* about food which God gave to Moses:

> *These are the animals you may eat: the ox, the sheep, the goat, the deer, the gazelle, the roe deer, the wild goat, the ibex, the antelope and the mountain sheep. You may eat any animal that has a divided hoof and that chews the cud. (Deuteronomy 14:4–6)*

However, there are animals that are forbidden:

> *You may not eat the camel, the rabbit or the hyrax. Although they chew the cud, they do not have a divided hoof ... The pig is also unclean; although it has a divided hoof, it does not chew the cud. You are not to eat their meat. (Deuteronomy 14:7–8)*

Fish are allowed, but not shellfish, calamari and eels because:

> *Of all the creatures living in the water, you may eat any that has fins and scales. But anything that does not have fins and scales you may not eat; for you it is unclean. (Deuteronomy 14:9–10)*

Clean birds are allowed but Deuteronomy chapter 14 has a long list of birds which are not allowed (mainly birds of prey and birds that eat dead animals; perhaps because Deuteronomy 14:21 says, 'Do not eat anything you find already dead'). This is followed by 'Do not cook a young goat in its mother's milk' (Deuteronomy 14:21).

Leviticus 17:13 adds this restriction: 'Any Israelite or any alien living among you who hunts any animal or bird that may be eaten must drain out the blood.'

As a result of the *mitzvot*, Judaism developed quite complicated food laws known as ***kosher*** (fitting or correct), which leads to the term ***kashrut*** (the state of being *kosher*) for keeping the laws. The main points are:

- Cows, sheep, goats, deer, chicken, turkey, duck and all fish (with fins and scales) can be eaten.
- Pigs, camels and shellfish must not be eaten (any such foods and anything that is not *kosher* is called ***treifah***).
- Animals must be slaughtered by the ***shechitah*** method of slitting the throat with a razor-sharp knife and draining out the blood (this is done by a specially trained slaughterer called a ***shochet***, who must also be learned in the Torah).
- When meat is brought home it must be soaked in salt water for 30 minutes, then rubbed in salt and drained before washing in cold water (nowadays this is often done by the butcher before the meat is sold).
- Kitchens should be in two halves, one for meat and one for dairy, with separate crockery, pans and utensils for each – many will have two sinks.

A McDonald's restaurant in Israel.

Activity

Look at the photo of a McDonald's above. Would a non-Jew be able to eat here? Would an Orthodox Jew be able to eat in an ordinary McDonald's?

Useful words

Kosher – fitting; food a Jew is permitted to eat
Kashrut – the state of being *kosher*
Treifah – not *kosher*
Shechitah – Jewish method of slaughtering animals
Shochet – a Jewish butcher

Activity

Look at the photo opposite. How do you know this is an Orthodox Jewish kitchen?

A double sink in a Jewish home: the red side is for meat and the green side is for dairy.

Divergent implications of the food laws

Keeping *kashrut* is very important for Orthodox Jews because:

- By eating non-*kosher* foods or not keeping a *kosher* kitchen they have broken many of the *mitzvot*. This importance can be seen on supermarket shelves where many items now have a label (called a ***hechsher***) showing that the food is *kosher*.
- It gives a sense of Jewish identity.
- It gives a bond with fellow Jews.
- It makes them think about God every time they decide to eat because they have to think about what God wants them to eat and how God wants them to prepare it.

Keeping *kashrut* is not as important for Liberal/Reform Jews because they believe that the laws of Moses are not God's direct commands, but rather they are a means for people to lead a holy life. Some will always eat *kosher* meat, but will not bother with the laws about meat and dairy and will not bother about eating non-*kosher* in the homes of non-Jews or in restaurants. Indeed, some Liberal Jews reject the whole concept of *kashrut* because they believe it is harmful for good relations between religions.

Useful words

Hechsher – a label certifying that a food is *kosher*

Summary

The Tenakh is the Jewish Bible: Torah, Nevi'm and Ketuvim. The Torah is the most important part as it contains the 613 commands (*mitzvot*) of the Law that Moses received from God. The Talmud contains the Oral Law explaining the Torah. The Torah contains the food laws which determine what can be eaten (*kosher*) and what cannot be eaten (*treifah*). The Orthodox Jews are much stricter about the food laws than the Liberal/Reform Jews.

Practice questions

c Explain two reasons why the Talmud is important for Jewish people. In your answer you must refer to a source of wisdom and authority.

d 'It's more important to get on well with people of other religions than to follow religious food laws that divide people.' Evaluate this statement considering arguments for and against. In your answer you should:

- refer to Jewish points of view
- refer to different Jewish or non-religious points of view
- reach a justified conclusion.

Topic 2.3b.3 Prayer

Purpose of Jewish prayer

Prayer is an attempt by humans to communicate with God.

Jewish people believe that prayer is very important because they believe that when they pray, they not only build up their relationship with God, but also believe they are serving God with their heart, so obeying God's commandment:

> *to love the Lord your God and to serve him with all your heart and with all your soul.* (Deuteronomy 11:13)

The Talmud tells Jewish people, 'What is service of the heart? That is prayer.'

Judaism teaches that through prayer, people have the opportunity to speak directly to God and that God will listen and respond to their prayers.

In a sense, there are only two types of prayer: formal prayers, where a set form of prayer is used; and informal prayers, where a person makes up their own spontaneous prayer to express their feelings to God (covered in Topic 2.3b.3, page 295).

The formal prayers of Judaism are contained in the **Siddur** (prayer book; there are different ones for Orthodox and Reform Jews) and are said in Hebrew by Orthodox Jews.

Prayer in the home

Much of Jewish worship and prayer is centred on the home. Some prayers at home are said as private prayers:

- When a Jew wakes up in the morning, they thank God for waking them before pouring water on their hands to purify themselves for the coming day.
- The day should end, as it should begin, by praising God – the *shema* is said followed by these words,

  > *may it be Your will that You should lay me down in peace and raise me up to good life and peace. Blessed are You God who lights up the whole world with His glory.*

- The **mezuzah** on each door of the house is a constant reminder of God's presence and God's blessing:

  > *You will be blessed when you come in and blessed when you go out.* (Deuteronomy 28:6)

  – so Jewish people touch the *mezuzah* and thank God whenever they pass it.
- Eating food requires prayers as Jewish people bless God before food:

  > *Blessed are you Lord our God, King of the universe who brings food out of the ground*

  and bless him again when they have finished eating.

Thinking points

In this topic you need to:

- think about the nature and purpose of prayer in the home, private prayer, prayer three times a day and the importance of having different forms of prayer, including prayer in Psalm 55:16–23
- be able to explain and evaluate the importance of having different types of prayer.

Useful words

Siddur – the daily prayer book
Mezuzah – small scroll of the *shema* fixed to the doorpost of the rooms in a Jewish house

Activities

1. Why do you think people pray?
2. Do you think it is a good idea to wear special things when you pray?

For me, I call to God, and the Lord saves me. Evening, morning and noon I cry out in distress, and he hears my voice. He rescues me unharmed from the battle waged against me, even though many oppose me ... Cast your cares on the Lord and he will sustain you; he will never let the righteous fall. (Psalm 55:16–22)

Useful words

Shacharit – morning prayer
Minchah – afternoon prayer
Arvit – evening prayer
Tefillin – leather boxes containing parts of the Torah strapped on the arms and head for prayers
Tallit – prayer shawl
Amidah – the standing prayer
Minyan – the number of men needed for synagogue services (usually ten)

The three daily prayers

During the day a Jew should pray a set formal prayer three times:

- ***shacharit*** is morning prayer
- ***minchah*** is afternoon prayer and
- ***arvit*** is evening prayer.

These prayers take place in an Orthodox synagogue but many Jews say the prayers at home. Orthodox men wear their ***tefillin*** and ***tallit*** for the *shacharit* prayers and will pray as a family group.

The format of the prayers is set out in the Siddur (daily prayer book) and each prayer includes the *shema*, and the ***amidah***, and readings from the Torah and the Nevi'im.

In Orthodox families, the prayers are said in Hebrew, but in Liberal/Reform families the prayers will be said in English. In Liberal/Reform synagogues women can make up a ***minyan***.

Private prayers

Judaism teaches that people should develop a relationship with God and that when they reach out to God, God listens and answers. In such a relationship prayers are not restricted to set forms and set times.

Jewish people pray whenever they feel the need to communicate with God, and obviously when they say these prayers, they use their own words. In private prayer, people can contact God when they want and can express their own thoughts and feelings rather than using other people's words. In such prayers they can ask for God's help for other people, and they can ask for God's help for themselves.

The importance of having different forms of prayer

Saying prayers in a set form, which have been used in this form for centuries, and at set times has many advantages:

- It stops prayer being focused on selfish concerns.
- It gives the worshipper a sense of being part of Jewish history.
- It gives the prayer a sense of community with Jews all over the world.
- It gives order and purpose to people's religious life.
- It helps people to pray who might find it difficult to know what to say.
- It gives people a feeling of stability and security by repeating familiar phrases in a familiar place.

Activity

Look at Psalm 55:16–22. How do you think these verses affect Jewish attitudes to prayer?

Saying prayers in your own words whenever you want to is important because people can only have a relationship with God if:

- they can contact God when they want
- they can express their own thoughts and feelings rather than other people's
- they can use their own words, so that they are saying what they want to say rather than using other people's words
- they can ask for God's help for other people
- they can ask for God's help for themselves.

Prayer in the home is important because the home is the heart of people's lives and praying as a family brings the family together.

Private prayer is important because people need to be able to pray to God in private so they can communicate with God one to one and express emotions they cannot express in front of others.

Public prayer is also important because praying with others in the synagogue gives a sense of belonging to a whole community of believers and an opportunity to feel the strength of the faith and make friends with others in the faith.

Practice questions

c Explain two reasons why it is important for Jewish people to have different forms of prayer.

d 'God doesn't need people to pray to him.' Evaluate this statement considering arguments for and against. In your answer you should:

- refer to Jewish points of view
- refer to different Jewish or non-religious points of view
- reach a justified conclusion.

Summary

Prayer is communicating with God, and Jews believe this is very important because it is obeying the *mitzvot* to love and serve God. There are set prayers for morning, afternoon and evening, and Jews also pray when they wake up, when they eat and when they go to bed. They believe it is important to have different forms of prayer so that prayer does not become a set ritual, but a search for God.

Topic 2.3b.4 *Shema* and *amidah*

Thinking points

In this topic you need to:

- think about the nature and importance of the *shema* and the *amidah*, when and how they are used and why, including Deuteronomy 6:4 and the *mezuzah*
- think about the similarities and differences between Christian and Jewish worship
- be able to explain the importance of the *shema* and *amidah* for Jews today.

Useful words

Shema – the declaration of Jewish belief in one God

Shema

Shema is known as the fundamental declaration of Judaism. Its main elements are:

> *Hear, O Israel, the L-rd is our G-d, the L-rd is One.*
>
> *Blessed be the name of the glory of His kingdom forever and ever.*
>
> *You shall love the L-rd your G-d with all your heart, with all your soul, and with all your might. And these words which I command you today shall be upon your heart. You shall teach them thoroughly to your children, and you shall speak of them when you sit in your house and when you walk on the road, when you lie down and when you rise. You shall bind them as a sign upon your hand, and they shall be for a reminder between your eyes. And you shall write them upon the doorposts of your house and upon your gates.*
>
> *The L-rd spoke to Moses, saying: Speak to the children of Israel and tell them to make for themselves fringes on the corners of their garments throughout their generations, and to attach a thread of blue on the fringe of each corner. They shall be to you as tzizit, and you shall look upon them and remember all the commandments of the L-rd and fulfil them, and you will not follow after your heart and after your eyes by which you go astray – so that you may remember and fulfil all My commandments and be holy to your G-d. I am the L-rd your G-d who brought you out of the land of Egypt to be your G-d; I, the L-rd, am your G-d. Amen.*

When the *shema* is said

The *shema* is said three times every day:

- once in the morning prayer
- once in the evening prayer and
- once before a Jewish person goes to sleep.

The first two paragraphs are written on the *mezuzah* scroll and so they are remembered, and sometimes spoken, every time a Jew goes into the house and from room to room. The first sentence is said whenever the Torah scroll is taken from the Ark.

Why the *shema* is said

The *shema* is important because it is also a declaration of the main points of the Jewish faith:

- There is only one God.
- People should love God and follow his commands.
- Those who serve God will receive blessings.
- The aim of Judaism is to become holy by fulfilling God's commands.

Activities

1. Look at the *shema*. How can you tell it comes from a Jewish prayer book?
2. Write a summary of the *shema*.

This belief that there is only one God who demands moral obedience is often called '**ethical monotheism**' and is the basis of Judaism.

> *Hear, O Israel: The Lord our God, the Lord is one. Love the Lord your God with all your heart and with all your soul and with all your strength. These commandments that I give you today are to be on your hearts. Impress them on your children. Talk about them when you sit at home and when you walk along the road, when you lie down and when you get up. Tie them as symbols on your hands and bind them on your foreheads. Write them on the doorframes of your houses and on your gates.* (Deuteronomy 6:4–9)

Useful words

Ethical monotheism – belief in one God who demands moral obedience
Amidah – the standing prayer

Mezuzah

A *mezuzah* has a parchment scroll on which is written Deuteronomy 6:4–9 and Deuteronomy 11:13–21 (God's promises for the Jews if they keep the *mitzvot*). The *mezuzah* is the scroll but it is usually kept in a container and these are fixed to the doorposts of the house and every room in the house except the bathroom. Jews are expected to touch the *mezuzah* every time they pass it to remind themselves of the Mosaic Covenant. The *mezuzah* reminds Jews that they are dedicated to God. Every time they touch it they remind themselves of the covenant God made with Moses and how they need to keep the *mitzvot*. It also reminds them of God's promise: 'You will be blessed when you come in and blessed when you go out' (Deuteronomy 28:6).

Amidah

Amidah is the second most important prayer and is sometimes known as 'the prayer'. It contains nineteen blessings, each of which ends with the words:

> *Blessed are you, O Lord.*

The first three blessings praise God:

- for being the God of Abraham, Isaac and Jacob
- for his power and might
- for his holiness.

The next six are personal requests for God:

- to grant wisdom and understanding
- to help Jews to return to a life based on the Torah
- for forgiveness for all sins
- to heal the sick
- to bless the produce of the earth
- to allow the ingathering of the Jewish exiles back to the land of Israel.

The next six are requests for the people of Israel. They ask God:

- to restore righteous judges as in the days of old
- to punish those who slander Jews
- to have mercy on all who trust in him
- to support the righteous
- to rebuild Jerusalem and to restore the Kingdom of David
- to bring the descendant of King David, who will be the Messiah.

Someone touching a *mezuzah* on a doorframe.

Some Jewish pilgrims pray at the historic Ghriba synagogue in Djerba.

Activity

Look at the photo. What prayer do you think is being said?

The final three blessings:

- ask God to accept the prayers
- ask God to have mercy and be compassionate
- thank God for the opportunity to serve the Lord.

The last prayer is the one for peace, goodness, blessings, kindness and compassion.

When and how the *amidah* should be said

Amidah means standing and the prayer should be said standing facing Jerusalem. The whole prayer is said for weekday daily prayers, with slight amendments on *Shabbat* and festivals.

Every *amidah* is divided into three central sections: praise, petitions and thanks. Immediately before reciting the *amidah*, it is traditional to take three steps backward and then forward again to symbolise entering into God's presence.

If the *amidah* is prayed in the synagogue, it is repeated aloud by the cantor, with the congregation reciting 'Amen' to each blessing, which will end (as it began) with a formal bow. In the middle section, after making a request to God, the congregation say, 'Holy, holy, holy is the Lord of Hosts, the whole world is filled with His glory' and rock up on the balls of their feet three times, for each word 'holy', symbolising the fluttering of the angels who recited this line of praise. Several more biblical verses are also recited, ending in the blessing, 'Praised are You, Adonai, the holy God.'

The final section of every *amidah* concludes with blessings of thanksgiving to God requesting him to grant peace, goodness, blessings and compassion upon everyone.

Why the *amidah* is said

The *amidah* is 'the prayer' because it fulfils all the requirements of a prayer which had been determined by the great rabbis. They declared that a worshipper should come before the Almighty first with words of praise, then should ask one's petitions, and finally should withdraw with words of thanks, which is exactly what the *amidah* does. As well as this, people have two needs, the spiritual and the physical, and the *amidah* asks God to fulfil spiritual needs such as forgiveness and physical needs such as food.

Why the *amidah* is important

The *amidah* is important for Jews because:

- It fulfils the prayer requirements set out by the great rabbis: praise, requests, thanks.
- It asks God to fulfil their spiritual needs.
- It asks God to fulfil their physical needs.
- It is the major prayer in the Siddur and so must be the major prayer for Jews.
- It helps Jews to fulfil their service to God.

Christian and Jewish worship

The main differences are between Orthodox Jewish worship and Christian worship. Worship in Liberal/Reform synagogues is very similar to Christian worship.

Differences:

- Jews should face Jerusalem for worship, whereas Christians can worship facing any direction (although most Catholic, Orthodox and Anglican churches face the east).
- Orthodox Jews worship in Hebrew, whereas Christians worship in their native language.
- Men and women worship separately in Orthodox Judaism, whereas the sexes worship together in Christianity.
- The Jewish special day for worship is Saturday, whereas the Christian special day is Sunday.
- Jews should worship three times a day at set times, whereas Christians are only required to go to church on Sunday, but are expected to pray every morning and evening.
- Christian worship usually has musical accompaniment and often has hymns, Orthodox Jewish worship does not.
- Christian worship often has visual stimuli (crosses, stained-glass windows, statues of Mary and the saints), Jewish worship does not

Similarities:

- Worship involves readings from the scriptures in both faiths.
- Weekly worship includes a sermon in both faiths.
- Worship involves the whole congregation saying a prayer together (even non-liturgical Christian worship includes saying the Lord's Prayer).
- Both worships involve praying for the needs of others.

Practice questions

c Explain two reasons why the *shema* is important for Jewish people. In your answer you must refer to a source of wisdom and authority.

d 'Prayer should just be a private matter between the individual and God.' Evaluate this statement considering arguments for and against. In your answer you should:

- refer to Jewish points of view
- refer to different Jewish or non-religious points of view
- reach a justified conclusion.

Activity

Do you think all the rituals associated with the *amidah* are a good idea for prayers to God?

Summary

The *shema* is the most important prayer for Jews as it reminds them of the oneness of God and the need for Jewish people to obey God's commands to receive his blessings. Jews remind themselves of the *shema* by touching the *mezuzah* every time they enter or leave a room. The *amidah* (standing prayer) is the second most important prayer and is said for the three daily prayers.

Topic 2.3b.5 Rituals and ceremonies

Thinking points

In this topic you need to:

- think about the importance of ritual; the nature, features and purpose of birth, marriage, Bar Mitzvah and Bat Mitzvah ceremonies, including Genesis 17, Genesis 21:1–8 and Leviticus 12
- consider the nature and importance of mourning ceremonies
- be able to evaluate and explain the importance of these rituals for Jews today and be aware of the different Jewish understandings of these.

Useful words

Brit Milah – the covenant of circumcision
Kvatters – people who carry the baby to Brit Milah
Sandek – person who holds the baby for Brit Milah
Mohel – person trained to perform Brit Milah

Jewish ritual

Rituals celebrating and marking important stages of life (birth, coming of age, marriage and death) are known as rites of passage. All societies seem to have such rites and in any society with its own religion, these rituals are religious. The rituals are important because they help both the person going through the ritual and the wider community hosting the ritual to come to terms with a changed status.

Birth ceremonies

Children are a great blessing in Judaism, indeed the very first *mitzvah* says Jews should have children:

> *Be fruitful and increase in number.* (Genesis 1:28)

Ceremonies for boys

Male children are circumcised eight days after their birth in a ceremony known as **Brit Milah**. This ceremony can take place in hospital, in the home or in the synagogue. If celebrated at home, there will often be ten adult males present to make a *minyan*.

The mother brings the baby in and hands him to the ***kvatters*** (bearers) – usually a married couple – who carry the child on a cushion to the ***sandek***, who holds the child for the procedure. The *sandek* is often the grandfather or a respected member of the congregation and it is a great honour to be chosen as a *sandek*. The ***mohel*** (circumciser) then carries out the procedure and dresses the wound. The father recites a blessing which remembers that God commanded circumcision so that children can enter the covenant. The *mohel* then blesses the child and names him before handing him back to the *kvatters*. Then there is a celebratory meal to welcome the child into the covenant.

Circumcision is a 'sign in the flesh' of the covenant God made with Abraham:

> *This is my covenant with you and your descendants after you, the covenant you are to keep. Every male among you shall be circumcised. You are to undergo circumcision, and it will be the sign of the covenant between me and you. For the generations to come every male among you who is eight days old must be circumcised.* (Genesis 17:10–12)
>
> *When his son Isaac was eight days old, Abraham circumcised him, as God commanded him.* (Genesis 21:4)

These verses mean circumcision is a *mitzvah* which marks the entry of Jewish males into the covenant. They also make a link with Jewish history reaching all the way back to Abraham. Circumcision has been important in Jewish history as both the Greeks and the Romans tried to ban it as a way of ending the Jewish nation, but the Jews were martyred rather than giving up the practice. The Tenakh gives no reason for circumcision other than to fulfil God's command.

Activity

Why do you think the Brit Milah is important for most Jews?

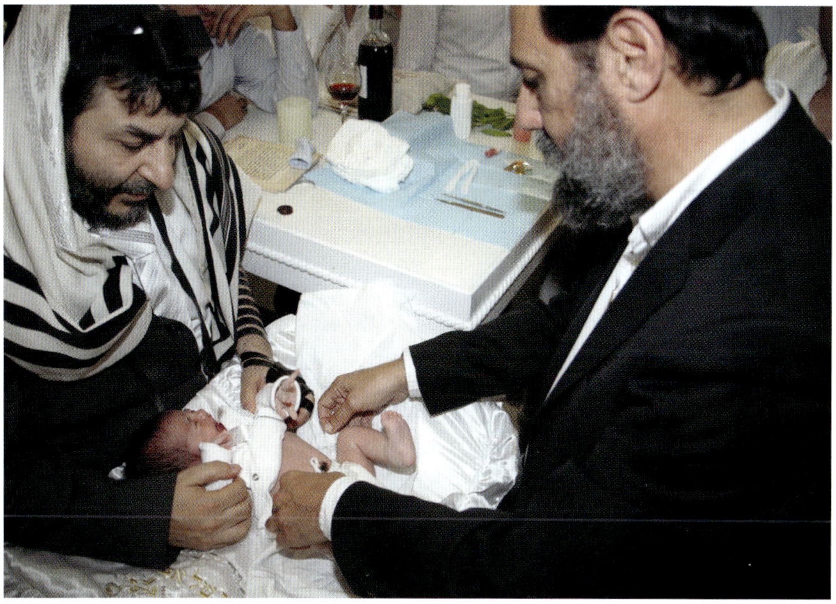

During a Brit Milah ceremony, a *mohel* (right) prepares an eight-day-old Jewish boy for circumcision. The infant is held in the lap of a *sandek*.

Although any adult male wanting to convert to Judaism must be circumcised, the ***halakhah*** makes clear that any male child born Jewish but not circumcised is still a Jew. Some very liberal Reform Jews do not circumcise their sons as they believe the covenant with Abraham was purely spiritual and so there is no need for a physical sign.

Useful words

Halakhah – the holy law of Judaism

Ceremonies for girls

Female children of Orthodox Jews have a special naming ceremony in the synagogue on the *Shabbat* following the birth. The rabbi blesses and names the child and there is a celebratory meal. Many Reform/Liberal synagogues have a special welcoming ceremony for girls. The ceremony is usually led by a rabbi who gives a blessing of welcome:

> *Blessed be the child whom we now welcome. We praise you, Eternal God, Sovereign of the universe: You hallow us with Your* Mitzvot, *and command us to bring our daughters into the Covenant of Life.*

The rabbi then names the child and after Kiddush over the wine, a few drops may be given to the child, after which the cup might be shared by the parents and family before the festive meal. This ceremony is known as Brit Bat.

Activities

1. Do you think the Brit Bat will ever be as important as the Brit Milah?
2. Look at the photo of the Brit Milah above. Who is carrying out the circumcision?

Marriage ceremonies

All Jews are expected to marry and have children because of the *mitzvah* that humans should be fruitful and increase the number of humans on earth.

Jewish marriage is based on these verses from the Torah:

> *The man said, 'This is now bone from my bones, flesh of my flesh; she shall be called woman for she was taken out of man.' For this reason a man will leave his father and mother and be united to his wife and they will become one flesh.* (Genesis 2:23–24)

Your wife has been given to you in order that you may realise with her life's great plan. A man who has no wife is doomed to an existence without joy, without blessing, without experiencing life's true goodness, without Torah, without protection and without peace. (Talmud)

Marriage is regarded as essential for people to become complete. The Talmud says that,

> *A man without a wife is incomplete. An unmarried woman is an unfinished vessel.*

The purposes of Jewish marriage are:

- to obey the *mitzvah* and have children
- for a man and woman to share a life of love and companionship
- for a man and woman to share sex with each other in the way God intended
- to establish a Jewish home so that children can be brought up as Jews and continue the Jewish faith.

The marriage ceremony usually has the following features, although there can be many variations between Orthodox and Reform, and Sephardi and Ashkenazi:

- The couple fast before the wedding as repentance for their past sins, as the wedding (*kiddushin* in Hebrew) will **sanctify** them and forgive their sins.
- The ceremony takes place under a canopy called a ***huppah***, which symbolises the couple's new home and unites them under one roof. The fact that it is closed on top and open at the sides symbolises how marriage needs both privacy and openness to friends and community.
- The bride and groom meet under the *huppah*.
- The rabbi blesses a glass of wine and thanks God for sanctifying Israel by his commands about marriage, and the bride and groom drink from the same glass.
- The groom puts a ring on the bride's finger with the words,

  > *Behold you are consecrated to me with this ring according to the Law of Moses and Israel.*

  This is what legalises the marriage according to the *halakhah* (Liberal Jews often have an exchange of vows and rings using the words 'with this ring I thee wed ...').
- The ***ketubah*** is read in which the groom promises to provide for his wife and specifies what she will receive in the event of his death or a divorce (marriage is a contract in Judaism so divorce is allowed).
- The rabbi recites seven blessings over a glass of wine; they include blessing God for wine, creation, making humans, making marriage, making children, and making the bride and groom rejoice.
- The bride and groom drink from the glass to show they will share everything together now they are man and wife.
- The bridegroom then stamps on the glass to remind everyone of the destruction of the Temple and that in the midst of joy some people are suffering and sorrowing.

A Jewish wedding ceremony can only take place between two Jews and so, if a non-Jew wishes to marry a Jew in a religious ceremony, they need to convert. However, some Liberal/Reform synagogues have special ceremonies for mixed (interfaith) marriages.

Useful words

Sanctify – to make holy
Huppah – wedding canopy
Ketubah – marriage contract

Activities

1. Read the Talmud passage about marriage above. What does it tell us about the Jewish attitude to marriage?
2. Outline the main features of a Jewish wedding ceremony.
3. Explain why marriage is important for Jewish people.

Bar Mitzvah

Bar Mitzvah (son of the commandment) is the term used for when a boy becomes responsible for his own actions and is regarded as an adult as far as religion is concerned. This means that after a boy's Bar Mitzvah he must put on ***tefillin*** for morning prayers, he can make up a *minyan*, he has to observe the fast days in full and he may be called up to read the *sidra* in synagogue services.

Bar Mitzvah is not about being a full adult in every sense of the word, ready to marry, go out on your own, earn a living and raise children. In Pirkei Avot in the Talmud, it says that while thirteen is the proper age for fulfilment of the Commandments, eighteen is the proper age for marriage and twenty is the proper age for earning a living.

A boy becomes Bar Mitzvah at the age of thirteen whether there is a special ceremony or not, but most Jewish families make sure their sons have a special ceremony. Before the ceremony a boy attends special Hebrew classes at the synagogue so that he can read the scriptures. The ceremony takes place on the first *Shabbat* after the boy's thirteenth birthday.

The main features of the ceremony are:

- The boy recites the blessing before the Torah reading.
- If possible, he reads the whole Torah passage for that day.
- The boy's father says, 'Blessed be he who hath freed me from the responsibility for this child'.
- The rabbi talks about the responsibilities of adult Jews and the joys of fulfilling the *mitzvot*.
- There is a celebratory meal.

There are no references to Bar Mitzvah in the Tenakh. The term first appears in the Talmud, which also refers to observing this rite of passage with a religious ceremony. The most complete references to Bar Mitzvah are in **Midrash** from the Middle Ages, for example:

> *The heathen when he begets a son consecrates him to idolatrous practices; the Israelite has his son circumcised ... and as soon as he becomes of age he brings him into the synagogue and school in order that he may praise the name of God, reciting the 'Brachu' (blessing) preceding the reading from the Law.* (Midrash Hashkem)

However, the nature and importance of Bar Mitzvah in modern Judaism mainly developed in the early twentieth century.

Bat Mitzvah

Bat Mitzvah (Daughter of the Commandment) ceremonies are very different in Orthodox Judaism from those in Liberal/Reform Judaism.

In Orthodox Judaism, girls attain their Bat Mitzvah at the age of twelve. However, they do not assume the same duties as boys (they cannot make up a *minyan*, wear *tefillin* or read the Torah in synagogue) so the ceremony is very different. Often a group of girls who have reached twelve years of age during the previous year are jointly addressed by the rabbi and each then reads a passage they have chosen from the Tenakh. This ceremony is sometimes called **Bat Chayil** (Daughter of Worth).

Useful words

Bar Mitzvah – son of the commandment; a Jewish boy's coming of age
Tefillin – a container for the *shema* scroll to put on the arms and head
Midrash – collection of rabbinic commentaries on the Tenakh
Bat Chayil – Daughter of Worth; name used by some Orthodox synagogues instead of Bat Mitzvah

Activity

Do you think there should be a difference between girls' and boys' Bar Mitzvahs?

Activity

Look at the photo. How do you know this is not an Orthodox synagogue?

A girl at her Bat Mitzvah ceremony reading from the Torah.

In Liberal/Reform Judaism, girls are treated exactly the same as boys and have exactly the same responsibilities, and so their Bat Mitzvah is just the same as a boy's. It happens at the age of thirteen and they are called up to read the Torah.

Death and mourning rituals

Death is obviously a major issue for everyone as it marks the end of someone's life and causes grief for family and friends. Judaism deals with death in four stages:

At the point of death

If it is known someone is dying, family should gather to help the person die as a Jew. The prayer book contains a special prayer. It begins,

> *'I acknowledge unto thee, O Lord my God and God of my fathers, that both my cure and my death are in thy hands', and ends, 'Hear O Israel: the Lord is our God, the Lord is one.'*

Ideally, every Jew dies with the last sentence of the prayer on their lips.

From death to the funeral

As soon as they hear of a death, close relatives make a tear in their clothes to fulfil the *mitzvah* which is the basis of much of the mourning ritual. The Torah records that when Jacob heard that his favourite son, Joseph, was dead,

> *Then Jacob tore his clothes, put on sackcloth and mourned for his son many days.* (Genesis 37:34)

Useful words

Chevra kaddisha – burial society
Tallit – a fringed garment worn by Jews

Synagogues usually have a burial society (***chevra kaddisha***) which helps the family at their time of grief. They are in charge of the ritual washing of the body, after which it is wrapped in a plain linen shroud covered with the dead person's ***tallit*** and then placed into a plain coffin. The funeral takes place as soon after death as possible; the Orthodox do not allow cremation. This is based on the verse about criminals who have been hanged,

A burial ceremony in Israel.

> *you must not leave his body on the tree overnight. Be sure to bury him the same day ... you must not desecrate the land the Lord your God is giving you* (Deuteronomy 21:23)

and God's warning to Adam,

> *until you return to the ground, since from it you were taken, for dust you are and to dust you will return.* (Genesis 3:19)

It is considered disrespectful to leave the dead person alone and someone stays with the body all the time until the funeral. During the time before the burial, mourners are exempt from the positive *mitzvot* as they will be too grief-stricken to think what they have to do.

The funeral itself is a very simple affair: some Psalms are read before a short prayer praising God for giving life and for taking it away. The rabbi usually gives a short speech about the dead person.

Everybody then accompanies the body to the grave, where prayers are said. It is customary for the family mourners to place a shovelful of earth into the grave, with all those attending the funeral then taking a turn. It is a *mitzvah* to help bury the dead. The family of the deceased may then be comforted by other mourners with the words: '**The Omnipresent** will comfort you among the mourners of Zion and Jerusalem.'

Everyone then washes their hands before leaving the cemetery as contact with the dead is considered unclean. At this point the family mourners move into the second stage of mourning – ***avelut***.

Useful words

The Omnipresent – a title used of God during mourning to remind that Jews that God is with the living and the dead

Avelut – the mourning period

Activities

1. Look at the photo. Outline what is involved in sitting *shiva*.
2. Do you think the Jewish mourning customs would help close relatives to cope with their loss?
3. Why do you think people often find it difficult to talk to someone who has lost a close relative or friend?

Useful words

Shiva – the seven days of intense mourning
Kaddish – the prayer recited publicly by mourners
Yarzheit – the anniversary day of someone's death

Jewish mourners.

Avelut: the period of mourning

On returning home, the mourners are served a meal of hard-boiled eggs, symbolising the idea that just as an egg has no opening so the mourners will be too grief-stricken to speak. *Avelut* has three stages:

- ***Shiva***: the first seven days are extreme mourning. Mourners stay in their homes except for going to synagogue on *Shabbat*, and do not cut their hair or nails; they sit on low chairs and do not listen to music, wear leather shoes or have sex. All mirrors are covered so that the mourners cannot pay attention to their appearance. They sit on low chairs because of this part of the story of Job:

  then they sat on the ground with him for seven days and seven nights. No one said a word to him because they saw how great his suffering was. (Job 2:13)

  A candle is kept burning day and night because of the verse in Proverbs 20:27:

  the candle of the Lord searches the soul of man.

  During the week, friends (and people from the synagogue) visit and bring food for the mourners. At the end of the week the mourners can return to normal life.
- For the next three weeks male mourners go to synagogue every day to pray ***kaddish***. During this time a headstone should be set up in the cemetery which must be simple, both to avoid idolatry and to show the equality of everyone in death.
- Those mourning a parent or a child observe a twelve-month period of mourning counting from the day of death. During this period most activity returns to normal, although male mourners continue to recite the mourner's *kaddish* as part of synagogue services and do not listen to or play music unless it is part of their job.

Yarzheit

This is the anniversary of the death and as long as mourners live they keep ***yarzheit*** on the anniversary of relatives' deaths. A candle is kept burning for a night and a day and *kaddish* is said.

How the Liberal and Reform Jews differ from Orthodox

Many Liberal/Reform Jews think that some of the Orthodox customs are out of place in the modern world. So they:

- allow more time to elapse before the funeral so all family members can attend
- allow cremation
- put on a black ribbon rather than tearing their clothes
- sit *shiva* only for one day or at most three days and do not use low chairs
- do not cover the mirrors
- do not stay in the house for seven days
- allow the playing of music.

The importance of rituals for Jews

This topic is all about Jewish rites of passage. A rite of passage is a ceremony which marks the transition from one phase of life to another (births and beginnings, reaching adulthood, partnerings, and endings or death). All religions and cultures mark and celebrate these passages in life, both because they are occasions which require marking and because they provide an opportunity for strengthening the society or religion concerned.

The Brit Milah and **Bat Brit** bring a child into the community of Judaism and are important in providing the parents with the promise of support in bringing up this new life in the Jewish faith.

The Bar and Bat Mitzvah are important because they give a young person the opportunity to take upon themselves the responsibility of being a Jew and ensure the continuity of the Jewish faith.

Jewish marriage ceremonies are important because they bring two people together in the Jewish faith and provide the opportunity for a new Jewish family to develop and continue the faith.

The death and funeral rituals are important because the death of a family member is a time of great grief but the rituals provide the comfort and hope for the future which help people to cope with this terrible time.

Practice questions

c Explain two reasons why the Bar Mitzvah is important for Jewish boys. In your answer you must refer to a source of wisdom and authority.

d 'We don't need rites of passage rituals nowadays.' Evaluate this statement considering arguments for and against. In your answer you should:

- refer to Jewish points of view
- refer to different Jewish or non-religious points of view
- reach a justified conclusion.

Useful words

Bat Brit – ceremony for female babies in Liberal/Reform synagogues

Summary

Rites of passage are rituals celebrating important stages in life. Birth ceremonies for Jews are Brit Milah (circumcision) but Liberal Jews also have a Brit Bat for girls. All Jews should marry because the *mitzvot* say they should. Jewish boys have a Bar Mitzvah ceremony at the age of thirteen when they can be part of the *minyan*. Girls have a Bat Mitzvah. Synagogues have a *chevra kaddisha* to help with death. Orthodox Jews do not allow cremation. *Avelut* is the period of mourning, the first seven days of which are keeping *shiva*. Jews keep *yarzheit* on the anniversary of a family member's death.

Topic 2.3b.6 *Shabbat*

Thinking points

In this topic you need to:

- think about the nature, history and purpose of celebrating *Shabbat* and how it is celebrated in the home and in the synagogue, including Exodus 31:12–18
- be able to explain why *Shabbat* is important for Jews today.

Activities

1. How do Jewish people welcome *Shabbat*?
2. Look at the photo below. Why might you need an app to find out when *Shabbat* begins and ends?

Useful words

Mishneh *Shabbat* – the part of the Talmud which contains all the regulations for *Shabbat*

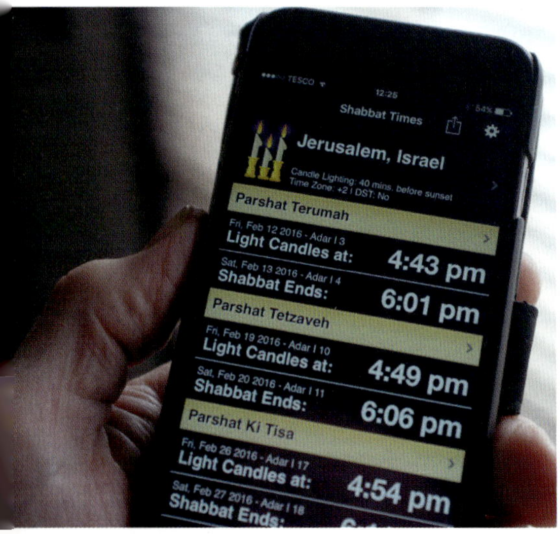

Checking *Shabbat* times using a smartphone app.

Nature, history and purpose of celebrating *Shabbat*

Shabbat means ceasing from work. In the Genesis account of creation, God created the universe, the earth, vegetation, animals and humans in six days and on the seventh day he rested. In celebration of this, God instructed that on the seventh day of the week Jewish people should rest from work:

> *Remember the Sabbath day by keeping it holy. Six days you shall labour and do all your work, but the seventh day is a Sabbath to the Lord your God. On it you shall not do any work, neither you, nor your son or daughter, nor your manservant or maidservant, nor your animals, nor the alien within your gates. For in six days the Lord made the heavens and the earth, the sea, and all that is in them, but he rested on the seventh day. Therefore the Lord blessed the Sabbath day and made it holy.* (Exodus 20:8–11)

The seventh day of the week is Saturday, but Genesis chapter 1 says that the day begins and ends with sunset and so *Shabbat* begins at sunset on Friday and ends at sunset on Saturday. As the timing of sunset varies, Jews in the UK discover the times from the synagogue, from a paper like the *Jewish Chronicle* or from a phone app.

Shabbat has been celebrated by Jewish people throughout their history, but the regulations as to what work is – and therefore what must be avoided on *Shabbat* – are set out as 39 categories in the **Mishneh *Shabbat*** in the Talmud. These have been interpreted for the modern world by the rabbis, for example one of the categories is lighting fire, so Orthodox Jews do not switch on lights because that is interpreted as lighting fire. This means that in an Orthodox home lights are switched on at sunset on Friday and stay on until sunset on Saturday unless on a timer. They do not cook on *Shabbat* and have special slow cookers so meals can be prepared before *Shabbat* begins. There are complex rules as to how to keep water hot and make tea and coffee from it. The Orthodox believe it is wrong to drive cars on *Shabbat* and so they usually live within walking distance of synagogue.

Liberal/Reform Jews take a much more relaxed attitude to *Shabbat* observance, although they would normally celebrate the Friday evening meal as a family and go to synagogue for the Saturday morning service. Most would not go to their job on *Shabbat* (although some would if it was part of their contract), but they would switch on lights and televisions, cook meals and drive to synagogue.

Jewish people celebrate *Shabbat* to:

- proclaim their belief that God created the world and then rested
- fulfil the *mitzvot* about *Shabbat*
- obey the fourth of the Ten Commandments
- spend time as a family

- spend time in worship, prayer and study
- think about what God intends life to be like and how they can fulfil God's wishes.

How *Shabbat* is celebrated in the home

Shabbat begins when the woman of the home lights the *Shabbat* candles and beckons with her arms to welcome *Shabbat* into the home. She covers her eyes and recites a blessing for the commandments, lights the candles and recites another blessing for her family before they go to service at the synagogue.

When the family return from the synagogue service, *Shabbat* worship continues at home with the *Shabbat* meal:

- The father of the household blesses the children and then recites Kiddush over the wine. The first part of Kiddush is reading the Genesis account of God resting on the seventh day. Wine is used to symbolise the sweetness and joy of the day. All the family join in the Amens, showing that they agree.
- There is a ritual cleansing of the hands before the father says the blessing over the bread. This is two specially plaited loaves called ***challot***, reminding the family of the time in the wilderness when God sent two lots of manna on *Shabbat*.
- After the blessing, the father cuts the bread, then dips a little in salt to recall the sacrifices at the Temple which were dipped in salt.
- Then the meal begins and between courses the parents tell Bible stories and the family sing songs.

Shabbat morning is spent at synagogue. The family then spend time together at home before the afternoon service in the synagogue.

When night falls the ***havdalah*** ceremony takes place to mark the end of *Shabbat*. *Havdalah* means separation and is a ceremony to mark the end of a holy day. At the end of *Shabbat* the father says a blessing over a cup of wine, then another over the *havdalah* spice box and a final one over a lighted candle. *Shabbat* begins and ends with wine and lighted candles. The spice box is passed round the family so that the memory of *Shabbat* lingers into the week. *Shabbat* is now over, the separation of the holy from the ordinary is ended and the new week begins.

How *Shabbat* is celebrated in the synagogue

Each Friday after the welcoming of *Shabbat*, synagogues should hold *Shabbat* evening prayers when *Shabbat* is greeted as a bride coming to meet her husband, the Jewish people. At the end of the service the rabbi takes a cup of wine and recites Kiddush to thank God for giving *Shabbat* to the Jewish people.

On *Shabbat* morning (Saturday) families go to synagogue for the morning prayer. The high point of the service is when the **Sefer Torah** (scroll of the Torah) is taken out of the Ark and carried to the *bimah* for the rabbi to read the ***sidra*** (section of the Torah so chosen that over a year the whole Torah will be read). Men are called from the congregation to recite a blessing at certain points of the reading, and at the end a man is called to read from one of the books of the prophets. After the Sefer Torah has been put back in the Ark, the rabbi gives a sermon.

This shop is closed for the *Shabbat*.

Useful words

Challot – plaited loaves used on *Shabbat* and festivals
Havdalah – ceremony marking the ending of *Shabbat*
Sefer Torah – the Torah scroll kept in the Ark
Sidra – a passage from the Torah

Activities

1. Outline what happens at the *Shabbat* meal.
2. How do Jewish people mark the ending of *Shabbat*?
3. Write an outline of the synagogue services for *Shabbat*.
4. Read the quotation from Exodus 31 on page 312. Does it help to explain why Orthodox Jews are so serious about keeping *Shabbat*?

Then the Lord said to Moses, 'Say to the Israelites, You must observe my Sabbaths. This is a sign between me and you for the generations to come, so that you may know that I am the Lord, who makes you holy. Observe the Sabbath, because it is holy to you. Anyone who desecrates it is to be put to death; those who do any work on that day must be cut off from their people. For six days work is to be done, but the seventh day is a day of sabbath rest, holy to the Lord. Whoever does any work on the Sabbath day is to be put to death. The Israelites are to observe the Sabbath, celebrating it for the generations to come as a lasting covenant. It will be a sign between me and the Israelites forever, for in six days the Lord made the heavens and the earth, and on the seventh day he rested and was refreshed.' (Exodus 31:12–17)

On *Shabbat* afternoon, prayers take place. These are shorter than the daily afternoon prayer, but the Sefer Torah is again taken out of the Ark and a short part of the next week's *sidra* is read.

Liberal/Reform synagogues have differences in the services. Prayers are said in English, not Hebrew, women attend all the services and sit with the men, the rabbi may well be a woman, and some of the prayers may be missed out.

Why *Shabbat* is important for Jewish people (the individual) today

- *Shabbat* offers Jewish people a chance to renew themselves both physically and spiritually as they rest from work and concentrate on religion.
- *Shabbat* gives a person time to think about what matters most to them and what they want life to be about.
- *Shabbat* provides time for a person to think about God and find out more about their faith.
- *Shabbat* provides an opportunity to socialise outside the demands and pressures of work. Friendships can be developed because of what people are, without any thought of how they might bring benefits.

Why *Shabbat* is important for the Jewish community

- *Shabbat* has been celebrated since the creation of the world and so is the oldest Jewish festival, making it important for the community to keep it going.
- *Shabbat* is God's gift to the Jewish people which binds them together – only Jews celebrate *Shabbat*.
- It reminds Jews of when they were slaves in Egypt:

  remember that you were slaves in Egypt and that the Lord your God brought you out with a mighty arm ... Therefore the Lord your God has commanded you to observe the Sabbath day (Deuteronomy 5:15)

  and refraining from work is a sign of freedom.
- *Shabbat* gives families time to spend together and provides an opportunity for families to grow together in their Jewish faith.

Summary

There are many *mitzvot* commanding Jews to rest on *Shabbat*, both as a sign of God's creation taking six days and because of God's covenant with Moses. *Shabbat* lasts from sunset on Friday to sunset on Saturday and there are special ceremonies in the home to welcome *Shabbat* and synagogue services on Friday evening and Saturday morning. No work should be done on *Shabbat*, but Orthodox and Liberal/Reform Jews have different ideas on this.

Practice questions

c Explain two reasons why *Shabbat* is important for Jewish people. In your answer you must refer to a source of wisdom and authority.

d '*Shabbat* should be about worshipping God, not keeping rules.' Evaluate this statement considering arguments for and against. In your answer you should:

- refer to Jewish points of view
- refer to different Jewish or non-religious points of view
- reach a justified conclusion.

Topic 2.3b.7 Festivals

Jewish festivals

Judaism has many festivals during the year, but these do not have exact dates in the Western calendar. The Jewish calendar has twelve months, but the months are determined by the moon and only have 29 days. This means that the lunar calendar goes out of sync with the solar calendar and so an extra month is added to the Jewish calendar every few years to keep it in line with the seasons of the year. Consequently, the timing of Jewish festivals varies from year to year, but stays in the same season. Jewish New Year, for example, is the first two days of the month of Tisri, but this can fall any time between early September and early October.

The main festivals are:

- New Year – Rosh Hashanah (September/October)
- Day of Atonement – Yom Kippur (September/October)
- Tabernacles – Sukkot (October)
- Rejoicing of the Law – Simchat Torah (October)
- Dedication – Hanukkah (December)
- Purim – (February/March)
- Passover – Pesach (March/April)
- Weeks – Shavuot (May/June).

All of these festivals have been celebrated since biblical times and they are important for Jews because:

- They celebrate important events in Jewish history:
  - Pesach celebrates how God saved the Jews from slavery in the Exodus
  - Sukkot celebrates the time the Jews were in the wilderness after escaping from Egypt
  - Hanukkah celebrates the preservation of the Jewish religion when the Greeks tried to destroy it
  - Purim celebrates the saving of the Jews in Persia as recorded in the Book of Esther
  - Shavuot celebrates the giving of the Law to Moses.
- They celebrate the special relationship the Jewish people have with God, for example Simchat Torah celebrates the Torah and the *mitzvot*, which are the basis of Jewish life. Rosh Hashanah celebrates God's kingship and his willingness to forgive his people's sins.
- They celebrate God being the creator and sustainer of nature, as Shavuot and Sukkot have connections with harvest.
- They give an opportunity for Jewish people to turn over a new leaf by repenting of their sins and determining a new start at festivals like Yom Kippur.

Thinking points

In this topic you need to:

- think about the nature, history and purpose of festivals, and the origins and meaning of Rosh Hashanah, Yom Kippur, Pesach, Shavuot and Sukkot, including interpretations of Leviticus 23
- be able to explain why these festivals are important for Jews today.

Activity

Why are festivals important in Judaism?

Activity

Do you think the way Jews celebrate New Year is better than the way the UK celebrates New Year?

Rosh Hashanah

Rosh Hashanah marks the beginning of the Jewish New Year. This is one of the holiest times of the year for Jewish people.

Origins

The celebration is one of the *mitzvot* as it is commanded in the Torah:

> *The Lord said to Moses, 'Say to the Israelites: "On the first day of the seventh month you are to have a day of sabbath rest, a sacred assembly commemorated with trumpet blasts. Do no regular work, but present a food offering to the Lord".'* (Leviticus 23:23–25)

Rosh Hashanah has been celebrated since biblical times, but the Talmud says it is to be celebrated as the day when God created the earth and created the human race.

The Torah says that on the 1st of Elul (the month before Rosh Hashanah), Moses went up Mount Sinai to receive new tablets of stone with the Ten Commandments written on them to replace the ones Moses had smashed when he found the Israelites worshipping the golden calf. Forty days later (the day now celebrated as Yom Kippur) he returned with the new tablets, showing that God had forgiven the people because they had repented.

Useful words

Shofar – a musical instrument
Book of Life – the book where one's quality of life for the coming year is recorded
Tashlich – casting away sins into running water

Features

During the month of Elul the ***shofar*** is blown every day in the synagogue. People think about their sins and their relationship with God so that they cast off their sins with feeling and have really thought about their resolutions for the new year.

Making New Year resolutions is not an optional extra for Jews, it is a requirement. New Year cards are exchanged and friends are greeted with the words, 'May you be inscribed for a good year'. This reflects the idea that God has a **Book of Life** in which he records the quality of people's lives and what he will record for the next year depends on what resolutions for improvement people make between Rosh Hashanah and Yom Kippur.

Rosh Hashanah is welcomed in the home by a Kiddush over foods containing honey in the hope that the New Year will be a sweet one; and the hope that there will be plenty of good deeds is expressed by eating fish which are found in shoals or pomegranates which have lots of seeds.

At the morning service, 100 notes of the *shofar* are blown to express the crying of the souls about past sins and the yearning of the soul to be reunited with God. After the service, families go to a river and in the ceremony of ***tashlich*** symbolically throw their sins into the water:

> *and you will cast all their sins into the depths of the sea.* (Micah 7:19)

A *shofar* with pomegranate and honey.

Meaning and importance

After thinking about their sins during the month of Elul, on Rosh Hashanah people should consider their relationship with God and with each other, and decide how they are going to make both of these better in the coming year.

Rosh Hashanah is the day when the Book of Life is opened and when God writes down the quality of people's lives:

> *See I have set before you this day life and good, death and evil ... choose life.* (Deuteronomy 30:1)

The book is open until the end of Yom Kippur, after which it is sealed and cannot be altered, so what people decide on Rosh Hashanah and confirm on Yom Kippur is what will be in the book for the coming year.

Choosing to be good can be a real struggle and when people fail and do things wrong they feel guilty. Rosh Hashanah is a chance to come before God, acknowledge what they have done wrong and show how they are going to do good in the coming year.

Yom Kippur

Yom Kippur (Day of Atonement) occurs ten days after Rosh Hashanah. These ten days are known as the '**Days of Awe**', when people reflect on what they promised at Rosh Hashanah and make sure that they put things right with anyone they have wronged.

Useful words

Days of Awe – the ten days between Rosh Hashanah and Yom Kippur

Kol Nidrei – annulment of vows made before Yom Kippur

Origins

Yom Kippur is commanded in the Torah:

> *The Lord said to Moses, the tenth day of the seventh month is the Day of Atonement. Hold a sacred assembly and deny yourselves, and present an offering made to the Lord by fire. Do no work on that day, because it is the Day of Atonement, when atonement is made for you before the Lord your God. Anyone who does not deny himself on that day must be cut off from his people.* (Leviticus 23:26–29)

Activity

What happens on Yom Kippur and how might this help a Jewish person to make a new start?

During the days of the Temple the priest sacrificed a bull as a sin offering to atone for sins he may have committed unintentionally throughout the year. Then he took two goats and presented them at the door of the tabernacle. Two goats were chosen by lot: one to be 'for the Lord', which was offered as a sacrifice, the other to be the scapegoat to be sent away into the wilderness. The high priest confessed the intentional sins of the Israelites to God, placing them symbolically on the head of the other goat, the scapegoat, who would symbolically take them away into the wilderness.

Yom Kippur involves a 25-hour fast, reflection of past sins, confession of sins and prayers for forgiveness. People wear simpler clothes and do not wear jewellery or leather shoes as they are forbidden in Leviticus.

On the eve of Yom Kippur, families have a special meal and make a family donation to the poor rather than sacrificing a chicken. Then they go to synagogue for a special evening service. This begins with the **Kol Nidrei** prayer, which used to be said by Jews at the time of the Spanish Inquisition to forgive them for pretending to be Christians so they would not be persecuted. This is followed by a confession of sins.

There are prayers of general confession, but people are expected to make their own confession in silence to God because confession should be personal to the sinner and God.

At home there is a *havdalah* ceremony just as at *Shabbat* to show that Yom Kippur is over.

Meaning and importance

- The *mitzvah* that Jews who do not deny themselves on Yom Kippur must be cut off means that this is regarded as the most important festival. Many Jews who never obey the *mitzvot* during the rest of the year fast and go to synagogue on Yom Kippur.
- Atonement has two meanings: reconciling God and man, and reparation for a wrong or an injury.
- Yom Kippur releases people from the guilt felt about the sins of the past.
- Yom Kippur makes people feel free to make a new start.
- The fasting takes people's minds off their physical needs so they can concentrate on the spiritual.
- Fasting encourages the self-discipline needed to keep the resolutions made at Rosh Hashanah.
- Fasting helps people to feel compassion for the poor who fast through necessity, not choice.

Sukkot (Tabernacles)

Sukkot begins just five days after Yom Kippur and many families start building the family *sukkah* (*sukkot* is the plural) as soon as they finish the family meal at the end of Yom Kippur.

Origins

After the Israelites escaped from Egypt in the Exodus, they spent 40 years living as nomads in the wilderness, in temporary huts (*sukkot*) roofed with palm leaves. This festival takes Jewish people back to those times.

The festival is commanded in Torah *mitzvot*:

> *On the fifteenth day of the seventh month the Lord's Festival of Tabernacles begins, and lasts for seven days. The first day is a sacred assembly; do no regular work ... So beginning with the fifteenth day of the seventh month, after you have gathered the crops of the land, celebrate to the Lord ... take a choice fruit from the trees, and palm fronds, leafy branches and poplars and rejoice before the Lord your God for seven days ... live in booths for seven days ... so that your descendants will know that I made the Israelites live in booths when I brought them out of Egypt.* (Leviticus 23:33–43)

Sukkot begins at the end of the fruit harvest in Israel. Families, and often the synagogues, make an outdoor *sukkah* with at least three walls and a covering of leafy branches. Depending on the climate, people either live in their *sukkah* for seven days or just eat their meals in it.

Useful words

Etrog – a citron fruit
Lulav – palm branch

On each day of the festival people meet in the synagogue carrying an ***etrog*** (a fruit that looks like a lemon) in one hand and a ***lulav*** (palm branch), myrtle and willow, as commanded in the *mitzvah*. They wave the *lulav* in all directions and there is much rejoicing since Sukkot is called 'the season

A *sukkah*.

of our rejoicing'. On the last day of Sukkot people process round the *bimah* seven times waving the *lulav* and carrying the *etrog*.

Meaning and importance

- It symbolises and encourages harmony, with families living in their *sukkah* as a unit.
- It is a link with the ancestors, reinforcing the idea that Jews belong to an ancient people.
- The four species symbolise God's presence everywhere and the blessings he showers on his people.
- The four species also symbolise four different types of people:
  - the *etrog* stands for people who both know the Torah and do good deeds
  - the *lulav* stands for those who are learned in Torah but do no good deeds
  - the myrtle stands for those who do good deeds but do not know the Torah and
  - the willow stands for those who are both ignorant of the Torah and selfish.

Activity

Look at the photo above. Why do Jews build one of these for Sukkot?

Pesach

Pesach is a seven-day festival at the beginning of spring. In the days before Pesach, houses are cleaned to remove all traces of leaven (yeast). Any food containing leaven is called ***chametz*** and children have special games hunting for any *chametz* in the house, which is all burnt before Pesach begins.

Useful words

Chametz – any food containing yeast/leaven

Origins

Pesach began with Moses, and the Torah recounts how, after Joseph had brought the Israelites into Egypt to escape famine, they were enslaved by the Pharaoh and made to work as slaves on building projects. Moses was called by God to bring the people out of Egypt. The Pharaoh refused and so God sent plagues on the Egyptians and after each plague the Pharaoh said the Israelites could go, but then changed his mind.

Before the tenth plague, the Israelites were told to sacrifice a lamb and spread its blood on their doorposts so the angel of death would pass over their houses, but when it came to Egyptian houses it killed the firstborn in each house. After this, the Pharaoh agreed to let the Israelites go and Moses led them out, but again the Pharaoh changed his mind and led his army in a chase after the Israelites.

When they came to the Red Sea, God parted the sea so that the Israelites could cross, but when the Egyptians followed, the waves came back and destroyed the army. So God saved Israel and gave the people their freedom, which is why Pesach is sometimes called the freedom festival.

There are Pesach *mitzvot* about the festival:

Activity

Why do Jewish people celebrate Pesach?

> *The Lord's Passover begins at twilight on the fourteenth day of the first month. On the fifteenth day of that month the Lord's feast of Unleavened Bread begins; for seven days you must eat bread made without yeast. (Leviticus 23:5–7)*
>
> *For seven days no yeast is to be found in your houses. And whoever eats anything made with yeast in it must be cut off from the community of Israel. (Exodus 12:19)*
>
> *Sacrifice as the Passover to the Lord your God an animal from your flock or herd. (Deuteronomy 16:2)*

Pesach has been celebrated by Jews ever since these events, which probably took place about 1250BCE.

Useful words

Seder – the Passover meal
Hagadah – book telling the story of the first Passover

Pesach begins an hour before nightfall, when the candles are lit and the festival is welcomed into the home. There is then a synagogue service where special prayers are said thanking God for freeing their ancestors from slavery in Egypt. Then the family return for the great meal of Pesach, which is called ***seder***. *Seder* means order and there is a special order to be followed in the meal as set out in the ***hagadah*** book. There are special foods on the *seder* plate which are only tasted, and there are a whole series of questions asked by the youngest family member and answered by the father. Then they have a proper meal featuring lamb. They sing songs about the Exodus and at the end of the meal they eat a piece of unleavened bread known as the *afikomen*.

Unleavened bread is eaten for seven days, then there is a *havdalah* ceremony after which those families who have been using special Pesach crockery wash it and put it away.

Meaning of the *seder* plate foods

Food	Meaning
Charoset	Paste made with nuts, fruit and spices to represent the mud bricks the Israelite slaves had to make in Egypt, and when eaten it gives the sweet taste of freedom
Bitter herbs (horseradish)	Represent the pain of slavery
Shank bone	A reminder of the lamb sacrificed at Passover
Burnt boiled egg	A reminder of the sacrifices offered in the Temple
Green herbs (parsley)	Green parsley represents freedom; it is dipped in salt water to represent the tears of the slaves and the sea they crossed to freedom
Lettuce	The leaves symbolise freedom and the bitter stalk slavery

A *seder* plate.

Activities

1. Look at the photo of the *seder* plate above. What do each of the foods represent?
2. Why might some people think Shavuot is the most important Jewish festival?

Meaning and importance

- Pesach is the freedom festival and is a great celebration of freedom and condemnation of slavery.
- It is also a celebration of God's power and God's control of history, for without the Passover and Exodus there would be no Jewish people.
- It is celebrated as the birthday of the Jewish nation and the *seder* meal is like a birthday party for the nation.
- It is a celebration of Jewish history and of the way God has preserved his chosen people.

Shavuot (also known as Pentecost or Weeks)

Shavuot is the Feast of Weeks. It is celebrated seven weeks after Passover, meaning that the first day of Shavuot is 50 days after Passover, hence the name Pentecost (Greek for the number 50).

Origins

Shavuot began as a harvest festival, marking the beginning of the wheat harvest. The Torah commands the Jews to offer the first fruits of the harvest to God:

> *When you have entered the land the Lord your God is giving you as an inheritance and have taken possession of it and settled in it, take some of the first fruits of all that you produce from the soil of the land that the Lord your God is giving you and put them in a basket … Place the basket before the Lord your God and bow down before him.* (Deuteronomy 26:1–11)

Happy Shavuot: a Jewish greeting card for this holiday.

Seven weeks after the events of the Exodus celebrated at Pesach, Moses was given the Torah on Mount Sinai, and this is now the main element of the festival – thanking God for the gift of the Torah.

Shavuot is the only festival without a specific *mitzvah* ordering its celebration. This is because the giving of the Torah is so important to the Jewish people that celebrating the giving of it is required by all 613 of the *mitzvot*.

Shavuot is a two-day festival and, as a festival, no work is done. The main things that happen at Shavuot are:

- Candles are lit to bring in the festival, on both the first and second evenings.
- Many people stay up to read the Torah on the first night of Shavuot.
- Everyone goes to synagogue on the first day of Shavuot to hear the reading of the Ten Commandments.
- People eat dairy foods rather than meat.
- On the second day of Shavuot, a special prayer for those who have died is recited in the synagogue.
- The Book of Ruth is read, as she was an ancestor of King David who was born on Shavuot and died 70 years later on Shavuot.
- Flowers and greenery are placed all around the synagogue, as Mount Sinai blossomed after God gave the Torah to the Israelites.

Meaning and importance

- The gift of the Torah is the most important thing in Jewish history. Following the 613 *mitzvot* of the Torah gives Jewish people their identity.
- It is thought that Shavuot completes Pesach, as Pesach was about the Israelites gaining physical freedom, but Shavuot celebrates the spiritual freedom brought by the *mitzvot*.
- Studying the Torah on the first night represents an attempt to put the past right and show people's eagerness to be given the Torah, as many of the Jews went to sleep the night before Moses brought them the Torah.
- Dairy produce is eaten rather than meat because people did not know what the laws about meat would be and so they made sure they did not break the laws by eating dairy products instead.
- The fruit and greenery represent not only the flowering of Sinai after the giving of the law, but also the *mitzvah* to present the first fruits to God.

Summary

Judaism has many festivals to celebrate the great events in Jewish history. The main ones are: Rosh Hashanah, celebrating the New Year; ten days later comes Yom Kippur, a whole-day fast giving people a chance to put things right for the New Year; Sukkot, remembering the 40 years in the wilderness; Pesach, remembering the Israelites' escape from Egypt; and Shavuot, celebrating the giving of the Torah to Moses.

Practice questions

c Explain two reasons why Pesach is important for Jewish people. In your answer you must refer to a source of wisdom and authority.

d 'You can't be considered a Jew if you don't fast and attend synagogue on Yom Kippur.' Evaluate this statement considering arguments for and against. In your answer you should:

- refer to Jewish points of view
- refer to different Jewish or non-religious points of view
- reach a justified conclusion.

Topic 2.3b.8 Features of the synagogue

The Jewish synagogue

A Jewish place of worship is called a synagogue, which is a Greek word meaning to gather together, or the place where people gather together.

It seems that synagogues began in the sixth century BCE when most Jews were in exile in Babylon and could not go to worship in the Temple in Jerusalem. In this situation, they had to develop places where they could meet for prayer, worship and study, and they became known as synagogues. However, most Jewish people refer to the synagogue either as 'temple' or '**shul**'.

Synagogues have features based on the layout of the Jerusalem Temple, especially the Ark of the Covenant, which was a precious box containing the tablets of the law received by Moses, lost when the first Temple was destroyed by the Babylonians (as featured in films such as *Raiders of the Lost Ark*).

After the destruction of the second Jerusalem Temple in 70CE, synagogues became more and more important. Some of the daily prayers such as *kaddish* can only be said when there is *a minyan* and so needed a synagogue. Young people needed to be taught the Hebrew language and the basics of the faith, and the synagogue was used for this. Finally, the synagogue became a community centre of the local Jewish community, providing socialising facilities for local Jews.

Nowadays the synagogue is a place of worship, an education centre and a community centre. Most synagogues run Hebrew classes for children, and have a hall which can be used for weddings, Bar Mitzvahs, mother and toddler groups, study groups, youth clubs, scouts, guides and so on.

Exterior synagogue design

A synagogue can be in any type of building and so the exterior can be of any design, except that it should:

- have either a Star of David  or a **menorah**  to show that it is Jewish
- have windows letting the light in so that worship is not a retreat from the world and to pour light as a sign of God's strength and guidance
- be built facing Jerusalem, where the Temple stood.

Interior synagogue design

All synagogues should have the following features:

- They should have a sink at the entrance for worshippers to ceremonially cleanse themselves before prayer.
- They have a Holy Ark (**Aron Hakodesh**), which is a cupboard fixed to the front wall, making it the focal centre of the synagogue. Sometimes it has an embroidered black and gold curtain in front, while others are painted black and have two gold lions on the doors representing the tribe of Judah from which will come the Messiah.

Thinking points

In this topic you need to:

- think about the nature, history and purpose of the design of the synagogue; how and why objects of devotion are used within the synagogue and how the synagogue is used by different communities, including reference to Exodus 27:20–21
- be able to explain the importance of the synagogue in Judaism.

Useful words

Shul – the name used for the synagogue by many Jews
Menorah – seven-branched candlestick
Aron Hakodesh – the Ark

Activities

1. Why did synagogues develop?
2. How would you know a building was a synagogue?
3. What compass direction should UK synagogues face?

Command the Israelites to bring you clear oil of pressed olives for the light so that the lamps may be kept burning. In the tent of meeting, outside the curtain that shields the ark of the covenant law, Aaron and his sons are to keep the lamps burning before the Lord from evening till morning. This is to be a lasting ordinance among the Israelites for the generations to come.
(Exodus 27:20–21)

A man holding a Torah scroll in a British synagogue.

- Inside the Ark are the Torah scrolls (Sefer Torah). A Torah scroll is about 60 metres long and is stitched at each end to a wooden pole so it can be wound and kept ready at the point of the next reading. The scroll is wound in a black and gold silk or velvet wrapping with a crown and bell on top of the poles, so that the congregation hear the bells when the scroll is removed from the Ark. Usually a shield decorated with the first two words of each of the Ten Commandments is placed on the front of the wrapped scroll.
- When reading the scroll the reader uses a ***yad*** (a pointer stick) to keep his place. This is important because the holy words of the Sefer Torah must not be stained or damaged by being touched by dirty fingers.
- They have a ***bimah*** (raised platform) with a desk for reading the Torah, a chair on one side for the rabbi and one on the other side for the ***chazzan*** or cantor who leads the prayers, and sometimes a pulpit for the rabbi to give the sermon. The *bimah* can be in the middle of the synagogue or in front of the Ark.
- Above the Ark is the ***ner tamid*** or everlasting light. This light is never put out and represents the *menorah* in the Jerusalem Temple, whose seven wicks were never allowed to go out.
- Many synagogues also have an actual *menorah* on a lampstand, but the *menorah* in the synagogue will generally have six or eight branches instead of the Temple *menorah*'s seven, because exact duplication of the Temple's ritual items is thought to be improper by the Orthodox.
- On the wall next to or above the Ark there is usually a plaque with the words of the Ten Commandments on it.

Useful words

Yad – pointer for reading the Sefer Torah
Bimah – the raised platform for Torah readings
Chazzan – the leader of worship who chants the prayers (also called a cantor)
Ner tamid – the everlasting light

How the synagogue is used by the different communities

The reason for the differences can be found in the introduction about Orthodox and Liberal/Reform Jews and Topic 2.3b.1 (page 288).

- In Orthodox synagogues there will be separate seating for women, sometimes with a screen between the men's and women's sections. In Liberal/Reform synagogues men and women sit together.
- In Orthodox synagogues the rabbi and cantor will always be men. In Liberal/Reform synagogues the rabbi and/or cantor may be women.
- In Orthodox synagogues there will be no musical instruments played on *Shabbat* because that would be work. In Liberal/Reform synagogues there may be an organ or a piano or a band for *Shabbat* worship.
- In Orthodox synagogues only males would be asked up to read. In Liberal/Reform synagogues both men and women can be asked up to read.
- In Orthodox synagogues prayers will be in Hebrew. In Liberal/Reform synagogues many of the prayers will be in English.
- In Orthodox synagogues there are prayers for the rebuilding of the Temple and the return of all Jewish people to the Holy Land. In Liberal/Reform synagogues these payers are not said.
- In Orthodox synagogues only men carry the Torah scrolls. In Liberal/Reform synagogues women or girls may be invited to carry the Torah scrolls.
- In Orthodox synagogues people will have walked to synagogue. In Liberal/Reform synagogues people will often come to synagogue by car.

Schedule of events and services at a synagogue in New York, USA.

Activity

Do you think it matters what a synagogue looks like? Remember to read Exodus 27:20–21.

How else the synagogue is used

Most synagogues have classrooms for learning Hebrew, lessons preparing for Bat or Bar Mitzvahs, and for meetings and lectures to learn more about the faith.

Many synagogues have a hall for wedding and Bar or Bat Mitzvah celebrations. It is also used for mother and toddler groups, senior citizens' clubs and other community activities.

Most synagogues also hold youth activities such as youth clubs, scouts and guides. They also run day camps during school holidays.

Practice questions

c Explain two reasons why the synagogue is used differently by different communities. In your answer you must refer to a source of wisdom and authority.

d 'The synagogue is the centre of Jewish life.' Evaluate this statement considering arguments for and against. In your answer you should:
- refer to Jewish points of view
- refer to different Jewish or non-religious points of view
- reach a justified conclusion.

Summary

The synagogue took the place of the Temple in Jewish worship and acts as a school and social centre for the Jewish community. Synagogues are built facing Jerusalem. The Torah scrolls are kept in the Holy Ark at the front of the synagogue where there is a *bimah* to read the Torah scroll from. All synagogues have a *ner tamid* or everlasting light to fulfil the *mitzvah* of Exodus 27. There are differences between Orthodox and Liberal/Reform synagogues.

How to answer questions

a) Describe two differences between Jewish forms of worship and forms of worship in the main religious tradition of Britain. [3]

The main religious tradition of Britain is Christianity. One difference is that Orthodox Jews worship in Hebrew, whereas Christians worship in their native language. Another difference is that men and women worship separately in Orthodox Judaism whereas the sexes worship together in Christianity.

A high mark answer because Christianity is identified as the main religious tradition and two differences are clearly described.

b) Explain two differences between Jewish and Christian forms of worship. [4]

One difference is that in Orthodox Jewish worship all the prayers are said in Hebrew, whereas in Christian worship everything is in the language of the country. In Jewish worship there are no images, but in Catholic and Orthodox worship there are likely to be crucifixes and statues of the Virgin Mary.

A high mark answer because two correct differences are given and each difference is developed.

c) Explain two reasons why circumcision is important for Jews. In your answer you must refer to a source of wisdom and authority. [5]

Circumcision is important because it is a 'sign in the flesh' of the covenant God made with Abraham in Genesis chapter 16. This made circumcision a *mitzvah* which marks the entry of Jewish males into the covenant. It has been particularly important in Jewish history as both the Greeks and the Romans tried to ban circumcision as a way of ending the Jewish nation, but many Jews were martyred rather than give up the practice.

A high mark answer because two correct reasons are given and each reason is developed with a reference to covenant, Genesis and *mitzvah* as sources of authority.

d) 'The Bar Mitzvah is where a Jewish boy becomes an adult.' [12 marks + 3 spelling, punctuation and grammar (SPaG) marks]

Some people may think that Bar Mitzvah is where a Jewish boy becomes an adult because it is the term used for when a boy becomes responsible for his own actions and is regarded as an adult as far as religion is concerned. Certainly, after his Bar Mitzvah, a Jewish boy must put on *tephilin* for morning prayers; he can make up a *minyan*; he has to observe the fast days in full and he may be called up to read the *sidra* in synagogue services. All of these show him being an adult.

However, others may disagree because Judaism does not regard a thirteen-year-old boy as an adult because he has had his Bar Mitzvah. In Pirkei Avot in the Talmud, it says that while thirteen is the proper age for fulfilment of the Commandments, eighteen is the proper age for marriage and twenty is the proper age for earning a living. Nowadays, most Jews would regard the Bar Mitzvah as making a Jewish boy responsible for his actions and for his religion but not a full adult.

It seems to me that few Jewish people would regard the Bar Mitzvah as making a boy an adult. I do not think anyone can be regarded as an adult at the age of thirteen and so I think that Bar Mitzvah makes a boy an adult for religion, but not for life.

A high mark answer because it gives three clear developed reasons for thinking that a boy becomes an adult at Bar Mitzvah. It then gives three reasons for disagreeing and then reaches a fully justified conclusion.

The answer would reach full marks for SPaG as spelling, punctuation and grammar are correct and a wide range of specialist vocabulary (*tephilin*, *sidra*, synagogue, Pirkei Avot, Talmud) is used appropriately.

SPaG

A high mark answer because the answer spells, punctuates and uses the rules of grammar with consistent accuracy and effective control of meaning. A wide range of specialist terms is used adeptly and with precision.

4 Peace and conflict

Area of study 2: Based on a study of Islam or Judaism

Topic 2.4.1a Muslim attitudes towards peace

Depending on your area of study you have a choice of either a) Islam or b) Judaism topics. These are indicated by the letters 'a' and 'b' in the topic headings. Please read the topic relevant to your area of study.

Thinking points

In this topic you need to:

- think about the nature and importance of peace for Muslims, Muslim teachings about peace, including Qur'an 25:63, and Islam as a religion of peace
- be able to explain and evaluate Muslim understandings of peace and how those may be understood in the life of a Muslim.

Useful words

Salaam – peace
Salaam alaykum – the Muslim equivalent of hello which means peace be with you
Divine guidance – being shown what to do by God

Activities

1. Why do Muslims believe that Islam is a religion of peace?
2. Why do you think some people might say that Islam is not a religion of peace?
3. Look at the quotation from Surah 25:63. What does this surah teach Muslims about conflict situations?

Islam, a religion of peace

The word Islam is derived from *'aslama'*, which means to surrender or submit, so Islam is the religion of submission to the will of God. However, the consonants *'s-l-m'* are those of **'salaam'**, which means peace, so there is a close connection between Islam and peace. Indeed, one meaning of the word Islam is peace. The greeting used by all Muslims when they meet each other is **'salaam alaykum'** – 'May peace be with you.'

The Qur'an itself makes plain that Islam is a religion of peace:

> *O You who believe! Enter into peace (Islam) wholeheartedly; and follow not the footsteps of the Evil One.* (Surah 2: 208)

Since the events of the 2001 '9/11' terrorist attack on the USA, and the increase in terrorism-related attacks around the world, the vast majority of Muslims have been keen to show that Islam is a religion of peace. Mahathir bin Mohamad, the former prime minister of Malaysia, said in 2002,

> *Clearly Islam the religion is not the cause of terrorism. Islam, as I said, is a religion of peace. However through the centuries, deviations from the true teachings of Islam take place. And so people who call themselves 'Muslims' kill despite the injunction of their religion against killing especially of innocent people.*

Muslim teachings about peace

Since the word 'Islam' is derived from the word meaning 'peace' in Arabic, Islam itself is a religion which its followers believe brings a peaceful life when people obey God's call and live by the moral values God sets. This is so that compassion, mercy, peace and love can be experienced all over the world. Muslims describe countries where Islam is the national religion as 'the abode of peace' and countries outside Islam are called 'the abode of war'.

> *And the servants of God, most gracious are those who walk on the earth with humility, and when the ignorant address them, they say, 'Peace!'* (Surah 25:63)

One of the attributes of God described in the Qur'an is 'peace and security', which means that for Muslims God's being itself is a manifestation of peace.

> *The Qur'an says that **divine guidance** is like a path of peace: 'God guideth all who seek His good pleasure to ways of peace and safety'.* (Surah 5:16)

Similarly, paradise, the ultimate destination for Muslims, is an abode of peace:

> *For them will be a home of peace in the presence of their Lord.* (Surah 6:127)

Abdul Rauf Campos-Marquetti (left), secretary for the Islamic Centre of Albuquerque, Rabbi Lynn Gottlieb (centre), of the Nahalat Shalom Synagogue and Mohammed Quraishi (right), president of the Islamic Centre of Albuquerque, pray together outside the mosque in Albuquerque, New Mexico, USA.

The Qur'an tells Muslims that, 'an **amicable** settlement ... is best' (Surah 4:128), and, according to Bukhari, whenever the Prophet had an option between two courses of action, he always chose the **non-confrontational** one.

Why peace is important for Muslims

Peace is important for Muslims because:

- Islam teaches that accepting Islam brings inner peace through submitting to the will of Allah.
- When Muslims have inner peace it encourages them to have peaceful relationships with other people.
- The Qur'an calls Islam '**Dar as Salaam**' – the House of Peace – and says that

  God doth call to the Home of Peace: He doth guide whom He pleaseth to a Way that is straight. (Surah 10:25)

  This verse is taken to mean that the House of Islam and the Home of Peace are the same thing.
- Islam teaches that true peace both within and between people comes from accepting Islam and living its ways.

Activity

Look at the photo of the meeting above. What does this photo show about Islam?

Jaber reported that the Messenger of Allah said, 'War is a deception'. (Hadith quoted by Bukhari and Muslim)

Useful words

Amicable – showing a polite and friendly desire to avoid disagreement and argument

Non-confrontational – tending to deal with situations calmly and diplomatically instead of being aggressive or hostile

Dar as Salaam – the House of Peace

The importance of peace for Islam means that peace should take a central place in a Muslim's life. Muslims should always look for an amicable solution to any conflict situations in which they find themselves. A Muslim is always likely to be non-confrontational, trying to keep the peace wherever and whenever possible. Of course, some Muslims choose to ignore the teachings of Islam about the importance of peace, and there is debate in Islam about whether those who choose the way of confrontation and conflict are true Muslims.

Practice questions

c Explain two reasons why Muslims believe that Islam is a religion of peace. In your answer you must refer to a source of wisdom and authority.

d 'Islam is the House of Peace.' Evaluate this statement considering arguments for and against. In your answer you should:

- refer to Muslim points of view
- reach a justified conclusion.

Summary

Islam can mean peace and the Qur'an says that Islam is a religion of peace. Muslims believe that Islam brings peace and Muslim countries are known as 'the abode of peace'. The Qur'an calls Islam the House of Peace and claims that true peace comes when people accept Islam and live in its ways.

Topic 2.4.1b Jewish attitudes towards peace

Jewish teachings about peace

The Hebrew word for peace is ***shalom***, but this word has several meanings:

- The primary meaning of *shalom* is peace, an absence of conflict and/or disagreement between individuals, groups or nations.
- The word also refers to health, well-being and welfare. The Jewish equivalent of hello is '*shalom aleichem*', often translated as 'well-being be upon you' or 'may you be well'.
- *Shalom* can also refer to a correct relationship with God. The Talmud says 'the name of God is "Peace" ', therefore, Jews should not greet each other with the word *shalom* in unholy places such as a bathroom.
- The word can also refer to a spiritual sense of security which comes when God's peace rests on a person.

The main teachings about peace come from the Tenakh, which emphasises that there is a close relationship between *shalom* and justice and truth:

> *righteousness and peace kiss each other.* (Psalm 85:10)

The Torah explains that peace is a major part of the covenant:

> *If you follow my decrees and are careful to obey my commands, I will send you rain in its season and the ground will yield its crops ... I will grant peace in the land, and you will lie down and no one will make you afraid.* (Leviticus 26:6)

Even in times of war, the Torah commands that peace must be the aim.

> *When you march up to attack a city, make its people an offer of peace. If they accept and open their gates, all the people in it shall be subject to forced labour and shall work for you. If they refuse to make peace and they engage you in battle, lay siege to that city.* (Deuteronomy 20:10–12)

Why peace is important for Jewish people

Shalom is important for Jewish people because:

- The basis of Judaism is the Mosaic Covenant based on the Torah, and the Talmud claims that, 'The entire Torah is for the sake of the ways of shalom' (Talmud, Shabbat, 10b). There is a **Midrash** which claims, 'The Torah was given to establish peace'. Further, the great rabbi Maimonides asserted, 'Great is peace, as the whole Torah was given in order to promote peace in the world' (Mishneh Torah).
- Peace is the ideal for all Jews. The perfect society, which Jews call the Messianic Age, is thought of as a time of peace when all weapons of war will be turned into instruments of peace. Isaiah actually gives the Messiah the title Prince of Peace (Isaiah 9:6) who will bring in such a time of peace and security that: 'They will beat their swords into ploughshares and their spears into pruning hooks. Nation will not take up sword against nation, nor will they train for war anymore' (Isaiah 2:5); 'The wolf will live with the lamb, the leopard will lie down with the goat' (Isaiah 11:6).

Depending on your area of study you have a choice of either a) Islam or b) Judaism topics. These are indicated by the letters 'a' and 'b' in the topic headings. Please read the topic relevant to your area of study.

Thinking points

In this topic you need to:

- think about the nature and importance of peace for Jews and Jewish teachings about the importance of peace, including Deuteronomy 20:10–12
- be able to explain and evaluate Jewish attitudes to peace.

Useful words

Shalom – peace
Midrash – a collection of rabbinic commentaries on the Tenakh

Activities

1. What does *shalom* mean?
2. Do you think peace is important for Jewish people?
3. What do you think of the quotation from the book of Deuteronomy?

Activities

1. Look at the image of the peace march. Why do you think these Jews in New York were protesting about Israel's bombing?
2. Look at the statement by Rami Elhanan below. Do you think you would feel like this if your child had been killed by a suicide bomber?

Members of the Jewish community in New York, USA, peace activists and Palestinians rally against Israel's bombing of Palestinian civilians.

Useful words

Parents' Circle – a group of Palestinian and Jewish families who have lost children in the conflict and are working for peace

Suicide bomber – terrorist who carries out a bomb attack, knowing that he or she will be killed by the explosion

Although all Jews agree that peace is important and should always be the priority in whatever a Jew does, there are differences about how to achieve this. Some Jews believe (from the experiences of the Jewish people in the Holocaust) that the best way to achieve peace is through strength and being prepared to confront, and even fight, those whose unjust behaviour threatens peace. Other Jews believe that peace comes through behaving justly and peaceably.

When someone kills your 14-year-old daughter, you want to get even and retaliate. This way is easy, but we are people not animals ... so there is also a second way. This is the way of understanding when you say, 'What can you do personally in order to prevent this hatred from affecting others? (Rami Elhanan, an Israeli and a member of ***Parents' Circle****, whose daughter was killed by a* ***suicide bomber****)*

Summary

Judaism teaches that peace brings health and spiritual security as well as an absence of conflict. The Torah teaches that peace is a part of God's covenant and the rest of the Tenakh teaches that justice and peace go together. Peace is very important for Jews because the rabbis taught that the Torah was given to promote peace.

Practice questions

c. Explain two reasons why Jews believe that Judaism is a religion of peace. In your answer you must refer to a source of wisdom and authority.

d. 'Judaism is a religion of peace.' Evaluate this statement considering arguments for and against. In your answer you should:
- refer to Jewish points of view
- refer to different Jewish or non-religious points of view
- reach a justified conclusion.

Topic 2.4.2a The role of Muslims in peacemaking

Muslim teachings about peacemaking

As we saw in the previous topic, Islam is a religion of peace. However, Islam also recommends its followers to be peacemakers.

The Qur'an recommends that Muslims end disagreements by making peace rather than by beginning further disputes and fights:

> *Repel evil with what is better: then will he between whom and thee was hatred become as it were thy friend and intimate! And no one will be granted such goodness except those who exercise patience and self-restraint.* (Surah 41:34–35)

> *Let there be no compulsion in religion.* (Surah 2:256)

Muslims are asked to take a balanced approach and seek **justice** as a way of making peace:

> *Fear God and keep straight the relations between yourselves.* (Surah 8:1)

> *If two parties among the believers fall into a quarrel, make ye peace between them ... The believers are but a single brotherhood: so make peace and reconciliation between your two contending brothers; and fear God.* (Surah 49:9–10)

The importance of justice, forgiveness and reconciliation in peacemaking

Muslims believe that justice is an important part of peacemaking because if a society and its laws are unjust, people will not obey them and will campaign against unjust laws causing trouble in society. For example, the civil rights campaign against laws refusing equality to black people in the southern USA in the 1960s disrupted normal life there. If the laws do not create a just society, people will think the legal system is not working and may start a civil war. For example, in Syria, the Syrian Sunni Muslims began a civil war because they thought the legal system of the Assad regime was treating them unfairly.

Muslims believe that forgiveness and **reconciliation** are important in peacemaking because:

- God is compassionate and merciful to sinners, and so Muslims should be merciful and forgiving to those who cause them offence.
- On the Day of Judgement God will deal with everyone as they deserve, but Muslims will be able to request his mercy. However, how can Muslims ask for God's forgiveness if they are not prepared to forgive?
- The Qur'an says that Muslims should forgive other people's sins against them and Muslims should obey the Qur'an as they believe it is the Word of God.

Depending on your area of study you have a choice of either a) Islam or b) Judaism topics. These are indicated by the letters 'a' and 'b' in the topic headings. Please read the topic relevant to your area of study.

Thinking points

In this topic you need to:

- think about Muslim teachings about peacemaking; and the importance of justice, forgiveness and reconciliation in peacemaking, including Surah 41:34–35
- understand the work of Muslims working for peace today; and what they do and why they try to work for peace
- be able to explain and evaluate the role of Muslims in peacemaking.

Useful words

Justice – the allocation of due reward and punishment

Reconciliation – bringing together people who were opposed to each other

Activities

1. Look at the photo of the London bus on page 333. What would seeing this bus make you think?
2. Do you think the Qur'anic command, 'Let there be no compulsion in religion' is a good idea?
3. Choose a Muslim organisation and explain how it works for peace today.

A Muslim woman holding a placard during a peace march.

- There are many hadith from the Prophet Muhammad about forgiving people who have offended others and bringing reconciliation to conflicts, and Muslims believe that they should follow the example of the Prophet.

Useful words

Ahmadiyya – a Muslim sect founded in Pakistan that is against war

The work of Muslims working for peace today

The **Ahmadiyya** sect is one of the Muslim groups which most clearly regards the message of Islam as a peaceful one. One of the mottos which appears on many of their publications is 'Love for all, hatred for none'. The Ahmadiyya movement began in Pakistan but has relocated its headquarters to London because of persecution in Pakistan. It is from London that this Muslim group promotes its message of worldwide peace.

The Ahmadiyya work for peace by:

- Holding an annual peace forum at which there is discussion with political leaders about how Islam could come together with other religions and tackle the causes of war, for example in 2014 there was discussion on how to attack the funding of terrorism.
- The group's leader, Hadhrat Mirza Marsoos Ahmad, goes around the world talking to major figures about peace and religion, for example in 2015 he met US leaders on Capitol Hill, the Dutch Parliament, and British MPs and government ministers.
- The group campaigns among Muslims on the need for human rights for everyone whatever their religion, especially in Muslim countries.
- Ahmadiyya is leading a campaign for Muslims to recognise the need for the separation of religion and the state to ensure the freedom of religion for all citizens.
- Ahmadiyya speaks out against any terrorist activities perpetrated in the name of Islam.

Another group teaching that Islam is a religion of peace is Muslim Peace Fellowship, founded in 1994. This group is dedicated to the theory and practice of Islamic non-violence and believes that *jihad* is the struggle to make a wise, just and compassionate society.

A red double-decker bus in London advertises 'United Against Extremism' by the Ahmadiyya Muslim community in the wake of the co-ordinated deadly terrorist attacks in November 2015, in Paris, France.

The Muslim Peace Fellowship was the first Muslim organisation specifically devoted to the theory and practice of Islamic non-violence and understands an 'unarmed struggle in pursuit of wise, just, and compassionate social transformation to be the original and enduring genius of the **Prophetic *jihad***'. The work of the group can be seen in some of its stated objectives:

- *To work against injustice and for peace in ourselves, our families, our communities, and our world.*
- *To affirm the commitment to peace on behalf of all Muslims.*
- *To explore and deepen our understanding of Islamic teachings about peace and nonviolence.*
- *To expose and transcend the vicious circle of religious stereotyping and false identity.*

(Muslim Peace Fellowship, https://mpf21.wordpress.com/about-2/)

The motto of the group 'Muslim Peace Fellowship' is the Qur'anic verse 'Let there be no compulsion in religion' (Surah 2:256).

Useful words

Prophetic *jihad* – *jihad* as understood and practised by the Prophet Muhammad

Activity

What do you think of the Muslim Peace Fellowship's understanding of *jihad*?

Practice questions

c Explain two reasons why forgiveness and reconciliation are important for Muslims. In your answer you must refer to a source of wisdom and authority.

d 'There can be no peace without justice.' Evaluate this statement considering arguments for and against. In your answer you should:

- refer to Muslim points of view
- reach a justified conclusion.

Summary

The Qur'an teaches that Muslims should be peacemakers and that the best way to do this is to try to remove injustice and forgive other people's sins, just as they hope God will forgive them. Two Muslim groups trying to bring peace to the world are the Ahmadiyya and the Muslim Peace Fellowship.

Topic 2.4.2b The role of Jews in peacemaking

Depending on your area of study you have a choice of either a) Islam or b) Judaism topics. These are indicated by the letters 'a' and 'b' in the topic headings. Please read the topic relevant to your area of study.

Thinking points

In this topic you need to:

- think about Jewish teachings about peacemaking; the importance of justice, forgiveness and reconciliation in peacemaking, including Pirkei Avot 1:18; and the work of Jews working for peace today, what they do and why they try to work for peace
- be able to explain and evaluate the role of Jews in peacemaking.

Jewish teachings about peacemaking

As we saw in the previous topic, Judaism is a religion of peace. However, Judaism also teaches that Jewish people should be peacemakers. The Tenakh teaches:

> *Turn from evil and do good; seek peace and pursue it.* (Psalm 34:14–16)

> *The Lord's justice will dwell in the desert, his righteousness live in the fertile field. The fruit of that righteousness will be peace; its effect will be quietness and confidence forever. My people will live in peaceful dwelling places, in secure homes, in undisturbed places of rest.* (Isaiah 32:17)

> *Look, there on the mountains, the feet of one who brings good news, who proclaims peace!* (Nahum 1:15)

The *amidah*, which is the central prayer of Judaism, concludes with these words:

> *He who makes peace in His heights, may He make peace for us and for all Israel. Now say, Amen.*

The great Rabbi Hillel said in Pirkei Avot 1:12:

> *Be of the disciples of Aaron, loving peace and pursuing peace, loving your fellow creatures and bringing them close to the Torah.*

> *Rabbi Shimon the son of Gamliel would say: By three things is the world sustained: law, truth and peace. As is stated (Zachariah 8:16), 'Truth, and a judgement of peace, you should administer at your [city] gates'.* (Pirkei Avot 1:18)

The importance of justice, forgiveness and reconciliation in peacemaking

Jews believe that **justice** is an important part of peacemaking because if a society and its laws are unjust, people will not obey its laws and will campaign against unjust laws causing trouble in society (for example, the civil rights campaign against laws refusing equality to black people in the southern USA in the 1960s disrupted normal life there). If the laws do not create a just society, people will think the legal system is not working and may start a civil war (for example, in Syria, the Syrian Sunni Muslims began a civil war because they thought the legal system of the Assad regime was treating them unfairly).

Judaism teaches that forgiveness and **reconciliation** are important in peacemaking because:

- In the ten days between Rosh Hashanah and Yom Kippur, Jews are expected to seek out anyone they have wronged and ask their forgiveness, so ending the conflict and becoming reconciled with them. They do this because on Yom Kippur, they are going to ask God to forgive them for all the wrongs they have done to God in the past year.

Useful words

Justice – the allocation of due reward and punishment

Reconciliation – bringing together people who were opposed to each other

Activities

1. Look at the quotation from Pirkei Avot 1:18. Do you think that justice and truth are essential before there can be peace?
2. Explain why Jews should be peacemakers.

Two demonstrators hold a banner for Jewish Voice for Peace in New York, USA.

- Judaism teaches that God forgives those who turn to him in true repentance, and the sign of true repentance is to seek forgiveness for your own sins and be prepared to forgive others their sins.
- The Tenakh encourages people to forgive those who wrong them and try to bring reconciliation, and Jewish people should follow the teachings of the Tenakh.
- The rabbis encourage Jewish people to forgive those who wrong them and become reconciled with them.
- The **Siddur** teaches that Jewish people should always try to forgive those who have wronged them when on their deathbed, before they ask God to forgive their sins.

The work of Jews working for peace today

To understand Jewish peacemaking, it is necessary to understand that there is conflict between Israel and the Palestinian people in the Middle East. The Palestinians want their own Palestinian state in areas which are currently controlled by Israel (known as the **Occupied Territories**). This was partly agreed in the Oslo Agreement (1993–5), but it has still not been put into practice as Israel is waiting for the Arab states to accept Israel's right to exist.

There are many Jewish organisations dedicated to working for peace, such as the Jewish Peace Fellowship and the Jewish Voice for Peace (both based in New York).

The Jewish Peace Fellowship is committed to non-violence, and it works for peace by:

- supporting **conscientious objectors** who refuse to be recruited into the Israeli military (all non-Arab Israeli citizens – men and women – over the age of eighteen must serve at least two years in the Israel Defence Forces)
- opposing Jewish involvement in all wars
- working for the reconciliation of Jews and Palestinians so that Israel can be at peace.

Activities

1. How do you think Jewish organisations should work for peace?
2. Look at the photo. What do you think protests like this can achieve?

Useful words

Siddur – the Orthodox prayer book

Occupied Territories – the Palestinian name for the West Bank and Gaza territories occupied by Israel since the Six-day War and the Yom Kippur War

Conscientious objector – a person who for reasons of conscience does not want to serve in the armed forces

The Jewish Voice for Peace is working to make peace by:

- ending the Israeli occupation of the West Bank, Gaza Strip and East Jerusalem
- bringing security and **self-determination** for Israelis and Palestinians
- achieving a just solution for Palestinian refugees based on principles established in international law
- organising the boycott, **divestment** and sanctions movement to encourage businesses involved in Israel's occupation of the West Bank to put pressure on the Israeli government to withdraw from the Occupied Territories.

Many Jews, especially those living in Israel, believe that they should work for peace by keeping Israel strong militarily so that eventually the Arabs and Palestinians will agree to Israel's right to exist.

Useful words

Self-determination – people deciding on their own future

Divestment – the process of selling off subsidiary business interests or investments

Practice questions

c Explain two reasons why forgiveness and reconciliation are important for Jews. In your answer you must refer to a source of wisdom and authority.

d 'There can be no peace without justice.' Evaluate this statement considering arguments for and against. In your answer you should:

- refer to Jewish points of view
- refer to different Jewish or non-religious points of view
- reach a justified conclusion.

Summary

Both the Tenakh and the Pirkei Avot teach that Jewish people should be peacemakers. They also teach that to make peace it is necessary to establish justice, be prepared to forgive and seek reconciliation as taught at Rosh Hashanah and Yom Kippur. The Middle East situation makes it difficult to make peace, but groups like the Jewish Peace Fellowship are trying to do this.

Topic 2.4.3 Attitudes to conflict

The problems caused by conflict

War and conflict cause many problems ranging from casualties and homes being damaged or destroyed to economic collapse. These problems are explored below.

Casualties

Death and injury, especially of civilian populations, are the most obvious problem. In the Second World War over 60 million people were killed, with about 60 per cent of the deaths being civilians. But current conflicts are no better. A United Nations report published in January 2016 says that nearly 19,000 civilians were killed in Iraq between January 2014 and October 2015, another 36,245 were injured and about 3.2 million people were **internally displaced**, including a million school-aged children. Much of the suffering was attributed to Isis, the Islamist terror group which has declared an Islamic caliphate across the vast stretches of territory it holds in Iraq and neighbouring Syria. In Syria it is estimated that the civil war which began in 2011 has claimed the lives of 181,000 soldiers, 70,000 civilians and at least 12,000 children.

Displacement

Conflict can create large numbers of refugees as civilians flee the war zones and often the armed forces involved forcibly move populations. During the Second World War, the Nazis deported between 7 million and 9 million Europeans, mostly to Germany. Within months of Germany's surrender in May 1945, the Allies **repatriated** to their home countries more than 6 million displaced persons. Between 1.5 million and 2 million displaced persons refused repatriation and ended up in refugee camps in Europe. The United Nations High Commission for Refugees (UNHCR) was set up in 1951 to help return home the estimated 1 million people still uprooted after the Second World War. The latest figures available show that the UNHCR was looking after 13 million refugees in mid-2014. Since then, the civil war in Syria has led to more than 3 million refugees from Syria fleeing to Turkey and Lebanon alone. Refugees from the Syrian conflict are fleeing to Europe overland from Turkey and refugees from the many conflicts in Africa are fleeing to Europe across the Mediterranean from Libya.

Expense

Economic problems are a major result of conflict. Wars cost money for weapons and military personnel, but they also disrupt the economy of the countries involved in the conflict, and cause social and economic problems in the countries where the refugees end up. The costs for governments hosting refugees include providing the influx of people with healthcare, education, housing and other social benefits. In the longer term, migrants could be absorbed into the labour force and eventually boost consumer demand, driving economic growth.

Thinking points

In this topic you need to:

- think about the nature of conflict and the problems it causes within society, and the causes of conflict
- consider *either* Muslim responses to the causes, including Qur'an 2:190, *or* Jewish responses to the causes, including Isaiah 2:1–5
- think about Situation Ethics and conflict
- be able to explain and evaluate different religious and non-religious responses to the problems caused by conflict.

Useful words

Internally displaced – being forced to move your home because of conflict, but staying in the same country

Repatriate – to return refugees to their place of origin

Activity

Can you think of any other problems conflict causes?

*There is hardly a conflict in the world today – Iraq, Russia, Indonesia, the Holy Land – without a religious dimension. And that is why finding common ground between different faiths is crucial for world peace ... It is important not to see all Muslims as supporting terrorism. This is like linking the Irish to terrorism because of the IRA. It doesn't work that way. Many Muslims in the world don't agree with terrorism. We can't condemn them all. I think religious differences are used to set people against each other. Religion isn't usually the cause of the conflict, but it's an added factor. The underlying problems are usually social or political. (Archbishop Michael Fitzgerald, president of the Vatican's Pontifical Council for **Inter-religious Dialogue**)*

Useful words

Inter-religious dialogue – discussions between different religions
Nationalism – a strong feeling of belief in the rightness of one's native country
Ethnicity – having the characteristics of a certain race or culture

Syrian refugees from Kobane in a camp in Turkey.

Causes of conflict

Although the Second World War, the last world war, ended over 70 years ago, wars are still occurring all over the world. The most generally accepted reasons for wars occurring are described below.

Religion

Wars often occur because of religious differences:

- There may be two religious groups, each of which wants to be dominant and each of which feels it has been badly treated by the other. For example, the war between Christians and Muslims in the Central African Republic.
- A specific area of a country may be largely one religion, but the country as a whole is a different religion. For example, the majority of Kashmir is Muslim, but Kashmir is part of India, which is Hindu. The Muslims of Kashmir are fighting to become part of the Muslim state of Pakistan.
- There are differences within a religion and one religious group attacks the other for having different beliefs. For example, the civil war in Syria where the government forces are Shi'a Muslims and the rebel forces are Sunni Muslims.

Politics, history and culture

A major cause of wars is connected with issues of politics (especially the concept of **nationalism**) and **ethnicity** (which is often connected with history and culture):

- One form of nationalism is the belief that each separate ethnic group should have its own country because it has a different culture. This leads minority ethnic groups to fight civil wars to establish an independent state. For example, the Tutsi rebels in the Democratic Republic of Congo and the ethnic Albanians in Kosovo.
- Another form of nationalism is to insist that any minority ethnic groups should be removed from the country so that the nation is only one ethnic group. This can lead to the genocide of an ethnic group such as the Tutsis in Rwanda in 1994.

Activity

Should religious people do more to help people fleeing conflict?

- Tensions between ethnic groups often arise in countries which have been artificially created as a result of colonialism. This has happened a lot in Africa where countries such as Sudan and Kenya were created artificially by European conquerors, leading to the current civil war in South Sudan.
- In the Democratic Republic of Congo ethnicity was used by two different political groups to gain power – one group supported by Uganda and Rwanda, the other supported by Zimbabwe, Angola and Namibia. The United Nations had to bring the two political groups together before it could begin to end the conflict.
- The Korean War began in 1950 when Communist North Korea invaded South Korea with the aim of uniting the country under communism. A truce was declared in 1953 after the United Nations fought a war against North Korea and China, but there is still no peace and there are still outbreaks of conflict.

Resources

Wars can often occur if a country has resources that another country wants or needs:

- Some people think that the two Gulf Wars occurred because the West wanted to make sure it would have access to the enormous oil reserves of the Middle East.
- There are two ongoing conflicts in Sudan whose origins probably lie in resources. The conflict in Dharfur is possibly about access to water, although there is also an ethnic element, with the Arab Sudanese government accused of carrying out ethnic cleansing of the black African people of Dharfur. The conflict in South Sudan is probably about ownership of the vast oil wealth, even though it was first thought to be a religious war between the Christian South and the Muslim North.
- Economic problems in one country can lead to conflict in another country. For example, the economic crisis in Zimbabwe has led to mass migration of refugees looking for food and work into South Africa. Some South Africans have objected and begun to attack the refugees.

At his Nuremberg trial, the Nazi war criminal Hermann Goering described how easy it is to organise a war:

> *Why, of course the people don't want war. That is understood. But, after all, it is the leaders of a country who determine the policy and it is always a simple matter to drag the people along, whether it is a democracy, or a fascist dictatorship, or a parliament, or a communist dictatorship. Voice or no voice, the people can always be brought to the bidding of the leaders. That is easy. All you have to do is tell them they are being attacked, and denounce the peacemakers for lack of* ***patriotism*** *and exposing the country to danger. (Hermann Goering, Nazi general, at his trial for war crimes, 1945)*

Activity

Look at the quotation from Goering below. Do you think patriotism (love for, or devotion to, one's country) can be dangerous?

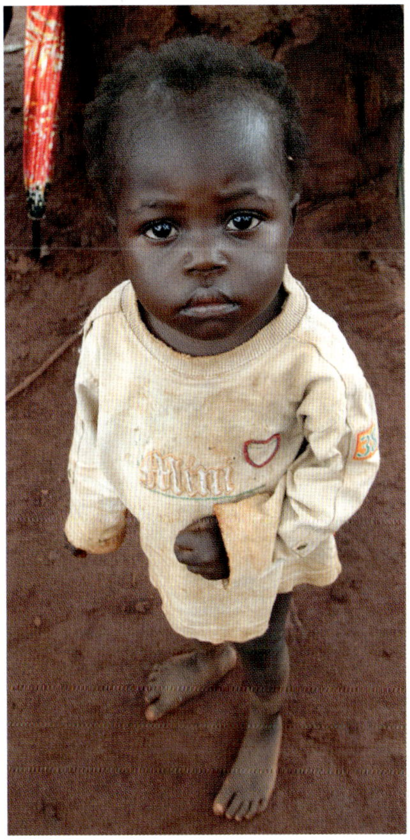

A refugee from the conflict in the Central African Republic.

> *Fight in the cause of God those who fight you, but do not transgress the limits; for God loveth not the transgressors. (Surah 2:190)*

Useful words

Patriotism – love for, or devotion to, one's country

This is what Isaiah son of Amoz saw concerning Judah and Jerusalem: In the last days the mountain of the Lord's temple will be established as the highest of the mountains; it will be exalted above the hills, and all nations will stream to it. Many peoples will come and say, 'Come, let us go up to the mountain of the Lord, to the temple of the God of Jacob. He will teach us his ways, so that we may walk in his paths.' The law will go out from Zion, the word of the Lord from Jerusalem. He will judge between the nations and will settle disputes for many peoples. They will beat their swords into ploughshares and their spears into pruning hooks. Nation will not take up sword against nation, nor will they train for war anymore. Come, descendants of Jacob, let us walk in the light of the Lord. (Isaiah 2:1–5)

Muslim responses to the causes of war

Most Muslims believe that if a war is just (see Topic 2.4.5, page 345) then a Muslim must fight in it. This means that Muslims must fight if they are attacked because this is what the Qur'an says, and Muslims believe the Qur'an is the Word of God. Also, Muhammad is the great example for Muslims of how to live their lives (the perfect exemplar) and he fought in wars of self-defence; therefore, so must Muslims.

However, to fight in a war, Muslims must be very clear about the causes of the conflict. Any war in which they could be classed as the aggressor could not be fought by a faithful Muslim. Muslims therefore could not be involved in the following sorts of conflict:

- a war to take resources from someone else
- forcing another country or people to become Muslim
- changing the political leadership or ideology of another country
- changing the culture of a country.

Muslims should always be wary of going to war because 'Jaber reported that the Messenger of Allah said, "War is a deception"' (hadith quoted by Bukhari and Muslim).

Jewish responses to the causes of war

Most Jews believe that if a war is just (see Topic 2.4.5, page 345) then a good Jew must fight in it. This means that Jews must fight if they are attacked because this is what the Torah says. The Talmud says that wars must be fought if they are *milchemet mitzvah* – that is, if God has commanded it. A *milchemet mitzvah* would occur if Jewish people are attacked by an enemy, if a pre-emptive strike will stop an enemy from attacking or if the war is going to the aid of a country that has been attacked.

However, to fight in a war, Jews must be very clear about the causes of the conflict. Any war in which they could be classed as the aggressor could not be fought by a good Jew, so they could not be involved in the following sorts of conflict:

- a war to take resources from someone else
- forcing another country or people to become Jewish
- changing the political leadership or ideology of another country
- changing the culture of a country.

Jews should always be wary of going to war because, as the Midrash says, 'The Torah was given to establish peace'.

Atheist and Humanist responses to the causes of war

Most Humanists believe that a good way to end wars is to get rid of religion. They believe that all religion is false because it is not based on reason and scientific evidence. So Humanists believe that a way of peacemaking is to challenge religious leaders and try to show believers where their religion is wrong, for example showing Muslims that they cannot prove the Qur'an is the Word of God and showing Jews that they cannot prove the Torah came from God.

Activity

How should *either* Muslims *or* Jews respond to the causes of conflict?

Humanists also believe in making the United Nations stronger so that it can end wars with a peacekeeping force and make the world a fairer place so that wars do not begin. Many Humanists are pacifists and so they would not fight in wars.

Many atheists have the same ideas about war as Humanists, but some would have a similar response to Muslims and Jews and fight in Just Wars.

Situation Ethics and war

The concept of Situation Ethics has been covered in Topic 1.2.6 (page 57). Muslims, Jews and Humanists often apply the idea to the causes of war. They will look at the causes and effects of a war and make a decision based on what will produce the most loving outcome. For example, they may be against war but if a country has been invaded and its people are being wiped out (ethnic cleansing), they may decide that the best solution is to declare war on the invaders. Likewise, people who think war can be justified might decide not to fight if the result will end in nuclear weapons destroying most of the world (see Topic 2.4.7, page 352).

Practice questions

c Explain two reasons why conflicts occur.

d 'Religion is the main cause of wars.' Evaluate this statement considering arguments for and against. In your answer you should:

- refer to Jewish or Muslim points of view
- refer to non-religious points of view and Situation Ethics
- reach a justified conclusion.

Summary

There are many different causes of conflict, including politics, history, culture and religion. Conflict in turn causes problems, such as casualties, displacement and financial problems.

Muslims will only fight in a war if they believe they have to, for example in self-defence.

Jews believe that they should fight in wars if they are just wars or if God commands it.

Jews and Muslims would not fight in a war where they could be classed as the aggressor.

Humanists believe that the best way to bring peace is to get rid of religion.

Topic 2.4.4 Pacifism

Thinking points

In this topic, you need to:

- think about the nature and history of pacifism
- consider *either* Muslim teachings about passive resistance and an example such as the Arab Spring *or* Jewish teachings about passive resistance and an example of its use, including Emanuel Ringelblum
- be able to explain and evaluate different religious and non-religious attitudes to pacifism.

Useful words

Pacifism – opposition to war
Militarism – belief that a country should have strong armed forces and be prepared to use them aggressively
Sermon on the Mount – Jesus' description of Christian living

He (Moses) said, 'O my Lord! I have power only over myself and my brother: so separate us from this rebellious people'. (Surah 5:28)

Activities

1. Where does the term pacifism come from?
2. Look at the photo of the Quakers. What do you think people would need to do to wage peace?
3. Write an outline of the history of pacifism.

What is pacifism?

Pacifism is opposition to war, **militarism** or violence. The word pacifism was coined by the French peace campaigner Émil Arnaud (1864–1921) and adopted by other peace activists at the tenth Universal Peace Congress in Glasgow in 1901.

The origins of pacifism go back to the Roman Empire, when several Roman writers wrote books against war. The most famous of these was Seneca the Younger, who criticised warfare in his book *Naturales Quaestiones* (written about 65CE).

Most modern pacifists can probably trace their origins to Christian teachings. Jesus taught in his **Sermon on the Mount** that Christians should not resist evil and that if they are hit on the right cheek they should turn and offer the left. Christian pacifists take this to mean that Christians should not fight and so cannot take part in wars.

In the Sermon, Jesus also taught that Christians should love their enemies. It seems impossible to love someone you are trying to destroy and so this teaching of Jesus also seems to mean that Christians should not be involved in wars.

For the first 300 years of Christianity, Christians refused to fight in wars. The great Christian leaders (for example, Origen, Tertullian and Cyprian) all argued that Christians must not be involved in war and must be pacifists.

These ideas re-emerged in the Reformation, when peace Churches such as the Religious Society of Friends (Quakers), the Amish, the Mennonites and the Church of the Brethren were established. These ideas played an important part in William Wilberforce's campaign to end slavery.

A group of Quakers at a peace rally near Parliament in London.

However, pacifism also developed among **Humanists**, beginning with Erasmus, who argued strongly against war in *In Praise of Folly* (1509), followed in the late eighteenth century by the philosophers Rousseau, Kant and Bentham, who argued that war is a waste of human resources.

During the late nineteenth century, peace groups were formed and international peace congresses promoted pacifism and the end of war. An important thinker who made a major contribution to pacifist thinking was Leo Tolstoy (1828–1910, the author of *War and Peace*), whose book *The Kingdom of God is Within You* gives a detailed history and defence of pacifism; a book which had a great influence on Gandhi and his non-violence movement to gain Indian independence without fighting.

Many pacifists became conscientious objectors during the two world wars and after the development of nuclear weapons they formed groups such as Campaign for Nuclear Disarmament (CND) in the UK and Peace Action in the USA to try to prevent a nuclear war.

Muslims and pacifism

Most Muslims would not agree with passive resistance. The Qur'an encourages all Muslims to 'struggle in the way of Islam'. The Arabic word for struggle is *jihad,* which is often translated as Holy War. However, Muslims believe in two forms of *jihad*: greater and lesser. The greater *jihad* is the struggle to make oneself perfectly Muslim. This involves Muslims struggling with themselves and their desires, and not fighting. Lesser *jihad* is the struggle with forces outside oneself to remove evil from society. Consequently, there is no idea of pacifism or turning the other cheek in Islam. The next topic shows that if Muslims are attacked, they are expected to fight back.

However, there is a tradition of **passive resistance** based on the story of Moses and Aaron. This is referred to in Surah 5:28 where the two brothers refused to fight the Israelites who rebelled against God and instead separated themselves from them. The democratic movements in Middle Eastern countries in the Arab Spring of 2011 were based on pacifism and passive resistance. Muslims protesting against the lack of democracy in their countries did so in a non-violent way. A major example of this was the demonstrations in Tahrir Square in Cairo which led to the overthrow of President Mubarak of Egypt. Although government forces used violence and the demonstrators sometimes responded with violence, in the main they succeeded in overthrowing the president by passive resistance. Although the rebellion in Tunisia was mainly non-violent, those in Syria and Libya which began with passive resistance are now full-scale civil wars.

A famous Muslim pacifist was Khan Abdul Ghaffar Khan (1890–1988). He was a friend of Gandhi and organised a non-violent movement campaigning for independence from British rule. He wanted a united independent India (just as Gandhi did) rather than Pakistan and Bangladesh being separate Muslim states.

Judaism and pacifism

Peace is the ideal for all Jews. Jews have always used '*Shalom alaikum*' – 'peace be with you' – instead of hello. The perfect society which Jews call the Messianic Age is thought of in terms of peace, when

> *He will judge between many peoples and will settle disputes for strong nations far and wide. They will beat their swords into ploughshares and their spears into pruning hooks. Nation will not take up sword against nation, nor will they train for war anymore. (Micah 4:3)*

Useful words

Humanist – a follower of the non-religious philosophy based on liberal human values

Passive resistance – non-violent opposition to authority

The Arab Spring refers to demonstrations and protests that took place across the Middle East in 2011. The purpose of these was to fight against social injustice and demand political freedom.

Activities

1. Do you think pacifism is a good idea?
2. Why do you think there are so few pacifists in *either* Islam *or* Judaism?

Albert Einstein (1879–1955): physicist, pacifist and Jew.

However, although Jews should seek peace, there is no concept of pacifism in Judaism. The Tenakh is full of accounts of wars in which God has been involved. Furthermore, most Jews feel that their experiences in the Holocaust, when the Jews had no army and very few weapons to defend themselves against the Nazis, meant that most Jews in Europe could only offer passive resistance, and that resulted in 6 million of them being murdered.

A great example of Jewish passive resistance was Emanuel Ringelblum (1900–44). He was a Polish historian and social worker who, along with 400,000 other Jews, was herded into the Warsaw Ghetto when the Nazis captured Poland at the start of the Second World War. Ringelblum decided that the best form of resistance was to keep an archive of everything the Nazis did which would later be able to be used as evidence against them when they lost the war. It is known as the Oneg Shabbat Archive. The papers were buried in milk churns and found after the war. They document the deportation and extermination of Polish Jewry and are compelling evidence of the Holocaust. However, the Jews in the ghetto abandoned passive resistance as more and more of them were killed and, in 1943, they fought back in the Warsaw Ghetto Uprising. Nowadays most Jews feel that their experiences in the Holocaust mean that they must keep a strong military to protect the Jewish people from any form of **anti-Semitism**.

Activity

Find out for yourself about the pacifism of *either* Khan Abdul Ghaffar Khan *or* Albert Einstein.

Useful words

Anti-Semitism – hostility to or prejudice against Jews

Humanism and pacifism

Humanists are opposed to war. They helped to set up the United Nations, and were the first directors of several of its agencies. Some Humanists are pacifists and have been conscientious objectors because human life is all the more valuable if you do not believe in an afterlife, and Humanists do not believe in life after death. Those Humanists who are not pacifists would think very carefully before supporting any war, because of the loss of life involved. Wars are hugely destructive, ruining lives, wasting resources and degrading the environment. Humanists think that wars fought over religion are ridiculous because they consider religion to be an absurd reason for killing other people. They also criticise the part that organised religions occasionally play in encouraging and supporting wars.

Summary

Pacifism is opposition to war and probably originated with the early Christians who refused to fight in wars. There was a growth in pacifism during the nineteenth century resulting in conscientious objectors in the world wars. Many Muslims and Jews disagree with pacifism because of the teachings of their holy books, but there are pacifist groups in both religions.

Practice questions

c Explain two reasons why there are so few pacifists in either Judaism or Islam. In your answer you must refer to a source of wisdom and authority.

d 'Pacifism and religion should go hand in hand.' Evaluate this statement considering arguments for and against. In your answer you should:

- refer to Jewish or Muslim points of view
- refer to different Muslim points of view and ethical theories
- refer to non-religious points of view
- reach a justified conclusion.

Topic 2.4.5 Just War theory

The nature and history of Just War

A Just War is a war that is fought for the right reasons and in the right way.

Although it is generally agreed that wars are bad because of their effects, it is also generally agreed that, in certain circumstances, wars are unavoidable and so can be justified. The theory used to decide whether a war is justified is associated with St Thomas Aquinas (*c.*1225–74) by Christians, but it was developed in Hinduism, Islam, Judaism and Buddhism long before that.

The Just War theory

Today, it is generally agreed that a war is just if:

- the cause of the war is just (for example, it is fought in self-defence when another country attacks, or it is trying to remove a great injustice such as **genocide**)
- it is being fought by the authority of the United Nations
- it is being fought with the intention of restoring peace
- it is begun as a **last resort** – that is, all non-violent methods of trying to end the conflict have been tried and failed
- there is a reasonable chance of success; it would be wrong to waste lives in a war if there is no chance of achieving its aims
- the methods used avoid killing civilians; although this would not ban such things as bombs aimed at weapons factories hitting hospitals accidentally, it would ban any methods which deliberately try to destroy civilian targets to make the civilian population afraid
- only **proportional methods** of response are used; for example, it would not be just to destroy a country with nuclear weapons because it had invaded a small island.

Situation Ethics and Just War

The nature of modern warfare means there are some difficulties involved in a war being regarded as just when modern weapons are used. Modern weapons make it almost impossible to avoid harming civilians and some would say it is virtually impossible to fight a Just War in the modern world.

Consequently, Muslims, Jews, Christians and non-religious people tend to use something like Situation Ethics to determine whether a war is just. They look at the circumstances of the war and try to determine whether not fighting the war would be more unjust than fighting it. If they determine that:

- the cause of the war is just
- attempts to solve the conflict peacefully have been tried
- there is a chance of success
- the military try to avoid civilian casualties as far as is humanly possible

Thinking points

In this topic you need to:

- think about the nature, history and importance of the Just War theory; the conditions of a Just War; whether Just War is possible with links to Situation Ethics; and Muslim or Jewish teachings on Just War
- be able to explain and evaluate different religious and non-religious attitudes to Just War.

Useful words

Genocide – the deliberate killing of a large group of people, especially those of a particular nation or ethnic group

Last resort – after all other methods have been tried

Proportional methods – using weapons of the same factor as those used against you

Activities

1. Do you think the Just War theory is important?
2. Can bombing which destroys people's homes ever be just?

Rescuers attempt to find survivors in a bombed home in Syria.

> *And why should ye not fight in the cause of God and of those who, being weak and ill-treated – men, women and children, whose cry is 'Our Lord! Rescue us from this town, whose people are oppressors; and raise for us from Thee one who will protect'. (Surah 4:75)*

Useful words

Aggressor – someone who attacks without being provoked

Weapons of mass destruction – weapons which can destroy large areas and/or large numbers of people

then they would consider a modern war to be a Just War. After all, it must be just for a country to defend itself if it is attacked by an **aggressor**. This argument is dealt with in Topic 2.4.7 (page 352): whether it is just to use **weapons of mass destruction** against an invader of one's country if their use will devastate the lives of millions of innocent people.

Muslims and Just War

There are strict rules in Islam about when a war can be fought justifiably by Muslims:

- It must be fought for a just cause (either Islam is being attacked, or people are suffering an injustice, or in self-defence).
- It must be a last resort (all possible non-violent methods of solving the problem must have been tried).
- It must be authorised and led by a Muslim authority.
- It must be fought in such a way as to cause the minimum amount of suffering.
- Innocent civilians (especially the old, the young and women) must not be attacked.
- It must be ended as soon as the enemy lays down their arms.

Most Muslims would agree that if a war fulfils these conditions then a Muslim must fight in it. The reasons for this view are:

- The Qur'an says that Muslims must fight if they are attacked and Muslims believe that the Qur'an is the Word of God.

- Muhammad is the great example for Muslims in how to live, and he fought in wars.
- Muhammad made many statements (hadith) about war which say that Muslims must fight in Just Wars.
- The Qur'an says that anyone who dies fighting in a Just War will go straight to heaven.

However, some Muslims feel that the nature of modern weapons means that no war can be a Just War, and so they oppose wars.

Judaism and Just War

Judaism teaches that it is acceptable for Jews to fight in a Just War, by which it means a war which fulfils these conditions:

- It is fought in self-defence against an enemy attack.
- It is a self-defensive pre-emptive strike to stop an enemy from attacking when they are about to attack.
- It is fought to help a country that has been attacked.
- The war must be a last resort.
- Non-violent solutions have been tried first.
- Civilians should not be targeted.
- There must be attempts to limit damage caused by the war.

Wars fought in self-defence or to help a country under attack are called ***milchemet mitzvah***, a war of command, and so must be fought. Wars fought for other just reasons are called ***milchemet reshut***, optional wars, and do not have to be fought, but if they are fought, they must fulfil all the other requirements of a Just War.

The reasons for Jewish attitudes to war are:

- A *mitzvah* is a command from God which all Jews have to obey, so they have to take part in a *milchemet mitzvah*.
- In the Tenakh there are many accounts of how Israel was able to keep its independence by defending itself when attacked.
- The experience of Jews before and during the Second World War, when they did not have a Jewish army, which resulted in 6 million Jews being murdered by the Nazis in the Holocaust.

Practice questions

c Explain two reasons why either Jews or Muslims will fight in a Just War. In your answer you must refer to a source of wisdom and authority.

d 'Religious people should never fight in wars.' Evaluate this statement considering arguments for and against. In your answer you should:

- refer to Jewish or Muslim points of view
- refer to non-religious points of view
- reach a justified conclusion.

Activities

1. Do you think it is possible to fight a Just War in the modern world?
2. Read the quotation from either Surah 4:75 on page 346 or Deuteronomy 20:19–20 and explain how it relates to the Just War theory.

When you lay siege to a city for a long time, fighting against it to capture it, do not destroy its trees by putting an axe to them, because you can eat their fruit. Do not cut them down. Are the trees people, that you should besiege them? However, you may cut down trees that you know are not fruit trees and use them to build siege works until the city at war with you falls.
(Deuteronomy 20:19–20)

Useful words

Milchemet mitzvah – a war of commandment which Jews must fight in

Milchemet reshut – optional war which Jews do not have to fight in but which must be fought in a just way

Summary

A Just War is one fought for the right reasons in the right way. The theory is old and is closely connected with religion. All religions say that their followers should only fight in a war if it is just. The development of modern weapons has made it more difficult to say that a war is just, because of the difficulty of protecting civilians.

Topic 2.4.6 Holy War

Thinking points

In this topic you need to:

- think about the nature of a Holy War and teachings about war and peace; and consider *either* Muslim teachings about war (Harb al-Maqadis), including lesser *jihad*, *or* Jewish teachings about war and peace, including ideas about *milchemet mitzvah*
- think about atheist and Humanist attitudes towards Holy War
- be able to explain and evaluate different religious and non-religious attitudes to Holy War.

Useful words

Crusade – a war for a religious or moral purpose

Activities

1. What is a Holy War?
2. Why do the crusades fit the criteria for a Holy War?
3. Look at the picture. Do you think Jesus would have led a Holy War?

The nature of Holy War

Religion and war have gone hand in hand for as long as history has recorded warfare. In the wars of the past, armies were blessed by priests as they set off for battle and very often carried signs of the faith with them. However, for a war to be regarded as a Holy War it needs to have the following features:

- It must be fought to achieve a religious goal.
- It must be authorised by a religious leader.
- It must promise a spiritual reward for those who fight in the war.

The nature of a Holy War can be seen in the first **crusade** (1095–9). It was called by Pope Urban II (so it was authorised by a religious leader) to free Jerusalem and the Holy Land from Muslim invaders and bring them back to Christian control (so it had a religious objective). Urban promised that those taking part would receive a reward in heaven and that any who died on the crusade would have their sins forgiven and so would go straight to heaven (so there was the promise of a spiritual reward for those taking part).

Many of the wars fought in the name of religion do conform to the Holy War conditions, but not all of them. Certainly, Holy Wars have had serious effects, as can be seen in the horrors that have been committed when followers of a religion have believed that their religion gave them the right to persecute or even fight wars against followers of other religions. When the Christian Church launched the Crusades to regain control of the Holy Land by killing Muslims in the sign of the cross, historians reckon that at least a million, and possibly as many as 3 million, people were killed.

Holy Wars have resulted in great bloodshed. The sixteenth-century French Wars of Religion fought between Catholics and Protestants had between 2 million and 3 million casualties. The Thirty Years' War, fought in seventeenth-century Europe between Catholics and Protestants, had

Peter the Hermit preaching the first crusade, *c.*1095.

at least 3 million casualties and possibly up to 11 million. At the present time, fighting between different Muslim groups in Iraq has led to as many as 100,000 casualties, while the United Nations estimates over 250,000 casualties in the conflict in the Syrian civil war, where most government supporters are Shi'a Muslims and most of the rebels are Sunni Muslims.

Muslim teachings about war and peace

Holy War is known as **Harb al-Muqadis** in Islam. According to the Shari'ah, a Holy War can be fought:

- to defend Islam
- to strengthen Islam
- to protect the freedom of Muslims to practise their faith
- to protect Muslims against attack
- to put right a wrong.

Any Holy War would be regarded as a lesser *jihad* because it would be part of the struggle to protect Islam and make the world the abode of peace.

However, Islamic lawyers today believe that a Holy War can only be called against an aggressor which threatens Islam; and even if a war follows this rule, it can only be called a Muslim Holy War if:

- it is a last resort (all possible non-violent methods of solving the problem must have been tried)
- it has been authorised and led by a religious leader chosen by the whole Muslim community and renowned for his piety and religion
- all the soldiers fighting in the war are faithful Muslims well versed in the teachings of Islam
- it has a prospect of success
- it will be fought in such a way as to cause the minimum amount of suffering
- it will protect innocent civilians, especially the old, the young and women
- it will be ended as soon as the enemy lays down their arms.

Most Muslims would agree that if a Holy War fulfils these conditions then a Muslim must fight in it. This is because the Qur'an says that Muslims must fight if they are attacked and Muslims believe that the Qur'an is the Word of God. Muhammad is the great example for Muslims in how to live, and although he fought in wars, the hadith from Muhammad about war show how it must be limited to be a Holy or Just War:

Do not kill any child, any woman, or any elder or sick person. (Hadith from Sunan Abu Dawud)

Do not kill the monks in monasteries, and do not kill those sitting in places of worship. (Hadith from Musnad Ahmad Ibn Hanbal)

Do not destroy the villages and towns, do not spoil the cultivated fields and gardens, and do not slaughter the cattle. (Hadith from Sahih Bukhari and Sunan Abu Dawud)

No one may punish with fire except the Lord of Fire. (Hadith from Sunan Abu Dawud)

Useful words

Harb al-Muqadis – Muslim Holy War

But when the forbidden months are past, then fight and slay the pagans wherever you find them, and seize them, beleaguer them, and lie in wait for them in every stratagem of war; but if they repent and establish regular prayers and practise regular charity, then open the way for them; for God is Oft-forgiving, Most Merciful. (Surah 9:5)

But if the enemy incline towards peace, do thou (also) incline towards peace, and trust in Allah. for He is One that heareth and knoweth (all things). (Surah 8:61)

The World March for Peace and Nonviolence. The march, which began in New Zealand on 2 October 2009, the 140th anniversary of Gandhi's birth, entered the northern Greek city of Thessaloniki as part of its 90-day journey that would eventually include all five continents. The event was organised by World Without Wars and Violence – an international organisation launched by the Humanist movement – which has been working since 1994 in the fields of pacifism and non-violence.

Jewish teachings about war and peace

Judaism teaches that Jews must fight in Holy Wars which meet the conditions of *milchemet mitzvah* because such wars are a *mitzvah*, and Jews should obey all the *mitzvot*. The conditions for a *milchemet mitzvah* are as follows:

- It has been commanded by God (as when God ordered Joshua to fight for the Promised Land).
- Jews are being attacked by an enemy.
- A pre-emptive strike is needed to stop an enemy from attacking Jews, but only when they are about to attack.
- War is needed to help a country that has been attacked.

Some Jews would be cautious about fighting a *milchemet mitzvah* because of the difficulties of knowing whether a war has been commanded by God. They would also want to be sure that it would be conducted in line with the requirements of the Just War theory.

Activities

1. Look at the banner above. Do you agree with it? Do you think it is a good campaign?
2. Look at the Humanist quotations on page 351. What do you think of them?
3. Look at either the Muslim or Jewish quotations from holy books. Do you think God would actually approve of Holy Wars?

However, Jews believe that their great King David fought Holy Wars to establish the kingdom of Israel and 2 Samuel 22 contains a song of praise David wrote thanking and praising God for giving him victory over his enemies:

> *I called to the Lord, who is worthy of praise, and have been saved from my enemies ... It is God who arms me with strength and keeps my way secure ... He makes my feet like the feet of a deer; he causes me to stand on the heights. He trains my hands for battle; my arms can bend a bow of bronze ... You armed me with strength for battle; you humbled my adversaries before me. You made my enemies turn their backs in flight, and I destroyed my foes ... The Lord lives! Praise be to my Rock! Exalted be my God, the Rock, my Saviour! ... He gives his king great victories; he shows unfailing kindness to his anointed, to David and his descendants forever.*

Faith: a firm belief for which there is no evidence. (Bertrand Russell, Human Society in Ethics and Politics, 1954)

My country is the world, and my religion is to do good. (Thomas Paine, The Rights of Man, *1791)*

Atheist and Humanist attitudes to Holy War

Both atheists and Humanists would regard the concept of a Holy War as indefensible. As far as they are both concerned, religion is misguided. There is no God and so the truth about life is to be found in reason and science. Most Humanists and atheists would accept the Just War theory as that is based on reason and moral values. However, to fight a war based on religious ideas and in response to a religious leader would seem ridiculous to both Humanists and atheists.

Practice questions

c Explain two reasons why either Jews or Muslims might regard a war as a holy war. In your answer you must refer to a source of wisdom and authority.

d 'No war should ever be called holy.' Evaluate this statement considering arguments for and against. In your answer you should:

- refer to Jewish or Muslim points of view
- refer to different Muslim points of view
- reach a justified conclusion.

Summary

A Holy War is a war fought for a religious goal, called by a religious leader and in which those who fight gain a spiritual reward. There have been many Holy Wars with lots of casualties.

Muslims believe that they should fight in Holy Wars if they are called to defend Islam because that is the teaching of the Shari'ah and the lesser *jihad*, but they must not harm children, women or the elderly.

Jews believe that they should fight in Holy Wars if they are called to defend Jewish people because such wars are *milchemet mitzvah* and are a command of God. However, they must be fought like a Just War.

Atheists and Humanists think that Holy Wars are wrong.

Topic 2.4.7 Weapons of mass destruction

Thinking points

In this topic you need to:

- think about problems and benefits of weapons of mass destruction (WMD), Muslim or Jewish attitudes towards the use of such weapons, and Humanist and atheist attitudes towards the use of WMD
- be able to explain and evaluate different religious, humanist and atheist attitudes to WMD.

Useful words

Biological weapons – weapons that make use of some kind of virus or disease to infect millions of people

Nuclear weapons – devices that explode through a nuclear reaction releasing a huge amount of energy

Intercontinental ballistic missiles – rockets that carry nuclear warheads over vast distances

Types of weapons of mass destruction

Nuclear, chemical and **biological weapons** are grouped together and referred to as weapons of mass destruction (WMD).

Nuclear weapons

Atomic bombs were first made towards the end of the Second World War. In 1945, the war in Europe had ended with the surrender of Germany, but the USA and Britain were still fighting the Asian war against Japan. They had to decide whether to attack Japan, risking losing hundreds of thousands of soldiers' lives, or to bring the war to a quick end by using their new weapon. On 6 August 1945, the Americans dropped an atomic bomb on Hiroshima, killing 84,000 people. The Japanese still did not surrender and three days later the Americans dropped a second bomb on Nagasaki, killing 40,000 people and bringing an immediate end to the war.

Since then, defence scientists have developed **nuclear weapons** considerably. The hydrogen bomb is 1000 times more powerful than the atomic bombs dropped on Japan. The neutron bomb (developed in the 1970s) is an enhanced radiation weapon designed to kill or disable people by radiation while leaving all the buildings intact.

The first atomic bombs were dropped from aircraft whereas modern nuclear weapons can be delivered by ballistic missiles, either from land sites or from submarines. These missiles have rocket motors to blast them above the earth's atmosphere, then follow an unpowered ballistic trajectory to their target (mainly still above the atmosphere). **Intercontinental ballistic missiles** have a range of up to 10,000 kilometres. The UK's missiles are known as Trident.

The United Nations has 190 member countries, but only eight are known or widely considered to have nuclear weapons. In order of their acquisition of nuclear weapons, these countries are as follows:

- the USA
- Russia
- the UK
- France
- China
- India
- Pakistan.

Most countries believe that Israel has nuclear weapons, but it has never officially acknowledged possession and is not known to have conducted a nuclear test. Most experts believe that Israel achieved a nuclear capability in the mid-1960s, and may currently possess anywhere between 100 and 300 nuclear warheads.

A team of military engineers wearing protective clothing clean up biological weapons in Libya under the supervision of the United Nations in 2012.

Chemical weapons

Any toxic chemical that can cause death, injury, temporary incapacitation or sensory irritation through its chemical action is considered to be a **chemical weapon**. The most dangerous of these are nerve agents (for example, sarin), blood agents (for example, hydrogen cyanide) and blister agents (for example, mustard gas); all of these are liquid but become gases when released. Chemical weapons incapacitate, injure or kill by affecting the skin, eyes, lungs, blood, nerves or other organs.

Biological weapons

Biological weapons include such things as bacteria, viruses and fungi when used as an act of war. These agents may be **lethal** or non-lethal, and may be targeted against a single individual, a group of people or even an entire population. An example of a biological weapon is the bacteria that cause the disease anthrax. If anthrax spores are breathed in they can lead to the inhalational form of the disease, which if untreated mostly results in toxic shock and death.

Useful words

Chemical weapon – a weapon that uses chemicals such as nerve and blood agents to kill or disable enemies

Lethal – sufficient to cause death

Mutually assured destruction – a strategy of stockpiling nuclear weapons by two or more opposing sides to deter the opposition from beginning nuclear strikes

MAD – mutually assured destruction

Benefits of WMD

Nuclear weapons have the potential to destroy the earth and many people believe that there have been no world wars since 1945 because of them. When two countries have nuclear weapons (as the USA and the Soviet Union did), they will hesitate to attack each other, because the other country could destroy them. This theory is known as **mutually assured destruction** (**MAD**).

Biological and chemical weapons do not destroy buildings, roads, bridges and so on (unlike nuclear weapons) and so they are an efficient way of destroying an enemy while leaving the infrastructure to be used by the attacker. Those using the weapons can be protected from their effects by using gas masks, protective clothing, shelters and decontamination procedures.

> *For me, I intend to let thee (an unjust murderer) draw on thyself my sin as well as thine, for thou wilt be among the companions of the fire and that is the reward of those who do wrong.*
> (Surah 5:32)

Problems of WMD

The major problem raised by WMD is that they deliberately target innocent civilians, including children, old people and women (groups specifically excluded from the effects of war by Holy and Just War theories).

Nuclear weapons are so powerful that they threaten the world with extinction. Recent scientific studies have found that a war fought with the current US and Russian nuclear arsenals would leave the earth virtually uninhabitable. The January 2010 edition of *Scientific American* warned that the detonation of 100 fifteen-kilotonne nuclear weapons in Indian and Pakistani megacities would engulf the entire planet with a thick smoke layer within ten days which could not be cleared by rain. It would block warming sunlight and create a kind of 'Ice Age', killing billions in the subsequent famine. These casualties would be in addition to the millions killed by the initial blasts and radiation. These 100 nuclear weapons only make up one per cent of the earth's nuclear arsenal!

Chemical and biological weapons can potentially kill as many people as nuclear weapons, although they act more slowly than bombs and missiles. Another problem is that chemical and biological weapons are difficult to deliver effectively and the subsequent effects of the attacks can only be guessed at. No one knows what will happen when large quantities are released into the atmosphere. The danger is that these weapons could be uncontrollable once released. Nothing could stop them from spreading outside the original target area.

Muslim attitudes to WMD

The very clear teachings of Islam on what constitutes a Just War seem to make it difficult for Muslims to justify using WMD. In Islam, war is a highly regulated field, as are other areas of life. Islam has given various rules to prevent atrocities, genocide or rape of women. Islam also forbids the killing of innocents or vulnerable populations not involved in war.

All of these rules of Islamic war make WMD unusable by good Muslims. Pakistan is the only Muslim country that has an arsenal of nuclear weapons, which it developed because it feared that its enemy, India, would feel free to attack if it could not defend itself. However, Pakistan has never given an Islamic justification for having nuclear weapons, whereas the spiritual leader of Iran, Ayatollah Khamenei, condemned WMD in October 2015:

> *The Islamic Republic of Iran, based on its fundamental religious and legal beliefs, would never resort to the use of weapons of mass destruction ... In contrast to the propaganda of our enemies, fundamentally we are against any production of weapons of mass destruction in any form.*

Activities

1. Outline the different types of weapons of mass destruction.
2. What do you think are the benefits of weapons of mass destruction?
3. How might Surah 2:205 be interpreted by Muslims opposed to weapons of mass destruction and by Muslims who think they should have weapons of mass destruction as a defence?

Jewish attitudes to WMD

Most Jews would be against using WMD because the Talmud (Shavuot 35b) explicitly prohibits the waging of war in a situation where the casualty rate exceeds a sixth of the population:

In view of this vital limitation of the law of self-defence, it would appear that a defensive war likely to endanger the survival of the attacking and the defending nations alike, if not indeed the entire human race, can never be justified. On this assumption, then, that the choice posed by a threatened nuclear attack would be either complete destruction or surrender, only the second may be morally vindicated. (Lord Jakobovits, former Chief Rabbi of Great Britain)

However, under Jewish law it would be possible to threaten to use a weapon that is prohibited, in the same way as to lie to save the life of an innocent person is permissible. The lie of nuclear deterrence is a way of saving many, many lives if it prevents an attack.

The Israel Defence Forces (IDF) have also developed the 'code of purity of arms', which its chief chaplain claimed to be derived from the Jewish *halakhah*. The document 'The Spirit of the IDF' contains the following statement:

Purity of Arms (Morality in Warfare) – The soldier shall make use of his weaponry and power only for the fulfillment of the mission and solely to the extent required; he will maintain his humanity even in combat. The soldier shall not employ his weaponry and power in order to harm non-combatants or prisoners of war, and shall do all he can to avoid harming their lives, body, honor and property.

This would seem to be a further ban on using WMD.

Corpses of men killed by nerve gas after a suspected chemical weapons attack in Damascus, Syria, in 2013.

Activities

1. Look at the photo below. What problems do chemical weapons cause?
2. How might Deuteronomy 20:19 be interpreted by Jews opposed to weapons of mass destruction?

When you lay siege to a city for a long time, fighting against it to capture it, do not destroy its trees by putting an axe to them because you can eat their fruit. Do not cut them down. (Deuteronomy 20:19)

Activities

1. Explain either Muslim or Jewish attitudes to weapons of mass destruction. Remember to use information from Topic 2.4.6 as well as from this topic.
2. Why are many religious people against weapons of mass destruction?

Humanists and WMD

No Humanist would support the use of WMD, but some would take the Jewish view that it is acceptable in a world of nuclear weapons to have nuclear weapons as a deterrent even if you would never use them.

The view expressed by Paul Sims in *The New Humanist* in 2013 explains the typical Humanist view:

> *To me, it seems obvious. If Humanists are committed to 'finding meaning, beauty and joy in the one life we have', and basing 'their moral principles on reason, ... on shared human values and respect for others' (to quote a couple of lines from the British Humanist Association's website), then surely we should be against the possession of weapons which provide the potential for the murder of millions, if not billions, of people and the destruction of the one planet we're able to call home.* (Paul Sims, British Humanist, writing in 2013)

Atheists and WMD

Atheists are split about WMD. Some are totally against WMD because they believe that this life and the earth is all we have, as they do not believe in God and an afterlife in heaven. Consequently, they do not think it is right to contemplate the use of weapons that could destroy life on the planet.

Other atheists think that it is acceptable for a country to possess WMD as a means of self-defence to frighten their enemies and so prevent them from attacking. They accept that the concept of MAD has kept the peace and so accept the need to possess such weapons. They do not believe in God or in a final judgement and so they are happy to have WMD and would be prepared to use them if the need arose.

Some people might use the ethical principle of utilitarianism (see Topic 1.4.8, page 144) to justify the possession of nuclear weapons. They might argue that the concept of MAD means that countries which possess nuclear weapons will never have to suffer horrendous consequences of war and therefore possessing a nuclear arsenal is right because it brings about 'the greatest happiness of the greatest number' of people. After all, everyone is happier living at peace than living through a war.

Summary

Weapons of mass destruction are weapons which can destroy large areas and large numbers of people. There are three types of WMD: nuclear, chemical and biological. The most destructive are nuclear weapons which can be sent thousands of miles by missiles. Countries which have nuclear weapons believe no one will attack them because it would result in the attacker's country being destroyed. This is known as MAD (mutually assured destruction). Some Muslims and Jews oppose WMD because of their beliefs about Just War. Others accept them because they keep the peace. Most Humanists are against possessing WMD but some accept possessing them to keep the peace.

Practice questions

c Explain two reasons why either Jews or Muslims might be against possessing weapons of mass destruction. In your answer you must refer to a source of wisdom and authority.

d 'Weapons of mass destruction might be dreadful, but having them keeps the peace.' Evaluate this statement considering arguments for and against. In your answer you should:

- refer to Jewish or Muslim points of view
- refer to non-religious points of view and ethical theories
- reach a justified conclusion.

Topic 2.4.8 Issues surrounding conflict

Violence

Conflict often results in violence and most violence actually occurs in the home. The Office for National Statistics said that in 2015 two women were killed every week in England and Wales by a current or former partner. It is estimated that one in four women in England and Wales will experience **domestic violence** in their lifetimes. Globally, one in three women will experience violence at the hands of a male partner. Twenty-five per cent of children in the UK have been exposed to domestic abuse and 62 per cent of children in households where domestic violence is happening are also directly harmed.

In countries where guns are easily available much conflict ends in violent death. In the UK there are only 0.23 gun-related deaths per 100,000 population, but in the USA there are 10.64 and in the small Latin American country of Honduras there are 67.18.

Crime often involves violence: burglary, robbery, rape, assault, kidnap, extortion, drug rackets and so on are all likely to be committed with violence.

War

For the issues surrounding war, use the information at the beginning of Topic 2.4.3 (page 337).

Terrorism

The word **terrorism** comes from the Latin verb *terrere*, meaning 'to frighten'. The United Nations has defined terrorism as any act

> *intended to cause death or serious bodily harm to civilians or non-combatants with the purpose of intimidating a population or compelling a government or an international organisation to do or abstain from doing any act.*

Since 1994 the United Nations has condemned terrorism on several occasions, with statements such as:

> *Criminal acts intended or calculated to provoke a state of terror in the public, a group of persons or particular persons for political purposes are in any circumstance unjustifiable, whatever the considerations of a political, philosophical, ideological, racial, ethnic, religious or any other nature that may be invoked to justify them.*

Probably the first organisation to use modern terrorist techniques was the Irish Republican Brotherhood who, from 1881 to 1885, used modern, timed explosives with the aim of sowing fear in British cities in order to achieve its political aims.

Thinking points

In this topic you need to think about violence, war and terrorism, including Muslim or Jewish, Humanist and atheist views and how Muslims or Jews have worked to overcome these issues. By the end of this topic you should be able to explain and evaluate Muslim or Jewish and non-religious attitudes to the issues surrounding conflict.

Useful words

Domestic violence – violence in the home, mainly men attacking their partners

Terrorism – criminal acts intended to provoke a state of terror in the public for political or religious purposes

Activities

1. Why do you think so much violence happens in the home?
2. What reasons do people have for becoming terrorists?

The twin towers of the World Trade Center in New York, USA, were attacked on 11 September 2001.

Some of the most notorious terrorist acts include the following:

- The 1998 bombings of the US embassies in Nairobi, Kenya and Dar es Salaam, Tanzania. Truck bombs, carrying up to seventeen tonnes of high explosives, were detonated within minutes of each other at the site of each embassy. While the intended targets were American property and personnel, the vast majority of the casualties were local people (303 killed, 4954 injured), although twelve Americans were killed, and both embassies were heavily damaged. The attack was carried out by the Egyptian Islamic Jihad group in retaliation for some of their members being imprisoned by US forces.
- The 1995 Oklahoma City bombing. On 19 April 1995, a truck bomb exploded in front of a federal office in Oklahoma City, USA. The resulting explosion tore into the building, demolishing much of it and killing 169 people and injuring 675 people. The bombing was carried out by two right-wing Americans, Timothy McVeigh and Terry Nichols, who claimed a hatred of the US government as their motivation.
- The '**9/11**' attacks. On 11 September 2001, nineteen members of Al Qaeda managed to hijack four airliners. Two of these planes were crashed into New York City's World Trade Center. A third plane was crashed into the Pentagon in Washington DC. The fourth plane, which is believed to have been headed for targets in Washington DC as well, crashed into a field in Somerset County, Pennsylvania, after passengers attempted to regain control of the plane from the hijackers. Both World Trade Center towers were demolished – literally crashing to the ground. The Pentagon was heavily damaged as well. There were 2993 people killed and 8900 injured.

Useful words

9/11 – the attacks in the USA on 11 September 2001

The number 30 double-decker bus in Tavistock Square, London, which was destroyed by a terrorist bomb on 7 July 2005.

- The 7 July 2005 London bombings (often referred to as **7/7**). These were a series of co-ordinated terrorist suicide bomb attacks in central London which targeted civilians using public transport during the morning rush hour. On the morning of Thursday 7 July 2005, four Islamist extremists separately detonated three bombs in quick succession aboard London Underground trains across the city and, later, a fourth on a double-decker bus in Tavistock Square. Fifty-two civilians were killed and over 700 more were injured in the attacks, the UK's first ever Islamist suicide attack.
- The Paris bombings. On the evening of 13 November 2015, a series of co-ordinated suicide bombings and mass shootings at cafés, restaurants and a music venue in central Paris, France, took place. The attackers killed 130 people, including 89 at the Bataclan theatre, where they took hostages before engaging in a stand-off with police, and another 368 people were injured. Isis claimed responsibility for the attacks, saying that they were in retaliation for French air strikes in Syria and Iraq.

Useful words

7/7 – the London bombings of 7 July 2005

Activity

Look at the photos on page 358 and above. What do you find most horrifying about terrorist attacks?

I advise you ten things: Do not kill women or children or an aged, infirm person. Do not cut down fruit-bearing trees. Do not destroy an inhabited place. Do not slaughter sheep or camels except for food. Do not burn bees and do not scatter them. Do not steal from the booty, and do not be cowardly. (Hadith reported in Malik's Muwatta 21:3:10)

Muslim views on violence

Muslims believe in a civilised society and they are against people using violence except under legal authority because:

- Islamic society is based on the rule of law and mutual respect between the members of that society. Clearly, violent people have no respect for people and so have no understanding of their responsibilities as members of society.
- Islam regards using violence without a just cause as sinful.
- Islam teaches that all Muslims are members of the *ummah* and should have equal treatment and respect. Any Muslim who is violent to a fellow Muslim is acting against the *ummah*.
- Islam teaches that it is the duty of Muslims to protect the weak and innocent, not attack them.
- Muhammad said in his final sermon, 'Every Muslim is a brother to every Muslim'. No one should be violent to their brother and so Muslims should not be violent.
- In a democracy, every person has human rights, including the right to be able to live free from fear. All the law schools teach that Muslims should defend human rights and so they should not be violent to others because that denies the victim's human rights.

Islamic teaching on the Just War (Topic 2.4.5, page 345) makes it plain that terrorism is difficult to equate with Islam. This has been made even clearer by Muslim scholars such as Hamza Yusuf. They make the following points:

- Islam must prohibit terrorism because Islam prohibits a Muslim from attacking innocent civilians, since the Prophet Muhammad said, 'Do not kill women or children or non-combatants and do not kill old people or religious people.'
- Throughout their history Muslims never allowed the killing of civilians, even in the midst of wars such as the Crusades.
- Suicide is ***haram*** in Islam. It is prohibited, like a mortal sin in Christianity, so a suicide bomber is going against Islam by killing themselves as well as bringing harm to the innocent.
- Murder is *haram* in Islam (it is condemned both in the Qur'an and in the hadith) and to kill civilians is murder.
- The Prophet said that there are people who kill in the name of Islam and go to hell. And when he was asked why, he said, 'Because they weren't fighting truly for the sake of God.'

The media's linking of terrorism and Islam has had some bad effects on ordinary Muslims. Muslim children in British schools have been bullied for being terrorists. In the week following the Paris attacks, Muslims living in Britain were reported to have suffered more than 100 racial attacks based on their religion. Most victims of UK hate crimes were Muslim girls and women aged 14–45 in traditional Islamic dress. The perpetrators were mainly white males aged 15–35.

Useful words

Haram – that which is forbidden

Activities

1. Do you think Muslims in the UK should be made to suffer for the actions of terrorists that have nothing to do with them?
2. What do you think religious people could do to prevent violence and terrorism?
3. How might a Muslim thinking about how they should react to violence and terrorism be affected by the hadith quoted by Malik?

How Muslims have worked to overcome these issues

The main work of Muslim organisations against violence has been covered in Topic 2.4.2a (page 331).

As far as terrorism is concerned, the vast majority of Muslims are against terrorism and work to prevent terrorism happening.

The Muslim Council of Britain has:

- paid for advertisements in the national press unequivocally condemning terror in the name of many UK Muslim groups
- encouraged community efforts to report criminal activities and co-operate with the police
- initiated a national process to explore grassroots responses to terrorism
- worked closely with Muslim communities and the police to develop a successful counter-terrorism policy.

The Ahmadiyya Muslims have condemned any form of terrorism, and co-operated with the police and Muslim communities to report any suspicious activities within the communities. As their leader said after the Paris attacks:

> *As far as Islam is concerned, it categorically rejects and condemns every form of terrorism. It does not provide any cover or justification for any act of violence, be it committed by an individual, a group or a government ... I most strongly condemn all acts and forms of terrorism because it is my deeply rooted belief that not only Islam but also no true religion, whatever its name, can sanction violence and bloodshed of innocent men, women and children in the name of God.*

In North America the Muslims Against Terrorism group works with Muslim and Christian organisations and arranged for a large group of imams to compose and sign a *fatwa* against terrorism. Muslims Against Terrorism has requested that the media not use phrases such as 'Islamic fundamentalists' or 'Muslim terrorists' regarding terrorist attacks, since they claim that such things do not exist. 'Islam is the religion of peace, love and mutual respect. Islam is the religion of moderation. Islam is the religion of human value and dignity.'

In India, over 70,000 imams signed a document condemning global terrorist activity, which stated that they do not consider groups like Isis to be true Islamic organisations, nor do they view members of these organisations as Muslims.

The Muslims Against Terrorism *fatwa*

Therefore, it is an obligation upon us (Imams) to inform all Muslims around the world that Muslims in Canada and the United States have complete freedom to practice Islam. There is no single city in Canada and the United States where MASAJIDS (Mosques) are not built. In all major cities Islamic schools provide education to Muslim children about Qur'an and the Islamic traditions. Thousands of Muslims perform Hajj every year and travel to Saudi Arabia with complete freedom and respect. In the month of Ramadan, both Canadian and the United States governments recognize the occasion and greet all Muslim citizens. Muslims pray five daily prayers in mosques without any fear or restrictions. Muslims have complete freedom to pay Zakat (poor due) to the charity or a person of their choice. Muslims have complete freedom to celebrate their festivals openly, publicly and Islamically. Muslims enjoy freedom of religion just like Christians, Jews and others. No one stops us from obeying Allah and His Messenger (Peace be upon him). No one stops us from preaching Islam and practicing Islam. In many cases, Muslims have more freedom to practice Islam here in Canada and the United States than many Muslim countries.

In fact, the constitutions of the United States and Canada are very close to the Islamic guiding principles of human rights and freedom. There is no conflict between the Islamic values of freedom and justice and the Canadian/US values of freedom and justice.

Therefore, any attack on Canada and the United States is an attack on the freedom of Canadian and American Muslims. Any attack on Canada and the United States is an attack on thousands of mosques across North America. It is a duty of every Canadian and American Muslim to safeguard Canada and the USA. They must expose any person, Muslim *or* non-Muslim, who would cause harm to fellow Canadians *or* Americans. We, Canadian and American Muslims, must condemn and stand up against these attacks on Canada and the United States.

May Allah save Canada, the United States and the entire world from the evil of wrongdoers. Ameen.

Activity

Read the *fatwa* above. What does this make you think about Muslim terrorists?

You hear, O Lord, the desire of the afflicted; you encourage them and you listen to their cry, defending the fatherless and the oppressed, in order that man, who is of the earth, may terrify no more. (Psalm 10:17–18)

Useful words

Anti-Semitic – racism directed against Jews

Jewish views on violence

Jewish people believe in a civilised society and are against people using violence except under legal authority because:

- Judaism is based on the rule of law and mutual respect between the members of society. Clearly, violent people have no respect for the people they victimise and so have no understanding of their responsibilities as members of society.
- Judaism regards using violence without a just cause as sinful.
- Judaism teaches that human beings are a creation of God made in God's image. Being violent to others is mistreating God's creation and so is wrong.
- Judaism teaches that it is the duty of Jewish people to protect the weak and innocent as part of loving your neighbour. Violence is the exact opposite of this as violent people attack and exploit the weak and innocent.
- In a democracy, every person has human rights, including the right to be able to live free from fear. All different forms of Judaism teach that Jewish people should defend human rights and so they should not be violent to others because violence denies the victim's human rights.

Judaism is against terrorism because it has suffered so much from attacks. The number of **anti-Semitic** incidents in the UK in 2015 reached the highest level ever recorded, with reports of violence, property damage, abuse and threats against members of Britain's Jewish population more than doubling. The Community Security Trust, a Jewish security charity which runs an incident hotline, recorded 1168 anti-Semitic incidents against Britain's 291,000 Jews in 2014, compared with 535 in 2013.

Judaism's religious texts teach compassion and peace rather than violence and hatred,

> *Judaism, from the days of the prophets, has proclaimed to mankind the ideal of universal peace, striving for spiritual and physical disarmament of all nations. Judaism rejects violence and relies upon moral education, love and sympathy.* (Columbus Platform of Reform Judaism)

Jewish teachings on peace (Topics 2.4.1b and 2.4.2b, pages 329 and 334) and Just War (Topic 2.4.5, page 345) show why Jews would find it difficult to support terrorism.

How Jews have worked to overcome these issues

There has been little Jewish terrorism until quite recently and so the main work of Jewish organisations against violence has been covered in Topic 2.4.2b (page 334).

However, the phenomenon of price tag attacks began around 2008. These are hate crimes carried out by extremist settler Jewish Israelis which target property associated with Arabs, Christians, secular Israelis and Israeli soldiers. The name was derived from the words 'Price tag' which may be scrawled on the site of the attack – with the allegation that the attack was a 'price' for settlements the government forced them to give up and revenge for Palestinian attacks on settlers. Churches have been attacked and in July 2015 a price tag arson attack against a Palestinian house in Jerusalem caused a fire that killed a father and his eighteen-month-old son.

These terrorist attacks have been condemned by the leading rabbis in Israel. Israel's Prime Minister Benjamin Netanyahu and President Reuven Rivlin both denounced the arson attack before visiting the surviving members of the family in hospital. A group of Muslim and Jewish leaders also went to see the family together. David Lau, Israel's chief Ashkenazi rabbi, made a public statement condemning 'this despicable murder' as contrary to all Judaism stands for.

The chief rabbi also condemned the attacks on Christian churches as totally against the values of Judaism and human ethics.

> *Judaism has a battle against idolatry, as a faith which claims to have a historic mission of bringing a blessing to the world. Torching churches is the exact opposite of that. It's a barbaric act which harms people, pulls the rug from under the moral claim which forbids harming Jews around the world, and mainly does nothing to promote the battle against idolatry.*

The American Jewish Committee (**AJC**) fights anti-Semitism and all forms of **bigotry**. It is based in the USA but has partnerships with Jewish communities worldwide. AJC works to enhance the well-being of the Jewish people and to advance human rights and democratic values for all, and so has condemned all terrorist activity, but especially those acts carried out in the name of religion. AJC has made alliances among diverse ethnic and religious groups and uses these to co-ordinate anti-terrorism.

Activities

1. Why do you think Humanists are against terrorism? (Don't forget to refer to Topic 2.4.3, page 337.)
2. How might Jews thinking about how they should react to violence and terrorism be affected by Psalm 10:17–18?'

Useful words

AJC – American Jewish Committee, working for fair treatment of all religions and ethnicities, especially Jews

Bigotry – intolerance to those who hold different opinions

Atheist and Humanist attitudes to conflict

The attitudes of atheists and Humanists to conflict in general are covered in Topic 2.4.3 (page 337).

As far as terrorism is concerned, Humanists feel it is fundamentally wrong for civilians to be directly targeted by violence to achieve political, social, economic or religious ends. They feel there can be no justification for trying to bring about a feeling of terror in a civilian population who have no opportunity to alter the situation in the way in which the terrorists want. Humanists believe that 'the end can never justify the means'. It does not matter how good the goal of a terrorist may be, to terrorise a civilian population (especially children) to bring it about has always got to be wrong.

The vast majority of atheists would agree with Humanists on terrorism, although those atheists who have a political belief that they treat as a religion (like the Cambodian Marxist Khmer Rouge) may feel that terrorism is justified.

Practice questions

c Explain two reasons why either Jews or Muslims might be against terrorism. In your answer you must refer to a source of wisdom and authority.

d 'Religion should do more to stop violence and terrorism.' Evaluate this statement considering arguments for and against. In your answer you should:

- refer to Jewish or Muslim points of view
- refer to non-religious points of view
- reach a justified conclusion.

Summary

Much of the violence not connected with war is domestic violence where women are the main victims. Terrorism is frightening the population for political or religious reasons. The most notorious recent terrorist attacks were the 9/11 attack in New York, the 7/7 attack in London and the Paris bombings of 2015. Muslims and Jews are against violence and terrorism because their religions teach the rule of law and that it is the duty of Muslims and Jews to protect the weak and innocent and not attack them. Jewish and Muslim leaders are working together to prevent terrorism. Humanists and most atheists think that violence and terrorism can never be justified.

How to answer questions

a) Outline three Muslim beliefs about war. [3]

First, the Qur'an says that Muslims must fight if they are attacked. Second, Muhammad, who is the great example for Muslims, fought in just wars; therefore, so should Muslims. Third, Muslims must not fight in any war in which they could be classed as the aggressor.

A high mark answer because three Muslims beliefs about war are clearly outlined.

b) Explain two reasons why Muslims work for peace today. [4]

Muslims work for peace because the Qur'an says they should. Surah 25 recommends that Muslims should be humble and 'when the ignorant address them, they say, "Peace!".'

The Qur'an also recommends that Muslims end disagreements by making peace rather than by beginning further disputes and fights. After all, God is compassionate and merciful to sinners, and so Muslims should be merciful and forgiving to those who cause them offence.

A high mark answer because two correct reasons are given and each reason is developed.

c) Explain two reasons why the Just War theory is important for Muslims. In your answer you must refer to a source of wisdom and authority. [5]

The Just War theory is important for Muslims because the Qur'an says they should fight in Just Wars: 'And why should ye not fight in the cause of God and of those who, being weak and ill-treated – men, women and children, whose cry is "Our Lord! Rescue us from this town, whose people are oppressors; and raise for us from Thee one who will protect"' (Surah 4:75).

The Just War theory is important because it is set out in the Shari'ah, which is the straight path that all good Muslims should follow.

A high mark answer because two correct reasons are given and each reason is developed with a reference to the Qur'an and the Shari'ah, which are sources of authority for Muslims.

d) 'Religious people should be pacifists.' Evaluate this statement considering arguments for and against. In your response you should:

- **refer to Muslim points of view**
- **refer to different Muslim points of view**
- **reach a justified conclusion. [12]**

Muslims such as the Ahmadiyya sect would agree, since their founder Mirza Ghulam Ahmad taught that there should be no violent form of *jihad* and coined the motto, 'Love for all, hatred for none' for the Ahmadiyya. These Muslims are pacifists who preach a message of worldwide peace. Another famous Muslim pacifist was Khan Abdul Ghaffar Khan, who worked with Gandhi in the non-violent movement for independence for India from British rule in colonial times.

Most Muslims would not agree with pacifism since the Qur'an encourages all Muslims to 'struggle in the way of Islam'. The Qur'an states that Muslims must fight if Islam is attacked. The Qur'an makes very plain that a Just War must be fought by Muslims, consequently there is little idea of pacifism or turning the other cheek in Islam.

[Continued]

It seems to me that although it may be true that some religious people should be pacifists, it cannot be true that all religious people should be pacifists because, for example, there are teachings in Islam which discourage pacifism.

A high mark answer because it two clear well-developed reasons for thinking that religious people should be pacifists. It then gives three reasons for Muslims disagreeing and then reaches a fully justified conclusion.

Glossary

7/7 The London bombings of 7 July 2005

9/11 The attacks in the USA on 11 September 2001

Abortifacients Substances that bring about a very early abortion

Abortion on demand The right to have an abortion whatever the woman's reasons

Absolution Through the actions and words of a priest or minister pardon of sins is assured

Abu Bak'r Muhammad's friend and first Caliph, who ordered the first collection of the Qur'an

Acquisitive crime Crimes such as stealing and burglary where the criminal wants to acquire someone else's property

Adalat God's attribute of justice

Adhan The call to prayer

Adoration Praising or adoring God for what he is

Adulation Extreme admiration

Adultery A sexual act between a married person and someone other than their marriage partner

Advent Season before Christmas remembering the first coming of Jesus and that he will come again

Aggressor Someone who attacks without being provoked

Agnostic Someone unsure as to whether or not God exists

Ahmadiyya A Muslim sect founded in Pakistan by Yirza Ahmad that is against war

AJC American Jewish Committee, working for fair treatment of all religions and ethnicities, especially Jews

Akirah Belief in the Last Day and life after death

Al-Hijra 1 Muharram, Islamic New Year's Day

Al'Jannah Heaven

Alien A foreigner, especially one who is not a naturalised citizen of the country where he or she is living

Allah The Arabic for God

Alms Charitable giving to the poor

Alpha The Christian course trying to convert non-churchgoers

Amicable Showing a polite and friendly desire to avoid disagreement and argument

Amidah The standing prayer

Amir al-Mu'minin Commander of the faithful, a title given by Shi'as to Ali and his descendants

Amputation Cutting off a limb

Anglicans Members of the Church of England or a Church in communion with the Church of England

Annulment A declaration by the Church that a marriage was never a true marriage and so the partners are free to marry

Anti-Semitic Racism directed against Jews

Anti-Semitism Hostility to or prejudice against Jews

Apostasy Giving up or denying your religious faith

Apostles Prophets or messengers: the titles given to those who brought God's message

Apostles' Creed A short statement of belief attributed to the disciples of Jesus

Apostolic Tradition The oral Gospel passed on by the Apostles to the Church

Apparent Age The idea that the world would have looked billions of years old when it was only a second old

Arafat The plain and hill eighteen kilometres from Makkah where the central part of *hajj* takes place

Ark Large cupboard at the front of the synagogue where the Torah scrolls are kept

Ark of the Covenant The holy container for the tablets of the commandments

Aron Hakodesh The Ark

Arvit Evening prayer

As'r Afternoon prayer

Ascension The return of Christ to heaven

Assisted suicide Providing a seriously ill person with the means to kill themselves

Atheist Someone who does not believe that God exists

Atonement Reconciliation between God and humans

Auschwitz A Second World War Nazi concentration camp in Poland where at least 1.1 million prisoners died

Avelut The mourning period

Ayatollah The highest ranking religious leader in Twelver Shi'ism

Baptismal vows The promises Christians (or their parents) make at their baptism

Barzakh The period between death and the Last Day

Bar Mitzvah Son of the commandment; a Jewish boy's coming of age

Bat Brit Ceremony for female babies in Liberal/ Reform synagogues

Bat Chayil Daughter of Worth; name used by some Orthodox synagogues instead of Bat Mitzvah

Believers' baptism Restricting baptism to those old enough to understand the meaning of the ritual

Bereaved Deprived of a close relation or friend through their death

Bigotry Intolerance to those who hold different opinions

Bimah The raised platform for Torah readings

Bioenergy Renewable energy made from materials derived from biological sources such as wood waste, straw, manure and sugar cane

Biofuels Fuels produced from plants

Biological weapons Weapons that make use of some kind of virus or disease to infect millions of people

Bismillah The words at the beginning of each surah, 'in the name of Allah, the Merciful, the Compassionate'

Blasphemy Speaking disrespectfully about God or sacred things

Book of Life The book where one's quality of life for the coming year is recorded

Brain death The brain is irreversibly damaged

Brit chayim Covenant of life ceremony for Reform girl babies

Brit milah Ceremony of circumcision for baby boys

Brit shalom Covenant of peace (ceremony welcoming uncircumcised male babies)

Caliph Leader of the Islamic community

Canaan Ancient name for the land of Israel

Canonise Make someone a saint

Capital offence A crime which can be punished by death

Capital punishment The death penalty for a crime

Catechetical programmes Religious instruction given in preparation for Christian baptism or confirmation

Catholic Catechism The official teaching of the Roman Catholic Church

Cenacle The Upper Room in Jerusalem where the Last Supper took place

Challot Plaited loaves used on *Shabbat* and festivals

Chametz Any food containing yeast/leaven

Chazzan The leader of worship who chants the prayers (also called a cantor)

Chemical weapon A weapon that uses chemicals such as nerve and blood agents to kill or disable enemies

Chevra kaddisha Burial society

Childbearing age The age when a woman is capable of having children

Christ's Passion The betrayal, arrest, trials and crucifixion of Jesus

Chukim *Mitzvot* with no reason given for them

Circumambulate Walk round, make a circuit

Civil divorce A divorce according to the law of the country but not the Church

Civil partnerships Legal ceremonies giving homosexual partners the same legal rights as husband and wife

Civil rights The rights of citizens to political and social freedom and equality

Clergy People ordained for religious duties in Christian Churches

Climate change Changes in global or regional climate patterns, attributed to the increased levels of carbon dioxide produced by the use of fossil fuels

Cohabitation Living together in a sexual relationship without being married

Colonise Where one race or culture takes control of another

Commodity Something that humans need or want

Compensation Paying someone back for a wrong done to them

Conception The fertilisation of the egg by the sperm

Condoms Thin rubber sheaths protecting against conception and STDs

Confession Prayers saying sorry for sins and asking God's forgiveness

Congregation The people assembled for worship

Conscientious objector A person who for reasons of conscience does not want to serve in the armed forces

Consensual sex When both parties freely agree to sexual activity

Conservation Protecting and preserving natural resources and the environment

Consummate Complete a marriage through sexual intercourse

Contemplation Communion with God

Contraception Methods of preventing pregnancy occurring from sex

Covenant An agreement between God and his people

Creationism The belief that the universe, and humans, were created in the way the Bible says

Creative purpose Sex as a means of creating a family

Creeds Statements of Christian belief

Crib A nativity scene with baby Jesus in a manger (crib)

Crusade A war for a religious or moral purpose

Custody One parent being made responsible for the care of the children

Cybercrime Criminal activities carried out by means of computers or the internet

Dar as Salaam The House of Peace

Days of Awe The ten days between Rosh Hashanah and Yom Kippur when Jews consider their deeds of the past year and resolve to do better in the coming year

Death penalty Execution ordered by a court of law

Decalogue The Ten Commandments

Decree An official order from a high authority

Dedication A ceremony involving a child being presented to the congregation and vows being made to encourage the child to follow the Christian life

Deity God

Desecrate Violate a sacred place or law

Destiny What has been set out to happen

Dhu al-Hijjah The twelfth month of the Islamic calendar, when *hajj* takes place

Diocese A Church area under the direction of a bishop

Divestment The process of selling off subsidiary business interests or investments

Divine guidance Being shown what to do by God

Doctrine of double effect The principle that it is acceptable to perform an action that has a side-effect as long as the intention was to achieve the good first effect

Domestic violence Violence in the home, mainly men attacking their partners

Dominant role The major, most influential part

Ecumenical Promoting Christian unity

Ecumenism Movement working for co-operation between the Churches and eventual Church unity

Ellul The final month of the Jewish year

Environment The surroundings in which plants and animals live and on which they depend for survival

Ethical monotheism Belief in one God who demands moral obedience

Ethnicity Having the characteristics of a certain race or culture

Etrog A citron fruit

Eucharist A Christian rite considered by most to be a sacrament

Euthanasia The painless killing of someone dying from a painful disease

Evangelisation Seeking to convert to Christianity

Ex nihilo From nothing

Exile When the Jewish people had to leave their homeland and live elsewhere

Exodus The Israelites' escape from slavery in Egypt

Extempore prayers Prayers said without preparation

Extramarital sex Sex acts outside marriage, usually referred to as adultery

Extraordinary minister A non-ordained man or woman who assists the work of priests

Fairtrade A group aiming to help producers in developing countries achieve better trading conditions and to promote sustainability

Faith Firm belief without logical proof

Faithful Staying with your marriage partner and having sex only with them

Fajr Dawn prayer

Fall of Man The idea that when Adam disobeyed God by eating the forbidden fruit, sin came into the world

Fallible memories Memory can be mistaken

Fard Actions which must be performed for a person to be regarded as good

Fatimid An Ismaili caliphate that ruled North Africa from 909CE to 1171CE

Finite resources Resources which can only be used once, for example oil, metals

First Communion The first time a person receives the sacrament of the Eucharist; children receive special lessons before this important occasion

Foetus A developing human in the womb from the end of the second month after conception (until then it is an embryo)

Foreknowledge Knowing what is going to happen long before it does

Fossil fuels Natural fuels (coal, oil and gas) formed over millions of years through the breakdown of the remains of living organisms

Fossil record The evidence provided in fossils for evolution

Franciscan A member of a religious order which follows the teachings and spiritual disciplines of St Francis of Assisi

Free will The idea that human beings are free to make their own choices

Freedom of expression The freedom to express your opinions in public (especially about politics and religion)

Friar A member of a religious order which does not own property and who has to either work or beg to earn a living

Fundamental principle The basic idea behind something

Gan Eden Heaven

Gehinnom Hell

Gender equality The sexes being treated equally

Geneticists Scientists in the study of heredity and genes

Genocide The deliberate killing of a large group of people, especially those of a particular nation or ethnic group

Gentiles Non-Jews

Gestation The process of a foetus developing inside the womb

Ghadeer Khum The Pool of Khum halfway between Makkah and Madinah

Global evangelism Preaching the Gospel to the whole world

Global warming The increase in the temperature of the earth's atmosphere (thought to be caused by the greenhouse effect)

Gospels The books of the Bible (Matthew, Mark, Luke and John), which are the only record of Jesus' life

Grace God's gift which gives the strength to be good and holy

Great Commission Jesus' last command to his disciples to go out and convert the world

Greenhouse effect The carbon dioxide from burned fossil fuels creates a barrier in the same way as the glass in a greenhouse: it allows the sun's heat through, but then traps it, causing the temperature to rise

***Hadd* punishments** The punishments for crime set down in the Qur'an such as cutting a hand off for theft

Hadith Sayings of the Prophet Muhammad

Haftarot Portions of the Nevi'im read after the Torah in services

Hagadah Book telling the story of the first Passover

Hajj Pilgrimage to Makkah, the fifth pillar

Hajji One who has completed the *hajj*

Halakhah Jewish law from the Written and Oral Torah

Halal That which is permitted

Haram That which is forbidden

Harb al-Muqadis Muslim holy war

Hashem The Name, a word used to refer to God without mentioning his name

Havdalah Ceremony marking the ending of *Shabbat*

Hawwa The first woman, Adam's wife (Eve)

Heaven A place of paradise in the presence of God

Hechsher A label certifying that a food is *kosher*

Hell A place of horrors where Satan rules

Heterosexual Attraction to the opposite sex

Hidden Imam The twelfth Imam who disappeared and is believed to be in contact with the ayatollahs

Higgs bosons The particles that make up the Higgs field, which gives evidence for the Big Bang

Holiness The state of being very moral and spiritual

Holocaust The mass murder of the Jews by the Nazis in the Second World War

Holy Communion The Christian service of thanksgiving using bread and wine (also called Eucharist or Mass)

Homage Acknowledgement of superiority

Homophobia Hatred or fear of homosexuals

Homosexuality Sexual attraction to someone of the same sex

Host Unleavened bread used in the Eucharist

Human dignity The belief that humans are persons, not things, and that they have self-knowledge and free will

Humane Treating with kindness and compassion

Humanist A follower of the non-religious philosophy based on liberal human values

Huppah Wedding canopy

Husayn Muhammad's grandson and the third imam of Shi'a Islam

Ibadah Worship

Iftar The meal breaking the fast at night

Ihram Pilgrim dress

Imam Prayer leader

Imamah Belief in the successors of the Prophet Muhammad. For Shi'as, Imam is a successor, but 'imam' with a small 'i' is a prayer leader for Sunnis

Imamate The office of the Imam

Iman Faith

Immaculate conception The Catholic belief that Mary was protected from original sin from the moment of her conception so that Jesus was not born with original sin

Immortality of the soul The idea that the soul lives on after the death of the body

Immutable Unable to be changed and unchanging over time

Incarnation The belief that God took human form in Jesus

Indeterminate life sentence Being imprisoned for the rest of one's life with no chance of ever being released

Infant baptism Baptising babies, with their parents and godparents making vows on their behalf

Infanticide Killing young children

Injil The Gospel given to Isa (Jesus)

Insh Allah If God wills

Inspired Stimulated by God to do things

Inter-religious dialogue Discussions between different religions

Intercede To use your influence to persuade someone in authority to forgive another person

Intercessionary prayers Prayers asking God's help for other people

Intercontinental ballistic missiles Rockets that carry nuclear warheads over vast distances

Internally displaced Being forced to move your home because of conflict, but staying in the same country

Isaac Abraham's son through Sarah, ancestor of Jewish people

Isha Night prayer

Ishaq Ibrahim's son Isaac, the father of the Jewish people

Ishmael Abraham's son through Hagar, ancestor of Arab people

Ismaili Shi'as who believe that the seventh Imam, Isma'il, was the final Imam

Israfil The angel who begins the Last Day by blowing his trumpet

IUD Intrauterine device (the coil); a type of contraceptive

Izra'il The angel of death

Jahannam Hell

***Jami* mosques** Mosques appointed for Friday prayers

Jibril The archangel Gabriel

Jihadi One fighting in a Holy War

Jummah Friday midday prayers

Justice Due allocation of reward and punishment, the maintenance of right

Ka'aba The shrine in Makkah which Muslims face to say prayers and which is the centre of *hajj*

Kabbalah Jewish mysticism

Kaddish The prayer recited publicly by mourners

Karbala Site of the battle where Husayn was killed by Caliph Yazid (100 km southwest of Baghdad)

Kashrut Keeping Jewish food laws

Ketubah Marriage contract

Ketuvim The books of the writings

Khalifahs Allah's stewards or vicegerents

Khums An additional charity tax for Shi'a Muslims

Khutba Sermon

Kiddush A prayer said over wine to sanctify *Shabbat*

Kitub Holy books (singular *kitab*)

Kol Nidrei Annulment of vows made before Yom Kippur

Kosher Food which a Jew is allowed to eat

Kvatters People who carry the baby to Brit Milah

Lailat al-Miraj The Prophet's night journey to Jerusalem and then to heaven

Last resort After all other methods have been tried

Laws Rules made by Parliament and enforceable by the courts

Laylat al-Qadr The Night of Power (destiny)

Lectionary A list of Bible readings to be read at certain times of the year

Legal representation A lawyer who makes sure an accused person is treated fairly and has their case put to best effect

Legitimate Lawful

Lethal Sufficient to cause death

Lethal injection Executing a criminal by injecting them with sufficient poison to kill them

Lifelong relationship The idea that marriage can only be ended by the death of a partner

Liturgical year The year in the Church's calendar based on the special festivals from Advent to Pentecost

Liturgy A set form of public worship

Lord's Prayer The prayer Jesus taught his disciples that begins 'Our Father'

Lulav Palm branch

Ma'sa The covered passageway between the hills Marwa and Safa, which pilgrims run between

MAD Mutually assured destruction

Madrasah Religious school or college

Maghrib Sunset prayers

Maimonides Medieval rabbi and philosopher (1135–1204) who wrote the Thirteen Principles

Makkah The city in Arabia where Muhammad was born

Malaikah Angels

Malicious Having or showing a desire to cause harm to someone

Mandub Actions which a Muslim will be rewarded for doing, but will not be punished if they do not do them

Martyr Someone who is killed because of their beliefs

Maryam The Virgin Mary

Material needs Such things as food, drink and clothing

Maternal To do with the mother

Maundy Refers to the washing of the disciples' feet

Maundy Thursday The day before Jesus was crucified (Good Friday)

Mawlid al-Nabi The birthday of the Prophet Muhammad

Meditation Thinking about religious matters

Menorah Seven-branched candlestick

Mentor An experienced and trusted adviser

Messianic Age A time when all nations will live at peace and there will be justice in the world

Mezuzah Small scroll of the *shema* fixed to the doorpost of the rooms in a Jewish house

Midrash Collection of rabbinic commentaries on the Tenakh

Mihrab Alcove in mosques showing the direction of Makkah

Mika'il The angel Michael

Milchemet mitzvah A war of commandment which Jews must fight in

Milchemet reshut Optional war which Jews do not have to fight in but which must be fought in a just way

Militarism Belief that a country should have strong armed forces and be prepared to use them aggressively

Mina The place ten kilometres from Makkah where pilgrims throw stones at Satan and make the sacrifice

Minaret The tower beside the mosque from which the call to prayer is announced

Minchah Afternoon prayer

Minyan The required number of adult male Jews needed for certain prayers to be said in the synagogue

Mishneh Commentaries on the Torah written about 200CE

Mishneh *Shabbat* The part of the Talmud which contains all the regulations for *Shabbat*

Mishneh Torah The code of law written by Maimonides

Mission dioceses An area of the country which requires spiritual and physical support from the Church for growth and development

Mission Metropolis The Catholic mission to start the re-evangelisation of Europe from the cities

Mitzvah Commandment (singular)

Mitzvot Commandments/laws (the singular of *mitzvot* is *mitzvah*)

Mohel Expert circumciser

Monogamous Having only one spouse at a time

Monogamy Marriage to only one person at a time

Moral evil Actions done by humans which cause suffering

Moral suffering Suffering caused by actions done by humans

Moral values The standards of good and evil, which influence people's behaviour and choices.

Mount Zion The holy hill in Jerusalem where the Temple was

Mu'tazilites Eighth-century Muslim theologians regarded as non-Muslim by most Sunni Muslims today

Mubah Actions which are permitted because nothing is said about them in the Qur'an or hadith

Muezzin The prayer caller who announces the call to prayer five times a day

Muharram The first month of the Islamic calendar

Mujtahid A Shi'a scholar with sufficient training and knowledge to interpret the Shari'ah

Muslim Law Schools The four schools which interpret the Shari'ah for Sunni Muslims

Mutually assured destruction A strategy of stockpiling nuclear weapons by two or more opposing sides to deter the opposition from beginning nuclear strikes

Nationalism A strong feeling of belief in the rightness of one's native country

Natural evil Things which cause suffering but have nothing to do with humans

Natural selection The idea that life evolved through mutations, making those life forms better suited to the environment survive, and the less well suited die out

Natural suffering Suffering which is caused by nature and has nothing to do with humans

Near-death experiences When people about to die have out-of-body feelings

Ner tamid The everlasting light

Nevi'im The books of the prophets

NFP Natural family planning

Ninety-nine names The titles or characteristics given to Allah in the Qur'an

Nisab The amount of income or wealth a Muslim needs to have before they are liable for *zakah*

Non-confrontational Tending to deal with situations calmly and diplomatically instead of being aggressive or hostile

Non-material Not physical

Nonconformist A Protestant in England who is not a member of the Church of England

Non-voluntary euthanasia Ending someone's life painlessly when they are unable to ask, but you have good reason for thinking they would want you to do so

Nubuwwah Prophets of God

Nuclear weapons Devices that explode through a nuclear reaction releasing a huge amount of energy

Occupied Territories The Palestinian name for the West Bank and Gaza territories occupied by Israel since the Six-day War and the Yom Kippur War

Omnibenevolent The belief that God is all-good

Omnipotence Unlimited power

Omnipotent The belief that God is all-powerful

Omniscience God's characteristic of being all-knowing

Omniscient The belief that God knows everything that has happened and everything that is going to happen

ONS Office for National Statistics

Oral Torah The unwritten Torah given to Moses by God

Ordained Either set down by God or to be made a priest

Ordinance Law

Ordination The act of conferring holy orders (making a priest)

Original sin The sin of Adam and Eve disobeying God, which some Christians believe is passed on to all humans at birth

Pacifism Refusing to fight in wars

Palaeontologists Scientists who study fossils

Palliative care Medical or nursing care that reduces pain and improves the quality of life of those who have terminal illnesses

Parable A story told to illustrate a religious or moral issue

Paranormal Unexplained events that are thought to have spiritual causes, for example, ghosts, mediums

Parents' Circle A group of Palestinian and Jewish families who have lost children in the conflict and are working for peace

Parish An area having its own church and clergy

Parish priest The clergy person responsible for a local church

Paschal candle The large candle kept in the church throughout Easter and first lit on Easter Day

Passive resistance Non-violent opposition to authority

Paternal To do with the father

Patriarchs The fathers of Judaism (Abraham, Isaac, Jacob, Moses)

Patriotism Love for, or devotion to, one's country

Penance An action showing sorrow for a sin

Perpetrator One who commits a crime

Physical needs Such things as housing and shelter from the elements

Piety Religious devotion

Polygamous Having more than one spouse at a time

Polytheism Worshipping many gods

Prayer groups Groups of Christians who join together to pray and increase their understanding of prayer

Precedence Priority in time, order of importance

Predestination The belief that everything that happens has already been decided

Premarital sex Sexual activity before marriage

Probation The release of a person from prison on the condition that they are monitored by a probation officer and don't break certain rules

Procreation Making a new life

Promiscuity Having sex with a number of partners without commitment

Prophesied Predicted events in the future

Prophetic *jihad* *Jihad* as understood and practised by the Prophet Muhammad

Proportional In the right relation to

Proportional methods Using weapons of the same factor as those used against you

Prostrated To put oneself flat on the ground so as to be lying face downwards, especially in respect of submission

Psalms A book of the Old Testament containing 150 sacred songs

Purgatory A place where Catholic Christians believe souls go after death to be purified

Purim Jewish holy day to celebrate the saving of the Jewish people from Haman, who was trying to kill all the Jews in Persia

Qibla Direction of the Ka'aba in Makkah

Quality of life The idea that life must have some benefits for it to be worth living

Rabbis Ordained Jewish religious leaders or teachers

Raka The set actions in the prayer ritual (plural *rakat*)

Ramadan Ninth month of the Islamic year; the month of fasting

Reconciliation Bringing together people who were opposed to each other

Re-evangelisation Trying to bring back Christianity to somewhere which was Christian but has left the faith

Rehabilitation Restoring to normal, productive life

Reincarnation The belief that, after death, souls are reborn in a new body

Reintegrate For someone to fit back in to society

Relics The physical remains of a saint or the personal effects of the saint or holy person

Reliquary A container for holy relics

Remarriage Marrying again after a divorce

Remembered lives Memories of a previous existence

Remembrance of Allah Thinking about God in a meditative way

Remission When a patient with a disease gets better

Renewable resources Resources which do not run out, for example hydroelectric power from water

Repatriate To return refugees to their place of origin

Resurrection The belief that, after death, the body stays in the grave until the end of the world, when it is raised

Retribution The idea that punishment should make criminals pay for what they have done wrong

Retributive justice Justice done by making the criminal pay for their crime

Revered Held in deep respect

Reverence An act showing religious respect

Risalah Belief in Allah's angels, prophets and holy books

Rosh Hashanah Jewish new year

Sacrament An outward ceremony through which God's grace is given

Sacred bond A joining together sanctified by God which cannot be broken by humans

Sadaqah Voluntary giving to the poor

Sahifa Ibrahim The holy book given to Ibrahim (Abraham)

Salaam Peace

Salaam alaykum The Muslim equivalent of hello which means peace be with you

Salafi Ultra-conservative reform movement in Sunni Islam

Salah Ritual prayers to be said five times a day, the second pillar

Salvation The act of delivering from sin or saving from evil

Sanctified Made holy

Sanctify To make holy

Sanctity of life The belief that life is holy and belongs to God

Sanctuary The most holy part of a religious building (can also mean a place of safety)

Sandek Person who holds the baby for Brit Milah

Sanhedrin The supreme religious authority in Israel at the time of Jesus

Sawm Fasting, the fourth pillar

Sects Group with different religious beliefs from those of a larger group to which they belong

Seder The Passover meal

Sefer Torah The Torah scroll kept in the Ark

Self-determination People deciding on their own future

Self-esteem A person's opinion of how good or important they are

Self-knowledge Knowing who you are and why you are here

Self-subsistent Without dependence on or support from anything else

Seminaries Educational institutions which prepare pupils for ordination as clergy

Sermon on the Mount Jesus' description of Christian living

Sermons Talks on a religious subject (usually based on a Bible passage)

Sex discrimination Treating people differently on the ground of their gender

Shabbat The Jewish holy day on Saturday, the seventh day of the week

Shacharit Morning prayer

Shahadah The Muslim creed and first pillar

Shalom Peace

Shari'ah The holy law of Islam which covers all aspects of life

Shaytan The devil

Shechitah Jewish method of slaughtering animals

Shema The declaration of Jewish belief in one God

Shirk The sin of associating other things with God; it is the worst sin

Shiva The seven days of intense mourning

Shoah The Holocaust

Shochet A Jewish butcher

Shofar Ram's horn

Shrine A place of worship that holds the tomb or relic of a saint

Shul The name used for the synagogue by many Jews

Siddur The Orthodox prayer book

Sidra The portion of the Torah read at *Shabbat* morning service

Simchat Torah The festival celebrating the giving of the Torah

Sin An act that is against God's will

Sirah A biography of the prophet Muhammad

Spouse Marriage/cohabitation partner

Stations of the cross Fourteen pictures representing stages of Christ's way to crucifixion

STD Sexually transmitted disease

Stewards People appointed to look after something on behalf of someone else

Stewardship Looking after something so it can be passed on to the next generation

STI Sexually transmitted infection

Stonewall A group which campaigns for the equality of lesbian, gay, bisexual and trans people across Britain

Subordinate Of inferior importance or rank

Suffragette A woman seeking the right to vote through protest

Suhur The meal just before fasting starts at dawn

Suicide bomber Terrorist who carries out a bomb attack, knowing that he or she will be killed by the explosion

Sunnah The example and way of life of the Prophet Muhammad

Supernova An explosion of a massive supergiant star

Supplication Prayers asking for God's help

Surah A chapter of the Qur'an (there are 114 surahs)

Tabernacle The holy place containing the Ark of the Covenant

Talbiya The *hajj* prayer which pilgrims say constantly

Tallit A fringed garment worn by Jews

Talmud Collection of Mishneh and other writing on the Jewish law

Tashlich Casting away sins into running water

Tawaf Seven circuits of the Ka'aba

Tawhid Belief in Allah's unity

Tawrat The holy book given to Musa (Moses)

Tefillin A container for the *shema* scroll to put on the arms and head

Temple The centre of worship built by Solomon in Jerusalem and destroyed in 70CE

Tenakh The Jewish scriptures

Terrorism Criminal acts intended to provoke a state of terror in the public for political or religious purposes

Thanksgiving Prayers thanking God

The Omnipresent A title used of God during mourning to remind that Jews that God is with the living and the dead

Theological Academic study of God and religious ideas

Thirteen Principles of Faith A summary of Jewish beliefs written by Maimonides

Tomb A burial place

Torah The books of Moses (Genesis, Exodus, Leviticus, Numbers, Deuteronomy), the most holy book of Judaism

Tosefta Rabbinic opinions extra to the Mishneh

Transgressions Breaking laws (especially God's laws)

Transubstantiation The belief that during the service of Mass (also called Eucharist or Holy Communion) the bread and wine transform into the body and blood of Jesus

Treason Attempting to overthrow a government or state

Treifah Not *kosher*

True Cross The actual cross on which Jesus was crucified

Two natures The belief that Jesus was both human and divine

Ummah The Muslim community (brotherhood of Islam)

United Nations (UN) An international organisation, founded in 1945, to increase co-operation between member countries

Unitive purpose Sexual activity as a source of joy and pleasure to unite a married couple

Usul ad-din The five roots of Shi'a Islam

Uthman The third caliph, who ordered the final official copy of the Qur'an

Vale of soul making The idea that God gave people this life to make their souls good enough for heaven

Veneration Treating with deep respect

Vestments Official robes for those leading Christian worship

Via Dolorosa 'The Way of Tears', the route Jesus took from Pilate's court to Golgotha

Vicar Another name for a parish priest

Vicegerency Looking after something on behalf of someone else

Vicegerent A person appointed to look after things on behalf of a ruler

Vicegerent Someone working as God's steward or representative on earth

Victims Those who have suffered from a crime

Virgin birth The belief that Jesus was not conceived through sex

Vocal prayer Prayer using words

Voluntary euthanasia Ending life painlessly when someone in great pain asks for death

Waquf A standing prayer during *hajj*

Weapons of mass destruction Weapons which can destroy large areas and/or large numbers of people

Wudu The ritual washing before prayers

Yad Pointer for reading the Sefer Torah

Yahya John the Baptist

Yarzheit The anniversary day of someone's death

Yazid The sixth caliph of Sunni Islam

Yom Kippur Jewish holy day, also known as the Day of Atonement

Yusuf The prophet Joseph (coat of many colours)

Zabur The holy book given to Dawud (David)

Zakah Charity tax, the third pillar

Zamzam well The well in the courtyard of the Great Mosque given by God for Hagar and Ismail

Zayd ibn Thabit Muhammad's chief secretary, who organised Uthman's Qur'an

Zuhr Midday prayers

Index

Photo credits:

p1 Peter Barritt/Alamy; **p2** RealyEasyStar/Fotografia Felici/Alamy; **p3** TravelStockCollection-Homer Sykes/Alamy; **p4** sedmak/Thinkstock; **p6** Art Directors & TRIP/Alamy; **p13** Wikimedia Commons; **p15** sedmak/Thinkstock; **p18** Art Directors & TRIP/Alamy; **p20** Manor Photography/Alamy; **p21** Stephen Barnes/Religion/Alamy; **p25** Wellcome Library, London/ http://creativecommons.org/licenses/by/4.0/; **p27** BrianAJackson/Thinkstock; **p28** WENN UK/Alamy; **p29** Prisma Bildagentur AG/Alamy; **p31** Zvonimir AtletiĐ/Alamy; **p32** Rosemary Harris/Alamy; **p35** Terry Harris/Alamy; **p36*t*** Victor Watton; **p36*b*** David Fisher/REX/ Shutterstock; **p38** Grant Rooney/Alamy; **p41** MRP/Alamy; **p43** Mark J. Terrill/AP/Press Association Images; **p45** Brian J. Ritchie/Hotsauce/REX Shutterstock; **p47*t*** CPA/SIPA/ REX/Shutterstock; **p47*b*** szeyuen/Thinkstock; **p48** Marmaduke St. John/Alamy; **p51** Victor Watton; **p53** BSIP/UIG Via Getty Images; **p54** Piotr Adamowicz/Alamy; **p59** wavebreakmedia/ Thinkstock; **p62** Philip Scalia Alamy; **p67** Michael Debets/Alamy; **p68** Alberto Pizzoli/ AFP/Getty Images; **p71** Angelo Hornak/Alamy; **p72** Friedrich Stark/Alamy; **p73** Gideon Mendel/Corbis; **p76** INSADCO Photography/Alamy; **p77** Network Photographer/Alamy; **p80** tatyana_tomsickova/Thinkstock; **p84** DeAgostini/Getty Images; **p85** Eldhorajan92/ CC BY-SA 4.0; **p86** CountrySideCollection - Homer Sykes/Alamy; **p87*t*** F1 Online/REX/ Shutterstock; **p87*b*** Debu55y/Alamy; **p89** Art Directors & TRIP/Alamy; **p91** robertharding/ Alamy; **p92** Matthew J. Lee/The Boston Globe via Getty Images; **p95** Borderlands/Alamy; **p96** TopFoto.co.uk; **p98*l*** Robert Gray; **p98*r*** David Humphreys/Alamy; **p99** Churches Together in England (www.cte.org.uk); **p102** Grzegorz Galazka/SIPA/REX Shutterstock; **p104** Chronicle/Alamy; **p105** Mark Boulton/Alamy; **p109** Steve Allen Travel Photography/ Alamy; **p110** Andreas Fink/CC BY-SA 3.0; **p111** Tighef/CC BY-SA 3.0; **p112** MR1805/ Thinkstock; **p113** cosmin4000/Thinkstock; **p117** breath10/Thinkstock; **p120** Junchang Lü & Stephen L. Brusatte/CC BY 4.0; **p125** B Christopher/Alamy; **p126** Todd Bannor/ Alamy; **p128** DonFord1/Thinkstock; **p129** ollega/Thinkstock; **p130** Quirky China News/ REX Shutterstock; **p133** Robert Gray; **p135** Purple Pilchards/Alamy; **p136** Jochen Sands/ Thinkstock; **p138** marc zakian/Alamy; **p141** Global Warming Images/Alamy; **p143** Andrew Fox/Alamy; **p144** Jose Gil/Alamy; **p145** Velar Grant/Alamy; **p149** robertharding/Alamy; **p151** Carlos Cazalis/Corbis; **p152** Art Directors & TRIP/Alamy; **p156** dbimages/Alamy; **p157** Art Directors & TRIP/Alamy; **p162** Zeynurbaba/Thinkstock; **p164** United Archives GmbH/Alamy; **p168** David Knopf/Alamy; **p171** robertharding/Alamy; **p172** Iulian Dragomir/ Alamy; **p173** ZUMA Press, Inc./Alamy; **p177** epa european pressphoto agency b.v./ Alamy; **p178** Art Directors & TRIP/Alamy; **p183** Purestock/Thinkstock; **p184** Alex Segre/ Alamy; **p187** tzahiV/Thinkstock; **p188** bestdesigns/Thinkstock; **p190** Image Source/Alamy; **p193** Wikimedia Commons; **p195** Debra Hershkowitz/Alamy; **p198*t*** Michael Burrell/Alamy; **p198*b*** Valeriy Kachaev/Thinkstock; **p199** Lebrecht Music and Arts Photo Library/Alamy; **p201** ESO/B. Tafreshi (twanight.org)/CC BY 4.0; **p205** Andrew Aitchison/In Pictures/Corbis; **p207** Geogast/CC BY-SA 3.0; **p211** World Religions Photo Library/Alamy; **p215** Roger Bamber/Alamy; **p217** talldwarf/Alamy; **p219** Tomwang112/Thinkstock; **p221** Britpix/Alamy; **p222** FotoMaximum/Thinkstock; **p225** mabe123/Thinkstock; **p226** Clive Postlethwaite/ REX Shutterstock; **p228** IPGGutenbergUKLtd/Thinkstock; **p229** alexeys/Thinkstock; **p232** darrensp/Thinkstock; **p236** Jason Kempin/FilmMagic/Getty Images; **p237** Paul Doyle/ Alamy; **p239** Kohl-Photo/Alamy; **p240** Ted Spiegel/Corbis; **p247** Adam Jones, Ph.D./CC BY-SA 3.0; **p248** Catrinus van der Veen/AFP/Getty Images; **p251** Raden Wardana/AFP/Getty Images; **p252** Kevin Holt/Daily Mail/REX Shutterstock; **p255** Oktober64/Thinkstock; **p258** Art Directors & TRIP/Alamy; **p261** Sally and Richard Greenhill/Alamy; **p262** World Religions Photo Library/Alamy; **p265** Louise Batalla Duran/Alamy; **p266** sam garza/CC BY 2.0; **p269** Suhaimi Abdullah/Getty Images; **p271** Robert Gray; **p274** Robert Gray; **p276** prmustafa/ Thinkstock; **p278** Saul Loeb/AFP/Getty Images; **p284** Still Works/arabianEye/Corbis; **p285** World Religions Photo Library/Alamy; **p287** Mauro Matacchione/Thinkstock; **p289** Yadid Levy/Alamy; **p290** Godong/Alamy; **p293** Paul Souders/Corbis; **p294** Art Directors & TRIP/ Alamy; **p299** tzahiV/Thinkstock; **p300** Fethi Belaid/AFP/Getty Images; **p303** Dan Porges/Getty Images; **p306** grahamandgraham/Thinkstock; **p307** David Silverman/Getty Images; **p308** Ira Berger/Alamy; **pp310, 311** Robert Gray; **p314** natushm/Thinkstock; **p317** chameleonseye/ Thinkstock; **p319*t*** blueenayim/Thinkstock; **p319*b*** museyushaya/Thinkstock; **p322** 67photo/ Alamy; **p323** Ira Berger/Alamy; **p325** magann/Thinkstock; **p327** Cary Herz/Getty Images; **p330** David Grossman/Alamy; **p332** Richard Milnes/Demotix/Corbis; **p333** amer ghazzal/ Alamy; **p335** Albin Lohr-Jones/Pacific Press/LightRocket via Getty Images; **p338** Joerg Boethling/Alamy; **p339** Jenny Matthews/Alamy; **p342** Matthew Chattle/Alamy; **p344** TopFoto; **p346** PixelPro/Alamy; **p348** The Print Collector/HIP/TopFoto; **p350** Craig Wherlock/Demotix/ Demotix/Corbis; **p353** KeystoneUSA-ZUMA/REX Shutterstock; **p355** Erbin News/NurPhoto/ REX Shutterstock; **p358** Spencer Platt/Getty Images; **p359** PA Photos/Topfoto.